From Benito Mussolini to Hugo Chavez

Intellectuals and a Century of Political Hero Worship

During the twentieth and twenty-first centuries, political dictators were not only popular in their own countries, but were also admired by numerous highly educated and idealistic Western intellectuals. The objects of this political hero-worship included Benito Mussolini, Adolph Hitler, Joseph Stalin, Mao Zedong, Fidel Castro and more recently Hugo Chavez, among others. This book seeks to understand the sources of these misjudgements and misperceptions, the specific appeals of particular dictators, and the part played by their charisma, or pseudo-charisma. It sheds new light not only on the political disposition of numerous Western intellectuals – such as Martin Heidegger, Eric Hobsbawm, Norman Mailer, Ezra Pound, Susan Sontag and George Bernard Shaw – but also on the personality of those political leaders who encouraged, and in some instances helped to design, the cult surrounding their rise to dictatorship.

Paul Hollander is Professor Emeritus of Sociology at the University of Massachusetts, Amherst, and an associate of the Davis Center for Russian and Eurasian Studies at Harvard University. Born in Budapest, he left Hungary in November 1956. He earned his BA from the London School of Economics and PhD from Princeton University. He received the Guggenheim Fellowship in 1974, and was a Visiting Scholar several times at the Hoover Institution. He has published fifteen books, most of them dealing with communist systems, totalitarianism, political violence, extremism, propaganda, and the political attitude of Western intellectuals.

From Benito Mussolini to Hugo Chavez

Intellectuals and a Century of Political Hero Worship

PAUL HOLLANDER
University of Massachusetts, Amherst

CAMBRIDGE
UNIVERSITY PRESS

CAMBRIDGE
UNIVERSITY PRESS

University Printing House, Cambridge CB2 8BS, United Kingdom

One Liberty Plaza, 20th Floor, New York, NY 10006, USA

477 Williamstown Road, Port Melbourne, VIC 3207, Australia

4843/24, 2nd Floor, Ansari Road, Daryaganj, Delhi - 110002, India

79 Anson Road, #06-04/06, Singapore 079906

Cambridge University Press is part of the University of Cambridge.

It furthers the University's mission by disseminating knowledge in the pursuit of education, learning and research at the highest international levels of excellence.

www.cambridge.org
Information on this title: www.cambridge.org/9781107415072

First published 2016

A catalogue record for this publication is available from the British Library

ISBN 978-1-107-07103-2 Hardback
ISBN 978-1-107-41507-2 Paperback

Contents

Preface

This book continues to explore several of my long-standing and converging interests. They include totalitarianism, communist systems, intellectuals and politics, the relationship between the personal and political, between political ideals and practices, the spiritual problems of modernity, and the apparently limitless capacity of idealistic human beings, notably intellectuals, to engage in wishful thinking and substantial political misjudgments.[1] I should hasten to add that the generalizations and propositions that follow in this book apply only to an undetermined but very visible and vocal *portion* of Western intellectuals. In the absence of opinion and other surveys addressed to "intellectuals" these proportions cannot be determined and quantified. Many intellectuals had and have political attitudes and sympathies quite different from those examined in this book (see also Chapter 8, pp. 308–309).

In addition to the interests sketched above, much of my work over my entire professional life involved the broader issues of illusions and reality, theory and practice, as well as deception and self-deception. These interests found expression not only in my writings about the political illusions of Western intellectuals but also in other realms of illusions: political propaganda, commercial advertising, secular religions, the "cult of personality" (deification of political leaders), and most recently in the

[1] It is an interest I share with Orwell, whose "main concern was the gullibility of the intelligentsia. How could so many educated minds believe all that fantasy and falsification?" (Robert Conquest in John Rodden ed.: *The Cambridge Companion to George Orwell*, Cambridge 2007, 129).

contemporary American pursuit of romantic love[2] – an apolitical and far less destructive pursuit of illusions.

The major earlier expression of my interests noted above may be found in *Political Pilgrims*, first published in 1981. It was written during the 1970s and as such was influenced by my experiences of that period, and its dominant social-political movements, observed in academic settings (Harvard and the University of Massachusetts, Amherst). Some readers may consider this book a follow-up of *Pilgrims* and in certain respects they would be correct, given the continuity of my preoccupations. But there are also substantial differences between these two books and their subject matter.

Political Pilgrims examined the appeals and attractions various communist systems had for many Western intellectuals. It included only brief discussions of the appeals of the leaders and founders of these systems. By contrast, the present volume focuses on attitudes toward and perceptions of the leaders of these systems that in many instances could be characterized as hero worship.

Second, and more importantly, the present study was broadened to include (among the political systems that impressed favorably groups of Western intellectuals) not only communist states but also Fascist Italy and Nazi Germany, as well as several contemporary authoritarian regimes and their leaders of varied ideological persuasion: Hugo Chavez of Venezuela, Saddam Hussein of Iraq, Omar Torrijos of Panama, the Kim dynasty of North Korea.

There have been several reasons for the expansion of my interests and the attendant shift of emphasis from systems to leaders. In the first place, while much has been written about the left-wing sympathies of Western intellectuals, much less has been known and written about corresponding attitudes (far more short-lived) toward other totalitarian and authoritarian systems such as Nazi Germany and Fascist Italy, among others. Given my general interest in the political attitudes and judgments of intellectuals, expanding the types of political systems they were attracted to promised further insight into the roots of their disposition that culminated in the misjudgments I explored in the more limited historical context of *Political Pilgrims*.

The new emphasis on "political hero worship," or, more precisely, the attractions of charismatic and often deified leaders, was intended to

[2] See my *Extravagant Expectations: New Ways to Find Romantic Love in America*, Lanham MD 2011.

highlight the secular-religious components of the attitudes I have been interested in for a long time. I expected that comparing the converging appeals of leaders of different political systems legitimated by different ideologies would lend support to the idea that the attitudes of the intellectuals here examined had more of a religious, or secular-religious, than political inspiration. A similar orientation can be readily identified in the religious-spiritual aspects of contemporary political beliefs and attitudes most strikingly found in the upsurge of radical-fundamentalist Islamist movements.

Another political-cultural phenomenon relevant to this study is the recent (winter 2015–spring 2016) popularity of Donald Trump among American voters. Arguably, these attitudes could also be classified as hero worship and as such deserve at least a brief comment in this study.

Unlike the figures dealt with in this book, Trump had no political power, no ideology, no discernible ideals, and no state-sponsored propaganda apparatus at his disposal. Nor did he appeal to intellectuals. At the same time, his popularity and admiration closely resemble the attitudes stimulated by the charismatic dictators dealt with in this book. It is noteworthy, as well as dismaying, that even in a democratic political culture, such as that of America, millions of people came to admire, support, and vote for an individual such as Trump, notwithstanding his complete lack of credentials or qualifications for the high office he has sought. It is equally remarkable that the same substantial portion of the population chose to ignore, or overlook, his numerous highly unappealing personal qualities – the inflated ego, his endless bragging, intolerance, authoritarian temperament, coarse language, lack of self-control, and demonization of opponents, among others.

Like genuinely charismatic figures, Trump was able to mobilize the most profoundly alienated, embittered, and frustrated segments of the population, who were ready to embrace an individual whose appeal rests solely on his boundless self-regard and willingness to make a wide variety of outlandish promises, offering simple, poorly articulated solutions to a wide variety of social, economic, and political grievances. Trump's wealth has also impressed many Americans who believe that great wealth is self-evident proof of impressive personal qualities.[3] Such a deeply internalized reverence for wealth, regardless of its sources and the character of those possessing it, helps to explain why his endless bragging and posturing

[3] But Trump is not exactly a self-made man having inherited huge amounts from his father – the foundation of his real estate empire.

failed to make a poor impression on his supporters. Many of those feeling deprived and victimized by the social system have been ready to identify with an individual such as Trump – rich, aggressive, and claiming to be a powerful supporter of the underdog.

Trump shares the key attribute of genuinely charismatic figures, namely an immense and irrational self-confidence that is a substitute for any specific credential or qualification for the political office he seeks. His crude and aggressive rhetoric, unembarrassed, vocal intolerance, and grandiose promises respond to the needs and grievances of the least educated, most frustrated, and most embittered portion of the electorate. As David Brooks recently wrote: "Trump's supporters aren't looking for a political process to address their needs. They are looking for a superhero. As the political scientist Matthew MacWilliams found, the one trait that best predicts whether you're a Trump supporter is how high you score on tests that measure authoritarianism."[4] The Trump phenomenon reminds us that political hero worship cannot be relegated to the past.

Although the focus of this book is the Western intellectuals' perception and admiration of various dictators, it was necessary to provide some information about the actual character and policies of the dictators in order to compare and contrast, as far as possible, the perceptions and images with psychological and biographical realities. The latter substantially, often spectacularly, diverged from the images and perceptions entertained by the intellectuals in question.

While it was not my intention to dwell on the nature of the political systems the dictators presided over – to avoid duplication of the topics dealt with at length in *Political Pilgrims* – it would have been difficult to analyze attitudes toward the dictators without reference to the major characteristics of the political and social systems they created and dominated. There was no danger of repetition when writing about Hitler's Germany and Mussolini's Italy and the other authoritarian systems and their leaders (discussed in Chapter 7) that were not dealt with in *Political Pilgrims*.

I have always been particularly interested in the respective influence (on the character of these systems) of their official ideology and the personality of their supreme leader. This study confirms that ideas and ideologies had considerable influence on the dictators and the elite groups sharing and supporting their power. I have also been curious (from an early age)

[4] David Brooks: "A Governing Cancer of Our Time," *New York Times*, February 26, 2016, A23.

about the part played by coercion and political violence in the maintenance and persistence of these systems, and the following will also shed some light on this matter.

I fully concur with an Iranian social scientist who had this to say about the part played by ideas vs. coercion in the maintenance of dictatorships:

> academic discussions of dictatorship ignore the stark reality of brute force and instead focus on *ideologies*; academics would have one believe that the people remain downtrodden because they misperceive the situation and directly or indirectly perpetuate their own powerlessness ... The disproportionate focus on ideas arises from the fact that many academics who have written about dictatorships have never lived in a dictatorship, nor have they experienced how people can be painfully aware of suffocating repression while living in a dictatorship but not be able to say or do anything about this terrifying reality because they fear torture, imprisonment and assassination ... These fears are justified.[5]

Professor Moghaddam and I share some personal experiences that help to account for our views as we both had lived in dictatorships, he in a theocratic one, myself in the Stalinist-communist variety.

There were several occasions over a long period of time when I benefited from exposing ideas related to this book to various audiences. In November 2001 I was a discussant at a Liberty Fund conference on "Communism and Intellectuals" in Kracow, Poland (all participants at Liberty Fund conferences are discussants). In November 2006 I spoke about the "Political Delusions of Western Intellectuals" at the Foundation for Economic Education in Irvington, NY; in March 2007 I gave a talk at the American Enterprise Institute in Washington, DC, entitled "Attraction and Abandonment: Political Morality and Communist Ideals." In May 2010 I gave a lecture in Bucharest at the Institute for the Investigation of the Crimes of Communism, entitled "Temptations of Communism and Western Intellectuals"; in November 2012 I participated in another Liberty Fund conference in Indianapolis on "Intellectuals and Society"; in March 2013 I gave a talk on "Intellectuals and Dictators" at a conference held at Boston College devoted to the topic of "Dreams of Total Power"; in February 2014 I gave a talk at the Center for Russian, East European and Eurasian Studies at Stanford University on the same topic. In September 2014 I addressed once more the same topic at a colloquium of the Sociology Department of the Central European University in Budapest. In September 2016 I gave a

[5] Fathali M. Moghaddam: *The Psychology of Dictatorship*, Washington DC 2013, 4.

lecture on the subject of this book at the Hungarian Academy of Science in Budapest.

Vladimir Tismaneanu helped to inspire this volume by inviting me several years ago to contribute a chapter to the volume he was going to edit on totalitarian dictatorships. I chose to write about intellectuals and dictators. The volume he edited has yet to be published.

I am grateful for the instructive and thoughtful comments, advice, and encouragement of Daniel Benveniste, Patrick Clawson, Anthony Daniels, Jorge Dominguez, Jeffrey Herf, Fred Hiatt, Christopher Hurn, John Kekes, Peter Kenez, Jonathan Mirsky, Norman Naimark, Richard Pipes, Laura Tartakoff, Ezra Vogel, Arthur Waldron, and Richard Wolin. Each of them read various parts of the manuscript related to their expertise and interests. The lengthy written comments of Jeffrey Herf, Arthur Waldron, and Richard Wolin were particularly helpful. I am pleased to note here that close to forty years ago Jorge Dominguez had also commented on parts of *Political Pilgrims*. Doubtless, all these responses improved various aspects of the book, even if not all of the advice of the readers was taken.

Peter Kenez and Mark Kramer read and endorsed the detailed proposal Cambridge University Press requested. I greatly appreciate their support. I am also grateful to Alexandra Sprague for her help in formatting the manuscript and miscellaneous computer problem-solving and Gene Fisher for solving problems resulting from my using a computer program different from that of the publisher.

1

Introduction: Intellectuals and Politics

> Politics in a dictatorship begins in the personality of the dictator.
>
> *Li Zhisui*[1]

> Distinguished intellectuals, gifted poets, and influential journalists summoned their talents to convince all who would listen that modern tyrants were liberators and that their unconscionable crimes were noble, when seen in the proper perspective.
>
> *Mark Lilla*[2]

> One of the most perplexing attachments to be found among proponents of the high cause of liberty, humanity and a new world of peace, justice and love, is the admiration of absolute power and grandeur in the shape of the leader, hero, or conqueror.
>
> *Renee Winegarten*[3]

The personality of the leader matters far more in a dictatorship than in a democracy. Unencumbered by the constraints of institutions, legal norms, and public opinion, the dictator's personality exerts much greater influence on the exercise of power than that of elected leaders. In this study attention will be paid both to the actual personality of the dictators

[1] Li Zhisui: *The Private Life of Chairman Mao: The Memoirs of Mao's Personal Physician*, New York 1994, x.

[2] Mark Lilla: *Reckless Mind: Intellectuals in Politics*, New York 2001, 198. Lilla also wrote: "As Continental Europe gave birth to two great tyrannical systems ... communism and fascism, it also gave birth to a new social type, for which we need a new name: the philotyrannical intellectual ... What is it about the human mind that made the intellectual defense of tyranny possible in the twentieth century? (Ibid., 197–198.)

[3] Renee Winegarten: *Writers and Revolution: The Fatal Lure of Action*, New York 1974, 99.

(insofar as evidence permits) and their images, or perceptions, and especially the positive impression they made on many Western intellectuals.

There is considerable evidence (presented below) indicating that many well-known twentieth-century intellectuals admired dictators of various ideological persuasion, as well as the political system they represented. Such admiration, often merging into hero worship, was an integral part of a substantial body of political misjudgments.[4] Misjudgments of this kind were not limited to intellectuals: artists, scientists, journalists, clergymen, businessmen, and politicians too were capable of making them. In the following I will make occasional reference to the latter as well, especially when their misjudgments were similar to those of the intellectuals.

The admiration of dictators and dictatorships was seamlessly integrated: the attractions of individual dictators were inseparable from the appeals of the social-political system they symbolized, and the pages that follow reflect this connection. I did not come across a single case of a political system that was found admirable, but not its leader, or conversely, reverence for the dictator unaccompanied by positive sentiments about the system.[5]

What Milovan Djilas, a leading Yugoslav communist functionary (and subsequently critic of the system), said of Stalin applies, in all probability, to other dictators as well, as discussed below, and accounts for their appeal: "He was the incarnation of an idea, transfigured ... into pure idea, and thereby into something infallible and sinless."[6] Most of the dictators possessed of such appeals were Fascist, Nazi, and Communist, and each made an indelible impact on the political movements and systems they represented. Francois Furet wrote: "Both Bolshevism and Fascism, as vast collective passions, were personified by personalities who were ... exceptional ... common to the three great dictatorships of the era was that each of their destinies was determined by the will of an individual."[7]

Here the question may also be raised if is there anything we might learn from this study about dictators, as distinct from learning about the

[4] For a book-length analysis of such misjudgments, see Paul Hollander: *Political Pilgrims: Western Intellectuals in Search of the Good Society*, New Brunswick NJ 1998 (first published by Oxford University Press, New York 1981).

[5] A partial exception to this generalization may be found in discussions of the relationship between the Soviet system and the personality of Stalin. Following his death and the revelations of his misrule, some Western intellectuals (not unlike Khrushchev in his 1956 speech at the 20th Party Congress) sought to legitimate the Soviet system by ascribing all, or most, of its defects to the personality and flawed policies of Stalin, thus separating the leader from the system.

[6] Milovan Djilas: *Conversations with Stalin*, New York 1962, 57.

[7] Francois Furet: *The Passing of an Illusion*, Chicago 1999, 164–165.

intellectuals who sympathized with them? Given the premise of this study, namely, that many intellectuals misperceived and misjudged the dictators, it would seem unlikely that we could learn much of interest or importance from their writings about the actual characteristics of dictators. Nevertheless, while we are likely to learn far more about the intellectuals from their attitudes toward dictators, we may also learn something about dictators from the same sources, despite their skewed aspects. Insofar as the dictators encouraged intellectuals (and others) to take a flattering view of them and basked in the official cults created by their institutions of propaganda, we might learn of their self-conceptions and the qualities they wished to propagate about themselves. If so, the dictators had *some* influence on the way they were seen by intellectuals.

To be sure, intellectuals and members of other elite groups are not the only people capable of admiring dictators; many dictators have been hugely popular with the ordinary people they ruled, at any rate for certain periods of time. As Ian Kershaw wrote, "the adulation of Hitler by millions of Germans ... meant that the person of the Fuhrer ... formed a crucial integratory force in the Nazi system of rule."[8] Albert Speer too noted about Hitler's popularity (also applicable to other charismatic dictators) that "the mass exultation was not called forth by rhetoric or suggestion, but solely by the effect of Hitler's presence. Whereas individuals in the crowd were subject to this influence only for a few seconds at a time, Hitler himself was eternally exposed to the worship of the masses."[9] While this broader phenomenon is also a matter of great interest, the attitude of intellectuals is particularly intriguing and in need of explanation since, as most of us believe, dictators do not deserve admiration from any quarter, least of all by intellectuals. Dictators are justifiably seen as personifications of oppression, lawlessness, and a seemingly insatiable hunger for power and adulation. Insofar as they attain legitimacy and popularity, it is usually ascribed to their skill in deceiving their supporters, or the false consciousness of their subjects.

The relationship between dictators and intellectuals raises broader questions about politics and intellectuals that cannot be answered in isolation from the major political, historical, and cultural currents of the periods concerned,[10] and without revisiting the conflicting conceptions of the nature of intellectuals.

[8] Ian Kershaw: *The "Hitler Myth": Image and Reality in the Third Reich*, Oxford, UK 1987, 1.

[9] Albert Speer: *Inside the Third Reich*, New York 1970, 48.

[10] Joachim Fest wrote: "The weakness and readiness to capitulate [to dictators – P.H.] can be understood only against a background of ... the whole position and function of

REVISITING CONCEPTIONS OF INTELLECTUALS

It is both tempting and problematic to generalize about intellectuals and their political attitudes. The major source of information about these attitudes is their own writings and public statements since "intellectual" is not a category used in empirical opinion research.[11] Most people who may qualify as intellectuals have no occasion or reason to disclose their political beliefs and attitudes toward dictators and the political systems they represented. But there have been other intellectuals, much smaller in number, interested in, and drawn to, these political figures, who chose to write and make public statements about them. A few of them even met various dictators and exchanged ideas with them. The generalizations that follow are obviously limited to such intellectuals, many of whom used to be prominent and influential.

I had no intention or ability to prove that *most* intellectuals, or intellectuals in general, misjudge political matters and are inclined to revere, admire, or worship dictators. However, a substantial but undetermined portion of Western intellectuals did display such attitudes.

Conceptions of intellectuals may be divided between the favorable or idealized and the critical or skeptical. The former emphasize (as did Karl Mannheim) their supposed autonomy and commitment to the disinterested exploration and questioning of a wide range of ideas. Richard Hofstadter, who held this view, designated intellectuals as "special custodian[s] of values like reason and justice."[12] Paul Baran advocated a similarly idealistic conception:

> The desire to tell the truth is ... only one condition for being an intellectual. The other is courage, readiness to carry on rational inquiry to wherever it may lead ... An intellectual is thus in essence a *social critic*, a person whose concern

intellectuals in modern society, which ... explains the susceptibility of these classes to totalitarian solutions. Among these motivations are the ambivalent attitude of intellectuals to power and their tendency to embrace utopian systems or ideological concepts" (*The Face of the Third Reich*, New York 1970, 249).

[11] There are, however, surveys of the political attitudes of certain occupational categories (such as college teachers) that include many intellectuals and provide information about their political attitudes. In the United States such surveys consistently reflected a left-of-center disposition of the majority.

[12] Karl Mannheim: *Ideology and Utopia*, New York 1936; Hofstadter quoted in Helena Rimon: "Paradoxes of 'Free Floating' and Controversy of Betrayal: Intellectuals' Reflections on Themselves against a Background of Terror," *Terrorism and Political Violence*, Vol. 25, No. 4, 2013, 532.

is ... to help overcome obstacles ... to the attainment of a better, more humane and more rational social order.[13]

Edward Said saw "the figure of the intellectual as a being set apart, someone able to speak the truth, a ... courageous and angry individual for whom no worldly power is too big and imposing to be criticized and pointedly taken to task." In this exalted view, "the real, or 'true' intellectual is ... always an outsider, living in self-imposed seamlessly integrated exile on the margins of society."[14] Said himself was a university professor at Columbia University, author of many widely reviewed and highly praised books, many of them required reading in hundreds of college and university courses.[15] Numerous books were written about him, courses on his ideas were offered at several universities, and he was a frequent guest on television talk shows and a popular speaker at professional meetings and on college campuses. Apparently all this was compatible with seeing himself as the true intellectual living on the margins of society.

The skeptical view of intellectuals emphasizes their lack of realism, propensity to abstract thinking, groundless generalization, a frustrated power-hunger, and an irresistible propensity to pontificate. The following summary characterization, *not* intended as criticism, captures some of these attributes: "Gramsci, like Lukacs is a man driven by the *dream* of totality, unity and coherence."[16] Notwithstanding the fuzziness of this dream (at any rate as summed up in the quotation), it can be readily associated with philosopher-kings, intent on creating social systems that will embody these dreams, whatever their exact nature.[17]

[13] Baran cited in Rafael Rojas: *Fighting over Fidel: The New York Intellectuals and the Cuban Revolution*, Princeton NJ 2016, 105.

[14] Said quoted in Jeremy Jennings and Anthony Kemp-Welch eds.: *Intellectuals and Politics: From the Dreyfus Affair to Salman Rushdie*, London 1997, 1–2. David Brooks commented on the "exalted view" of intellectuals "influenced by the Russian notion of the *intelligentsia*, a secular priesthood ... who participated in national life by living above it in a kind of universal space of truth and disinterestedness, rendering moral judgments on the activities below ... only by staying aloof from society that they could see it clearly and honestly, so they believed" (*Bobos in Paradise*, New York 2000, 143–144).

[15] See Joshua Muravchik: *Making David into Goliath: How the World Turned Against Israel*, New York 2014, 99.

[16] Neil Harding: "Intellectuals and Socialism," in Jennings and Kemp-Welch eds., 208 (emphasis added).

[17] Tocqueville was probably the first to discern some of these defining characteristics of intellectuals: "Their very way of life led these writers to indulge in abstract theories and generalizations regarding the nature of government ... For living as they did, quite out of touch with practical politics, they lacked the experience which might have tempered their enthusiasms ... Thus ... there was gradually built up in men's minds an imaginary

There is disagreement about the compatibility of being a true intellectual and a holder of power, given the likelihood that the possession of power and dispassionate truth-seeking are difficult to reconcile. Russell Berman wrote:

> a certain enlightenment utopia imagined a world ruled by reason as a formula for universal peace and prosperity. Only the brightest ... could hold the reins of power, their intelligent schemes could banish the benighted habits of humanity ... Intellectuals, finding themselves at a distance from political centers, succumb to a will to power, a desire to control. Should they succeed, their effort to impose their plans on the social world often take a repressive turn.[18]

By many definitions Joseph Goebbels was an intellectual, or, as one author put it, "an intellectual among thugs."[19] He had a doctorate in literature and philosophy, writing his dissertation on German romantics; he was the author of books and plays before becoming the chief propagandist of Hitler. He had a consuming interest in ideas, and fully agreed with Lenin about using ideas as weapons. He was a dedicated moralizer and believer in a utopian social system of the future. We tend to recoil from thinking of him as an intellectual because he was powerful and a deeply committed supporter of the Nazi regime who inspired and devised many of its policies. It may be equally shocking for those who believe that higher education confers immunity against inhumane attitudes that the 1942 Wansee Conference (devoted to planning the Final Solution, that is, the extermination of European Jews) "was attended primarily by people with academic titles; *two thirds had university degrees and over half bore the title of doctor, mainly of law*."[20]

There is no useful and widely agreed upon occupational definition of intellectuals, since they may be found in a variety of occupations that have something to do with the creation and dissemination of ideas.[21] Being an intellectual is largely a matter of possessing certain attitudes, in

ideal society in which all was simple, uniform, coherent, equitable and rational" (Alexis de Tocqueville: *The Old Regime and the French Revolution*, Garden City NY 1955, 141, 147).

18 Russell Berman: "Intellectuals and Power," *Telos*, Summer 2007.

19 Louis L. Snyder: *Hitler's Elite*, New York 1989, 99.

20 Ivan Klima: *My Crazy Century*, New York 2013, 476. The data he quoted came from Mark Roseman: *The Wannsee Conference and the Final Solution: A Reconsideration*, New York 2004.

21 Thomas Sowell defines intellectuals as people "whose end products are ideas" and who create "a general set of presumptions, beliefs and imperatives – a vision that serves as a framework for the way particular issues and events ... are perceived by the population at large" (*Intellectuals and Society*, New York 2011, 503–504).

particular a social-critical disposition combined with a moralizing bent. The social-critical impulses of intellectuals are, as a rule, aimed at their own society and sometimes culminate in its wholesale rejection, in feelings of alienation. But the latter can be compatible with high levels of material comfort, security, and a respectable social status, at any rate in our times, and in pluralistic Western societies, as in the case of Edward Said. Reinhard Bendix observed that there is a "mismatch between their [the intellectuals'] comfortable life-style and their theoretically based despair ... public messages of despair are again and again sent ... by people living in relative comfort."[22]

A more devastating view of intellectuals (the intelligentsia of his times and country) was expressed by Anton Chekhov through one of his fictional characters:

> The vast majority of the intelligentsia that I know don't search for anything, don't do anything and aren't capable of labor. They call themselves the intelligentsia but they talk ... to their peasants as if they were animals ... don't read anything serious, do absolutely nothing ... they philosophize, but meanwhile before their very eyes, the workers ... sleep without pillows, thirty or forty in a single room, everywhere there are bedbugs, stench, dampness, immorality ... So apparently all these good conversations we have serve only to delude ourselves and others.[23]

In a similarly critical spirit Joseph Epstein wrote of Dwight Macdonald that he was "the intellectual par excellence, which is to say that without any specialized knowledge he was prepared to comment on everything ... and always with what seemed an unwavering confidence." Epstein further suggested that "another of MacDonald's core ideas was that the job of intellectuals was to keep up critical pressure, especially on his own country, which, by definition, can never be good enough." Macdonald believed – as did many other intellectuals – that their "first priority" was dissent from what they considered the conventional wisdom and the status quo. Irving Howe, another well-known intellectual, also believed, as Epstein put it, that "the intellectual was always an outsider, and intellectual life was really only valid when one lived it as a member of a minority. This minority was to be in permanent opposition,

[22] Reinhard Bendix: *Embattled Reason: Essays on Social Knowledge*, Vol. II, New Brunswick NJ 1989, 424, 426. In a similar spirit it was observed of Norman Mailer that "he was a play outlaw," that is to say, his rebelliousness was compatible with high income, celebrity status, and overall security (See Louis Menand: "The Norman Invasion," *New Yorker*, October 21, 2013, 96). The same phenomenon was captured in the concept of "tenured radicals" (the title of Roger Kimball's 1990 book).

[23] Anton Chekhov: *The Cherry Orchard*, Indianapolis 2010, 29–30 (first published 1913).

in state of perpetual dissatisfaction with the world as it is."[24] Tom Wolfe considered the enlarged capacity for moral indignation their essential attribute: "From the very onset the eminence of this new creature, the intellectual ... was inseparable from his *necessary* indignation. It was his moral indignation that elevated him to a plateau of moral superiority."[25] In turn, cultivating such a sense of moral superiority has been an essential part of nurturing a favorable self-conception.

More recently, Franklin Foer wrote that "feelings of embattlement are the very qualities that would attract a romantic like Howe to a career as an intellectual: the nobility of the lonely stand, the feverish devotion to the unappreciated idea."[26] Likewise Jean-Paul Sartre believed that the uncritical and politically disengaged intellectual was not a genuine intellectual but "a mere 'technician of practical knowledge' or a 'theoretician of the bourgeois class.'" Gramsci shared this view, calling the politically committed intellectual "organic," a term of approval.[27]

Such idealized views of the intellectual are reminiscent of the older conception of the (pre-Soviet) Russian intelligentsia, in particular "the sense of moral responsibility" central to it. As Isaiah Berlin has written, the Russian intelligentsia "was founded ... on the idea of a permanent rational opposition to the status quo," and he also suggested that this intelligentsia "was generated by truly oppressive regimes."[28] But he did not believe that conditions in contemporary pluralistic Western societies were like those in Russia, implying that modern Western intellectuals differ, or ought to differ, in their outlook from the Russian intelligentsia of the past, as *their* social criticism has not been a response to dire, repressive conditions such as used to prevail in nineteenth-century Russia. What Berlin did not point out is that many contemporary Western and especially American intellectuals have often *claimed* (especially since the 1960s) to be oppressed and threatened by the status quo in order to authenticate their social criticism and political protest. It is likely that

[24] Joseph Epstein: *Essays in Biography*, Mount Jackson VA 2012, 191, 207, 234. More generally Epstein noted "the intellectuals' overdependence on ideas, and their consequent detachment from reality" ("Intellectuals – Public and Otherwise," *Commentary*, May 2000, 49).

[25] Tom Wolfe: *Hooking Up*, New York 2000, 117. See also Jillian Jordan et al.: "The Point of Moral Outrage," *Sunday Review*, *New York Times*, February 28, 2016.

[26] Franklin Foer: "Partisan Reviewer," *New York Times Book Review*, January 18, 2015, 16.

[27] Sartre quoted in Kepa Artaraz: *Cuba and Western Intellectuals Since 1959*, New York 2009, 155; on Gramsci, ibid., 157–158.

[28] Isaiah Berlin: *The Power of Ideas*, Princeton NJ 2000, 104, 108, 207.

to the extent that present-day American public intellectuals are familiar with the social-political roles and attributes of the Russian intelligentsia of the past, they would strongly identify with them.[29]

To sum up, intellectuals are well-educated, idealistic people of a social-critical disposition and high expectations, preoccupied with moral, cultural, political, and social issues, mainly employed (at the present time) by academic institutions in departments of humanities and social sciences.

As regards the attitudes probed in this study, an important distinction has to be made between those intellectuals who lived in countries ruled by dictators and those who observed them from a safe distance. The attitudes of these two groups require, at last in part, different interpretation. The positive views of dictators held by intellectuals who did not live under the repressive political systems may seem at first glance more puzzling. These views were also more disinterested and idealistic, less colored by opportunistic motives, including fear. Western intellectuals who sympathized with dictators had little to gain, or lose, by the public expression of such sentiments. It helps to understand their attitude to point out that they knew very little about the actual conditions in the idealized countries or about their leaders, and were not subject to any pressure to praise them. By contrast intellectuals who lived in Nazi Germany, Fascist Italy, the Soviet Union, communist China, and Cuba were obligated, at any rate in their public utterances, to express nothing but unwavering reverence and support for these systems and their rulers; at the same time they were far better informed about the realities of these societies. But it is also true that during the early years of these systems – especially in Germany and Italy – there was strong and genuine support for them among intellectuals (as well as the general public) that cannot be reduced to opportunistic motives. Many of these intellectuals were, at least in the earlier stages in the evolution of these systems, idealistic and took pride in the apparent material and social progress being made.[30]

Somewhat unexpectedly, a characterization of the attitude of Egyptian intellectuals toward Nasser's regime seems to apply to many intellectuals who lived in the dictatorships here discussed. Tawfig al-Hakim, an Egyptian writer, "spoke for most Egyptian intellectuals describing how,

[29] In recent decades "public intellectual" has been increasingly substituted for "intellectual," conveying a conception of the intellectual I suggested above.

[30] This proposition applies probably more to Nazi Germany and Fascist Italy than to the communist states. In any event, in entrenched totalitarian systems it was difficult to gauge how genuine such enthusiasm was.

despite the forced conformity, censorship, hypocrisy and repression of the Nasser era, the regime 'bewitched us with the glitter of hopes that had fascinated us for a long time, and they intoxicated us with the wine of "attainment" and "glory"'."[31]

The phenomenon discussed in his study compels reflection and exploration because we do not expect intellectuals to sympathize with dictators, let alone admire them – we expect them to possess sound political and moral judgment. Edward Shils, the distinguished sociologist, believed that

> intellectuals possess an unusual sensitivity to the sacred, an uncommon reflectiveness about the nature of their universe and the rules which govern their society ... [they are] inquiring and desirous of being in frequent communion with symbols which are more general than the immediate concrete situations of everyday life ... This interior need to penetrate beyond the screen of immediate concrete experience marks the existence of the intellectuals in every society.[32]

Regrettably enough, the many available instances of the dubious, sometimes severely impaired political judgments of intellectuals do not support the view of Shils. For example, it may be noted here "that one of the greatest European universities [Cambridge, UK] ... had provided the USSR with its most devoted and effective agents ... symbolic of the force of the Communist idea in the twentieth century."[33] Furet was referring to Philby, MacLean, Burgess, and Blunt, all of whom became Soviet spies devoting their lives to serving the Soviet system. He could have added Eric Hobsbawm to this roster of prominent pro-communist intellectuals who studied at Cambridge University since he too was a lifelong Soviet sympathizer, without becoming a spy.

We expect (or used to expect) more of intellectuals; we think of them as an elite group, a moralizing elite, free of illusions and delusions and endowed with an enlarged capacity for differentiating between good and evil, as well as between appearance and reality. We don't expect intellectuals to suspend the use of their critical faculties under certain conditions: for example, when they are taken on a political conducted tour,

[31] Quoted in Barry Rubin: *Modern Dictators*, New York 1987, 73.

[32] Edward Shils: *The Intellectuals and the Powers and Other Essays*, Chicago 1972, 3. For a sweeping critique of intellectuals based on a very small and somewhat questionable sample, see Paul Johnson: *Intellectuals*, New York 1988. His views are further discussed in Chapter 8.

[33] Furet, 272. Indicative of similar conditions in another elite institution, in the late 1940s reportedly "one student in four at the *Ecole Normale* (Superior, in France) was a member of the Communist cell" (Francois Fejto: "Letter from Paris," *Encounter*, December 1982, 60).

and contemplate dictators surrounded by an orchestrated cult. Rarely did the intellectuals here discussed express shock, distaste, or revulsion when they encountered these "cults of the personality," as Khrushchev called the officially mandated worship of Stalin. However, many of them had changed their positive attitude in later years without necessarily acknowledging it in public.

It has also been widely believed that intellectuals have a special interest in free expression and are fiercely committed to its defense – how could they function otherwise? If so, the obvious and compelling question arises: how did they manage to admire and support dictators who invariably restricted or altogether abolished free expression? A. James Gregor, among others, pondered this puzzle:

> There is really no satisfactory answer to questions of why such individuals [i.e., intellectuals – P.H.] remain loyal to political systems marred by moral failures. Why did not the Founding Fathers ... withdraw their support when the system ... institutionalized slavery – after they had all committed themselves to the moral conviction that "all men were created equal"? Why did not Nikolai Bukharin absent himself from the regime that had massacred untold numbers of innocents ...? And what of all the Chinese intellectuals who continued to support Mao Zedong after the madness of the "Great Proletarian Revolution"? And what of the countless Western intellectuals who found so much to admire in Stalinism and Maoism even after their respective barbarisms became common knowledge?[34]

Stanley Aronowitz, the author of a sympathetic study of C. Wright Mills, the leftist sociologist, was among those apparently *not* puzzled by (or unaware of?) such attitudes, although he had high expectations of intellectuals. He wrote: "The political intellectual, an endangered species throughout modern history, assumed the role of tribune: his mission was to expose the distortions, half-truths, and outright lies that were the steady diet offered by official propaganda."[35] He meant such propaganda in capitalist countries and did not seem to be aware of, or concerned with, the attitude of leftist intellectuals toward the "official propaganda" of countries ruled by leftist dictators. He might have found it difficult to explain why the same intellectuals who denounced the defects and misrepresentations prevalent in their own (Western) societies refrained from denouncing corresponding – or more massive – falsehoods emanating from leftist dictatorships. In his largely admiring intellectual biography

34 A. James Gregor: *Giovanni Gentile: Philosopher of Fascism*, New Brunswick NJ 2001, 99.

35 Stanley Aronowitz: *Taking It Big: C. Wright Mills and the Making of Political Intellectuals*, New York 2010, 190.

of Mills (who was an early supporter of Castro), Aronowitz offered a qualified defense of his own political misjudgments.[36] His own largely uncritical view of Mills is among the illustrations of the illusions often harbored about the political insight and acuity of intellectuals.

This book seeks to answer several questions. Is the admiration of dictators by intellectuals similar or different from the admiration by ordinary people, by non-intellectuals? Do intellectuals admire dictators because of their personality, ideas, or the political system they symbolize and represent? What particular attributes of the dictators do intellectuals find the most appealing? How do they justify the admiration of dictators in light of the dissonance between their supposed commitment to free expression and the policies they pursued?

How can we explain these conflicting attitudes? Do larger cultural-political trends account for them, or are they rooted in the nature or personality of intellectuals, in their shared attributes that include ambivalence about their social role, identity problems, and an unease about being thinkers and talkers rather than doers?[37] Sartre's "acute bouts of bourgeois self-hatred"[38] are among the illustrations of this phenomenon, as are his efforts to overcome the status of being a mere "talker" by selling Maoist publications on the streets of Paris.

What is it in the nature of many intellectuals, especially the public (or political) intellectuals, that makes them susceptible to the appeal of dictators and the political systems they represent? These question cannot be answered without further reflections about the nature and essential qualities of intellectuals.[39]

Intellectuals, for the most part, are not highly specialized; they are primarily social critics and professional moralizers, idealistic and therefore chronically dissatisfied with their own society, or the world as a

[36] Aronowitz seemed uninformed of certain conditions prevailing in Cuba. For instance, he asserted that Cuban "citizens remained armed" (ibid., 210) and that the so-called "committees for the defense of the revolution" provided opportunities for criticizing the authorities (ibid., 211). In fact the major function of these committees was grassroots supervision and spying. As to the armed citizens, only those whose loyalty to the system was beyond the slightest doubt had been armed.

[37] For a more recent analysis of the shared attributes of intellectuals, including their identity problems and aversion to capitalism, see Alan S. Kahan: *Mind vs. Money: The War Between Intellectuals and Capitalism*, New Brunswick NJ 2010.

[38] Richard Wolin: *The Wind from the East: French Intellectuals, the Cultural Revolution and the Legacy of the 1960s*, Princeton NJ 2010, 216.

[39] I reviewed various definitions and conceptions of intellectuals in *Political Pilgrims* (see 40–73). For a recent discussion of the varied and often conflicting conceptions and defining characteristics of intellectuals, see also Rimon cited.

whole, which doesn't measure up to their ideals. Albert Hirschman's observations about human nature are especially applicable to them and highly relevant to their critical disposition: "humans, in contrast to animals, are never satisfied, that is their very nature to be intrinsically unsatisfiable, insatiable ... disappointment is the natural counterpart of man's propensity to entertain magnificent vistas and aspirations." In a similar spirit Thomas Sowell wrote of intellectuals that "their vision of the world is not only a vision ... as it exists and a vision of what the world ought to be like, it is also a vision of *themselves* as a self-anointed vanguard, leading toward a better world."[40] The political disposition of many Western intellectuals has probably also been influenced by their uncertain social status and corresponding identity problems reflected in their alternating embrace of elitism and egalitarianism. Many of them used to believe that in the idealized totalitarian dictatorships these identity problems were, or would be, resolved: intellectuals would become integrated, cease to be isolated from the masses, taken seriously, and assured of their social-cultural functions by the philosopher-king dictator in charge. Leszek Kolakowski wrote: "what is usually called the alienation of intellectuals, their often described feeling of being uprooted, of not belonging, may produce ideological needs which are expressed in joining and articulating anti-intellectual tendencies in existing movements."[41]

If this study succeeds in documenting the uncritical and favorable attitude many intellectuals held toward dictators and the political systems they represented, it may also suggest a rethinking of the defining attributes of intellectuals. In light of the information here gathered, and contrary to widely held views and the conventional wisdom, a substantial number of intellectuals will have to be thought of not as skeptics but potential, or actual, true believers; not hard-nosed social critics but credulous supporters of repressive political systems; not individuals possessed of a penetrating sense of reality committed to unmasking and demystification but seekers of utopian social-political ideals and arrangements. Such a revised conception of intellectuals will have to include the wish to believe, and a propensity for ideologically determined moral indignation. A compelling need to escape the profane and the attendant pursuit

[40] Albert Hirschman: *Shifting Involvements: Private Interests and Public Action*, Princeton NJ 1982, 11, 23; Sowell, 544. Intellectuals could also be described as "those who demand that their society should be judged by the highest possible standards" (Frank Parkin: *Middle Class Radicalism*, Manchester, UK 1968, 30).

[41] Leszek Kolakowski: "Intellectuals Against Intellect," *Daedalus*, Summer 1972, 14.

of self-transcendence may offer the best explanation of the attitudes here examined.[42]

Sharp fluctuations of moral absolutism and moral relativism are also among the attitudes of intellectuals revealed in this study. The moral absolutism is reserved for the stern judgments of their own society, while a pragmatic moral relativism appears when they give the benefit of the doubt to certain dictators and their political systems as long as they find them fundamentally praiseworthy and well intentioned. It follows that the centrality and consistent use of the critical faculties of intellectuals has often been overestimated. In reality the operation of these faculties is largely determined by their basic values and emotional disposition. The spectacular misjudgments of various twentieth-century political systems and their leaders reflect a readiness to suspend, or altogether abandon, their supposedly well-honed critical faculties on particular occasions. Like other mortals, intellectuals are influenced by their predisposition that gives rise to selective perception and selective criticism. Such a disposition was at times made explicit and supported by cultural relativism and the associated unwillingness to be judgmental.

For example, Andrew Young, US ambassador to the United Nations under President Carter, averred: "We must recognize that they [the Soviet policymakers – P.H.] are growing up in circumstances different from ours. They have, therefore, developed a completely different concept of human rights."[43] This used to be the non-judgmental mantra among sympathetic visitors to various dictatorial societies, especially communist ones.

Further back in time, Beatrice and Sidney Webb collected vast amounts of "information" or "data" for their huge study of the Soviet Union (*Soviet Communism: A New Civilization*, 1937), but

> it never seemed to have occurred to [them] that some of the things they had collected might have been false. They accepted them as they were, word for word, whether they dealt with the constitution, the judicial apparatus, political organizations, agricultural collectivization, or the Five-Year Plan. They wrote as though

[42] I made a similar point in *Political Pilgrims* (p. 29), a study that focused not on hero worship but on the misapprehension of communist political systems as a whole: "Behind the metaphors of wholeness, identity and community lies a craving for a universe that has meaning, purpose and direction. Apparently such a craving is ... more pronounced among intellectuals than among 'ordinary people.' Of late it appears that intellectuals find it less tolerable ... to live in a world of 'disenchantment' from which 'the ultimate and sublime values have retreated'," as Max Weber put it.

[43] Quoted in Carl Gershman: "The World According to Andrew Young," *Commentary*, August 1978, 18.

a real country could be described and analyzed according to what it said about itself, inaugurating what would be a long-lived academic tradition.

Nor did the Webbs make reference to any author critical of any aspect of the Soviet system:

The result, [was] the two-volume *Soviet Communism*, with its benign spirit and credulity ... Nothing was missing, not even a justification of the single party in the name of democracy, for they saw the party as acting exclusively by means of persuasion ... Stalin had "not even the extensive power which the Congress of the United States [had] temporarily conferred upon President Roosevelt ..." in the Soviet Union they [the Webbs] had seen in its infancy the withering away of the state![44]

Kolakowski wrote: "It is impossible today to read without horror the panegyric of Sidney and Beatrice Webb ... who in the days of the most ferocious Stalinist terror, glorified the democratic Soviet regime and proclaimed its superiority over the British democracy."[45]

In the second half of the twentieth century, postulating *moral equivalence* between Western pluralistic societies and communist dictatorships (especially the Soviet Union) became a common manifestation of the intellectuals' inability, or unwillingness, to use their critical or analytical faculties and make important distinctions. Arthur Koestler called it "neutralism," but it was more a pretense of neutralism. He wrote: "Neutralism was indeed the most refined form of intellectual betrayal ... It showed a forgiving attitude towards totalitarian terror but denounced with unforgiving venom any failing or injustice in the West. It equated the Hollywood purges of suspected Reds in the film industry with purges which decimated the Soviet population."[46]

In a totally different context bizarre double standards were used by the once-famous 1960s radical, Kwame Ture (formerly Stokely Carmichael), who spent much of his youth protesting racial and other injustices in American society. He moved to Guinea in Africa:

"a country with less political freedom than the one he left behind," and supporting the authoritarian President Toure, Ture embraced ideology "at the expense of his identity as an intellectual maverick and political contrarian." And Ture's "vision of an idealized Africa," Mr Joseph [his biographer] writes, "bound by a

44 Furet, 154–155.
45 Kolakowski, 19.
46 Arthur and Cynthia Koestler: *Stranger on the Square*, New York 1984, 95.

unifying culture, ideology and economic system seemed at times to veer toward magical thinking."[47]

SOME EXPLANATIONS

Explanations of the misperception and idealization of dictators and their political system here dealt with has to take into account the universal human capacity for self-deception. I do not believe that the intellectuals involved intended to deceive any particular audience. They generally believed what they said, or wrote. The capacity for self-deception, aided by selective perception and wishful thinking, is a plausible enough explanation and the essential precondition of the misjudgments here discussed.

Intellectuals disenchanted with their own society and the familiar social world yearned to find superior alternatives, and it was this desire that led to the suspension of their critical faculties, to overlooking the great flaws of both the dictators and their political systems. For example, as Saul Bellow observed, Sartre's "hatred of the bourgeoisie was so excessive that he was inclined to go easy on the crimes of Stalin."[48] Sartre was by no means an exception.

Robert Trivers, an evolutionary biologist, has written about the general processes of self-deception relevant for understanding the attitudes here discussed:

> At the heart of our mental lives, there seemed to be a striking contradiction – we seek out information and then act to destroy it ... our sense organs have evolved to give us a marvelously detailed and accurate view of the outside world ... But once this information arrives in our brains, it is often distorted and biased to our conscious minds. We deny the truth to ourselves. We project onto others traits that are in fact true of ourselves ... We repress painful memories, create completely false ones, rationalize immoral behavior, act repeatedly to boost positive self-opinion.[49]

[47] Quoted in Felicia Lee: "He Cried Out 'Black Power,' Then Left for Africa," Arts Section, *New York Times*, March 24, 2014. Ture was also an admirer of Castro and his system. On one of his visits to Cuba he "spent three days in conversations with Fidel," who put him "under my protection" and considered him an ally and a major source of information about the radical black movement in the United States (see Tom Hayden: *Listen Yankee! Why Cuba Matters*, New York 2015, 130).

[48] Saul Bellow: *It All Adds Up*, New York 1994, 107.

[49] Robert Trivers: *The Folly of Fools: The Logic of Deceit and Self-Deception in Human Life*, New York 2011, 2.

Trivers suggested that self-deception is often bred by self-righteousness[50] – an attitude idealistic intellectuals often find hard to avoid. Self-righteousness contributes to self-deception, especially when cognitive dissonance has to be dealt with. The latter arises when, for example, intellectuals disposed to venerate a particular dictator and his regime come across information that conflicts with their favorable disposition. The preferred solution is to ignore or discredit such information.

Mario Vargas Llosa suggested that it is the elitism of intellectuals that leads them to the misjudgments here examined: "Camus wrote that a very intelligent man in some areas can be stupid in others. In politics intellectuals have been very stupid, in many cases ... They don't like mediocrity. And democracy is an indication of mediocrity; democracy is to accept that perfection doesn't exist in political reality."[51]

Further questions may be raised about the sources of the apparent (if often transient) affinity between some intellectuals and dictators. Were these intellectuals attracted to particular political systems because they were impressed by the personality of the dictators who were in charge of them, or, to the contrary, was it the nature of these systems that impressed them in the first place and led them to the admiration of their founders, and leaders, the dictators? Did the admiration of dictators by intellectuals have practical consequences, helping to legitimate them and the political system they dominated?[52]

It is important to emphasize that the dictatorships which appealed to many Western intellectuals in the twentieth century were not ordinary authoritarian regimes but, as a rule, totalitarian ones, which proclaimed commitment to secular-religious beliefs and the sweeping transformation of social institutions and even human nature. Hans Borkenau, among others, noted the religious undertones of these commitments: "The essence of these revolutionary creeds is the belief that the final day of salvation has come, that the millennium on this earth is near ... that complete virtue, simplicity and happiness can be brought about by violence."[53]

50 Ibid., 298.

51 "The Politics of Literature: An Interview with Mario Vargas Llosa," *Daily Beast*, online October 10, 2013.

52 For example, it has been suggested that Walter Duranty's adulatory views of Stalin and the Soviet system exerted "great influence in shaping American attitudes toward the Soviet Union" and even helped to persuade Roosevelt to open diplomatic relations with it (Francine de Plessix Gray: "The Journalist and the Dictator," *New York Times Book Review*, June 24, 1990).

53 Borkenau quoted in Michel Burleigh: *Sacred Causes*, New York 2007, 121.

Dictators of more circumscribed aspirations and more limited power, such as Franco, Salazar, Chiang Kai-shek, Peron, or Somoza, did not exert the same attraction. Omar Torrijos of Panama was an exception – by no means a major historical figure, he lacked consuming ideological commitments, but nonetheless stimulated the admiration and friendship of Graham Greene.[54]

The late Eric Hobsbawm, the widely respected British historian, provides a striking example of the overwhelming importance many intellectuals attached to the *professed ideals* (or good intentions) of the leaders and the political system they admired. In 1994 an interviewer asked him if he would have supported the Soviet system had he known of its mass murders of the 1930s. He responded, after some apparent hesitation, that he would have done so, because of "the chance of *a new world being born in great suffering* would still have been worth backing."[55] It was an attitude shared by Irving Howe (not a supporter of the Soviet Union), for whom too the *ideals* of socialism seemed to be more important than the results of the attempts to realize them. As Hilton Kramer put it, "for Howe, it seems, the socialist idea was far too precious to be subjected to anything as vulgar as the judgment of history." Sartre also succeeded in saving the nobility of the ends from the taint of the means: "Through the special alchemy of the Sartrean dialectic, crimes committed in the name of socialism were forgiven as contingent derelictions, when they were not simply denied, and all attempts to hold their perpetrators to moral account were dismissed as an example of 'bad faith'."[56]

[54] See Graham Greene: *Getting to Know the General*, New York 1984. Greene also admired other (communist) authoritarian systems such as the Soviet Union, Castro's Cuba, and Nicaragua under the Sandinistas, but only with Torrijos did he have an intimate personal relationship (see Chapter 7, pp. 259–263). Gabriel Garcia Marquez was another friend of Torrijos, who was "a faithful reader" of his books (see Enrique Krauze: "In the Shadow of the Patriarch," *New Republic*, November 4, 2009, 45).

[55] Quoted in Robert Conquest: *Reflections on a Ravaged Century*, New York 2000, 10–11 (emphasis added). One may detect religious undertones in Hobsbawm's implied connection between suffering and its rewards, the better new world. See also my review of Eric Hobsbawm: *Interesting Times: A Twentieth Century Life* in *National Interest*, Summer 2003. Presumably it was also Hobsbawm's durable pro-Soviet sentiments that led him to affirm (in the British communist newspaper, the *Daily Worker*, November 9, 1956) that he approved, "though 'with a heavy heart'," the Soviet troops crushing the Hungarian Revolution in 1956 (quoted in Roger Scruton: *Fools, Frauds and Firebrands*, London 2015, 18).

[56] Hilton Kramer: *The Twilight of Intellectuals: Culture and Politics in the Era of the Cold War*, Chicago 1999, 151, 286.

THE DISCONTENTS OF MODERNITY, POLITICAL HERO WORSHIP, AND CELEBRITY INTELLECTUALS

The common foundation of the sympathetic attitude toward fascism and Nazism, on the one hand, and communism, on the other, was a profound alienation that predisposed many intellectuals to a hopeful, benefit-of-the-doubt attitude toward political systems that promised to offer thrilling, radical alternatives, preferably revolutionary change.[57] Alastair Hamilton suggested that "the barrier between those who chose Communism and those who preferred Fascism seems to me, in many cases, so slim that we are less than ever entitled to say that a certain type of man, a certain type of psychology tended toward Fascism."[58]

Disillusionment with or a questioning of modernity was the broadest common denominator of these attitudes. Peter Berger argued that "*intellectuals constitute a group particularly vulnerable to the discontents of modernity*." [my emphasis] By the same token they have also been particularly susceptible to the appeals of socialism that included "the theme of renewed community" and "promised all the blessings of modernity *and* the liquidation of its costs, including most importantly, the cost of alienation." For all these reasons the affinity between intellectuals and socialism was suffused "with moral passion, in many instances with profoundly religious hope."[59] Arguably Czeslaw Milosz had in mind the same intellectuals and their discontents when he wrote: "judging by the rage and contempt emanating from books, paintings and films – never before have so many people taken up indictment as a pastime ... A conviction of decadence, the rotting of the West, seems to be a permanent part of the equipment of enlightened and sensitive people for dealing with the horrors accompanying technological progress."[60]

[57] See also Raymond Aron: *The Opium of Intellectuals*, London 1957. The passage of time made no dent on the validity of his proposition.

[58] Alastair Hamilton: *The Appeal of Fascism: A Study of Intellectuals 1919–1945*, London 1971, xvi.

[59] Peter L. Berger: "The Socialist Myth," *Public Interest*, Summer 1976, 5, 7, 9, 11. In a similar spirit Leszek Kolakowski wrote that Marxism "was a dream offering the prospect of a society of perfect unity, in which all human aspirations would be fulfilled and all values reconciled ... The influence that Marxism has achieved ... is almost entirely due to its prophetic, fantastic and irrational elements ... [it] performs the function of religion ... Marx combined his romantic dreams with the socialist expectation that all needs would be fully satisfied in an earthly paradise" ("Epilogue," in *Main Currents of Marxism*, New York 2005, 1206, 1208, 1209).

[60] Czeslaw Milosz: "The Agony of the West," in *Visions from San Francisco Bay*, New York 1975, 114.

Many of the intellectuals referred to below would have agreed with Sayyid Qutb's critique of Western societies inspired by his radical Islamic outlook:

At this time an outcry has arisen everywhere, a warning alarm about the fate of humankind in the thrall of a materialist civilization devoid of faith and human spirit – the white man's civilization ... Humanity today is standing at the brink of an abyss ... because humanity is bankrupt in the realm of values ... which foster true human progress and development. This is abundantly clear to the Western world, for the West can no longer provide the values necessary for the flourishing of humanity.[61]

Curiously enough, the sentiments expressed by Hillary Clinton in her 1969 Wellesley College commencement speech have an unexpected affinity with the beliefs of Qutb quoted above, as do the underlying sentiments characteristic of the period when she made them:

We are, all of us, exploring a world that none of us even understands and attempting to create within that uncertainty. But there are some things we feel, feelings that our prevailing, acquisitive and competitive corporate life ... is not the way for us. We're searching for a more immediate, ecstatic and penetrating mode of living ... Every protest, every dissent ... is unabashedly an attempt to forge an identity in this particular age.

She also expressed a determination to lift "the burden of inauthentic reality."[62] Qutb and Hillary Clinton shared a concern with the spiritual impoverishment of the Western world and especially American society. Less surprisingly her feelings were paralleled by the communitarian longings of the 1960s radicals. Todd Gitlin, former president of the Students for a Democratic Society (SDS), wrote: "There was a longing to 'unite the fragmented parts of personal history' ... to transcend the multiplicity and confusion of roles that become normal in a rationalized society: the rifts between work and family, between public and private, between strategic, calculating reason and spontaneous expressive emotion."[63] Richard Wolin observed a convergence of longing for sustaining communal bonds at both ends of the political spectrum that was not limited to German and French intellectuals:

a critique of the West formerly purveyed by thinkers on the German right during the 1920s became popular among the French intellectual left in the 1960s. As set

[61] Quoted in Pankaj Mishra: *From the Ruins of Empire: The Intellectuals Who Remade Asia*, New York 2012, 262, 270.

[62] Quoted in Jonah Goldberg: *Liberal Fascism: The Secret History of the American Left from Mussolini to the Politics of Meaning*, New York 2004, 320.

[63] Quoted in ibid., 181.

forth by ... Oswald Spengler, Ernst Junger and Carl Schmitt this critique took aim at a moribund and decadent bourgeois "civilization." These critics sought to replace the latter with a new form of Gemeinschaft or community that would prove capable of meeting the challenges of a technological age.

Tony Judt also drew attention to such sentiments: "During the twilight of the Third Republic [in France], 'Left and Right alike felt a distaste for the lukewarm and were fascinated by the idea of violent relief from mediocrity.'"[64] It is not difficult to see how such sentiments paved the way for the rise of hero worship, the admiration of charismatic, resolute, problem-solving political leaders, who offered relief from mediocrity.

Modernity, needless to say, also meant secularization and, as Roger Griffin put it, had an "anomy-generating impact" associated with the "progressive loss of a homogenous value-system."[65] Another aspect of modernity that disturbed intellectuals was the moral relativism that was associated with a permissive pluralistic political and cultural setting. Czeslaw Milosz had the opportunity the observe these attitudes among intellectuals first in his native communist-dominated Poland, later in Western Europe and the United States where he lived for much of his life. He wrote:

> Westerners, and especially Western intellectuals, suffer from a special variety of *taedium vitae*; their emotional and intellectual life is too dispersed. Everything they think and feel evaporates like steam in an open expanse. Freedom is a burden for them. No conclusions they arrive at are binding ... The result is constant uneasiness. The happiest of them seem to be those who become Communists.[66]

Even as belief in a divine care-giver declined, the need for religious beliefs and certainties did not, and has found new expression in the hoped-for redeeming power and benevolence of secular rulers upon whom attributes earlier reserved for deities came to be projected.[67] As William Pfaff put it, there was a "desire to find a postreligious moral

64 Richard Wolin: *The Seduction of Unreason: The Intellectuals' Romance with Fascism from Nietzsche to Postmodernism*, Princeton NJ 2004, 246–247; Judt quoted in ibid., 158.

65 Roger Griffin: *Modernism and Fascism: The Sense of Beginning under Mussolini and Hitler*, New York 2007, 116, 344.

66 Czeslaw Milosz: *The Captive Mind*, New York 1953, 79.

67 Jan Plamper wrote: "the death of God was the precondition for the deification of man and the types of modern personality cults to which the Stalin Cult belongs" (*The Stalin Cult: A Study in the Alchemy of Power*, New Haven CT 2012, 24).

explanation for life ... [as] the myth of secular salvation has generally replaced religion in Western high culture" and "secular utopian thought" came "to inspire a lethal dogmatic idealism." He also grasped that "the idea of total and redemptive transformation of human society through political means, the most influential myth of Western political society from 1789 to the present day, remains with us." Longing for such "redemptive transformation" also permeated the agenda of terrorist groups such as the Red Brigades of Italy, who vowed "to liberate man finally from bestial exploitation, from necessary labor, from misery, from fatigues, from social degradation."[68]

Worshiping powerful leaders in the twentieth century became, for numerous intellectuals and non-intellectuals alike, a substitute for the religious veneration of divinity. It remains an open question as to what extent intellectuals here discussed were influenced by the quasi-religious propaganda of totalitarian states in their hopeful attitude toward these leaders.[69]

The dictators subject to the veneration (temporary or enduring) of intellectuals were, for the most part, charismatic, or somewhat charismatic, and this obviously increased their appeal. Here it may be useful to recall Max Weber's widely used definition of charisma and the charismatic leader:

> The provisioning of all demands that go beyond those of everyday routine ... has had a charismatic foundation ... The natural leaders in distress have been holders of specific gifts of the body and spirit; and these gifts have been believed to be supernatural, not accessible to everybody ... the holders of charisma ... must stand outside the ties of this world, outside routine occupations, as well as outside the routine obligations of family life ... the charismatic hero does not deduce his authority from codes and statues ... nor does he deduce his authority from traditional custom ... charismatic domination ... is revolutionary

[68] William Pfaff: *The Bullet's Song: Romantic Violence and Utopia*, New York 2004, 15, 23, 188, 189, 288.

[69] It is of some interest that – unlike the argument presented above – as of 1970 Arthur Schlesinger Jr. made the dubious suggestion that "ours is an age without heroes" and that World War II somehow discredited all heroes, "precipitat[ing] a universal revulsion against greatness." He made no distinction between dictators like Stalin, Hitler, and Mussolini on the one hand and leaders such as Churchill, F.D. Roosevelt, and de Gaulle on the other. He believed that in the postwar period "the sheer weight of such personalities on one's existence" could no longer be felt (quoted in Theodore L. Gross ed.: *Representative Men: The Cult Heroes of Our Time*, New York 1970, 13–14). Schlesinger obviously overlooked the impact of figures such as Mao, Castro, or Pol Pot and conflated their kind of greatness with that represented by figures such as Roosevelt and Churchill.

> and transvalues everything; it makes a sovereign break with all traditional or rational norms.[70]

Weber also wrote that "The holder of charisma ... demands obedience and a following by virtue of his mission ... The term 'charisma' will be applied to a certain quality of an individual personality by virtue of which he is set apart from ordinary men and treated as endowed with supernatural, superhuman, or at least specifically exceptional powers or qualities."[71]

More recently a political leader was defined as charismatic if he "possess[ed] a coherent vision of the future – a picture of how the world ought to be, based on a special insight into the nature of reality," or a "certainty of vision." Laurence Rees further suggested that "the single most important precondition for the creation of Hitler's charisma was his ability to connect with the feelings, hopes and desires of millions of his fellow Germans." The proposed credentials of the charismatic leader include "the conviction that goals could be achieved primarily by willpower and by faith."[72] Many of these attitudes and attributes are applicable to the totalitarian leaders of the past century and to the forms of domination they exercised, unknown in Weber's lifetime.

Most important among the stimulants of hero worship is the belief that certain individuals (who become, or are, the leaders or dictators) possess unique, superhuman gifts, that they are redeemers capable of resolving all the problems and difficulties their predecessors, more conventional politicians, were incapable of solving. Georges Bataille was among the Western intellectuals who "believed in the need for a spiritual elite to restore the dimension of social solidarity that was wanting in modern society."[73] The heroic leader obviously belonged to this elite.

In another approach to the same societal needs, Michael Ignatieff suggested that

> heroism is essential to politics. We live for the hour when a politician stands up ... and we recognize ... that here is a person prepared to take risks, tell us what we don't want to hear, face possible defeat for a principle, tackle insuperable odds, and by doing so show us that politics need be not just the art of the possible.[74]

Also characteristic of the modern dictators here considered is that, almost invariably, they aspired to the role of philosopher-king, to be seen as great

[70] Max Weber: *Essays in Sociology*, London 1948, 245, 248–249.

[71] Quoted in S.N. Eisenstadt ed.: *Max Weber on Charisma and Institution Building*, Chicago 1968, 20, 48.

[72] Laurence Rees: *Hitler's Charisma*, New York 2012, 10, 44, 131, 219.

[73] Quoted in Wolin 2004, 117.

[74] Michael Ignatieff: "The Hero Europe Needed," *Atlantic*, March 2015, 96.

thinkers, fonts of wisdom – they wanted to be more than holders of concentrated power. Even Qaddafi of Libya felt obligated to write a book, the *Green Book*, that was a "complete guide to remaking society; along with guidelines for government and the economy ... musings on education, black people, sports, horsemanship and stagecraft." Not surprisingly such ambitions and dispositions had a special appeal for intellectuals.[75]

Hero worship had another important source, a compensatory need stimulated by aspects of modernity that reduce opportunities for heroic self-assertion. Many intellectuals, perhaps more than other groups, missed and craved these opportunities in the prosaic, liberal capitalist societies. As Alan Bloom observed, "civil societies dedicated to ... self-preservation cannot be expected to provide fertile soil for the heroic or the inspired. They do not require or encourage the noble ... One who holds the economic view of man cannot consistently believe in the dignity of man or in the special status of art and science." Ian Buruma and Avishai Margalet made a similar point: "What is lacking in the democratic Occident is sacrifice and heroism. Unlike Mao, Hitler or Stalin, democratic politicians lack 'the will to grandeur.' ... The anti-heroic, antiutopian nature of Western liberalism is the greatest enemy of religious radicals, priest-kings, and collective seekers after purity and heroic salvation."[76]

Robert Nisbet suggested that there has been a "retreat of the heroic from the life of Western societies ... between heroism and modernity there has been a fateful conflict. The acids of modernity, which include egalitarianism, [and] scepticism ... have eaten away much of the base on which heroism flourished." Hans Speier also noted the connection between modernity and the decline of the heroic dimensions of life: "There is a sharp contrast between heroic society and modern social organization. Power now is centralized and largely anonymous; law has restrained self-reliance ... A truly bewildering specialization of work ... has created a web of interdependence ... We are divorced from the naive and full assertion of life."[77]

[75] Jon Lee Anderson: "King of Kings," *New Yorker*, November 7, 2011, 48. See also Craig Calhoun: "Libyan Money, Academic Missions and Public Social Science," in *Public Culture*, September 2016, 29, Duke University Press; also Jon Wiener: "Professors Paid by Qaddafi: Providing 'Positive Public Relations'" in *The Nation*, March 5, 2011; also Jeevan Vasagar: "Academic linked to Gaddafi's fugitive son leaves LSE" in www.guardian.co.uk, October 31, 2011.

[76] Bloom quoted in Saul Bellow: "Writers, Intellectuals, Politics: Mainly Reminiscence," in *It All Adds Up*, New York 1994, 111–112; Ian Buruma and Avishai Margalit: *Occidentalism: The West in the Eyes of Its Enemies*, New York 2004, 57, 72.

[77] Robert Nisbet: *Twilight of Authority*, New York 1975, 102, 109; Hans Speier: "Risk, Security and Modern Hero Worship," in *Social Order and the Risks of War*, New York 1952, 125, 126.

Speier further argued that while in modern societies externally imposed risks have multiplied, opportunities for freely chosen risk, integral to heroism or heroic self-assertion, diminished. Vicarious identification with seemingly heroic dictators promised to satisfy these unmet needs both among ordinary people and intellectuals seeking opportunities for idealistic self-assertion. Georges Bataille also discerned a connection between modernity and hero worship, as he proposed that "revival of the charisma and myth would serve as a salutary counterweight to the centrifugal tendencies of modernity."[78]

It is important to remind the reader that modern conditions have also made it possible to replicate charisma, to "manufacture" and stimulate a synthetic hero worship by techniques and technologies that have become newly available. Some of the dictators discussed below clearly benefited from these opportunities, creating or strengthening their own cult. Sidney Hook wrote, well before the advent of television and computers, that "Today, more than ever before, *belief* in the hero is a synthetic product. Whoever controls the microphones and printing presses can make or unmake belief overnight. If greatness be defined in terms of popular acclaim ... then it may be thrust upon the modern dictator. But if it is not thrust upon him, he can easily arrange for it."[79] While this claim is somewhat exaggerated, modern hero worship (including that of non-political celebrities) has an inauthentic component contributed by the new techniques of propaganda, advertising and "public relations." At the same time it is undeniable that the two major cults of dictators of the previous century, those of Hitler and Stalin, "relied on the active and willing participation of millions, who suspended their disbelief and endorsed and magnified the overblown personalities constructed by the authorities."[80]

There may be an additional reason accounting for the popularity of dictators, as John Gray (among others) has suggested: "Tyranny offers relief from the burden of sanity and a license to enact forbidden impulses of hatred and violence. By acting on these impulses and releasing them in their subjects tyrants give people a kind of happiness, which as individuals they may be incapable of achieving."[81]

While, as argued above, aspects of modernity stimulated hero worship, the roots of the phenomenon are deep and preceded modernity, or

[78] Bataille, quoted in Wolin 2004, 176.

[79] Sidney Hook: *The Hero in History*, New York 1943, 10.

[80] Richard Overy: *The Dictators: Hitler's Germany and Stalin's Russia*, New York 2004, 119.

[81] John Gray: *The Silence of Animals*, New York 2013, 57.

its more recent manifestations. Thomas Carlyle, the British philosopher, had no use for a conception of history dominated by impersonal social forces and was an unembarrassed admirer of great heroes. Writing in 1840, he preferred to believe that "Man is heaven born; not in the thrall of Circumstances, of Necessity, but the victorious subduer thereof." He further argued:

> We cannot look ... upon a great man, without gaining something by him. He is the living light-fountain ... The light which enlightens ... Worship of a Hero is transcendent admiration of a Great Man. I say great men are still admirable ... there is, at bottom, nothing else admirable! No nobler feeling than this of admiration for one higher than himself ... Hero worship, heartfelt prostrate admiration, submission ... for a noblest godlike Form of Man, – is not that the germ of Christianity itself? ... in these circumstances ... "Hero-worship" becomes a fact inexpressibly precious ... There is an everlasting hope in it ... Had all traditions ... creeds, societies that men ever instituted, sunk away, this would remain.

Carlyle did not seem to entertain the possibility that hero worship could be a form of false-consciousness, a form of escapism, that the wrong kinds of individuals might be admired for the wrong reasons, as they had been throughout history and especially in more recent times. The heroes he venerated included Mohammed, Dante, Shakespeare, Rousseau, Cromwell, and Napoleon, but he found "the hero as king" – that is to say, the political leader – "the most important of Great Men ... He is practically the summary of *all* the various figures of Heroism: Priest, Teacher, whatsoever of earthly or spiritual dignity we can fancy to reside in a man."[82]

Carlyle's view of heroes was of a Romantic derivation: he was strongly influenced by German romanticism; he translated a novel of Goethe and wrote a book about Schiller. He disliked emerging modernity and, like all Romantics, believed that some dramatic form of deliverance from the problems of life and society was within reach. He wishfully overestimated the impact a single individual could have on social arrangements and the improvements he could bring to society. His ideas were popular with Nazi ideologues: "Nazi propagandists saw in Carlyle a respectable support for their beliefs"; his *On Heroes* was required reading for students. Both Hitler and Goebbels read his works and were inspired by them.[83]

[82] Thomas Carlyle: *On Heroes, Hero-Worship and the Heroic in History*, Berkeley CA 1993 (first published 1841), xxxiv–xxxv, 3–4, 11–12, 169, 174.

[83] M.K. Goldberg: "Introduction," in ibid., lxxii–lxxiii.

Romantic hero worship was also in evidence in the second half of the twentieth century. Intellectuals like Norman Mailer expressed an unembarrassed, heartfelt longing for heroes and bitterly complained that his society failed to provide them: "So, Fidel Castro, I announce to the City of New York that you gave all of us who are alone in this country ... some sense that there were heroes in the world ... You were the first and greatest hero to appear in the world since the Second [World] War."[84] Revolutionary heroes like Castro did not hesitate to use violent means to accomplish their objectives, a disposition that too appealed to Mailer, who believed that violence is often a form of authentic self-expression.[85]

While intellectuals, for the most part, have been reluctant to engage in acts of violence in the pursuit of their political aspirations and ideals,[86] many admired strong men who did not hesitate to resort to it in order to accomplish their political objectives. A handful of intellectuals such as Trotsky, T.E. Lawrence, Andre Malraux, Gabriele D'Annunzio, and Regis Debray became what Saul Bellow called "intellectual activists."[87] They held some political power for periods of time and occasionally participated in armed conflicts. There were substantial differences between the extent and nature of their political activism and the dangers they exposed themselves to.

Slavoj Zizek, self-styled revolutionary, social critic, and celebrity philosopher of our times, provides a singular example of the refusal of some

[84] Norman Mailer: *Presidential Papers*, New York 1963, 67, 68.

[85] For further explorations of Mailer, violence, and intellectuals, see Lionel Abel: "Murder and the Intellectuals," *Commentary*, November 1981; Naomi Munson and James Atlas: "The Literary Life of Crime," *New Republic*, September 9, 1981. George Watson also argued that violence holds "an emotional attraction" for intellectuals who often regard it as a mark of authenticity. He wrote: "for many intellectuals the gun confers heroism" (George Watson: "Were the Intellectuals Duped?" *National Review*, November 7, 1975, 1230, 1231).

[86] There have been numerous exceptions. One was the largely unknown involvement of intellectuals in assassinations organized by the NKVD (the Soviet political police) in the 1930s documented by John Dziak among others (see Stephen Schwartz: "Intellectuals and Assassins: Annals of Stalin's Killerati," *New York Times Book Review*, January 24, 1988). Other cases include the murderous Shining Path guerilla movement in Peru that "was headed and founded by professors" and the violent Red Brigades of Italy that enjoyed similar support among academics (Conquest, 220). Equally noteworthy is that "15 out of 25 leaders of the *Einsatzgruppen* [units that specialized in the killing of Jews in territories occupied by Nazi Germany during World War II – P.H.] had doctorates. These were ... members of the German academic elite" (Niall Ferguson: *The War of the World: History's Age of Hatred*, New York 2007, 397).

[87] Bellow 1994, 103.

intellectuals to modify their political beliefs in light of changing historical circumstances and evidence. Zizek insisted that "the misfortunes of the fate of revolutionary terror confront us with the need – not to reject terror *in toto*, but – to reinvent it." In the same book he averred that "the problem here is not terror as such – our task today is precisely to reinvent *emancipatory terror*."[88] Zizek did not explain what he meant by this new Orwellian concept, but presumably it was purifying terror, the terror of good intentions. He also wrote:

> in every authentic revolutionary explosion there is an element of "pure" violence, i.e. an authentic political revolution cannot be measured by the standard ... to what extent life got better for the majority afterward – it is a goal-in-itself, an act which changes the very standards of what "good life" is, and a different (higher, eventually) standard of living is a by-product of a revolutionary process, not its goal ... one should directly admit revolutionary violence as a liberating end-in-itself.[89]

Among well-known intellectuals, only Sartre and Mailer were similarly enthralled by this fantasy of a mystified, liberating violence that would prove the authenticity of those engaging in it, including the committed intellectual. Zizek, like Sartre and Mailer, had no difficulty beholding the troublesome relationship between ends and means – strongly felt good intentions took care of the problem and guaranteed authenticity.

Zizek's pronouncements exemplify an unusually extreme and irrational attitude toward political violence, inspired by what seem to be deep secular-religious convictions. His determination to "remain faithful to the legacy of the radical left" led him to propose that "the terrorist past has to be accepted as *ours*."[90] His peculiar views (often expressed in jargon-ridden, convoluted prose) did not interfere with his becoming a major intellectual-academic celebrity of the Western world.[91] A small sampling of more of his startling propositions follows:

[88] Slavoj Zizek: *In Defense of Lost Causes*, London 2008, 7, 174 (emphasis added).

[89] Zizek: "Foreword," to Bob Avakian and Bill Martin: *Marxism and the Call of the Future*, Chicago 2005, x. As a critic of Zizek pointed out, for him "the utopian dimension is so precious that it is worth any number of human lives. To the tens of millions already lost in Russia, China, Cambodia and elsewhere, Zizek is prepared to add however many more are required" (Adam Kirsch: "The Deadly Jester," *New Republic*, December 3, 2008, 32).

[90] Zizek, *In Defense of Lost Causes*, 160.

[91] See Paul Hollander: "Slavoj Zizek and the Rise of the Celebrity Intellectual," *Society*, July–August 2010. For another critical discussion of Zizek, see John Zmirak: "Slavoj Zizek Offers Smut for the Smart," *Modern Age*, Summer 2015.

> The Stalinist terror of the 1930s was a humanist terror; its adherence to a "humanist" core was not what constrained its horror, it was what sustained it, it was its inherent condition of possibility ... far from being the greatest catastrophe that could have befallen Russia, Stalinism effectively saved what we understand as the humanity of man ... in what is arguably the most intelligent legitimization of Stalinist terror, Merleau-Ponty's *Humanism and Terror* ... the terror is justified as a kind of wager on the future ... if the final result of today's horror will be the bright Communist future, then this outcome will retroactively redeem the terrible things a revolutionary has to do today. [Hobsbawm shared these feelings, see pp. 176, 177 – P.H.][92]

Zizek admired Che Guevara because (among other reasons), in the midst of the Cuban missile crisis, "he advocated a fearless approach of risking the new world war which would involve (at the very least) the total annihilation of the Cuban people – he praised the heroic readiness of the Cuban people to risk its own disappearance." Needless to say the Cuban people were not consulted on this matter and it is unlikely that they were ready to endorse their own annihilation in a nuclear conflagration. Not surprisingly Zizek was also drawn to Mao and the Cultural Revolution he initiated. In his opinion Mao (like Che Guevara) deserved praise for his "courage" to confront unflinchingly the possibility of a nuclear showdown: "one should recall Mao Zedong's message to the hundreds of millions of downtrodden, a simple and touching message of courage – do not be afraid of the Big Powers ... the same message of courage sustains also Mao's (in)famous stance towards the prospect of a new atomic world war."

The gist of Mao's "courageous" stance was the proposition that given the large population of China, plenty of Chinese would survive a nuclear war while its less numerous enemies would perish (see p. 177).

In turn, the Cultural Revolution impressed Zizek because it "did contain elements of an enacted utopia" and was "the last truly great revolutionary explosion of the twentieth century." The violence it entailed was greatly preferable and morally superior to the violence of capitalist systems: "What were the violent and destructive outbursts of a Red Guardist caught in the Cultural Revolution compared to the true Cultural Revolution, the permanent dissolution of all life-forms which capitalist reproduction dictates?"[93]

92 Zizek, *In Defense of Lost Causes*, 214–215, 211, 224.

93 Slavoj Zizek: *Violence*, New York 2008, 209.

Zizek's beliefs appear to be rooted in an unshakeable conviction that nothing exceeds the evils of capitalism and the violence it generates.[94] It was a conviction shared to varying degrees by many Western intellectuals who were attracted to dictators of different political persuasion and who had in common an anti-capitalist disposition. John Gray sheds further light on the roots of Zizek's beliefs and especially his popularity:

> A feature of hyper-capitalism of recent years is that it abolishes historical memory. The squalor and misery of communism are now as remote to most people as life under feudalism. When Zizek and others like him defend communism – "the communist hypothesis" as they call it – they can pass over the fact that the hypothesis has been falsified time and again, in dozens of different countries, because their audience knows nothing of the past. Hence the appeals of Zizek's works ... avidly consumed by young people in Europe and beyond.[95]

Zizek is prominent among intellectuals who remain enamored with ideals that have their distant roots in Marxism but can no longer be plausibly associated with any existing political system, whatever it calls itself. As Robert Hughes has written, "the effort to save some notionally 'pure' essence of Marxist ideas from their results in the real world still goes on ... in America – because America unlike Russia or China or Cuba, has never had a Marxist government, or anything resembling one, so that the millenarian hope and fantasies of Marxism never had a chance to be tested."[96]

While sympathy for repressive communist systems has greatly diminished (for obvious reasons) since the collapse of the Soviet Union, the *idea* of communism has retained its attraction for some Western intellectuals, such as Zizek. These sentiments were reliably captured by a conference called "The Idea of Communism," held in London at the Birkbeck Institute for the Humanities in 2009, which, its organizers believed, "had huge political importance."[97] Alain Badiou, one of the participants, considered Khrushchev's critique of Stalin "misguided" and blamed him for contributing to "the decline of the Idea of communism." He further blamed Khrushchev for "pav[ing] the way for the 'New Philosophers' of

[94] Zizek wrote: "it is the self-propelling metaphysical dance of capital that runs the show, that provides the key to real life developments and catastrophes. Therein lies the fundamental systemic violence of capitalism, much more uncanny than any direct pre-capitalist socio-ideological violence" (*Violence*, 12–13).

[95] John Gray: "Commonwealth by M. Hardt and A. Negri; First as Tragedy Then as Farce by S. Zizek" [review], *The Independent*, November 20, 2009.

[96] Robert Hughes: *Culture of Complaint: The Fraying of America*, New York 1993, 76.

[97] "Introduction: The Idea of Communism," in Costas Douzinas and Slavoj Zizek eds.: *The Idea of Communism*, London 2010, viii.

reactionary humanism a decade later." Zizek concluded the conference volume by proclaiming that "without the perspective of communism, without this Idea, nothing in the historical and political future is of such a kind as to interest the philosopher."[98]

The less durable celebrity status of the late Louis Althusser, the French interpreter and devotee of Marxism, also deserves mention here. As Tony Judt wrote, "he was a guru, complete with texts, a cult and true believers ... How could it be that so many intelligent and educated people were taken in by this man?" He was supposed to reshape and rejuvenate revolutionary theory and transform the understanding of Marx. His "special contribution was to remove Marxism altogether from the realm of history, politics and experience and thereby to render it invulnerable to any criticism of the empirical sort." He was also always "a deeply troubled person" who in 1980 murdered his wife, was found mentally unfit to be tried, and was placed into a psychiatric institution, released after three years. Judt ended his review of Althusser's memoir asking "what does it say about modern academic life that such a figure can have trapped teachers and students for so long in the cage of his insane fictions...?"[99]

The case of another celebrity intellectual, Paul de Man (Sterling Professor of Humanities and chairman of the Comparative Literature Department at Yale, at the peak of his career), while of lesser political significance, offers another striking illustration of the questionable judgment of academic intellectuals. De Man's celebrity status was, in all probability, also linked to his being the leading proponent of "deconstructionism," a murky and pretentious literary theory that was the rage in departments of English in the 1970s and 1980s. It was a theory that appealed to the (selective) cultural-political relativism of the period.

As characterized by Robert Alter (Professor of Comparative Literature at the University of California, Berkeley), one of the few not enamored by de Man:

> In the 1970s and 1980s, he was a central figure ... in American literary studies, in which doctoral dissertations ... could scarcely be found without dozens of citations from his writings ... de Man was a person who flagrantly disregarded rules and obligations, shamelessly and repeatedly lied about himself and had a criminal past ... he was an extraordinarily gifted con man, persuading the most discerning intellectuals that he had credentials he did not possess and a heroic personal history, rather than a scandalous one ... De Man produced a fictitious curriculum

[98] Ibid., 10, 210–211.

[99] Tony Judt: "The Paris Stranger," *New Republic*, March 7, 1994, 33, 34, 36 37.

vitae ... [and] he would embellish his fictitious autobiography further ... he never wrote a book, only two collections of articles.

On top of misrepresenting his academic credentials, de Man also turned out to be a Nazi collaborator in his native Belgium during World War II: "writing for the collaborationist press gave him a sense of himself as a literary critic, and it is in this guise that he introduced himself in New York [upon his arrival in 1948] ... He claimed to be friendly with several prominent Parisian thinkers whom in fact he did not know." Alter also noted that "De Man left Belgium for the United States because he was fleeing the authorities. Eventually he was tried in absentia, found guilty of fraud and embezzlement and sentenced to six years."

Both Alter and de Man's biographer, Evelyn Barish, seem to believe that there was a connection between de Man's character (and amorality) and "the literary theory that made him famous." Alter wrote:

Barish, like others before her, proposes a link between his negation of history [associated with deconstructionism – P.H.] and his career of deception, between his denial of the continuity of the self and his suppression of his own past ... between his insistence that the written or spoken word never tells anything about the intention of its originator and his assumption of a new identity.[100]

Saul Bellow suggested another source of de Man's popularity among academic intellectuals: "De Man, like his master Heidegger ... believed that there was nothing further to be said or done for this civilization of ours and that whatever hastened its disintegration was historically justified ... In doing so de Man won the admiration of hundreds of intellectuals."[101] Doubtless, this point of view – of considerable political significance – contributed to his popularity among academic intellectuals.

Finally, de Man's celebrity status was enhanced by his turgid, impenetrable style of writing that many academic intellectuals mistook for profundity. As Alter put it:

In his writing, abstruseness, bristling abstraction, and disorienting use of terms make his essays often difficult to penetrate. This was part of the key to his success: to his American admirers, with their cultural inferiority complex, it seemed that if things were difficult to grasp, something profound was being said ... He got away with it because of the gullibility of American scholars, their confused

[100] Robert Alter: "Blindness and Hindsight: The Sordid Truths About an Academic Deity," *New Republic*, April 7, 2014, 35, 36, 38, 39.

[101] Saul Bellow: *Letters*, ed. by Benjamin Taylor, New York 2010, 453.

sense that they needed a guide, preferably European, who would show them how to break the chains of convention.[102]

Several other academic authors, most of them European or of European origin, also benefited from a similar reverence for obscurity confused with profundity. They include Jurgen Habermas, Martin Heidegger, Georg Lukacs, Herbert Marcuse, and the American Talcott Parsons.

Louis Menand, like Alter, came to the conclusion that de Man had "the record of a sociopath" and his behavior was "that of a man who lacks a normal superego."[103]

The less recent celebrity status of Margaret Mead, the famous anthropologist, rested largely on her contribution to the myth of the Noble Savage and his liberated sex life. Mead was acclaimed for her "discovery" of the joyous, conflict-free sex life of adolescents in Samoa, a Pacific island. Her book, first published in 1928, anticipated some of the popular counter-cultural beliefs of the 1960s. It also made a major contribution to the myth of the happy, uncorrupted, noble savage that had captivated Western intellectuals for generations, especially anthropologists. The latter, in particular, were drawn to the idea that the way of life of pre-literate tribal people was ethically and morally superior and preferable to the social arrangements prevailing in modern Western societies. Ernest Henri Baudet wrote:

> the "noble savage" or a tenuous prefiguration of him, has been present in our culture from earliest times ... The glorification of all things primitive, the cultureless as a characteristic of the true, the complete, the only and original bliss: that is one of the fundamentals of our Western civilization ... The natural goodness that developed so harmoniously in others formed a striking contrast to our errors and corruption.[104]

The key to the attraction of the noble savages was their presumed authenticity, a quality many Western intellectuals, especially the anthropologists, yearned for, but could not find in their own debased societies.

Mead, in her best-selling *Coming of Age in Samoa*, found what she was disposed to find: gentle, contented Samoans leading a free and pleasant sex life, unencumbered by the arbitrary rules and restrictions imposed on the unfortunate people living in Western societies. Mead also found these authentic natives largely non-violent, but if they

[102] Alter, 39.
[103] Louis Menand: "The de Man Case," *New Yorker*, March 24, 2014, 90.
[104] Henri Baudet: *Paradise on Earth: Some Thoughts on European Images of Non-European Man*, New Haven CT 1965, 10–11, 51.

were, it was the result of colonial domination, of the impact of Western civilization. Mead's findings were subsequently challenged by another anthropologist, Derek Freeman, better acquainted with the customs and way of life of the Samoans.[105] More recently, Steven Pinker, the social psychologist, observed that "Mead painted a Gauguinesque portrait of native peoples as peaceable, egalitarian, materially satisfied, and sexually unconflicted. Her uplifting vision of who we used to be – and therefore who we can become again – was accepted by otherwise skeptical writers as Bertrand Russell and H.L. Mencken."[106] Life in pre-literate tribal societies was not quite as idyllic and tranquil as Mead would have her readers believe.

A totally different – but equally remarkable – misreading of human nature and needs was encapsulated in a remark of B.F. Skinner, the once-famous behaviorist psychologist, who suggested "in the 1970s that people should be rewarded for eating in large communal dining halls [as they did in some areas of Mao's China – P.H.] rather than at home with their families, because large pots have a lower ratio of surface area to volume than small pots and hence are more energy efficient."[107]

THE PERSISTENCE OF QUESTIONABLE POLITICAL JUDGMENTS: A SMALL SAMPLE

While in more recent times the propensity to admire dictators has found fewer expressions (due to the shortage of suitably qualified candidates), it is not difficult to find other examples of noteworthy political misjudgments and illusions of similar origin.

The fame of Rigoberta Menchu is one such case, and another instructive example of the results of the wish to believe, of the willful suspension of disbelief and a determination to support political beliefs even after their factual basis has been exposed as illusory. Menchu, a supposedly poor, uneducated Guatemalan woman, published an autobiography that detailed her sufferings under the right-wing military government of Guatemala and the loss of members of her family during the military

105 Derek Freeman, *Margaret Mead and Samoa: The Making and Unmaking of an Anthropological Myth*, Cambridge MA 1984; also by the same author: *The Fateful Hoaxing of Margaret Mead: A Historical Analysis of Her Samoan Research*, Boulder CO 1999.

106 Steven Pinker: *The Blank Slate: The Modern Denial of Human Nature*, New York 2002, 26.

107 Skinner quoted in ibid., 246.

campaign against the leftist guerillas.[108] In 1992 she was awarded the Nobel Peace Prize; in the years that followed she received numerous honorary degrees and her book has been required reading in anthropology, women's studies, Latin American history, and political science in many American colleges. According to Menchu, her book "has inspired some 15,000 scholarly papers ... [and] has been translated into twelve languages."[109] Subsequently David Stoll, an American anthropologist and researcher of Guatemalan peasant society, came upon information that made clear that many of her autobiographical allegations were fabricated.[110] They included the claim that she had been a child laborer, that she was uneducated, that she had witnessed the death of her brother and that the Guatemalan military forces were solely responsible for the violence that engulfed rural areas. Stoll's well-documented revelations inspired outrage by numerous American academic intellectuals for whom Menchu has become an icon, a personification of the virtuous victim whose image combined the noble savage, the righteous revolutionary, and victim of right-wing oppression supported by the United States.

Following the disclosures of Stoll, the chairman of the Spanish Department at Wellesley College averred that "Rigoberta Menchu has been used by the right to negate the very important space multiculturalism is providing in academia. Whether her book is true or not, I don't care. We should teach our students about the brutality of the Guatemalan military and the US financing it."[111] These were sentiments very similar to those expressed when it turned out that Tawana Brawley, a young black woman, in 1988 falsely claimed that white men raped her: what mattered, for some commentators, was not her false accusation but that many black women had been raped by white men at other times, on other occasions.[112]

Most remarkable about the Rigoberta Menchu case was not her initial, uncritical celebration and embrace by leftist intellectuals but their

[108] *I Rigoberta Menchu: An Indian Woman in Guatemala*, New York 2000.

[109] Quoted in Charles Lane: "Deceiving Is Believing," *New Republic*, March 8, 1999, 36.

[110] David Stoll: *Rigoberta Menchu and the Story of All Poor Guatemalans*, Boulder CO 2008.

[111] Quoted in Lane, 36.

[112] See for example Stanley Diamond: "Reversing Brawley," *Nation*, October 31, 1988. At the present time a similar attitude prevails on many campuses when allegations of rape are readily believed even when factual evidence is dubious or disproved. Specifics of victimization become less important than the somewhat vague idea that a "rape culture" exists that victimizes a greatly inflated number of women (See for example Heather Wilhelm: "The 'Rape Culture' Lie," *Commentary*, March 2015).

subsequent refusal to modify their beliefs in light of new information that called into question her truthfulness. Especially striking was the repeated insistence (on the part of her defenders) that it did not matter whether or not she told the truth as long as she conveyed an important political message, or lesson. Once more, the wish to believe overpowered both the available factual information and the presumed capacity of intellectuals to use their critical faculties. As one commentator put it:

> the book's vision of simple, virtuous peasants and evil, blood-drenched landlords is the sort of political cartoon that was irresistible ... The credulity with which Menchu's ghastly fairy-tale was greeted in the West must also be explained in broader cultural and psychological terms ... [she] pulled the wool over so many eyes because she reconstructed herself romantically in the image of Western civilization's most enduring symbol of innocent victimhood ... the noble savage ... these intellectuals "transmuted" the noble savage into the "good revolutionary."[113]

Dismissing Stoll's revelations was also made easier by the postmodernist belief in "the instability of meaning inherent in any text" and the proposition that "subalterns," that is, victims or underdogs (such as Rigoberta Menchu), understand truth and facts differently than privileged Westerners. Astonishingly enough, some of her defenders argued that "To say that Rigoberta Menchu lied is taken to mean that no social injustice takes place in Guatemala."[114] In other words, questioning the veracity of her allegations was equated with supporting the social injustices and repression perpetrated by the military regime in Guatemala.

Daphne Patai emphasized that "Menchu's story ... resembles other cases in which political commitments have generated public support not linked to standards of evidence," such as the false claims of rape by Tawana Brawley and the false accusations against the Duke University lacrosse players. In both of these cases defenders of the putative victims argued that even if nobody was raped, such incidents *could have* taken place, and had, on other occasions. Even if Menchu misrepresented her background and invented certain incidents, Guatemala under the military regime was an unjust and repressive society and any allegation that confirmed it deserved support.

Angel Davis has been another academic political celebrity since the 1960s, a radical academic intellectual with a long record of political

[113] Dante Liano quoted in Daphne Patai: "We, Rigoberta's Excuse-Makers," *Academic Questions*, Summer 2012, 199, 201.

[114] Ibid., 205.

activism. Her being a black woman has doubtless buttressed her credibility and idealization. She is currently a distinguished Professor Emerita of the History of Consciousness at the University of California, Santa Cruz. As she recalled, "[Herbert] Marcuse taught me that it is possible to be an academic, an activist, a scholar and a revolutionary."[115] Her political record includes her less well-known support of "The People's Temple," better known as Jonestown in Guyana, whose leader, Jim Jones (she called him "my friend"), she addressed on a radio-phone on September 10, 1977 and with whom she agreed that there was a conspiracy against the group.[116] It may be recalled that some 900 members of the group committed mass suicide urged on by Jim Jones.

Davis used to be a member of the American Communist Party and was running mate as vice-presidential candidate of Gus Hall, head of the party, in 1980 and 1984. In 1979 she was awarded the Lenin Prize by the Soviet authorities. Even before gratefully accepting it, she visited the Soviet Union in 1973 and, not surprisingly, was given VIP treatment.[117] Her visit was chronicled in a sixty-page-long Soviet publication printed in 45,000 copies.[118]

Davis also admired Castro's Cuba, where she found "the sense of human dignity palpable," among many other joyous experiences and thrilling impressions.[119] Aside from her loyalty to the former Soviet Union that was *not* typical of 1960s radicals, she did personify the radicalism of the period and has been rewarded by academic positions, awards, and invitations as commencement speaker. Reportedly she charges $20,000 per speech. More recently she was invited to Birkbeck College, University of London, to give the Annual Law Lecture. Her chosen title was "Freedom Is a Constant Struggle."[120]

115 Quoted in *San Diego Reader*, October 21, 2010, accessed from Wikipedia. For a brief, critical survey of her academic career and political beliefs as of 1995, see Peter Collier: "Angela Davis as Tenured Activist," *Heterodoxy*, April 2, 1995.

116 "Statement of Angela Davis," September 10, 1977, online (accessed December 6, 2015).

117 Alexander Solzhenitsyn wrote after her trial (she was acquitted of smuggling a weapon to an imprisoned Black Panther) and subsequent visit to the Soviet Union: "for an entire year, we heard nothing … except [of] Angela Davis … children in school were told to sign petitions in her defense … she was set free … [and] came to recuperate in Soviet resorts." He also noted that when she was asked to intervene on behalf of imprisoned Czech dissidents, she answered: "'They deserve what they got. Let them remain in prison'" (*Warning to the West*, New York 1975, 60, 61).

118 Olga Chechetkina: *Andzela v Sovetskom Souze* [Angela in the Soviet Union], Moscow 1973.

119 Angela Davis: *An Autobiography*, New York 1974, 203.

120 Alan Johnson: "What Does Angela Davis Know about Freedom?" *Telegraph Blog*, online, October 25, 2013.

Even more noteworthy has been what Ronald Radosh called "The Rehabilitation of New Left Terrorists," exemplified by the case of Kathy Boudin (who served twenty-two years for her participation in the Brink's robbery and murder of two policemen) being appointed as Adjunct Professor at Columbia University's School of Social Work.[121] The academic career and good fortunes of Bill Ayers, a former head of the SDS and co-founder of the Weather Underground, has been even more remarkable. He is distinguished Professor Emeritus of Education and Senior University Scholar at the University of Illinois, Chicago, and author of several well-received books. He has few, if any, second thoughts about the violence carried out by his organization.[122]

Questionable, or profoundly wrongheaded, political judgments find expression not only in groundless idealization or the suspension of critical faculties, but also in overly harsh or irrationally hostile attitudes toward particular political actors and systems. Anti-Americanism is one such disposition I discussed elsewhere.[123] A few examples of the latter may suffice for the present discussion. The first one is the huge volume written by Oliver Stone and Peter Kuznick entitled, rather inaccurately, *The Untold History of the United States* (2010), which closely followed in the footsteps of a very similar undertaking by Howard Zinn.[124]

The Stone–Kuznick volume was compiled with the avowed intention to present a highly unfavorable portrait of the United States through much of its recent history. It was designed to rebut books and school curricula "that trumpet US achievements" and instead to focus on "what the United States had done wrong – the ways in which it betrayed its mission." The authors proposed that American society has been dominated by those "driven by personal greed and narrow-self-interest" at the expense of "those who extol social values like kindness, generosity, compassion, sharing, empathy and community building."

[121] Ronald Radosh: "Rehabilitation of New Left Terrorists," online, posted December 29, 2013.

[122] For more on Ayers, see Paul Hollander: "Resisting Disillusionment," in *The End of Commitment: Intellectuals, Revolutionaries and Political Morality*, Chicago 2006, 320–334. For further reflections of the same mentality, see also my review titled "Unrepentant" of Mark Rudd: *Underground: My Life with SDS and the Weathermen* in *Claremont Review of Books*, Fall 2009.

[123] See Paul Hollander: *Anti-Americanism: Irrational and Rational*, New Brunswick NJ 1995 and Paul Hollander ed.: *Understanding Anti-Americanism*, Chicago 2004; see also Paul Hollander: *The Only Superpower: Reflections on Strength, Weakness and Anti-Americanism*, Lanham MD 2009.

[124] Howard Zinn: *A People's History of the United States*, New York 2010 (first published in 1980).

The authors also made clear that they considered anti-communism a far greater moral and political defect and threat than communism. They routinely characterized anti-communists as "virulent" or "rabid," dismissing their views as self-evidently wrongheaded. Richard Pipes (the Russian historian at Harvard University) is a "virulently anti-Soviet Polish immigrant," apparently further discredited by his Polish background. The same applies to Zbigniew Brzezinski, "son of a Polish diplomat and probably the most unreconstructed anti-Communist." Social-economic status and religiosity were also used to suggest that particular individuals of similar disposition were not to be trusted, such as William Casey, director of CIA under Reagan, "a multimillionaire Wall Street lawyer and devout Irish Catholic."[125]

As to former President Bush and Vice-President Cheney, the authors suggested that while "for most Americans, 9/11 was a terrible tragedy; for Bush and Cheney it was also an incredible opportunity – a chance to implement the agenda that their neoconservative allies had been cooking up for decades." While the authors didn't approve of 9/11, their avid anti-capitalism led them to designate the World Trade Center one of "the premier symbols of US imperial power," the Pentagon being the other. Not only is the United States the major, rather, the only global oppressor and exploiter, it is a virtual police state characterized by blighted domestic social conditions, powerless, exploited masses and rampant social injustices.

Stone and Kuznick excel in asserting time and again that there is no global problem, type of misery, or suffering that cannot be blamed on the United States, the "global hegemon," and on its long-standing insatiable thirst for power and global domination. The major explanation of these policies is the greed that fuels and underlies capitalism. They also implied that major American political figures and their advisors are exceptionally unattractive human beings, even aside from their capitalistic greed and power-hunger.

While the authors repeatedly suggested that "from the Soviet vantage point, US behavior was quite alarming" and for good reasons, they never conceded that there ever was a time or occasion when Soviet behavior might have been a justifiable source of apprehension for American policymakers. Their pro-Soviet inclination, as well as limited information about conditions in Eastern Europe, is further reflected in their belief that "with

125 Oliver Stone and Peter Kuznick: *The Untold History of the United States*, New York 2012, xii, 396, 402, 427.

Communists having played a leading role in antifascist resistance movements beleaguered Europeans [meaning East Europeans] often welcomed Soviet troops and liberators."[126]

Communists did not play a leading role in every East European resistance movement, and even if they did, it would not and did not follow that the rest of the population rejoiced at the arrival of Soviet troops. And even if some of them did, such rejoicing did not last long since the same troops, upon their arrival, immediately embarked on a spree of raping and looting, not only in East Germany but even in friendly Yugoslavia, prompting Milovan Djilas to raise the issue with Stalin when he met him.[127] The only group unambiguously pleased by the arrival of the Soviet troops in Eastern Europe were the surviving Jews. Even their enthusiasm waned as time went by and the communist authorities adopted increasingly intolerant and repressive policies.

Presumably the key to this lengthy and detailed indictment (750 pages) is the authors' unwavering conviction that the United States betrayed its historic mission, sentiments that closely follow in the footsteps of Howard Zinn's volume noted above.

Another example of exceptionally intense and irrational anti-Americanism found expression in Jean Baudrillard's 2001 article that "not only developed a justification of the nineteen suicide attackers, but also seemed to express a certain admiration for them. He wrote that September 11 'represents both the high point of the spectacle and the purest defiance' and that therefore, 'it could be forgiven.'"[128] An earlier visit to the United States filled him with feelings of profound revulsion over what he considered the essential and rampant inauthenticity of American culture and society: "America is a world completely rotten with wealth, power, senility, indifference, puritanism, and mental hygiene, poverty and waste, technological futility and aimless violence ... there is no culture here ... the only country where quantity can be extolled without compunction ... Here everything human is artificial ... This country is without hope."[129]

[126] Ibid., 501, 500, 417, 188.

[127] Djilas, 110–111.

[128] Baudrillard quoted in Janet Afary and Kevin B. Anderson eds.: *Foucault and the Iranian Revolution: Gender and the Seductions of Islamism*, Chicago 2005, 170.

[129] Jean Baudrillard: *America*, London and New York 1988, 23, 66, 87, 100, 121. Wolin wrote about this book: "one of the strange features of this narrative is that although he describes a myriad of tourist sites, he reproduces not a single conversation with a 'real' American ... [his] theoretical perspective on American life was fully worked out before he departed" (Wolin 2004, 305).

Slavoj Zizek's anti-Americanism was of a similar "essentialist" character, rooted in the belief that American values are responsible for and explain all the evil the United States perpetrates in the world:

Abu Ghraib was not simply a case of American arrogance toward a Third World people: in being submitted to humiliating tortures, the Iraqi prisoners were effectively *initiated into American culture*. They were given a taste of its obscene underside ... what we are getting when we see the photos of the humiliated Iraqi prisoners ... is precisely a direct insight into American values, into the very core of the obscene enjoyment that sustains the US way of life.[130]

Much earlier, Bertrand Russell's somewhat hysterical anti-Americanism was apparently stimulated by his conviction that the United States was the most dangerously irresponsible superpower, the preeminent threat to global peace and a highly repressive society. He believed that

Members of the FBI join even mildly liberal organizations as spies and report any unguarded word. Anybody who goes so far as to support equal rights for colored people, or to say a good word for the UN is liable to a visit by officers of the FBI and threatened, if not with prosecution, at least with blacklisting and a consequent inability to earn a living. When a sufficient state of terror has been produced by these means, the victim is informed there is a way out, if he will denounce a sufficient number of his friends, he may obtain absolution.[131]

In 1961 Russell had also asserted that "on a purely statistical basis, Macmillan [British prime minister] and Kennedy are about fifty times as wicked as Hitler." Paul Johnson correctly observed of him that "when his sense of justice was outraged and his emotions aroused, his respect for accuracy collapsed."[132]

At the time of the Cuban missile crisis in 1962, Russell "denied that there were such missiles in Cuba and dismissed the photographs as fakes. He denounced the American heads of state as 'worse than Hitler' and as the crisis deepened, wrote: 'You are going to die because rich Americans dislike the government Cubans prefer. Do not yield to ferocious and insane murderers.' "[133]

Somewhat surprisingly, Russell had earlier held fiercely anti-Soviet views that found expression in advocating preventive war against the Soviet

130 Zizek, *Violence*, 176.

131 Quoted in Sidney Hook: "Bertrand Russell and Crimes Against Humanity," in *Philosophy and Public Policy*, Carbondale IL 1980, 212.

132 Quoted in Paul Johnson, 209, 203.

133 Cited in ibid., 211.

Union.[134] These wild fluctuations of his beliefs and judgments suggest, among other things, that one must resist the temptation to overestimate the rationality of intellectuals.

Recent hostility among Western intellectuals toward Israel is another example of a political disposition that blends rational and highly emotional elements. I am not suggesting that Israeli policies deserve no criticism (in particular the expansion of settlements on the occupied West Bank), but I believe that many of the critiques, inspired and magnified by an underlying animosity, have been excessive and often groundless.

Thus members of the American Studies Association voted to impose an academic boycott on Israel to protest its treatment of Palestinians in the occupied territories. Curtis Martez, president of this organization and Associate Professor of Ethnic Studies at the University of California, San Diego, admitted that "many nations, including many of Israel's neighbors, are generally judged to have human rights records that are worse than Israel's or comparable, but, he said, 'one must start somewhere.' "[135] Why with Israel?

The explanation may be found in the gradual transformation of the image of Israel from a small, beleaguered country into triumphant regional military superpower that occurred after the Six Day War in the late 1960s. The denigration of Israel came to be paralleled by the idealization of Palestinians, as a new paradigm of victims and victimizer emerged. Edward Said (among others) succeeded in "redefining Arabs and Muslims as the moral equivalent of blacks" and the preeminent victim group of the present. Similar sentiments were expressed by Muslim gang members in Denmark as reported by a Danish sociologist: " 'Part of their identity is that they are living in the same reality as the oppressed black man in the American ghettos...' And this belief feeds a narrative of victimization that becomes a self-fulfilling prophecy."[136]

[134] Hook, 210–211. See also Russell in the *Saturday Review*, October 16, 1948. On his advocating such a preventive war, see also Ronald W. Clark: *Bertrand Russell and His World*, London 1981, ch. 19.

[135] R. Perez-Pena: "Scholars' Group to Discuss Result of Vote on an Academic Boycott of Israel," *New York Times*, December 15, 2013; see also R. Perez-Pena and Jodi Rudoven: "Boycott by Academic Group Is a Symbolic Sting to Israel," *New York Times*, December 17, 2013.

[136] Quoted in Joshua Muravchik: *Making David into Goliath: How the World Turned Against Israel*, New York 2014. See also Paul Berman: *Power and the Idealists*, New York 2005, 53–54, concerning New Left attitudes toward Israel, and Charles Krauthammer: "Judging Israel," in *Things That Matter*, New York 2013, 251–257.

Joshua Muravchik also suggested that some leftist intellectuals found a substitute for the proletariat in the followers of Islam,[137] and Richard Wolin thought that "in the Western political imagination the role of the 'wretched of the earth' needed to be entirely recast ... since September 11, in many instances that role has been filled by representatives of political Islam. Thus Al Qaeda and its allies ... have been retrofitted as the new freedom fighters: as the new *lumpenproletariat*."[138] Similar sentiments found expression in the solicitousness toward Muslim student groups on American college campuses and in the insistence that Islamic religious doctrines and beliefs have nothing whatsoever to do with the acts of violence committed on their behalf and in their name by groups and individuals who insistently and vocally legitimate their violence by these beliefs and doctrines.

Disputes about the influence of Muslim religion (as conveyed in the Koran) on jihadist violence are reminiscent of past disputes about the relationship between Marxist theory and the practices of communist states. While we obviously cannot hold Marx responsible for the gulag and the KGB, it does not follow that his ideas had *nothing whatsoever* to do with the nature of the existing communist systems. For one thing, he bequeathed to them the doctrine of class struggle and a conviction that a largely flawless social system can be created and that its creation demands and justifies sacrifices, including violence and repression. Moreover, in both of the voluminous writings of Marx and the Koran, quotations can be found to support diametrically opposed interpretations of these doctrines, their peaceful as opposed to pugnacious character.[139]

In the case of Israel and the Palestinians (as in many others), moral judgment and indignation have been predetermined not by the magnitude and quality of the moral transgressions committed but by the respective identity of the wrongdoers and their victims, putative or genuine. Over the last few decades Israel (alongside the United States) has become the primary target of a reflexive moral indignation of large portions of Western intellectuals and other elite groups, and, correspondingly, the Palestinians became their favored victim group outside their own countries.

Concerning the Muslim gangs in Denmark, see William Wheeler: "The Jihadist of Copenhagen," *New Republic*, September–October 2015, 25.

137 Muravchik, 118, 197.

138 Richard Wolin: "The Counter-Thinker," *New Republic*, August 12, 2010, 33.

139 See also Paul Hollander: "Marx and the Koran," *Weekly Standard*, February 21, 2015.

As Muravchik pointed out, by 2009 sympathy toward Israel in Western Europe and the United Nations was "a distant memory":

British teacher unions proclaimed academic boycotts of Israel; mainline Protestant churches in the United States divested from companies doing business with Israel; Norwegian supermarkets boycotted Israeli goods; Sweden's largest newspaper concocted … stories that Israel was slaughtering Palestinians to harvest and sell their organs … a former president of the United States [Carter] issued a book accusing Israel of … apartheid … a Palestinian state became a kind of Holy Grail … while almost no one gave a fig for the aspirations of the Kurds or Tibetans … no reasonable person could argue that Israel's abuses equaled, much less exceeded, those of scores of regimes that practiced violence, repression and racial and religious discrimination without being rebuked by UN bodies … censure of Israel accounts for one-fifth to one-quarter of all motions passed by the General Assembly … of all General Assembly resolutions that criticize a particular country, three quarters apply to Israel.[140]

Prevalent sentiments toward Israel in the United Nations were reflected in the choice of Richard Falk as "special rapporteur" of the Human Rights Council of the UN concerned with Israeli violations of Palestinian human rights. Falk is Professor Emeritus of International Law at Princeton University, and one of the most vocal adversaries of Israel and avowed supporter of the Palestinian Solidarity Movement. He did not consider comparing (that is, equating) the treatment of Palestinians by Israel with the "Nazi record of collective atrocity" to be "an irresponsible overstatement."[141] Falk has also been one of the few Western admirers of Ayatollah Khomeini.[142]

Hostility toward Israel among academic intellectuals and student groups is both reflected and deepened by the widespread use as college texts of the writings of authors such as Edward Said, Noam Chomsky, and Judith Butler – each of them harboring a long-standing hostility toward Israel.[143]

The opera *The Death of Klinghoffer* (performed in New York City, among other places) testifies to the influence of these trends on elite culture. The opera strongly suggests a moral equivalence between the grievances of Arab terrorists and their murder of Klinghoffer, an old,

140 Muravchik 2014, ix–x, xii–xiii, xi. See also Ron Prosor: "The UN's War on Israel," *New York Times*, April 1, 2015. The article notes, among the other examples of double standards, that the UN Commission on the Status of Women condemned only Israel for its alleged mistreatment of women and had nothing to say about the treatment of women in Muslim countries. Such partiality has also been shown in the UN reports of Israel's alleged human rights violations in its war with Hamas. For a rebuttal of one such report, see Richard Kemp: "The UN's Flawed Gaza Verdict," *New York Times*, June 25, 2015.

141 Muravchik, 77, 78.

142 Richard Falk: "Trusting Khomeini," *New York Times*, February 16, 1979.

143 Muravchik, 231.

wheelchair-bound American Jew. As one critic pointed out, in the opera "the terrorists are allowed ecstatic flights, private musings, self-justifications ... Mamoud [one of them] ... discloses that his mother and brother were killed in Palestinian refugee camps – a back story that might seem designed to justify the character's own violence."[144] The daughters of Mr. Klinghoffer wrote: "Imagine if Mr Adams had written an opera about the terrorists who carried out the 9/11 attacks, and sought to balance their worldview with that of those who perished in the twin towers."[145] According to another critic, the most revealing message of the opera was that "in depicting a morally unambiguous event in a morally ambiguous manner, *Klinghoffer* signals that even the most heinous attacks on Israel or Jews have now become essentially debatable matters."[146]

It has been argued that hostility toward Israel is rooted in antisemitism, but this need not be the case, except among Arab-Islamic populations. Israel's close alliance with the United States and its position as an outpost and symbol of Western values and institutions surrounded by Third World countries may be a sufficient explanation. Buruma and Margalit wrote: "Israel has ... become the prime target of a more general Arab rage against the West, the symbol of idolatrous, hubristic, amoral, colonialist evil, a cancer in the eyes of its enemies that must be expunged."[147] In addition, Israel's transformation from a small, seemingly weak nation into a regional military superpower, reflected in its victories in the wars of 1948, 1967, and 1973, greatly contributed to being cast in the role of arrogant and ruthless aggressor.

In the final analysis it is impossible to determine to what degree, if any, antisemitism underlies or colors the current Western hostility toward Israel. Far less questionable is that the policies of some academic organizations, and all those advocating various punitive economic sanctions, entail double standards as they single out Israel for transgressions that are far more severe and widespread in much of the world, and especially in the Islamic countries hostile to Israel.

Several patterns emerge from this preliminary discussion of the political attitudes of groups of Western intellectuals. The most obvious is that over time they made many erroneous political judgments with great confidence. The intellectuals dealt with believed that certain dictators

144 Alex Ross: "Long Wake," *New Yorker*, November 3, 2014, 88, 90.
145 "'Klinghoffer': The Opera and the Furor" [Letter], *New York Times*, June 21, 2014.
146 Jonathan S. Tobin: "Why *The Death of Klinghoffer* Matters," *Commentary*, December 2014, 34.
147 Buruma and Margalit, 138–139.

personified idealistic, purposeful, and just political systems. They knew little of the gulf separating the dictators' professed goals and ideals from the prevailing social-political realities in the countries concerned. They admired attributes the dictators did not possess – a disposition rooted in ignorance, imagination, and selective perception. Their attraction to dictators and their political system was influenced by a strongly felt discontent with modernity as they experienced it in their own societies. These sentiments, combined with a distaste for, or hatred of, capitalism, contributed to a compensatory hero worship of the perceived enemies of capitalism.

The highly patterned and often bizarre misperceptions may be further explained by the pressing need to find alternatives to the social, political, and cultural conditions that groups of Western intellectuals found deplorable in their own society. Last but not least, it is also possible that many individuals who gravitate to the role of public intellectual are predisposed, to some degree, to a discontent with long-standing, familiar social arrangements (perhaps with their own way of life as well). Their apparent capacity for wishful thinking and projection may be further traced to secular-religious impulses and to an overestimation of the social and political determinants of individual happiness and a meaningful life.

As one might expect, the examination of the relationship between various dictators and intellectuals that follows will shed far more light on the disposition of intellectuals than on the personalities – as distinct from the images – of dictators. Nonetheless, even the idealized and wrongheaded views of dictators will help to better understand their appeals (enduring or temporary) and the circumstances that were conducive to their rise to power.

2

Mussolini, Fascism, and Intellectuals

Mussolini ... tapped into the powerful subterranean human impulse to violent collective action for a utopian goal.

William Pfaff[1]

Beyond question an amazing experiment is being made here, an experiment in reconciling individualism and socialism, politics and technology. It would be a mistake to allow feelings aroused by ... the harsh deeds and extravagant assertions that accompanied the Fascist process ... to obscure the potentialities and lessons of the adventure ... [of] destiny riding without any saddle and bridle across the historic peninsula.

Charles Beard[2]

In the 1930s travelers returned from Mussolini's Italy, Stalin's Russia and Hitler's Germany praising the hearty sense of common purpose they saw there, compared to which their own democracies seemed weak, inefficient and pusillanimous.

Michael Ignatieff[3]

[1] William Pfaff: *The Bullet's Song: Romantic Violence and Utopia*, New York 2002, 40.

[2] Beard quoted in John P. Diggins: "Flirtation with Fascism: American Pragmatic Liberals and Mussolini's Italy," *American Historical Review* [cited hereafter as *AHR*], January 1966, 494.

[3] Michael Ignatieff: "Are the Authoritarians Winning?" *New York Review of Books*, July 10, 2014, 53.

FIGURE 1. Classical preening portrait; posture and facial expression convey immense self-confidence bordering on arrogance.

THE FASCIST CRITIQUES OF MODERNITY AND CAPITALISM

It is important to emphasize at the outset that the attraction of Western intellectuals to right-wing dictators and dictatorships was far less widespread and durable than similar attitudes toward communist dictators and their political systems that persisted past World War II and in some instances up to the present. Correspondingly, there has been far less public awareness of and scholarly research about these largely forgotten expressions of political misjudgment. Nonetheless these more fleeting attitudes are also of importance and somewhat unexpectedly help to better understand the far more intense and durable attraction of the communist systems.

Half-a-century ago Stephen Spender correctly pointed out that "some of the greatest modern writers sympathized with Fascism ... [because it]

FIGURE 2. Inspecting girls belonging to the fascist youth organization; supposed to illustrate Mussolini's benevolence and affinity with the younger generations.

offered political answers to criticisms of modern technological society made by the cultured and the lovers of past civilization."[4] Likewise Leon Surette observed that "fascism was not perceived in the 1920s as the face of evil – neither by the man in the street, by the media, or by the leaders of democratic nations."[5]

Richard Wolin proposed a far-reaching reevaluation of fascism and its appeals to intellectuals:

> It would be comforting to think that ... fascism was an anti-intellectual phenomenon attractive only to criminals and thugs ... Many of the [European] continent's leading lights were clamoring to mount the fascist political bandwagon ... An enumeration of fascism's literary and philosophical sympathizers ... would include Ernst Junger, Gottfried Benn, Martin Heidegger, Carl Schmitt, Robert Brasillach, Pierre Drieu La Rochelle, Louis-Ferdinand Celine, Filippo Marinetti, Gabriele d'Annunzio, W.B. Yeats and Wyndham Lewis ...
>
> [P]ostmodernism has been nurtured by the doctrines of Nietzsche, Heidegger, Maurice Blanchot and Paul de Man – all of whom either prefigured or succumbed to the proverbial intellectual "fascination with fascism." ... [A]n antidemocratic

4 Stephen Spender: "Foreword," in Alastair Hamilton: *The Appeal of Fascism: A Study of Intellectuals*, London 1971, x.

5 Leon Surette: *Dreams of Totalitarian Utopia: Literary Modernism and Politics*, Montreal 2011, 97.

orientation popular during the 1930s was making an eerie comeback – this time, however, under the auspices of the academic left.[6]

In the same volume, Wolin undertook "to shed light on the uncanny affinities between the Counter-Enlightenment and postmodernism." He argued that during the 1960s, "Counter-Enlightenment views that heretofore had been the exclusive preserve of the European right came to permeate the standpoint of the postmodern left ... the postmodernists ... aimed their sights ... at 'reason,' 'humanism,' modernity, – the same targets that, for decades, had been privileged objects of scorn and derision among proponents of the counter-revolutionary right." He mentions among these postmodernists Foucault, Derrida, Lyotard, and Baudrillard.

"An uncompromising rejection of political liberalism"[7] was central to the beliefs embraced by both fascist and communist leaders, ideologues, and their supporters. Roger Griffin made a similar point:

so widespread was the disaffection with the official cult of material, liberal progress ... that intellectuals and artists all over Europe were attracted to the idea that their own bid to break free from a stultifying "normality" was part of a wider impulse, a sea change in history ... For some the very notion of the "modern" was infused with a sense of cultural regeneration.[8]

Malcolm Muggeridge further reminds us of the converging attitudes toward fascism and communism in the early 1930s:

As many adhering to the Left journeyed to the USSR, there to offer thanks and admire all that they were shown, so did their corresponding type of the Right make Hitler their hero and the Third Reich ... If the Rev. Hewlett Johnson detected in the Soviet regime the highest extant realization of Christian principles, Major Yeats-Brown made the more guarded statement that it was his "honest conviction that there is more real Christianity in Germany today than there ever was under the Weimar Republic..." Corresponding to the ladies who met Russians whose eyes glowed proudly when Stalin's name was mentioned, were other ladies who had met Germans whose eyes similarly glowed when Hitler's name was mentioned ... against Lord Passfield [Sidney Webb] reverent in Moscow, might be set Lord Rothermere reverent in Munich.[9]

[6] Richard Wolin: *The Seduction of Unreason: The Intellectual Romance with Fascism From Nietzsche to Postmodernism*, Princeton NJ 2004, xi–xii.

[7] Ibid., 5, 279, 310.

[8] Roger Griffin: *A Fascist Century: Essays by Roger Griffin*, New York 2008, 4–5.

[9] Malcolm Muggeridge: *The Sun Never Sets: The Story of England in the 1930s*, New York 1940, 281–282.

We are also reminded in a more recent study that "both fascism and communism, were ... utopian vision and bearers of great hopes."[10] In a similar spirit, a disillusioned supporter of the Soviet Union came to the conclusion that "men must have an ideal, however debased or false, to die for."[11]

It was the concept of totalitarianism that focused attention on and systematized the similarities between both the institutional characteristics and appeals of Nazism and communism. Tzvetan Todorov wrote:

> The family resemblance between Nazism and Communism is indisputable, and justifies ... our treatment of them as two varieties of a single species, totalitarianism. But they were also significantly different from each other ... One way of broaching the question of the difference between Nazism and Communism is to say that realities were much closer to each other than the images they projected of themselves.[12]

It was a profound disappointment with modernity, in addition to the economic difficulties of the period following World War I, that made the major contribution to the growing appeals of both fascism and Nazism on the one hand and those of the Soviet system on the other. Modernity, somewhat paradoxically, for many of its critics, amounted to decadence, that is to say, the decline of social cohesion, community, public morality, and cultural vitality. Last but not least, it opened the chasm of nihilism and meaninglessness.

Contrary to earlier confident expectations, the spectacular progress of science and technology did not make life more meaningful and contented. As Max Weber approvingly quoted Tolstoy: "Science is meaningless because it gives no answer to our question, the only question important for us: 'What shall we do and how shall we live?' "[13]

While there has been much ambivalence toward, or outright rejection of technology among critics of modernity located at different points of the political spectrum, fascist, Nazi, and communist systems alike eagerly flaunted their technological accomplishments as sources of legitimacy. As Griffin wrote, "at every turn Fascist rhetoric sought to forge the link in

[10] Jonah Goldberg: *Liberal Fascism: The Secret History of the American Left from Mussolini to the Politics of Meaning*, New York 2007, 7.

[11] Freda Utley: *The Dream We Lost: Soviet Russia Then and Now*, New York 1940, 296.

[12] Tzvetan Todorov: "Two of a Kind," in *Hope and Memory: Lessons from the Twentieth Century*, Princeton NJ 2003, 82.

[13] *Max Weber: Essays in Sociology*, ed. by H.H. Gerth and C. Wright Mills, London 1948, 143.

the public's mind between dynamism, technology, the *Duce*, and the New Italy."[14]

These technological accomplishments included superhighways (*autostrada*), hydro-electric plants, the draining of marshes, and improved public transportation (trains running on time). Nazi Germany too built superhighways (*autobahn*) and a wide range of superior weapon systems, and mass-produced a cheap, popular car, the Volkswagen.

In communist countries the worship of technology reached even more extreme forms with poetic invocations of tractors driven by women, the romance of smokestacks of factories spreading over the formerly somnolent countryside, and gigantic power-plants straddling rivers and producing huge amounts of electricity. None of these systems – communist, Nazi, and fascist – displayed any concern with the impact of technological modernization on the environment, nor were their admirers concerned with such matters, including Western visitors and political tourists.

None of these systems and their supporters were unconditionally opposed to modernity, only to those of its aspects that were "associated with decadence; namely cultural pluralism, liberalism and materialism."[15] As Griffin further argued, "Nazism was not anti-modern, but celebrated technology as the externalization of the Faustian drive and Aryan creativity of the German people."[16] Giovanni Gentile correctly pointed out that "the crisis of the rationalist, progressive, Enlightenment model ... has led us to recognize that authoritarianism and modernity, irrationalism and modernity, fascism and modernity are not at all incompatible."[17] There was an often overlooked (or outright denied) affinity between the Marxist and Romantic-conservative critiques of modernity, capitalism, and bourgeois society – an affinity that illuminates and helps us to understand the connections between romanticism, nationalism, Nazism, and communism.

It is the Romantic rejection of modernity that may be the most significant component and common denominator of the political attitudes probed in this study. While we tend to associate romanticism with the idealization of the past, with right-wing movements and systems – mainly Nazi and fascist – "romanticism unfolds from one end of the political

[14] Griffin 2008, 35.

[15] Ibid., 36. For a comprehensive treatment of the phenomenon, see Jeffrey Herf: *Reactionary Modernism: Technology, Culture and Politics in Weimar and the Third Reich*, Cambridge, UK 1984.

[16] Ibid., 41.

[17] Gentile quoted in Roger Griffin ed.: *Fascism*, Oxford, UK 1995, 296.

gamut to the other," Michael Löwy and Robert Sayre argued. They also pointed out that there is a "significant ... romantic dimension" in Marxist thought.

The profound and growing disillusionment with modernity – shared across the political spectrum by alienated intellectuals – overlapped with what Georg Lukacs designated as "romantic anti-capitalism," the combination of romanticism and anti-capitalism. Michael Löwy and Robert Sayre wrote:

> Besides nostalgia for a lost communitarian paradise, the other major dimension of Marxist thinking that is undeniably Romantic in inspiration is the critique of certain fundamental aspects of industrialist-capitalist modernity ... this critique is not limited to private ownership of means of production: it is much broader, deeper and more radical. The entire existing mode of industrial production and the whole bourgeois society are called into question – with arguments and attitudes similar to those of the Romantics.[18]

The questioning of modernity found further, popular expression in the love of nature and the German youth movement, the *Wandervogel*, "that grew into the most popular youth movement in pre-war Germany," dedicated to a return to, and recovery of, nature.[19] It brought together young people on hikes and camping trips, reaffirming both traditional values and a new nationalism. It resembles present-day environmental movements similarly critical of modernity, but unlike the *Wandervogel*, present-day environmentalists are preoccupied with capitalism as the major threat to the environment.

The most important and strongly felt common denominator of both the communist and Nazi critiques of capitalism and modernity was the distress over the decline of community, the distortion of human relationships, and the spreading impersonality associated with, or rooted in, the so-called "cash nexus," or "commodification." As Saul Bellow put it, "many human attachments cut in the process of liberation will have to be restored and renewed,"[20] and both Nazism and fascism eagerly volunteered to do so.

A German journalist, Sebastian Haffner discerned similarities between Nazi Germany and communist East Germany, in their approach to

[18] Michael Löwy and Robert Sayre: *Romanticism against the Tide of Modernity*, Durham NC 2001, 10, 82, 83, 95.

[19] Laurence Rees: *Hitler's Charisma*, New York 2012, 34.

[20] Saul Bellow: *It All Adds Up*, New York 1994, 128.

community building, designating them as "two peas in a pod." In both settings, he wrote, a large portion of the population

took part in extra-domestic communities or "collectives" ... the songs that were sung and the speeches that were made were different in the Third Reich from those in the GDR [German Democratic Republic] today. But the activities, rambling [hiking], marching and camping, singing and celebrating, model making and PT and firearms drill, were indistinguishable, just as much as the undeniable sense of security, comradeship and happiness which flourished in such communities.[21]

Arguably, these spiritual concerns and critiques were more intensely felt – even among those on the left – than indignation over specific social injustice, exploitation, and inequality. As Löwy and Sayre observed:

Romanticism represents a critique of modernity, that is, of modern capitalist civilization, in the name of values and ideals drawn from the past (the precapitalist, premodern past) ... Many romantics felt ... that all the negative characteristics of modern society – the religion of the god Money ... the decline of all qualitative, social and religious values ... the tedious uniformization of life; the purely utilitarian relations among human beings among themselves and with nature – stem from the same source of corruption: market quantification.

They also noted that the Romantic critics of modernity rejected "reification ... the solitude of individuals, uprootedness, alienation through merchandise, the uncontrollable dynamics of machines and technology ... the degradation of nature."[22]

The fascist version of these critiques of modernity and capitalism led to a new search for, and appreciation of, the heroic dimensions of life, to hero worship. William Pfaff wrote: "Fascists understood the thirst for heroism better than anyone else ... [they] understood that war is about death, and that when people's lives are sterile they consciously or unconsciously welcome war ... a liberation from the boredom of life."[23]

The Romantic outlook was compatible with both left- and right-wing dispositions because it accommodated individualistic as well as communitarian ideals and aspirations. The friendship of Andre Malraux, the novelist, ostensibly a man of the left,[24] and Pierre Drieu la Rochelle, also

[21] Haffner, quoted in John Gray: *The Silence of Animals*, New York 2013, 53–54.

[22] Löwy and Sayre, 17, 35, 251.

[23] Pfaff, 54.

[24] It was observed of Malraux that his "vision as a whole ... reveals a certain affinity with Stalinism ... The affinity with Stalinism lies in the elitist tendency that runs throughout Malraux's work: the cult of the hero and the purely passive conception of the people. The latter constitute a malleable mass to be manipulated by the leader-hero, whom they worship with a quasi-religious devotion" (Robert Sayre: "'L'Espoir' and Stalinism," in Brian Thompson and Carl A. Viggiani eds.: *Witnessing Andre Malraux*, Middletown CT 1984, 138).

a writer, and an avowed supporter of fascism, was symptomatic of seemingly implausible affinities nurtured by a shared revulsion from modernity. Renee Winegarten wrote:

> both were exponents of self-realization and the cult of risk ... steeped in Nietzsche ... both [were] romantics haunted by the tragic sense of life ... In heroic neo-romanticism, a writer who chose the Communist side, like Malraux, and one who chose the Fascist side, like Drieu, sometimes appear to be separated by a hair's breadth ... they were united in their unshakeable hatred of bourgeois society ... Some form of political or revolutionary commitment was also, for Drieu as well as Malraux, a substitute for a lost religious mysticism.[25]

Paul Nizan, a friend of Malraux, suggested that "for Malraux ... revolution was simply a remedy against anguish, it was not, 'as for the masses of the people, a historical necessity.' "[26]

Drieu admired Malraux as "a man of action" who rejected "the anti-heroic tenor of modern life." For Drieu, political commitment merged into the Romantic belief in the "life-enhancing" quality of risk-taking, in living dangerously. Malraux shared these beliefs and occasionally tried to act on them, for example by participating in the Spanish Civil War by piloting a plane. Gabriele D'Annunzio, the Italian fascist writer discussed below, another notable "man of action," also flew planes in World War I.

Drieu, in particular, personified the Romantic protest against modernity, the "encroaching urbanization and the dehumanizing machine." Like many other politically inspired and impassioned intellectuals, occupying different positions on the ideological spectrum, he was "never really concerned with politics as the art of the possible, only as an emotional outlet, as a mean of fulfilling his dreams, desires and aspirations." Not surprisingly, he shared with Malraux a critique of democracy and, especially, contempt for the bourgeois liberal parliamentary system.[27] Frederick Brown wrote of Drieu that he "felt alive only within the radical circle of a hero."[28]

Sayre also pointed out that the novel was permeated by the perspective of "the fellow traveler of Stalinism" and that the major characters in the same novel reflected Malraux's world view, at any rate at the time the book was written (ibid., 132).

25 Renee Winegarten: *Writers and Revolution: The Fatal Lure of Action*, New York 1974, 215–216, 275–276, 291.

26 Nizan quoted in Curtis Cate: *Andre Malraux: a Biography*, New York 1995, 202.

27 Renee Winegarten: "The Fascist Mentality: Drieu la Rochelle," in Henry A. Tuner Jr. ed.: *Reappraisals of Fascism*, New York 1975, 215, 218, 220, 226.

28 Brown quoted in David A. Bell: "The Trump of War: When Literature Supported Atrocity," *New Republic*, June 9, 2014, 65.

It is notable that when fascist and communist movements seized power, opportunities for heroic self-assertion on the part of intellectuals greatly diminished.

In contrast to what they discerned and abhorred in their own society, many Western intellectuals believed that communist systems succeeded in modernizing without the well-known adverse side-effects of the process, and ushered in new and superior forms of community.[29] Italian fascism had similar appeals, seen as an alternative form of modernization promising the sweeping regeneration and revitalization of society. Griffin wrote:

> a key element in the genesis ... and praxis of fascism was played by the "sense of a beginning", the mood of standing on the threshold of a new world ... Far from being intrinsically anti-modern, fascism only rejects "the allegedly degenerative element of the modern age" and ... "it represents an *alternative modernism* rather than a rejection of it." ... [F]ascism itself can be seen as a political variant of modernism ... fascism took it upon itself not just to change the state system, but purge civilization of decadence, and foster the emergence of a new breed of human beings.[30]

Elsewhere Griffin wrote that "the myth of the regenerated national community" was presented as the solution for the basic problems of liberal-capitalist modern society.[31] But there was even more to the appeals of fascism, with Giovanni Gentile proposing that "Fascism ... while being a party, a political doctrine is above all a total conception of life."[32]

It is to be emphasized once more that, notwithstanding the points made above, the appeals of fascism and Nazism and their leaders proved to be far more limited and evanescent than those of communist systems and their leaders. Several circumstances explain why this was the case. As time went by, evidence accumulated discrediting both the domestic and foreign policies of Nazi Germany, as well as the ideology of Nazism and Hitler himself. Nazi Germany became increasingly seen as the most repugnant political system of the twentieth century, or "as Goebbels once accurately predicted, the Nazis have largely monopolized the spot reserved for human evil in the Western contemporary imagination."[33] The growth of information about the large volume of atrocities, including the

[29] Communist systems were credited with the superior forms of modernization unaccompanied by alienation (see also Peter L. Berger: "The Socialist Myth," *Public Interest*, Summer 1976).

[30] Roger Griffin: *Modernism and Fascism: The Sense of Beginning under Mussolini and Hitler*, New York 2007, 1, 2, 6.

[31] Griffin 2008, 33.

[32] Gentile quoted in Griffin ed. 1995, 54.

[33] Michael Burleigh: *Moral Combat: Good and Evil in World War II*, New York 2011, 551.

Holocaust, carried out by Nazi Germany made it especially difficult to cling to a favorable image of these systems (allied to one another) and their leaders.[34]

World War II in particular made it impossible for Western sympathizers to persist in their positive attitudes toward regimes that were at war with their own countries. Moreover, the political system of both Nazi Germany and Fascist Italy was destroyed in the course of this war and thus nothing was left to idealize. But probably the most important explanation of the difference in the attitudes of Western intellectuals was that neither Nazism nor Italian fascism offered the kind of respectable, inspiring, and universalistic ideology Marxism appeared to be. Neither the increasingly apparent human costs, nor the exodus of millions of refugees, nor the economic inefficiencies, nor the final collapse of Soviet communism managed to delegitimate the Marxism that inspired and ostensibly legitimated these systems. Saul Bellow wrote: "One way or another, they [intellectuals] clung to the texts that had made intellectuals of them. The Marxist fundamentals had organized their minds and gave them an enduring advantage over unfocused rivals ... What you invest your energy and enthusiasm in when you are young you can never bring yourself to give up altogether."[35]

Disillusionment with modern Western societies was the major source of the attraction of *both* fascism and communism. In both cases the point of departure was the strongly felt conviction that Western liberal-capitalist societies were historically doomed and in a prolonged and profound crisis. These beliefs were especially plausible in the early 1930s. More generally speaking, radicals located at different points of the political spectrum shared a long-standing visceral hostility toward bourgeois society and its liberal values.

In the 1960s and 1970s these convergences became, once more, apparent, as Richard Wolin has written:

> a critique of the West formerly purveyed by thinkers on the German right during the 1920s became popular among the French intellectual left in the 1960s ... This transposition of the conservative revolutionary critique of modernity from Germany to France gave rise to a phenomenon that might be aptly described as *left Heideggerianism*. Thereby, a critique of reason, democracy and humanism

[34] The atrocities committed by Fascist Italy were far more limited: the major and best-known were committed during the invasion of Ethiopia.

[35] Saul Bellow: "Writers, Intellectuals, Politics: Mainly Reminiscence," in *It All Adds Up*, New York 1994, 104–195.

that originated on the German Right during the 1920s was internalized by the French left.

Needless to say, it was not only the French left that "internalized" these critiques. It was a short step from these critiques of modernity to the more recent radical rejections of American society and culture, that is to say, to anti-Americanism, as, again, Wolin pointed out: "Ironically, images of America once a staple of the European Counter-Enlightenment have been assimilated and recycled by the multicultural left. The subterranean affinities between these two intellectual traditions, European right and contemporary cultural left, reveal a disconcerting chapter in the history of political ideas."

Wolin further argued that these affinities extend to postmodernism as well (which may, or may not, be considered part of "the contemporary cultural left"). His book here cited sought "to shed light on the uncanny affinities between the Counter-Enlightenment and postmodernism ... Many of these texts [of Derrida, Foucault, Deleuze, and Lyotard] were inspired by Nietzsche's anticivilizational animus ... According to the conventional wisdom both poststructuralism and postmodernism are movements of the political left. One of the goals of this study is to challenge this commonplace."[36]

For all these reasons it is important to emphasize the often overlooked fact that intellectuals attracted to fascism shared with their more numerous leftist colleagues a profound distaste for capitalism and that their anti-capitalism and aversion to modernity were closely linked.[37] As noted above, anti-capitalism had (and still has) two major components: one is the protest against injustice, exploitation, and inequality, and the other is the revulsion from impersonality, the impoverishment of human relationships, or the "commodification" of human beings – the latter more closely associated with modernity and what has been called "romantic anti-capitalism." Arguably Romantic anti-capitalism has been more characteristic of the ideas, movements, and political systems of Nazi or fascist derivation.

While there were significant differences between Nazism and Italian fascism, and their respective appeals,[38] both had in common with

36 Wolin 2004, 8, 11, 246–247, 284.

37 By contrast, Soviet and pro-Soviet ideologues of the period insisted that fascism (Nazism included) was the end product of capitalism, or its most recent manifestation. Obviously this idea helped to overlook, or ignore, the anti-capitalist sentiments many supporters and ideologues of fascism and Nazism harbored.

38 Gregor argued that the ideology of fascism has been largely misunderstood in the Western world and that it had far less in common with Nazism than has been generally believed.

communist systems and their ideologies a pervasive collectivism. The latter had a strong appeal for Western intellectuals concerned with their social isolation and the decline of community in their society. Intellectuals have been particularly receptive to the critiques of capitalism that focused on its destructive impact on human bonds and disinterested personal relationships.

THE APPEALS OF MUSSOLINI AND FASCIST ITALY ABROAD

According to John Diggins, a historian who wrote extensively about American attitudes toward Fascist Italy, "Mussolini's Fascist dictatorship drew more admiration from democratic America than from any other Western nation," and some of these sentiments rested on Mussolini's image "as the savior of capitalism."[39] In 1927 the journal *Literary Digest* asked its readers: "'Is there a dearth of great men?' The person named most often to refute the suggestion was Benito Mussolini, followed by Lenin."[40] We do not know how many people responded to the question and how many readers this journal had. In any event, Diggins believed that "mainstream America's interest in Mussolini far outstripped that of any other international figure in the 1920s." He wrote:

> the pragmatic posture of the Italian statesmen elicited enthusiastic acclaim from a number of American students of politics who regarded Mussolini as something of a ... philosopher-king ... For the generation of the twenties, Mussolini appeared to many as the harbinger of a new political movement, one that rejected the tired dogmas of democracy and the paralyzing principles of liberalism ... Nowhere is this point of view better illustrated than in the reaction of Lincoln Steffens to the

He wrote: "there remains a residue of opinion that continues to deny Fascism the same reasoned beliefs that everyone readily grants to the political movements and systems of Joseph Stalin or Mao Zedong ... It became commonplace to attribute to Fascism a unique irrationality, accompanied by a ready recourse to violence." Important differences between the two ideologies and political systems included a far less virulent racism and antisemitism in the fascist case, as well as the absence of biological determinism that was central to Nazism. Gregor also noted that Fascism did not provide rationale for the mass murder of Jews (see his *Mussolini's Intellectuals: Fascist Social and Political Thought*, Princeton NJ 2005, ix, 1, 4, 226, 258). He further argued that there were considerable differences between the treatment of intellectuals in Nazi Germany and Fascist Italy, the latter being far less repressive (see his *Giovanni Gentile: Philosopher of Fascism*, New Brunswick NJ 2001, 67–68). Likewise, according to Jonah Goldberg, "many of the leading scholars of fascism and Nazism ... have concluded that Italian Fascism and Nazism, while superficially similar ... were in fact different phenomena" (Goldberg, 53).

[39] Diggins, *AHR*, 487.

[40] Goldberg, 27.

> advent of Fascism ... Steffens came to regard Mussolini as one of the few men who emerged from the war enlightened by realism rather than betrayed by idealism ... Mussolini like Albert Einstein, succeeded because he challenged ancient axioms. The leaders of the Bolsheviks and Fascists were men of action.[41]

Steffens' readiness to believe in the accomplishments of dictatorships was further reflected in his better-known enthusiasm about the Soviet system in the early 1920s.

Diggins suggested that "the potential force of hero worship among the American people" was another factor in the early popularity of Mussolini's system. He wrote: "With the dashing force of charisma as well as an appeal to native folk values, he [Mussolini] appeared to Americans as a redeemer of virtue, a restorer of conservative order and tradition, a self-made man of iron will."[42] If he was capable of impressing Americans as a redeemer, it is hardly surprising that Italians thought of him as such.

Of all the dictators considered in this study, Mussolini and Fidel Castro lent themselves best to the kind of hero worship that "could gratify the vicarious need for excitement ... Mussolini, the man of action also became a hero of typically masculine mind ... courageous, resolute, bold."[43] The British ambassador reported in 1923 that "he [Mussolini] has been 'driving about through Rome in a two-seater with a well-grown lion cub sitting beside him.' "[44] An Italian anarchist intellectual, Leda Rafenelli, wrote "after hearing him [Mussolini] speak for the first time, that 'Benito Mussolini ... is the socialist of the heroic times. He feels, he still believes, with an enthusiasm full of virility and force. He is a Man.' "[45] Harold Laski wrote of him that "it was as the symbol of that revivification that Mussolini came to do battle with the old order ... he represented the passionate optimism of youth."[46]

Diggins had no doubt that Mussolini was the classical charismatic leader, emerging at a time of "insecurity and moral crisis" and "deriving

[41] Diggins, *AHR*, 489–490, 491, 492.

[42] John P. Diggins: "Mussolini and America: Hero-Worship, Charisma and the 'Vulgar Talent'," *Historian* [cited hereafter as *Historian*], August 1966, 584.

[43] Ibid., 578.

[44] Lucy Hughes-Hallett: *Gabriele d'Annunzio: Poet, Seducer and Preacher of War*, New York 2013, 510.

[45] Rafanelli, quoted in Goldberg, 33.

[46] Harold J. Laski: "Lenin and Mussolini," *Foreign Affairs*, September 15, 1923, 49.

his authority from his spectacular display of power ... triumph[ing] over impersonal legal forms and debilitating parliaments."[47]

Another major factor contributing to the popularity of Fascist Italy at the time was the Great Depression. Diggins wrote: "While this country [the U.S.] seemed to founder and drift, the Corporate State [Italy] held out an attractive picture of direct action and national planning." Moreover, Mussolini after 1933 "appeared to be doing for Italy what the American President [FDR] was doing for his country."[48] The Depression played the same part in prompting favorable comparisons of the United States and other Western capitalist countries with the Soviet Union. Nonetheless, in the final analysis it was Mussolini's image as redeemer that impressed most deeply Americans of different political persuasion. He was "the new leader who reaffirmed old values and virtues ... the spiritual savior ... the wise and mature leader," and – especially important for Americans – a "self-made man."[49]

Herbert Croly, editor of the *New Republic*, was also enamored by Fascist Italy and the "*elan* of Italian nationalism which ... would enable Italians to master themselves through a renewal of moral vision ... [it was] 'a political experiment which aroused in a whole nation an increased moral energy and dignified its activities by subordinating them to a deeply felt common purpose.' "[50]

It is noteworthy that the apologetics of Mussolini's Italy sometimes included cautioning against ethnocentric judgments, that is to say, against using criteria based on the standards of one's own society. Thus an editorial in the *New Republic* warned that it would be a mistake to judge harshly the new regime since "one could not measure the political actions of another country by one's own standards and values. Fascism had given the Italians a sense of unity and direction, a national self-consciousness and awakened the country's potential."[51] Remarkably similar warnings against and apprehensions about being overly judgmental and ethnocentric were also entertained by sympathetic visitors of communist countries and helped to stifle the exercise of their critical faculties.

An especially good example of the appeals of Fascist Italy for some American intellectuals is provided by the views of Lawrence Dennis,

47 Diggins, *Historian*, 583.
48 Diggins, *Historian*, 573.
49 Ibid., 577.
50 Croly quoted in Diggins, *AHR*, 497.
51 Croly quoted in ibid., 495.

an American author and diplomat.[52] In the early 1930s he reached the conclusion that "the old system [in the United States] is doomed" and fascism was the only "alternative to ultimate social disintegration and chaos" since "the existing system in the United States [was] unworkable." He had expected the United States to become fascist: "The question really boils down to one of whether we shall get fascism through the war, or fascism before the war and without getting into the war."

His profound distaste for American capitalism found expression in the belief that in the United States "economic power is used for oppression and mischief" and in his assertion that "what the Constitution protects is not the right of the hungry to eat but the right of the rich to keep what they have and to eat while the poor starve."

Dennis had boundless confidence in the benefits fascism would bring to American society. His conviction about these benefits rested on three subsidiary beliefs (each in turn questionable): (a) that fascism is more efficient and pragmatic; (b) that it will make better use of elite groups, and will govern with the help of these superior elite groups; and (c) that a fascist system will enhance social solidarity by its communitarian-patriotic ethos. He further argued that fascism did not have a "millenarian," that is, utopian, component and focused instead on the present and the most appropriate means to accomplish short-term goals:

> Fascism sees no inevitable millennium but merely says, "Given existing conditions in the leading capitalist countries, here is a formula for order and abundance which can be made to work and which most people can be made to like..." Fascism triumphs because it is ... a formula for fulfillment, which people are happy to turn to from liberal formulas of defeat, frustration and inhibition both of government and private initiatives.

In the fascist state, "national interest efficiently pursued" contrasted with "the anarchy of innumerable powerful minority interests" that prevailed in liberal societies. A specific benefit of fascism was supposed to be that "the fascist state, through government-assisted unions of workers,

[52] The largely unknown, unusual background and beliefs of Lawrence Dennis deserve a brief summary. He was half black (white father, black mother) and through much of his life passed as white. Educated at Philip Exeter Academy and Harvard, he joined the foreign service. Subsequently he published several books and a newsletter and became a strong supporter of Nazi Germany and Fascist Italy. He was invited to and attended the 1936 Nuremberg Nazi Party Congress where he met Alfred Rosenberg, the Nazi ideologue. He also met Rudolph Hess, another highly placed Nazi. On another occasion he had a personal audience with Mussolini (see Gary Young: "The Fascist Who 'Passed' for White," *Guardian*, April 4, 2007).

government regulated associations of employers, and special executive tribunals for hearing appeals and complaints, can afford far more redress and correction than the liberal State with its judicial process available only to the rich individual and the large corporation."

Dennis further wrote that "We shall assume that an ideal fascism for America must provide for maximum economic production and consumption with a steady rise in living standards ... without either a class or civil war or the expropriation of all private rights in the instruments of production." Whereas under capitalism

> the worst abuses of power are committed with the aid of courts and law enforcement ... Fascism attaches importance only to the guarantee afforded by ... a consciousness of national solidarity, by a certain sense of noblesse-oblige ... Fascism, in other words, so far as the control of the elite in the national interest or the protection of people is concerned pins its faith on character rather than on codes.

At last, in another flourish of wishful thinking, Dennis proposed that "the great contribution of fascism to mass welfare is that of providing a formula of national solidarity within the spiritual bonds and iron discipline of which the elite and the masses of any given nation ... can cooperate for the common good."

It is notable that most of these critiques of capitalism and American society could also have been made by leftists, or Marxists, and in fact many such critiques were advanced by them. The difference in his and the leftist world view lies in the remedies proposed. Those advocated by Dennis are vague and unconvincing, such as the rise of an incorruptible, selfless elite, a nation united by communitarian sentiments and values, and the emergence of a benevolent and strong state devoted to the common good.

While there are many favorable references in Dennis' writings to Lenin, Mussolini, and Hitler (almost always jointly mentioned), he cautioned that neither Mussolini nor Hitler could authoritatively "define what fascism in America would be like." He refrained from the tempting suggestion that a powerful, charismatic leader would personify and bring about all the admirable goals and policies he ascribed to fascism and a fascist elite. Nonetheless he was convinced of the spiritual blessings such a leader would provide for his people: "Hitler can feed millions of his people acorns, and, yet, if he integrates them in a spiritual union with their community, they will be happier than they were while receiving generous doles from a regime which gave them no such spiritual integration."[53]

[53] Lawrence Dennis: *The Coming of American Fascism*, New York 1936, vii, viii, 12, 46, 100, 104–106, 136, 161, 163, 225–226, 252, 254, 306.

Admiration of Mussolini – unlike that of the other dictators discussed later – was less closely integrated with sympathy for the political system and its ideology that he represented. As Diggins wrote: "Americans found certain features of Fascism repugnant, but Mussolini himself continued to generate personal acclaim ... Americans admired not Fascism but Mussolinism, not the revolutionary ideology but the cult of personality."[54] Diggins also pointed out that "of the many splendid images which Mussolini enjoyed in America none received greater attention from intellectuals than his pose as the pragmatic statesman." Correspondingly, "Fascism's appeal to the liberals ... was found in its experimental nature, anti-dogmatic temper, and moral elan."[55] Charles Beard, the historian, was among these liberals, demonstrating the capacity for wishful thinking and projection that will be encountered throughout this study among the intellectuals discussed: "This [Fascist Italy] is far from the frozen dictatorship of the Russian Tsardom; it is more like the American check and balance system and it may work out in a new democratic direction."[56]

Above all, Mussolini appealed to many intellectuals, Michael Burleigh wrote, because of his

> quasi-religious conception of politics, in which a dedicated elite would help regenerate mankind from the social and cultural ills that were commonly held to debilitate it ... Fascism ... was an attempt to transcend the narrow horizons of conventional class or interest politics ... in favor of an all-embracing anti-politics based on a series of potent myths whose veneration was taken to religious heights.[57]

Emilio Gentile, the major theoretician of fascism, "meticulously documented the concerted efforts by the Fascist regime to create a state religion ... Italian Fascism sought to create a civic and political religion ... whence a 'new man' would emerge, regenerated and totally integrated into the community."[58] The creation of a "new man" was also an avowed objective of communist states.

Different intellectuals found, or rather projected, different virtues or traits upon Mussolini. As Diggins put it, "Mussolini and Fascism ... could be many things to many men."[59] According to Irving Babbitt, Mussolini's "puritanical will may be needed to save us from the American equivalent

[54] Diggins, *Historian*, 560, 582.

[55] John P. Diggins: *Mussolini and Fascism: The View from America*, Princeton NJ 1978, 211, 231.

[56] Beard quoted in Diggins, *AHR*, 494.

[57] Michel Burleigh: *Sacred Causes*, New York 2007, 55, 57–58.

[58] Griffin 2008, 11.

[59] Diggins 1966, 488.

of Lenin," whereas "Santayana saw in Fascism a higher organic Italian culture." Lincoln Steffens, who (for a while) admired *both* fascism and communism, "believed that Mussolini's charismatic dictatorship of the Right could lead to a new realistic path to the goals of the Left."[60] Likewise Wyndham Lewis "was not alone in admiring Mussolini's fascism, but he was eccentric in his endorsation [*sic*] of *both* fascism and Soviet communism." Surette further argued that

> Both fascism/nazism and communism represented themselves as revolutionary, and both claimed to represent the common man against the interests of commerce and industry ... Agreeing with the socialists that the status quo is not supportable ... [W.] Lewis's solution ... was benevolent tyranny, as exemplified by Lenin's rule in the Soviet Union and Mussolini's in Italy.[61]

Wallace Stevens in 1935 admitted to being "pro-Mussolini" and supported the Italian invasion of Ethiopia: "The Italians have as much right to take Ethiopia from the coons [!] as the coons had to take it from the boa-constrictors."[62] Oswald Spengler, the famous German historian, initially also had a favorable impression of Fascist Italy, and of Mussolini in particular, and sent him five of his books in 1925.[63] Reportedly even "Freud sent Mussolini a copy of a book he wrote with Albert Einstein, inscribed, 'To Benito Mussolini, from an old man who greets in the Ruler, the Hero of Culture.' "[64]

Probably Ezra Pound was the most fervent and deeply committed foreign admirer of Mussolini. He moved to Italy in 1924 and during World War II became a propagandist for the regime, making radio broadcasts. He considered Mussolini and the system he created vastly superior to the decadent Western societies and their leaders. Although far from being a Marxist, Pound detested capitalism, and believed that Fascist Italy would purify Europe of its corruptions. He averred that Fascist Italy was the only country capable of "opposing ... the infinite evil of the profiteers and the sellers of men's blood for money."[65] It was also his peculiar conviction that Mussolini had much in common with Thomas Jefferson and continued "the task of Thomas Jefferson."[66] Pound further asserted that

[60] Babbitt and Steffens quoted in Diggins 1978, 209, 210, 224.

[61] Surette, 100, 146, 156.

[62] Quoted in Diggins 1978, 245.

[63] Hamilton, 116–117.

[64] Simonetta Falasca-Zamponi: *Fascist Spectacle: The Aesthetics of Power in Mussolini's Italy*, Berkeley CA 1997, 53.

[65] Ezra Pound: *Jefferson and/or Mussolini*, New York 1935, 61.

[66] Quoted in Hamilton, 288.

"The heritage of Jefferson, Quincy Adams, old John Adams ... is HERE, NOW in the Italian Peninsula ... not in Massachusetts or Delaware."[67] His strange world view found further expression in the belief that World War II "was not caused by any caprice on Mussolini's part, nor on Hitler's. This war is part of the secular war between usurers and peasants, between usurocracy and whomever does an honest day's work with his own brain or hands."[68]

For Pound the attractions of Mussolini and Fascism were inseparable: "The first act of fascio was to save Italy from people too stupid to govern ... The second act was to free it from parliamentarians ... from groups too politically immoral to govern." Rather implausibly he averred that "neither Lenin nor Mussolini show themselves primarily as men thirsting for power." His faith in Mussolini was boundless: "Mussolini's miracle had been that of awakening the sense of responsibility ... By taking more responsibility than any other man (save possibly Lenin) ... Mussolini has succeeded in imparting ... this sense to others."[69] Evidently Pound also admired and respected Lenin.

British intellectuals who admired Mussolini (or "had shown a positive interest in the Italian experiment") included Rudyard Kipling, H.G. Wells, and Hilaire Belloc. Hamilton suggested that "Belloc and Gilbert Chesterton ... believed in a more equal distribution of wealth which they thought the Jews were obstructing and Mussolini was on the way to attaining." William Butler Yeats, while rejecting Marxism, was attracted to fascism and admired Giovanni Gentile, its foremost intellectual legitimizer and supporter.[70]

Hilaire Belloc (1870–1953), the prolific British writer, poet, literary critic, one-time member of parliament, and sailor, was also a devout Catholic and critic of parliamentary democracy and, more generally, of modernity. He found in Mussolini and the system he created in Italy a glorious alternative to the Western European social systems, and especially the British one he held in great contempt. He credited Mussolini with the "resurrection of the country" (that is, Italy). He was also impressed by "his interest in his job, not in his name", that is, in not being egomaniacal. It was an especially groundless opinion. He further wrote:

Society in Italy had to reach the point of acute peril before that reaction took place which saved the country ...

[67] Pound, 12.
[68] Pound quoted in Hamilton, 289.
[69] Pound, 39, 94, 99.
[70] Hamilton, 257, 258, 270, 278.

> I made a sort of pilgrimage to see Mussolini, the head of the movement ... I had the honour of a long conversation with him alone, discovering and receiving his judgments. What a contrast with the sly and shifty talk of your parliamentarians! What a sense of decision, of sincerity, of serving the nation ... Meeting this man after talking to the parliamentarians in other countries was like meeting with some athletic friend of one's boyhood after an afternoon of racing touts; or it was like coming upon good wine in a Pyrenean village after compulsory draughts of marsh water.

As to Mussolini's contempt for majority rule (which Belloc shared): "Mussolini's reaction ... was, I think, against the ludicrous abuse of the doctrine of the majority which has brought Europe to its present pass; for there is nothing so wicked, or so senseless or so degrading but a majority ... generally a sham majority."[71]

Mussolini's decisiveness, dynamism, will, lack of doubt in his mission, and self-assured composure represented for Belloc an alluring counterpoint to the inefficient, hesitant, corrupt, and compromise-ridden politicians of democratic political systems he was familiar with. The religious metaphors he used further revealed his perceptions of Mussolini: he "resurrected" Italy and Belloc went on a "pilgrimage" to meet him.[72]

Jonathan Raban observed that Belloc's program "for the regeneration of England" was "explicitly Fascist, and the real hero of his story is Mussolini." As a critic of modernity and parliamentary democracy, Belloc craved "a miraculous return to a 'homogenous' society," such as Mussolini's Italy promised to be, in his eyes. Raban also noted that *Nona*, Belloc's sailboat, was "held up as a tiny scale model of how an idyllic society might be; it is a ship of state in miniature, and the simple virtues of life at sea are set in counterpoint against the corruption and depravity of modern England."[73]

Belloc's friend and intellectual ally G.K. Chesterton shared both his views of the moral corruption of Western societies and a corresponding, compensatory admiration of Italian fascism. After visiting Italy in 1929 and interviewing Mussolini, Chesterton wrote, rather imaginatively: "the very faces of the crowd carrying the eagles or the fasces are not the shifty obliterated faces of the modern mob, but those of the old

[71] Hilaire Belloc: *The Cruise of the Nona*, New York 1983 (first published 1925), 161, 163–164, 166, 268.

[72] Not surprisingly Belloc also admired Franco, calling him "the man who saved us all" (quoted in Michael Burleigh 2007, 157).

[73] Jonathan Raban: "Introduction," in Belloc, vi, viii, ix.

Roman busts ... So far as a man may give the sense of his experience in a single phrase: he has seen the return of the Romans." While Chesterton had more reservations about fascism than Belloc, he felt it represented authority employed in the interest of the nation and not big employers: "Mussolini['s] ... was a despotism cleansed of capitalists. An authority acting 'independently of both Trade Magnates and Trade Unions and capable of giving orders to both.' "[74]

George Bernard Shaw was one of those Western intellectuals who admired *both* Mussolini and Lenin, as well as Stalin, and the political systems each created. Hamilton wrote: "After sending Lenin his latest book with a flattering dedication in 1921 he [Shaw] praised 'the inspired precision' with which Mussolini 'denounced liberty as a putrefying corpse.' ... To condemn Mussolini for the assassination of Matteoti was absurd, according to Shaw, for many great statesmen were forced ... to murder inconvenient opponents."[75] As another author observed, "Shaw's main theme was the inadequacy of democracy. Dictatorship, he claimed, was more efficient and more of the people. 'Italy is governed by a man of the people...'."[76]

Shaw is an outstanding example of Western intellectuals whose political sympathies were overdetermined by their visceral rejection of their own society and consequently were drawn to almost any political movement or system that shared their hatred of it. Shaw was convinced that both Mussolini's Italy and Lenin's (and Stalin's) Soviet Union represented rejuvenation and all-round progress. Lincoln Steffens shared this outlook: "For Steffens and countless other liberals, Mussolini, Lenin and Stalin were all doing the same thing: transforming corrupt, outdated societies."[77]

Shaw personifies the stunning contrast (characteristic of the attitudes of many alienated Western intellectuals here discussed) between the merciless criticism many of these intellectuals routinely and reflexively aimed at their own society and an embarrassing credulousness they displayed about the claims of idealized political systems, such as the Soviet one. It never seems to have occurred to Shaw, the great cynic, that the conducted tour of the Soviet Union he took might not have been the best

[74] Quoted in Jay P. Corrin: *G.K. Chesterton and Hilaire Belloc: The Battle Against Modernity*, Athens OH 1981, 178, 179.

[75] Hamilton, 271.

[76] Richard Griffiths: *Fellow Travellers of the Right: British Enthusiasts for Nazi Germany 1933–9*, London 1980, 20.

[77] Goldberg, 103.

way to obtain reliable information about that country and its government.[78] Numerous compatriots of his shared his blinders.

H.G. Wells, like Shaw, was attracted to both the Soviet Union and Fascist Italy, although he had some reservations about the latter. He appreciated the fascist preoccupation with "discipline and public service" and "a considerable boldness in handling education and private property for the public benefit. Fascism indeed was not an altogether bad thing ... and Mussolini left his mark on history."[79]

Sir Charles Petrie, author of a book on Mussolini (among others), considered him "the greatest figure of the present age, and perhaps one of the most notable of all time." Sir John Squire, editor of the *London Mercury*, compared Mussolini favorably to Napoleon, crediting him with "more compassion." The British *Saturday Review* on February 3, 1934, carried a full-page picture of Mussolini and designated him "the World's most benevolent Ruler ... [who] dragged Italy out of the mire of Socialism and made it the most successful and prosperous country in Europe." Other articles in the same publication "praised the Duce [leader] who 'sets an example of kindness to animals and birds.' " The same publication, and its owner Lady Houston in particular, warmly supported Italy's invasion of Abyssinia.[80]

James Barnes, author of several books about fascism, was among the English supporters of Italian fascism who combined a nostalgia "for a more perfect past" with "a concern for ... the victims of the capitalist system" in the present. His views were strongly influenced by those of Belloc and Chesterton: "Like them he wanted fairer distribution of wealth, social peace and the downfall of the international financier. Fascism, for him, meant a return to the Catholic Middle Ages ... Mussolini's moral power had made the whole Italian people full of moral strength." Elsewhere Barnes wrote of Mussolini and Italian fascism that "by great fortune, the movement also produced the man, gifted with all the true marks of a leader ... who could read deep into the soul of the people and thereby able to drive the movement closer and closer to the Italian Nation's true traditions, ridding it ... of its impurities and moderating its excesses." It was said of Barnes that he "emerged in the 1920s as one of the most fervent British

[78] Shaw was among the most gullible of the political pilgrims dealt with in the book of the same title (see especially ch. 4).

[79] Quoted in Griffin ed. 1995, 59.

[80] Ibid., 22, 24, 25, 210–211.

apologists of Fascism [and] ... a close friend and devotee of Ezra Pound."[81]

Emil Ludwig (1881–1948), the popular German writer of the same period, was impressed, like Shaw, by both Mussolini and Stalin and he met and interviewed both (for the Stalin interview, see pp. 136–137). His impressions and assessments of Mussolini reflect a generic political hero worship that seem transferable to the other dictators encountered later in this volume. It is hard to know if this was the case because the dictators here considered were in fact similar to one another, or because they were homogenized in the perception of sympathetic Western intellectuals such as Ludwig, who projected upon them similarly idealized attributes.

Mussolini, as Ludwig saw him, possessed an abundance of heroic qualities. He was one of those rare human beings who "undertake a life of action in the grand style" and is dominated by a "feeling of having a mission to fulfill." He was especially impressive because he "yearned ... for the establishment of a definitely new order of things. And if he sought power it was not for its own sake but rather that he might help in building up this new order after which he yearned." At any rate, that was what Ludwig believed.

In these as in some other regards, Mussolini was no different from other modern dictators who also intended to fundamentally transform their societies, if not the whole world. Such undertakings required vast amounts of power, which made it difficult to distinguish individual power-hunger from the idealistic commitment to the creation of a new social order.

Mussolini had no doubt that his people were following him "to a man in case of necessity" and believed that "they all looked up to him as to a father." According to Ludwig, he was a man of great pride and possessed high levels of self-esteem. Ludwig wrote: "Such a life, directed only by energy and pride, can maintain itself free of all scepticism only by faith in its own mission." This sense of mission helped to explain to Ludwig why Mussolini worked sixteen hours a day, "as did the great Russian leader whom the Fascist leader resembles in essentials." It is not clear if Ludwig alluded here to Lenin or Stalin, but probably it was Stalin since Ludwig met him and wrote about him.

[81] James Bradshaw and James Smith: "Ezra Pound, J.S. Barnes ('The Italian Lord Haw-Haw') and Italian Fascism," *Review of English Studies*, September 20, 2013, 15.

Ludwig also discerned and apparently admired in Mussolini the disposition to live dangerously, and a belief in destiny that coexisted with activism and risk-taking. Mussolini remarked to him that "Nobody may challenge Destiny more than once. Anyhow, everybody meets the death that is in harmony with his character" – a peculiarly misplaced romantic notion.[82]

Mussolini, like some other contemporary dictators, had artistic proclivities,[83] which found expression not only in playing the violin but in his attitude toward the masses. He averred, as quoted by Ludwig, that:

> I feel the masses in my hands as they think, or if I mingle with them ... then I feel a part of this mass of people. And yet I have a certain aversion to them, as the artist has towards the material he works on. Sometimes the sculptor will smash the marble in rage because it does not lend itself with sufficient pliancy to the shape he wishes to evoke from it ... The important thing is to rule the masses as an artist dominates his material.[84]

The impressive attributes of Mussolini that Ludwig discerned were also manifest in tangible accomplishments enumerated by Ludwig:

> Giant ships ... are now sailing under the Italian flag ... An entirely new air fleet has been constructed. Three new universities have been founded, the old modernized ... The standard of all elementary schools has been raised ... Attendance fees have been reduced or entirely abolished, and in the South illiteracy has been almost entirely wiped out. In Rome, Ostia and Pompei ... new archeological treasures have been brought to light. With an energy that rivals the Russian example, the private interests of the worker, his wife and children, have been taken under the care of the state, even to the extent of looking after their pleasures.

On top of all these achievements, Ludwig, who described himself as "a convinced pacifist," anointed "Mussolini a guarantee of peace in Europe in spite of his bellicose utterances."

[82] In his own death Mussolini failed to live up to such heroic ideas. He was captured while trying to escape from Italy to Switzerland (from where he intended to fly to Spain). He was executed by Italian partisans near Lake Como, his corpse subsequently taken to Milan where it was hung by his ankles, displayed for public viewing.

[83] At any rate he was perceived as having such proclivities by some of his admirers. For example, Ezra Pound claimed that "Mussolini was himself an artist" (quoted in Surette, 281).

[84] Here it may be noted that the romantic admiration of the artist, and by extension the artistically inclined dictator, had a sinister aspect often overlooked by his admirers. Isaiah Berlin wrote: "This attitude has a darker side too: worship not merely of the painter or the composer or the poet, but of the more sinister artist whose materials are men – the destroyer of old societies, and the creator of new ones – no matter at what human cost: the superhuman leader who tortures and destroys in order to build on new foundations" (*The Power of Ideas*, London 2000, 204).

Last but not least, Ludwig was also impressed by Mussolini's physical features:

At first one is somewhat surprised to notice the delicate and almost feminine hands. But that feeling changes the moment he grasps the hand of the guest. It is a manly and firm shake. The deep black eyes and the large domed forehead are in striking contrast. And here you have an illustration of the basic contradiction that underlies Mussolini's whole nature. Like every man of creative genius, he is a combination of masculine and feminine qualities, the Act and the Dream.[85]

Curzio Malaparte, the Italian writer-journalist (who later abandoned his fascist sympathies), aptly summed up the appeals of fascism for many Western intellectuals, such as Emil Ludwig:

The Fascist revolution [is] a whole process of revision of the present civil, cultural, political and spiritual values. [It is] A radical and objective criticism of … everything modern … the final goal of the Fascist revolution is the restoration of our natural and historical civilization which has been degraded by the triumphant rise of the barbarism of modern life.[86]

A similar observation of Mussolini by Diggins could be generalized to account for the appeal of *all dictators* considered in this volume: "Mussolini's dominant image was … that of the redeemer. He and his men represented all that was healthy and redemptive in Italian life."[87] In a similar vein, Falasca-Zamponi suggested that

At a time when some critics attacked democratic ethics for being fundamentally materialistic and utilitarian and for precipitating the fall of spiritual values, Mussolini's call for high ideals attracted the attention of intellectuals and politicians … Mussolini's claim to spiritualism, his activism and his nonconformist political theories attracted the attention of many critics of the liberal system who were looking for a "new man."

… Mussolini detached himself from earthly matters and seemed to offer an almost spiritual image of himself … driven by a superior goal.[88]

Inside Italy the cult of Mussolini flourished. Walter Laqueur wrote:

In Mussolini's lifetime, no less than 400 books about Il Duce were published … Mussolini was predestined, elected, called by God and history … He was also the new man, the greatest man who ever lived, or at least the highest incarnation of the Italian race … He was a colossus, a titan … Like Stalin he

[85] All quotations from Emil Ludwig: *Nine Etched from Life*, Freeport NY 1934, 320, 324, 327, 329, 330, 333, 335, 336, 337, 341.

[86] Malaparte quoted in Hamilton, 53.

[87] Diggins 1978, 59.

[88] Falasca-Zamponi, 43, 45, 76.

> was frequently compared to an eagle ... His knowledge was encyclopedic and universal; like Stalin he was considered omniscient and omnipresent ... he had a limitless capacity for work. He virtually never slept. He was a champion swimmer, flier, horseman, fencer, driver, cyclist, and so on.[89]

A Catholic prayer was adapted to express worshipful attitudes toward Mussolini:

> I believe in the high Duce ... And in Jesus his only protector – Our Savior was conceived by a good teacher and an industrious blacksmith – He was a valiant soldier ... He came down to Rome ... he reestablished the state. He ascended into the high office – He is seated at the right hand of our Sovereign ... I believe in the wise laws – The Communion of Citizens – The forgiveness of sins – The resurrection of Italy – The eternal force. Amen.[90]

Falasca-Zamponi further noted that Mussolini was depicted as "an 'elected' person who enjoyed the direct assistance of God ... Most often ... the regime's characterizations blurred the difference between Duce and God and Mussolini appeared as an omnipotent being with supernatural powers." His mystique (like Stalin's) included the belief that he hardly ever slept and a light was always left on in his office at night to support this idea.

Mussolini was also at ease with wild animals, being photographed visiting lions in their cages. Like lesser heroes such as D'Annunzio and Malraux, he too was an avid and talented pilot. His superhuman qualities were further attested to by refusing anesthesia during surgery. He was also credited with stopping the lava flow from the volcano Etna by his mere presence during a visit to Sicily, saving a village from destruction. Attributions of immortality, his "ability to escape death" were part of his cult. At last, "besides omnipotence and immortality, Mussolini's divine character was conveyed by his omnipresence. Through photographs, graffiti, radio and cinema, Mussolini appeared everywhere and, like God, permeated places and objects of everyday life."[91]

ITALIAN INTELLECTUALS AND MUSSOLINI

Although, as indicated above, numerous Western intellectuals and public figures were attracted to Mussolini, not surprisingly he had far more enthusiastic supporters among Italian intellectuals than among those abroad, especially after he became allied with Hitler. They included many

[89] Walter Laqueur: *Stalin: The Glasnost Revelations*, New York 1990, 186–187.

[90] Prayer quoted in Falasca-Zamponi, 64–65.

[91] Ibid., 66, 68, 70–71, 73, 78.

of the "most prominent modern artists, architects, designers and technocrats."[92] In March 1925 a congress of fascist intellectuals in Bologna concluded with a manifesto (drafted by Giovanni Gentile) that gave full support to Mussolini's policies, stressing "the vitality of Fascism and exalt[ing] the Italian nation." It was signed by the major figures of the period.[93]

Benedetto Croce (who subsequently became an opponent of the Fascist regime) averred, at one point, that "I consider so excellent the cure to which Fascism has submitted Italy that my main worry is that the convalescent may leave her bed too soon and suffer a serious relapse."[94] Even toward the end of the war, when the fortunes of the Axis powers were rapidly declining, "those traditionally considered 'intellectuals' – the scholars, literary figures, artists and journalists – made themselves available" to Mussolini to assist him in recreating the fascist regime in Northern Italy.[95]

Luigi Pirandello, the well-known Italian playwright, was "one of the many intellectuals to be seduced by Mussolini's charm, for the Duce knew the art of telling his visitors exactly what they wanted to hear ... [he] knew how to flatter artists. When Ezra Pound met him in 1933 he found a copy of his *Cantos* lying on Mussolini's desk." It was a technique also widely used in communist countries to impress visiting foreign intellectuals.

Pirandello believed that Mussolini had a special affinity with artists and art: "I have always had the greatest admiration for Mussolini and I think I am one of the few people capable of understanding the beauty of this continuous creation of reality performed by him ... Mussolini is one of the few people who knows that reality only exists in man's power to create it." Pirandello also claimed to believe that Mussolini "had solved the antinomy between life and form."[96]

He was far from the only intellectual or artist who believed that the admirable dictator was a "philosopher king" endowed with artistic impulses and talents as well. Falasca-Zamponi wrote that "the tight connection Mussolini envisaged between politics and art ... was not merely a product of picturesque literary pretension ... To the contrary, the link

[92] Griffin, 18–19. He also wrote: "Fascism ... became a magnet to an ever wider gamut of modernists ... keen to feel part of a dynamic, ongoing, open-ended process of cultural transformation that seemed to be heading ... towards a new 'order' " (ibid., 216).

[93] Hamilton, 56–57.

[94] Croce quoted in Hamilton, 44.

[95] Gregor 2005, 227.

[96] Hamilton, 46–47.

between politics and art constituted the central element of Mussolini's political vision." Mussolini himself explicitly linked arts and politics:

> That politics is an art there is no doubt ... Also because in politics there is a lot of intuition. "Political" like artistic creation is a slow elaboration and sudden divination ... Both work with the material and the spirit ... In order to give wise laws to a people it is also necessary to be something of an artist.

Elsewhere he expressed admiration of Lenin for being the consummate artist-politician: "Lenin is an artist, who has worked with human beings as other artists work with marble or metal."[97]

Several of the dictators considered in this volume harbored artistic ambitions and self-conceptions. While Hitler in his youth aspired to be a painter, Mussolini was an "accomplished" violinist and wrote a play,[98] while Mao wrote poems. Romain Rolland "portrayed Lenin as an artist of the revolution not ruthless professional revolutionary."[99] Following his rise to power Hitler advised architects and also thought of himself as a great thinker, and "came to regard himself as the 'philosopher Fuhrer.' "[100]

In addition to these pursuits all of these dictators have written copiously about weighty social and political matters, and their writings were designated, in the countries they ruled, as part of the essential doctrinal foundation of these systems. They were often perceived by the intellectuals attracted to them as fellow intellectuals of superior qualities and accomplishments who transcended the gulf between talk and action, theory and practice. John Gunther, an American journalist, suggested that Mussolini was "the only modern ruler who can genuinely be termed an intellectual."[101] Attributions of towering intellect were even more frequent in the case of the communist dictators, as will be seen later.

Gentile was the most committed and influential supporter of Mussolini and fascism and he was, in turn, highly appreciated by Mussolini, who "had unequivocally committed himself to the Gentilean notion of the totalitarian state in which 'everything [was] in the state, nothing outside the state, and nothing against the state.' " This idea was similar to Fidel Castro's proposition that everything was permissible within the

97 Falasca-Zamponi, 15, 21.

98 See Diggins 1978, 241, 242. As another author put it, "Mussolini was Romanticism's godlike 'artist-creator' transposed from the sphere of the arts to the arena of politics" (Jan Plamper: *The Stalin Cult*, New Haven CT 2012, 12).

99 James Fisher: *Romain Rolland and the Politics of Intellectual Engagement*, Berkeley CA 1988, 238.

100 Yvonne Sherratt: *Hitler's Philosophers*, New Haven CT 2013, xviii.

101 Gunther quoted in Diggins 1978, 61–62.

Revolution, but nothing outside of it. As Gregor further observed, "for Gentile, the concept of human beings as 'communal' creatures always remained central to his moral and political doctrine. The moral injunction to fully realize oneself ... could be achieved only in community – within the state ... Gentile saw in Fascism the "true realization of ... thought and action"[102] – arguably its major appeal for intellectuals and very similar to the appeal of the (alleged) unity of theory and practice in the policies and objectives of communist systems. Gentile was appointed minister of education by Mussolini in 1923.

It was another major appeal of fascism that it sought to gratify, and succeeded in gratifying, nationalistic longings: "For Gentile, and for the intellectuals who initially committed themselves to Fascism, Mussolini and his movement embodied Italy's effort to find its place in the sun in a world environment in which all the advanced industrial powers had already established themselves."[103] This aspiration was very similar to that of communist states such as the Soviet Union and China, which wished to "catch up with" and "overtake" Western capitalist countries.

There was also an affinity between collective, nationalistic self-assertion and legitimacy conferred by political violence. Falasca-Zamponi wrote:

> A Janus-faced approach to force – on the one hand ... "surgical," on the other as "regenerating" – allowed the fascist movement to propose itself as the national savior ... Subsequently in the aftermath of Mussolini's takeover, the blood of the dead [a reference to World War I – P.H.] continued to be invoked and served to legitimize the regime's actions ... By magnifying the fascists' blood and sacrifice, the regime sanctified violence as the premise for Italy's renewal, the foundation for a morally regenerated society.[104]

Thus it was not surprising that the invasion of Ethiopia was welcomed by prominent intellectuals such as Gabriele D'Annunzio, the politically active Italian poet who congratulated Mussolini for invading Ethiopia, as did Pirandello, who called him "The Author of his great feat [i.e., the invasion] ... A true man of the theater, a providential hero whom God granted Italy at the right moment."[105]

Vilfredo Pareto, the famous Italian sociologist, was also favorably inclined toward fascism. In his view, most of its supporters "followed a line of conduct in the pursuit of an almost mystical ideal: the celebration

[102] A. James Gregor: *Giovanni Gentile: Philosopher of Fascism*, New Brunswick NJ 2001, 52, 63.

[103] Hamilton, 58, 96.

[104] Falasca-Zamponi, 36.

[105] Pirandello quoted in Hamilton, 69.

of national sentiment and the power of the State." He was also impressed by the new elites; unlike in much of Europe, "in Italy Fascism has effectively embarked on a solution by substituting a new ruling class for one which had shown itself to be completely inept ... In Italy Fascism has succeeded in ... giving to the nationalist religion the goal of defending the State and bringing about a social renewal."[106]

The favorable views of Mussolini on the part of both intellectuals and ordinary people cannot be dismissed altogether as delusional projections, or products of the institutionalized cult. Like Hitler, Mussolini was a genuinely charismatic figure, a dynamic speaker who galvanized his audiences and projected decisiveness and courage; moreover, in the earlier period of his rule material-economic conditions did improve. He was also a virile and vibrant figure: "fencing, riding, skiing or wrestling submissive lions and tigers in the zoo ... [he] could pilot aircraft ... was perpetually seen rushing about, at the control of planes or speeding by on motorbikes or in racing cars."[107]

Gabriel D'Annunzio, the Italian writer (1863–1938), is another important political figure who belongs to this chapter, although his relationship to Mussolini was ambivalent. While his enormous popularity, influence, and active participation in World War I sets him apart from typical intellectuals, he did personify many of their essential attributes in an extreme form. He was a powerful public intellectual (before the concept was invented), a celebrated national hero, and a potential role model for intellectuals striving for authenticity and longing to connect words and deeds, theory and practice.[108] He devoted much of his life to attempting to restore what he perceived as the lost heroic dimensions of life driven by an unconcealed hunger for power and glory. Sheri Berman, a political scientist, wrote: "His poems, plays, novels and journalism conveyed a disgust and boredom with the contemporary world and a longing for a more heroic era."[109]

D'Annunzio was far more open and unembarrassed about being attracted to and glorifying violence than intellectuals tend to be, including

[106] Pareto quoted Griffin ed. 1995, 249–250.

[107] Michael Burleigh, *Sacred Causes: The Clash of Religion and Politics from the Great War to the War on Terror*, New York 2007, 63.

[108] "During the war years and at Fiume d'Annunzio repeatedly alluded to his previous life as 'mere poet' ... as though literature was something he had toyed in the past but then outgrown. He was a warrior, a Commandant. He told his legionaries that there was no melody in him but that of their marching songs" (Hughes-Hallett, 482).

[109] Sheri Berman: "Fascist Designs," *New York Times Book Review*, September 1, 2013, 19.

even those who felt – like Norman Mailer and Sartre – that it was purifying and authenticating. D'Annunzio was a genuine megalomaniac and, unlike most intellectuals, he did not merely fantasize about power but held power for a period of his life when, after World War I, he was the leader of troops occupying the contested city of Fiume.

D'Annunzio was also a charismatic figure, fiery speaker, and major influence on Mussolini. According to one commentator, "[he] manipulated crowds with speeches from a balcony ... made use of gestures and salutes ... stirred up audiences with oratorical crescendoes ... Mussolini studied and absorbed these tactics."[110] Under D'Annunzio's influence, "in Fiume ... a kind of permanent festival had been installed, a form of political theater, animated by D'Annunzio with a speech nearly every day, eliciting from the public the spontaneous response, the emotional public dialogue, which was his key political invention, his legacy to Mussolini."[111]

D'Annunzio is among those who defy the conventional images and stereotypes of the intellectual. There was nothing "marginal" about him, nor was critical skepticism one of his defining characteristics. He was a great success as a writer, poet, playwright, public figure, political activist, and war hero who ended his life in luxurious retirement in a villa on the shores of Lake Garda. D'Annunzio personifies the restless intellectual who wants to change the world and has nothing but contempt for timid, compromising politicians. His political attitudes and beliefs are also noteworthy because they cannot be easily classified as either right or left. While briefly a right-wing member of the Italian parliament, on one occasion he literally "passed to the other [socialist] side of the chamber," explaining that "he was not of the right, or of any other fixed position. 'I am a man of life, not of formulae.' "[112]

He was animated by a vigorous rejection of the liberal bourgeois society the left and the right shared, and, more broadly speaking, by the revulsion from many aspects of the modern world. The latter did not extend to modern technology – especially planes, cars, and the efficient weapons he admired and occasionally made use of. He had "once complained of the tedium of a life in which tame commercialism had replaced the 'magnificent crimes' of a grander, bloodier age." He believed that only " 'a great conflict of the races' can purge society of its decadence ... Violence on

[110] David Gilmour: "He Dared the Undarable," *New York Review of Books*, March 6, 2014, 22.

[111] Pfaff, 175.

[112] D'Annunzio quoted in Hughes-Hallett, 205–206.

a massive scale was the only remedy. Now at last, the torrent of cleansing blood was about to flood across Europe." He was a strong advocate of Italy's entering World War I and despised politicians reluctant to do so. He felt strongly that there had to be a "'necessary hatred' against those who deny their nation's greatness" and believed in "the grandeur of 'action' regardless of its purpose." He told a friend "'I adore war' and wrote to another friend 'For me and for you and for those like us, peace today is a disaster.'"

His affinity with war and violent political conflict had obvious Romantic undertones. He believed that "the most intense experience of life ... was 'to be bought only with the coin which has life on one side and death on the other.'" His biographer wrote: "War brought him peace. To set out on a dangerous mission was, for him, to achieve 'an ecstasy' he compared with that known by the great mystics."

He had a complex, competitive, and mutually suspicious relationship with Mussolini, as he considered himself the "inventor" of fascism. He wrote to Mussolini: "'In the movement which calls itself 'fascist' has not the best been engendered by my spirit? Was not the present upheaval heralded by me...?'." Despite his reservations, in 1936 he congratulated Mussolini for defeating Ethiopia: "'You have subjugated all the uncertainties of fate and defeated every human hesitation.'"

Mussolini visited him several times at his lavish retreat on Lake Garda, showered him with gifts, and authorized the government to pay the considerable expenses of maintaining and expanding the luxurious estate D'Annunzio was constantly remodeling. He granted him every favor he asked for except building a private airport. In 1926 he was promoted to general. Mussolini also had agents keeping an eye on him while allowing the public to "believe that d'Annunzio was wholeheartedly behind the new regime ... At times d'Annunzio assumed a paternal stance pointing out (correctly) how much Mussolini and his followers learned from him. Mussolini was more than happy to agree." When he died, Mussolini "claim[ed] the role of chief mourner ... to ensure that ... in death he will be securely claimed for the fascist cause."[113]

Although widely ignored in our times and barely known in the United States, D'Annunzio would have been at home in the protest movements and the counter-culture of the 1960s; the young protestors and activists of that period would have found his lifestyle and vivid denunciation of liberal-bourgeois society appealing and congenial.

[113] Hughes-Hallett, 28, 300, 309, 360, 372, 378, 428, 486, 509, 541, 542.

In many ways D'Annunzio resembles Andre Malraux, who admired him[114] and was a much better-known European public intellectual and skillful political operator, whose self-esteem too was boundless and who also aspired to power and public influence, and succeeded in realizing these aspirations to a considerable degree. They also had in common a talent for self-dramatizing and self-promotion, for attracting publicity. Both possessed an adventurous streak (D'Annunzio's stronger) and believed that living dangerously was ennobling and proved one's authenticity. They also believed that art and politics ought to cross-fertilize one another, and are, or ought to be, linked in some creative way – a disposition that was characteristic of several of the dictators here discussed.

Hughes-Hallett wrote:

> though he was an author first and foremost, d'Annunzio was never solely a man of letters. He wanted his words to spark uprisings and set nations ablaze … To watch d'Annunzio's trajectory from neo-Romantic young poet to instigator of radical right-wing revolt against democratic authority is to recognize that fascism was not a freakish product of an exceptional historical moment … both Mussolini and Hitler learned a great deal from d'Annunzio … D'Annunzio believed he was working to create a new and better world order, a "politics of poetry." So did observers from every point on the political spectrum, from the conservative nationalists … to V.I. Lenin, who sent him a pot of caviar and called him the "only revolutionary in Europe." … Mussolini encouraged the writing of a biography of D'Annunzio entitled *The John the Baptists of Fascism.*

D'Annunzio's political activism culminated in the occupation of the city of Fiume in September 1919 as the leader of a band of irregular troops. It was his "penultimate adventure" and "sacred entry." His biographer wrote, "From now on he would 'create not with words, but with human lives.' His life as a hero was about to begin."

Fiume, which was part of the Austro-Hungarian Empire defeated in World War I, had a large Italian population, and following the war its political status was unsettled. Italian nationalists and public opinion demanded that it become independent or annexed by Italy, but the victorious allies intended to make it a part of the new state of Yugoslavia. D'Annunzio, given his nationalist credentials and heroic military exploits during the war, was invited to lead the irregular troops that seized the city. He established a city-state that endured for a little over a year

114 Pfaff, 227.

(1919–1920) and became the hotbed of what today would be called the European counter-culture:

> In Fiume under his command a political rally might segue ... into a street party and thence into a love-in. To be young and passionate was a patriotic duty ... Fiume was like a city in the throes of Dionysiac possession, and d'Annunzio was its god ... Women pelted ... [him] with flowers when he marched out with his legionaries ... The American vice-consul in Triest reported that Fiume was "completely beflagged." Lights blazed all night. Portraits of d'Annunzio hung ... all around the main plaza. Banners reading "Italy or death" were suspended over every street ... D'Annunzio was everywhere, speechifying, reviewing troops ... tirelessly displaying himself to the crowds ... and for the two film crews who followed his every move ... Every day he would appear on the balcony to address the hundreds of people ... gathered in the square beneath. He treated them as a conductor treats his chorus, or a priest his congregation. He gave them cues; they responded.

Anticipating Fidel Castro, "he would become transported by his own oratory ... [he] referred to these 'colloquies' as his 'parliament in the open air' and the 'first example of direct communication ... between the people and their ruler ... since Greek times."

His troops were mostly young, undisciplined, and "cultivated eccentricity," and included many teenagers and "juveniles proud to be delinquent ... Some of the new arrivals ... were looking to found, not a newly independent Fiume, not a Greater Italy, but a new world order. Others simply sought excitement."[115] As Michael Ledeen wrote, "For him, Fiume was the beginning of a spiritual blaze that would consume all of the rotting and decrepit western world and that would purity the West."[116] D'Annunzio fantasized about Fiume igniting "'desires of revolt the world over' ... His mission was directed against all the world's evil ... It was universalist." He announced that "'on the verge of old age I have been reborn as the Prince of Youth.'"[117]

In the end he left Fiume under Italian political and military pressure and moved back to Italy and a very active retirement at Lake Garda.

Of all the major dictators included in this study, Mussolini was, arguably, the least reprehensible (besides Omar Torrijos of Panama, a far less important figure discussed in Chapter 7) with much less blood on his hands than was the case of his colleagues discussed below. Moreover, his economic policies (like those of Hitler) benefited his nation, at any rate until he invaded Ethiopia and entered World War II.

[115] Hughes-Hallett, 5, 6, 7, 8, 313, 408, 413, 418, 419, 424–426, 449, 458.
[116] Ledeen quoted in Pfaff, 172.
[117] Hughes-Hallett, 420, 447.

Both Fascist Italy and Nazi Germany introduced economic policies that were more efficient and beneficial (at any rate in the short run) for their respective populations than corresponding Soviet policies, or those of other communist systems that emerged after World War II. With few exceptions, communist states pursued disastrous economic policies that were embarked upon for doctrinal reasons and marked by high levels of mismanagement.

Mussolini's power and popularity derived in part from the social and political conditions that prevailed in Italy following World War I, as well as the more elusive discontents of modernity noted in the previous chapter. The nature of his cult, as those of similar figures discussed later, prompts reflections on the social-psychological preconditions of political hero worship.

The hero worship of Mussolini (and of the other dictators) raises the question as to what enabled, or compelled, multitudes of people, many of them highly educated (including numerous intellectuals), to believe that particular individuals of uncertain qualifications would bring about dramatic and highly desirable changes in their society (or the whole world). Why was it so tempting to believe that these new leaders would be capable of fundamentally transforming not only social, political, and economic institutions and practices, but human relationships and human nature as well?

To explain these matters by the charisma of these leaders raises the further question as to why the same multitudes projected upon them the quality we came to call charisma. Arguably, a large, probably overwhelming portion of charismatic attributions were delusional, nothing but wishful fantasies that no actual human being was capable of realizing.

As the familiar argument goes (see pp. 22–23) charismatic leaders typically arise in times of severe social-political crises and dislocations, when popular longing for simple, quick, and radical solutions becomes intense and widespread. These attitudes culminate in the belief that certain individuals of indistinct qualifications – the new leaders – will become redeemers, who will resurrect, revitalize, and reinvigorate decadent, corrupt, morally bankrupt social systems and establish social justice, variously defined. While deteriorated objective conditions (lost war, domestic disorder, economic crisis, inflation, unemployment, etc.) play an important part in the rise of these hopes and beliefs, in the final analysis modern political hero worship, and the attributions of charisma it entails, are nurtured by dormant religious impulses that surface in the virtual deification of the dictators here discussed.

3

Hitler, Nazism, and Intellectuals

> Above all, what Hitler offered his audience was redemption. In his speeches he talked less about policy and more about destiny. It was a privilege to live at such a decisive time in history. The Nazis were on a "splendid crusade" that would "go down as one of the most miraculous and remarkable phenomena in world history" ... the forthcoming journey offered every German a chance to find meaning in their lives.
>
> *Laurence Rees*[1]

> The Fuhrer alone *is* the present and future German reality and its law ... The Fuhrer has awakened this will in the entire people and has welded it into a single resolve.
>
> *Martin Heidegger*[2]

HITLER'S APPEALS IN GERMANY

While it has been well established and widely known that Hitler enjoyed broad popular support in Germany it is not well known that his supporters included large numbers of academic intellectuals and other highly educated groups. Even less is known about the sympathy, sometimes outright admiration he enjoyed among many intellectuals outside Germany. Sympathy among the latter was less widespread and less durable; nonetheless it did exist for a period of time and included some notable Western intellectuals, as will be shown below.

[1] Laurence Rees: *Hitler's Charisma*, New York 2012, 99–100.

[2] Quoted in Richard Wolin ed.: *The Heidegger Controversy: A Critical Reader*, Cambridge MA 1993, 47, 49.

FIGURE 3. Varied facial expressions reflect strong feelings which complemented Hitler's oratorical skills and helped to impress his audiences with his authenticity.

FIGURE 4. Hitler radiating warmth and kindness toward girls greeting him.

Although the cult of Hitler was distinguished by its intensity and spontaneity, it had several features in common with the cults of other twentieth-century dictators, notably that of Stalin. Richard Overy wrote:

> They [Hitler and Stalin] were driven ... by a profound commitment to a single cause, for which ... they saw themselves as the historical executor ... Both were driven by a remarkable determination to fulfil what they saw as a necessary place in history ...
>
> Hitler's cult of personality was not something grafted on to German political culture, but derived its appeal from a wide ... expectation of a German redeemer ... the two dictators approached the construction of their images in very similar ways. Both presented themselves as modest, simple men ... This pose allowed both men to appear simultaneously accessible and distant ... Hitler and Stalin were ... presented as men burdened by high office, working ceaselessly for the nation or the revolution, all-seeing, all-knowing ... the two dictatorships constructed moral orders that preached the absolute value of the collective and the absolute obligation to abandon concern for the self in the name of the whole.[3]

The similarities between Italian fascism and Nazism were far more obvious, less controversial, and more widely recognized than similarities between Nazism and Soviet communism. Mussolini, among others, was convinced of these shared attributes:

> Not only have Nazism and Fascism the same enemies ... but they share many conceptions of life and history. Both believe in violence as a force determining the life of peoples ... and hence reject the doctrines of so-called historical materialism ... Both of us [i.e., himself and Hitler] exalt work in its countless manifestations as the sign of the nobility of man, both of us count on youth, from which we demand ... discipline, courage, tenacity, patriotism and scorn for comfortable life.[4]

It is of some interest that in addition to the similarities between their cults and self-presentation, Hitler and Stalin thought well of one another and might have been aware of the similarities between their respective systems. According to John Lukacs, "Hitler respected (and later increasingly admired) Stalin ... Conversely there is evidence of Stalin's admiration for Hitler."[5] Reportedly Lenin and Mussolini also thought well of one another.[6]

[3] Richard J. Overy: *The Dictators: Hitler's Germany and Stalin's Russia*, New York 2004, 22, 53, 105, 112, 119, 301.

[4] Mussolini quoted in Roger Griffin ed.: *Fascism*, Oxford, UK 1995, 79.

[5] John Lukacs: *The Hitler of History*, New York 1997, 163. On Hitler's admiration of Stalin, see also Daniel Chirot: *Modern Tyrants: The Power and Prevalence of Evil in Our Times*, New York 1994, 134.

[6] Jonah Goldberg: *Liberal Fascism: The Secret History of the American Left from Mussolini to the Politics of Meaning*, New York 2007, 34.

Notwithstanding Overy's propositions quoted above, of all the dictators discussed in this book, Hitler's appeals to intellectuals may seem to be the most puzzling. Claudia Koonz, an American historian, wrote:

> seasoned observers could not imagine how intellectuals would be attracted to a politician who regularly made them the butt of his wisecracks – ridiculing them as "eggheads" and "despondent weaklings" plagued with self-doubt. Why would tenured professors in German universities welcome the dictatorship of a man who had dropped out of school before finishing secondary education, who at age 44 never held a steady job ... and who had never been elected to public office?[7]

Likewise Louis P. Lochner, an American journalist and bureau chief of the Associated Press in Berlin during the 1930s, "could not understand the students who were repeatedly driven to frenzied applause by Hitler's oratorical skills. Lochner felt he had been confronted with a phenomenon he could not explain. He wondered 'how a man ... who screamed, raged and stamped his feet could make such deep impression on young intellectuals.' "[8] These observations indirectly support the suggestion that "the central myth of Hitler's dictatorship was the claim that he possessed a unique affinity with the German people,"[9] which presumably included many intellectuals.

As to Hitler's appeal to intellectuals, it has been also argued – in contrast to the points quoted above – that he "must be regarded as a genuine intellectual," that his "will to knowledge and the will to power" were fused, and this fusion "in a single drive allows us to reintegrate Hitler into the larger history of Western civilization, so that he takes his place alongside Marx and Freud" – a questionable proposition. More persuasively, the same author also suggested that "what made Hitler unique (pathological if you will) was not the nature of his convictions but the intensity with which he held them."[10] While the latter helps us to understand Hitler's appeal, it is redundant since charisma always entails intensity. In any event Hitler's appeal – neither to the masses, nor the intellectuals – by itself supports the claim that the substance of his ideas equaled those of Marx and Freud, as the author quoted above proposed.

Before proceeding further, an important distinction is to be made between Hitler's reputation and popularity among German intellectuals and those in other countries. It is far easier to explain the former

[7] Claudia Koonz: *The Nazi Conscience*, Cambridge MA 2003, 47.

[8] Lochner quoted in Mathias Schmidt: *Albert Speer: The End of a Myth*, New York 1984, 32.

[9] Overy, 113.

[10] Lawrence Birken: *Hitler as Philosopher*, Westport CT 1995, 1, 2–3.

than the latter. In the following I will attempt to suggest some explanations of the favorable impressions he made (initially) among intellectuals outside Germany, despite the unattractive attributes noted by other commentators.

As we embark on this attempt to better understand the appeals of Hitler (both abroad and in Germany), we need to remind ourselves that human beings have always shown a remarkable capacity to hold a wide range of inexplicably bizarre beliefs – religious, political, and superstitious. This capacity has survived the spectacular advances of science, affirmations of rationality, the better understanding of both the physical and mental world, and the process of secularization. As has often been noted, human beings believe what they want to believe, and various political or religious leaders deemed charismatic greatly benefit from this disposition.

The most conspicuous present-day example of the widespread revival of irrational beliefs has been the upsurge of fanatical Islamic religious teachings including the serene conviction that the indiscriminate slaughter of civilians deemed "infidels" will bring bountiful other-worldly rewards to the perpetrators. It is a belief that keeps replenishing the ranks of suicide bombers. The same conviction is reflected in the exclamation "God is Great" that regularly accompanies bursts of murderous violence performed by these true believers.[11] In comparison to such convictions, the German people's confidence in Hitler's capacity to redeem and unify the nation, solve all social and economic problems, win wars, and purify society of undesirables is more comprehensible.

Hitler's charisma and the secular-religious attractions of Nazism converged. A French author wrote: "similarities between the two liturgies [i.e., the Christian religious and the Nazi – P.H.] fostered many interpretations of Nazism as a secular religion: the fuhrer-prophet announced to the distraught masses the possibility of salvation through purification and the advent of a world free of conflict and threats, the 'thousand-year-Reich'."[12] Hitler himself said that "Those who see in National Socialism nothing more than a political movement know scarcely anything of it. It is even more than a religion: it is the will to create mankind anew."[13]

In all probability it was these secular-religious impulses and themes, and their combination with the new emphasis on the nation as the key

[11] See also Paul Hollander: "Marx and the Koran," *Weekly Standard*, February 23, 2015.

[12] Pierre Aycoberry: *The Social History of the Third Reich 1933–1945*, New York 1999, 72.

[13] Quoted in *A Fascist Century: Essays by Roger Griffin*, New York 2008, 42.

community, that broadened and deepened the appeal of Nazism and made it comparable to that of communist systems. Lawrence Birken wrote: "Another characteristic of Nazism which makes it appear simultaneously traditional and modern ... was its combination of an almost religious faith with a revolutionary secularism ... Hitler represented the continuation of an essentially Enlightenment style of thought ... this-worldliness ... underpinned by quasi-religious elements."

An optimistic future-orientation was another trait Nazism shared with communist systems and their official beliefs:

> The most attractive feature of Hitler's ideology was ... its optimism ... He [Hitler] was a secular messiah proclaiming a German version of the "good news." ... Hitler's success, at least in part, stemmed from the fact that he preserved (even as he vulgarized) the optimism of the philosophes [of the Enlightenment – P.H.] in an increasingly pessimistic world ... Hitlerism was defense against nihilism ... Hitler thus saw himself as a kind of secular Jesus the new messiah.[14]

Thus moral regeneration and revitalization were the most prominent themes and promises integral to the rise and appeals of Nazism, as they were to Italian fascism. Both Mussolini and Hitler were charismatic leaders capable of playing convincingly the role of the redeemer.

Roger Griffin shed further light on these developments:

> Hitler had a consistent vision of the NSDAP's [National Socialist Party] mission to transcend the decadence of contemporary history by inaugurating a new era ... The Third Reich was thus, like Fascist Italy and Bolshevik Russia ... a totalitarian *modernist state* ... Another empirically documented aspect of Nazism ... as a modern revitalization movement is the prominent role played by ... ritual and spectacle aimed at sacralizing the entire socio-political process of national transformation and hence creating ... a "political religion" ... The focal point of Nazism's political religion was ... the Fuhrer cult ... Hitler as a "messianic figure" ... a "death transcending hero" ... the redeemer of the *Volk* ... the Hitler cult [was] a source of "secular salvation".[15]

Alan Bullock shared this view: "Hitler saw himself as called upon by Providence to rescue the German people from the humiliation and decadence of Weimar." Both Hitler and Stalin "saw themselves not as tyrants ... but as leaders prepared to devote their entire lives to a higher cause." He further suggested that there was "a convergence between the

[14] Birken, 16, 42, 68.

[15] Roger Griffin: *Modernism and Fascism: The Sense of Beginning under Mussolini and Hitler*, New York 2007, 264, 267, 271, 272.

Stalin cult and the Hitler myth, in both ... there was present the same yearning for a substitute religion, for a messiah in the guise of a leader."[16]

A darker interpretation of the rise of Hitler was offered by a German writer, Friedrich Percyval Reck-Malleczewen, a critic of Nazism who was executed at Dachau: "Hitlerism is only a symptom, indicating a deep disturbance of cosmic proportions in the world: that we have now come to the end of five centuries of rationalism and free thought; that in the area occupied by mankind, a new factor, the irrational has again made its appearance."[17]

Albert Speer, major executor of the economic policies of the regime and close associate of Hitler, reached the conclusion that Hitler had, almost to the very end, an irrational self-confidence and sense of mission that, he believed, was mandated by "divine Providence." Even in totally hopeless situations, he averred that "at the last moment Fate would suddenly turn the tide in his favor ... He was by nature a religious man, but his capacity for belief had been perverted into belief in himself." In a speech made in June 1944 when it was apparent that the war was being lost, Hitler said:

> I often feel that we will have to undergo all the trials the devil and hell can devise before we achieve Final Victory ... I may not be a devout churchgoer, but deep within me I am nevertheless a devout man. That is to say, I believe that he who fights valiantly obeying the laws which a god has established and who never capitulates ... such a man will not be abandoned by the Lawgiver. Rather, he will ultimately receive the blessing of Providence.[18]

Hitler's view of himself as a (former) aspiring artist (painter) had probably also influenced his self-conception as a charismatic political leader, inspired by both artistic and political sensibilities. Goebbels shared these sentiments, suggesting that "politics is 'the highest and most comprehensive art there is ... we who shape modern German policy feel ourselves to be artists.' "[19] He also had this to say about the relationship between artists and the regime:

> The German artist today feels himself freer ... than ever before. With joy he serves the people and the state who have accepted him ... National Socialism has wholly won over German creative artists...
>
> How could the German artist not feel sheltered in the state! Socially secure, economically improved, esteemed by society he can now serve his great plan in peace and without the bitterest cares for his livelihood. He no longer speaks to

[16] Alan Bullock: *Hitler and Stalin: Parallel Lives*, New York 1991, 343, 354, 366.

[17] Friedrich Percyval Reck-Malleczewen: *Diary of a Man in Despair*, London 1970, 26.

[18] Quoted in Albert Speer: *Inside the Third Reich*, New York 1970, 357, 555.

[19] Quoted in Susan Sontag: *A Susan Sontag Reader*, New York 1982, 317.

empty rooms ... In this hour, we all look reverently upon you, my Fuhrer, you who do not regard art as a ceremonial duty but as a sacred mission and a lofty task.[20]

Andrei Zhdanov, charged with regulating Soviet cultural life after World War II, would have heartily endorsed these sentiments as guides to Soviet cultural policies.

Adolf Spemann, a prominent German publisher of the period, also believed that education and culture had been appropriately subordinated to political criteria: "The great master of the education of his people, Adolf Hitler, has in a few years transformed our souls." Under the new dispensation the publisher has become "a cultural-politician ... the servant of the writer has been changed into a deputy of the state."[21] In the same spirit a school principal averred: "We German educators must rid ourselves altogether of the notion that we are primarily transmitters of knowledge."[22] Gerhard Kruger, a philosopher, was another staunch supporter of the politicization of higher education who advocated the struggle against the remnants of liberal thinking and bemoaned treating "the intellect ... [as] the only yardstick for admission" to the university. He also wrote: "True socialism [i.e., National Socialism] shakes the fundamental concepts of life as it has been lived up to now ... There are no autonomous institutions and concepts. Even the university and learning must ... be imbued and renovated by the revolution. And here is the great task of the student body ... to be the storm troop."[23]

These claims about the new position of the artist and intellectual under National Socialism resonated with the longings of alienated, left-leaning Western intellectuals who dreamed of becoming integrated into a communitarian socialist society. Many of them believed that such a process had actually taken place in the Soviet Union, and later on, in China and Cuba. Susan Sontag commented on these often-overlooked aspects and attractions of Nazism that were integral to its connection to the discontents of modernity:

it is generally thought that National Socialism stands only for brutishness and terror. But this is not true. National Socialism – more broadly, fascism – also stands for ... ideals that are persistent today under other banners: the ideal of life as art ... the dissolution of alienation in ecstatic feelings of community ... The

20 Quoted in George L. Mosse ed.: *Nazi Culture: Intellectual, Cultural, and Social Life in the Third Reich*, New York 1968, 158.

21 Quoted in ibid., 160.

22 Quoted in ibid., 280.

23 Quoted in ibid., 306, 308.

exaltation of community does not preclude the search for absolute leadership; on the contrary, it may inevitably lead to it.[24]

Saul Friedlander too subscribed to the belief that fascism "was a revolt against modernity ... a rebellion designed to create a deliberately archaic utopia." He noted that in Nazi propaganda nature predominates; there is no iconography of factories, combines, or large dams and electrification, unlike in its Soviet counterpart. (Germany already had such assets, taken for granted, that needed no further popularization.) The appeals of Nazism were to be found "in the power of emotions, images and phantasm." He further proposed that "the emotional hold Hitler and his movement maintained on many Germans to the bitter end ... the spell it wove for so many people ... defies all customary interpretation within the framework of a historiography in which political, social or economic explanations predominate."[25]

Recollections of the impact of Hitler on ordinary Germans testify to widely experienced sensations evoked by his charisma, and help us to understand why few of his contemporaries were able to take a critical view of him. A "worker" found it "impossible to describe the experience of seeing and hearing the Leader for the first time ... from that day on I had no other purpose than to fight for him until the victory was won." Another of his devoted supporters recalled the impact of reading Hitler's *Mein Kampf* (My Struggle): "The more I became absorbed in it, the more I was gripped by the greatness of the thoughts expounded therein. I felt that I was eternally bound to this man." A listener to one of his speeches who saw him for the first time wrote: "Those hours are never to be forgotten. The Leader spoke ... His words went straight to the heart. I wanted to be a true follower. The Leader spoke of the threatened ruin of the nation and of the resurrection under the Third Reich. What matter personal interests, and social status? How insignificant had all parties become to my eyes!"[26]

William Shirer, an American reporter, testified to Hitler's charisma as he observed the German crowds responding to him:

"They reminded me of the crazed expressions I saw once in the back country of Louisiana on the faces of some Holy Rollers ... They looked at him as if he were

[24] *A Susan Sontag Reader* 1992, 319–320.

[25] Saul Friedlander: *Reflections of Nazism: An Essay on Kitsch and Death*, New York 1982, 14, 29, 120.

[26] Theodore Abel: *The Nazi Movement: Why Hitler Came to Power*, New York 1966 (first published 1938), 214, 240, 298. This study was based on autobiographical writings of supporters of the Nazi movement obtained by the author.

a Messiah, their faces transformed into something positively inhuman. If he had remained in sight for more than a few moments ... many of the women would have swooned from excitement." The next day, Shirer began to understand how Hitler was generating such fanatical admiration. At the opening meeting of the Party Congress ... he noted that the Nazis were putting on "more than a gorgeous show; it also had something of the mysticism and religious fervor of an Easter or Christmas Mass in a great Gothic cathedral."[27]

Another eyewitness, the American journalist Virginia Cowles, confirmed Shirer's observations and impressions:

> Then Hitler began to speak. The crowd hushed into silence, but the drums continued their steady beat ... the multitude broke into a roar of cheers. Some of the audience began swaying back and forth, chanting "*Sieg Heil*" over and over again in a frenzy of delirium. I looked at the faces around me and saw tears streaming down people's cheeks.[28]

It is important to emphasize that, as these observations make clear, Hitler's cult was not imposed on the population, it was not a creation of the machinery of propaganda, although the latter sought to strengthen and deepen it. "The 'heroic' Hitler image was as much an image created by the masses as it was imposed on them," Ian Kershaw, the British historian wrote. He further argued that "the legend of warmth and protectiveness" Goebbels sought to construct around the image of Hitler "evidently tapped a vein of pseudo-religious, 'secular salvation' emotions forming a not insignificant strand of popular psychology which, alongside the naive propensity to personalize politics ... contributed to ... the receptivity to the Fuhrer cult."[29] That is to say, the propaganda apparatus reinforced but did not create the widespread public disposition to venerate Hitler:

> Posters and magazine illustrations, newsreels and films proclaimed Hitler as the man from the trenches, with the common touch, not only a many-sided genius with a sense of destiny, but also a humble, even simple human being who had few needs, spurned wealth and display, was kind to children and dealt compassionately with old comrades fallen on hard times. Solider, artist, worker, ruler, statesman, he was portrayed as a man with whom all sectors of German society could identify.[30]

[27] Quoted in Andrew Nagorski: *American Eyewitnesses to the Nazi Rise to Power*, New York 2012, 173.

[28] Quoted in Overy, 111.

[29] Ian Kershaw: *The "Hitler Myth": Image and Reality in the Third Reich*, Oxford, UK 1987, 4, 73.

[30] Richard J. Evans: *The Third Reich in Power 1933–1939*, New York 2005, 122–123.

Omniscience, omnipresence, and infallibility were the key characteristics of the image of Hitler his cult sought to project (as did the cults of the other dictators here discussed) and promote, in part by the wide distribution of his photographic images installed in every office.[31] The official propaganda also found expression in textbooks for children. In a German schoolbook for children aged 11–12, a witness described a flight of Hitler on a stormy day in 1932:

> And yet, what a feeling of security is in us in the face of this fury of the elements! The Fuhrer's absolute serenity transmits itself to all of us. In every hour of danger he is ruled by his granite-like faith in his world-historical mission, the unshakeable certainty that Providence will keep him from danger … Even here he remained the pre-eminent man, who masters danger because in his innermost being he has risen far above it.[32]

Another example of the Hitler cult, and its similarity to religious observances, was the vow of allegiance, resembling a prayer, that members of the *Hitler Jugend*, the Nazi youth organization, were obligated to recite daily with their evening meal:

> Fuehrer, my Fuehrer, given me by God
> Protect and preserve my life for long
> You saved Germany in time of need,
> I thank you for my daily bread.
> Be with me for a long time, do not leave me,
> Fuehrer, my Fuehrer, my faith, my light
> Hail to my Fuehrer.[33]

There was a similarity between the nature and function of the cults of Hitler and Stalin, as Overy further argued:

> The mobilization of cults to endorse personal rule brought other political dividends. Both Stalin and Hitler were freed from moral restraint. The idea that politics could be reduced to expressions of the leader's will allowed the construction of a distinctive moral universe. The rightness of both dictators was assumed from the myths of infallibility and omniscience generated by the cults of personality … In each dictatorship a unique moral universe was constructed in order to justify and explain what appear otherwise to be the most sordid and arbitrary acts … The dictatorships believed that they gave expression to a higher morality.

Overy correctly pointed out that "hero-worship infected all areas of public life."[34]

[31] Overy, 115–116.
[32] Quoted in Mosse ed., 292.
[33] Quoted in Louis L. Snyder: *Hitler's Elite*, New York 1989, 181.
[34] Overy, 122, 125, 265, 299.

HITLER AND GERMAN INTELLECTUALS

The adulation of Hitler was not confined to the masses. Among German intellectuals, especially academics, there was enthusiastic support for Nazism and its creator and symbol, Hitler, possibly more fervent than in the population at large.[35] These attitudes, needless to say, were in stark contrast to the long-standing idealized views of intellectuals as people of an unfailingly critical disposition, who see through the demagoguery of politicians and dictators and are committed defenders of political freedom.

The German intellectuals' support for Nazism might have been the most notorious historical instance of intellectuals abdicating their role and responsibility as social critics and supporters of an open, pluralistic society and free expression.[36] Sympathy for Nazism among German academic intellectuals and their students has not received the attention it deserves, although it is a critical part of the historical evidence, suggesting that a reconsideration of the conventional views of the attributes and political role of intellectuals is warranted. For example, "as early as 1924 ... two Noble Prize winners, Philip Lenard and Johannes Stark, were among the signatories of a newspaper appeal in support of Hitler, who, they said ... appear to us like God's gifts out of time that has long passed in which races still were purer, men still greater, minds less deceived.' "[37]

University students were among the most zealous early supporters of the Nazi movement: "In 1927, during a time of general prosperity, 77% of Prussian students insisted that the 'Aryan paragraph' – barring Jews from employment – be incorporated into the charters of German universities ... 60% of all German undergraduates supported the Nazi Student Organization."[38]

Max Weinreich pointed out that "The Nazis set out with a comparatively small number of outsiders but soon were joined by mounting

[35] According to Daniel Chirot, "liberal professions and students" were over-represented in the Nazi Party, 10 percent of the population but 20 percent of party members (see Chirot, 80). Pierre Aycoberry had a somewhat different view: "the academic community did not exactly carry nazism to power. But neither did it defend the values of the mind against the rising tide of barbarians ... In the main it 'cultivated an atmosphere in which any 'national' movement could claim to be a 'spiritual revival' " (Aycoberry, 21).

[36] For a study of the subservience of German academic philosophers, see Yvonne Sherratt: *Hitler's Philosophers*, New Haven CT 2013.

[37] Quoted in Martin Gilbert: "Foreword," to Max Weinreich: *Hitler's Professors*, New Haven CT 1999, v–vi.

[38] Richard Grunberger: *The 12-Year Reich: A Social History of Nazi Germany 1933–1945*, New York 1995 (quoted in Goldberg, 167).

numbers of people of regular academic standing, some of them scholars of note. As time progressed, the bulk of university scholars, of scholarly periodicals, of publishing houses was entirely Nazified."[39] Even scholars in the humanities "jumped on the Nazi bandwagon."[40]

Hannah Arendt, in her generally positive review of Weinreich's book, wrote that "the list of German scholars who collaborated with Hitler is not complete: many more names, especially from the humanities could have been added."[41] Joachim Fest provides further illustrations of the same phenomenon:

> As early as March 3 [1933] three hundred university teachers of all political persuasions declared themselves for Hitler in an election appeal, while the mass of students had gone over to the National Socialist camp considerably earlier. As early as 1931 the [National Socialist] party, with 50 to 60 per cent of the votes enjoyed almost twice as much support in the universities as in the country as a whole.[42]

Fest held German academic intellectuals responsible for lending legitimacy to the regime:

> The guilt of intellectual radicalism in helping to bring about National Socialism lies in the way it prepared public opinion for the regime's excessive claims in all fields, in its expulsion of reason, its devaluation of the image of man ... its consistent denunciation of all ethical principles ... presented under the guise of a fresh, undismayed, undeluded feeling for life.[43]

In the same spirit Wilhelm Ropke, the German economist and critic of Nazism, wrote that "there is scarcely another class in Germany that failed so fatally as that of the intellectuals in general" in resisting Nazism, and that "the faculties of social science provided a special opportunity for practicing intellectual treachery and preparing the way for Nazism."[44] Even more dismaying, that, as Richard Wolin has written, German historians "furnished the SS with indispensable logistical and demographic information that facilitated the planning and execution of the Final Solution."[45] A German author, Gotz Aly, also concluded that "the Nazi

[39] Weinreich, 240.

[40] Richard Wolin: *The Seduction of Unreason: The Intellectual Romance with Fascism from Nietzsche to Postmodernism*, Princeton NJ 2004, 90.

[41] Hannah Arendt: *Essays in Understanding 1930–1954*, New York 1994, 201.

[42] Joachim C. Fest: *The Face of the Third Reich: Portraits of the Nazi Leadership*, New York 1970, 252.

[43] Ibid., 261–262.

[44] Wilhelm Ropke: "National Socialism and Intellectuals," quoted in George Huszar ed.: *The Intellectuals*, Glencoe IL 1960, 346, 348.

[45] Wolin 2004, 89.

regime relied to an exceptional degree upon academically-trained advisers and ... made use of their skills." What he calls "The economy of the Final Solution" benefited from the advice of "German experts ... economists, agronomists, demographers, historians, planners and statisticians." In his view, "a careerist, academically-trained, intelligentsia," including "major intellects," played a part "in the extermination of millions of people," including "major intellects."[46]

Ian Kershaw observed that

> among the well-educated young Germans attending universities in the early 1920s were those who would qualify with doctorates in law, taking in and digesting ideas about the inner renewal of the German people by removing "harmful influences", just as detoxification revitalizes the human body. The most pernicious "harmful influence" that had to be removed, they learned, was that of the Jew. Some of those swallowing these ideas as students would later join the Security Police, become the planners of genocide and lead the murderous *Einsatzgruppen*.[47]

Further support for these assertions can be found in a recent study of what its author calls "SS intellectuals."[48] They were

> a group of eighty university graduates, economists, lawyers, linguists, philosophers, historians and geographers, some of whom pursued academic careers while simultaneously devising doctrines, carrying out political surveillance, or gathering intelligence ... Most of them were, from June 1941, involved in the Nazi attempt to exterminate the Jews of East Europe, as members of the mobile commando units known as *Einsatzgruppen*.

The author strongly suggests that they were not merely unthinking careerists, or bureaucrats, of the Eichmann stereotype who merely obeyed orders, but believers in what they were doing who related these activities to Nazi doctrines. Ingrao writes: "the essential interest of the men studied here is that they simultaneously produced a doctrinal discourse ... and carried out to their conclusion, at ground level, the practical consequences of this system of beliefs once they assumed command of the *Einsatzgruppen*." They were beholden to "the immense expectations of a revolutionary and redemptive movement ... which generated a visceral attachment on the part of these men to their own political commitment."

[46] Gotz Aly: "The Planning Intelligentsia and the 'Final Solution'," in Michael Burleigh ed.: *Confronting the Nazi Past*, New York 1996, 140, 141.

[47] Ian Kershaw: *Fateful Choices: Ten Decisions That Changed the World, 1940–1941*, New York 2004, 440–441.

[48] Christian Ingrao: *Believe and Destroy: Intellectuals in the SS War Machine*, Malden MA 2013. I could find no information about the sampling method, i.e., how those eighty "SS intellectuals" he wrote about were selected.

Ingrao repeatedly emphasizes that "SS intellectuals did indeed play a crucial role in the ... legitimation of genocide, justifying ... each new step in the rituals of genocide, and providing the perpetrators with doctrinal justification."[49]

Daniel Goldhagen suggested that many elite intellectuals provided old-style antisemitism with an up-to-date "scientific" underpinning: "they were an intellectual elite who, using pseudo-scientific reasoning, elaborated upon and brought the common German ideational strain to a logical conclusion. They merely gave gutter beliefs – which ran not only through the gutter but also through bourgeois German homes and German universities – a scientific form."[50] Pierre Aycoberry pointed out that those who initiated the extermination of Jews and Gypsies could rely on advisors who presented the final solution as a scientific project: "virtually every discipline contributed something to the stages of elimination (deportation, sterilization, execution) ... construct[ing] the path to Utopia."[51]

A further illustration of the academic intellectuals' support for the Nazi authorities was provided by Alfred Baumler, a philosopher, who presided over the notorious Berlin book-burning[52] in 1933 (carried out by the SA storm troopers), "crowing with pleasure in a rousing speech." He played a major role in the Nazification of universities as Alfred Rosenberg's "right-hand man" and became professor at the University of Berlin, the most prestigious in Germany, where he created the Institute for Political Education. Rosenberg was Hitler's trusted enforcer of the official ideology, "firmly established as Nazi 'philosopher in chief' " specializing in racial theories and the theoretical elaboration of antisemitism, and "hailed as the spiritual and philosophical educator of the Party." Another prominent academic who became a supporter of Hitler was Carl Schmitt, the legal philosopher, who, after initial reservations, joined the Nazi Party in 1933; he too endorsed the book burnings and became Hitler's

49 Ibid., "Preface," vii, viii, 69, 203.

50 Daniel Jonah Goldhagen: *Hitler's Willing Executioners: Ordinary Germans and the Holocaust*, New York 1997, 598, note 80.

51 Aycoberry, 299.

52 It is not widely known that book burnings were not limited to Nazi Germany. In communist China in the early 1950s, "with the literary inquisition came a great burning of books ... Lectures were given on 'How We Should Dispose of Bad books' ... entire collections were consigned to the flames ... [on one occasion alone] in May 1953 a giant bonfire lasting three days swallowed up 300,000 volumes representing 'vestiges of the feudal past.' " (Frank Dikotter: *The Tragedy of Liberation: A History of the Chinese Revolution, 1945–57*, New York 2013, 190.)

legal advisor. He was president of the National Socialist German Jurors, and worked hard to provide legal justification for Hitler's assumption of power in 1933 and for the murderous purge of opposition in 1934 that included members of the Nazi Party. He called Hitler "the highest judge and highest lawgiver" of the nation.[53] He was also noted for his "loathing for modernity."[54]

Hans Georg Gadamer, another famous German philosopher and old-style German nationalist, was among the more restrained supporters of the Nazi regime. He nonetheless signed, in 1933, "an internationally circulated petition of support for Hitler, organized by German university professors." In 1937 he "enrolled in a Nazi camp for political 'reeducation' for the sake of furthering his career" and also joined the National Socialist (Nazi) Teachers Association. He was among those who saw the victory over France in 1940 as a reflection of German social-cultural superiority over inferior French "civilization". Gadamer's support for the regime also found expression in an address he gave at the German Institute in occupied Paris that sought to win over French opinion leaders.[55]

As these examples indicate, German academic intellectuals supporting the Nazi government were well rewarded and this makes it more difficult to determine what combination of careerism, opportunism, and idealistic conviction motivated them and accounted for their conduct.[56] Their attitudes and circumstances contrasted sharply with those of the Western supporters of totalitarian systems (Nazi, Soviet, and other) who did not live under them. The material circumstances, social status, and professional reputation of these intellectuals did not depend on their attitude toward these political systems and they rarely benefited materially or otherwise from their sympathy for them.[57] No less misguided, these Western intellectuals were clearly far more disinterested and idealistic and often enjoyed strong subcultural support in their academic settings.

[53] Sherratt, 106, 71–72, 66, 69.

[54] Koonz, 57.

[55] Wolin 2004, 91, 122, 124–125.

[56] Likewise Koonz observed: "It is impossible to ascertain the mix of idealism, self-delusion and opportunism that prompted each man to embrace Nazi rule." She was referring to Heidegger, Schmitt and Gerhard Kittel, a theologian (Koonz, 48).

[57] Occasionally there were rewards and benefits. Some Western intellectuals had their books published in the countries concerned and were taken on luxurious conducted tours; a few received official prizes: Pablo Neruda and Jorge Amado, the Stalin Prize; Angela Davis; the Lenin Prize; Halldor Laxness, the Soviet-sponsored "World Peace Council Literary Prize."

Oswald Spengler, the famous German historian, despite his reservations about Hitler averred that he could not find anyone else to vote for in 1932, and subsequently had an interview with him. Ernst Junger, the famous writer, sent "dedicated copies of his war books" to Hitler, and in turn Hitler sent him his *Mein Kampf* and in 1927 offered him a National Socialist seat in the parliament, which Junger refused to accept.[58]

Carl Jung, the revered psychologist, too initially sympathized with Nazism, his attitude "shaped in part by the conviction that a new religion was needed to heal the modern soul," and Nazism appeared to offer such a secular-religious substitute. He also declared "in a lecture to the Berlin Psychoanalytic Institute ... following the Nazi seizure of power, that 'the Aryan unconscious has a higher potential than the Jewish.' "[59]

Another lesser-known case of a famous German academic intellectual who sympathized with Nazism was that of Konrad Lorenz, the Noble Prize-winning biologist: "He had joined the Nazi Party in June 1938 ... and quickly became a member of the party's Office of Race Policy. In September 1940 he was appointed professor and director of the Institute of Comparative Psychology at the University of Konigsberg ... He actively contributed to Nazi policies of repopulation and ethnic cleansing in Poland."[60]

Martin Heidegger, the philosopher, was probably the most prominent and committed academic supporter of Hitler and Nazism, who approved of Hitler's "wish to be unconditionally responsible for assuming the mastery of the destiny of our people." He joined the Nazi Party and accepted appointment as rector of Freiburg University. In his inaugural address he left no doubt as to his loyalty to the regime and Hitler in particular. In his capacity as rector he fully implemented Hitler's order to remove all non-Aryan faculty and cooperated with the Gestapo's investigation of politically suspect faculty members. In an article he wrote for the student newspaper, he averred: "The Fuhrer himself and he alone is the German reality, present and future, and its law ... Heil Hitler." He had his publisher remove his dedication to his former Jewish mentor, Edmund Husserl, from his book *Being and Time*.[61] Heidegger "saw in Hitler the embodiment of the ethnic regeneration for which he had longed." Even after he ceased to be rector he retained the chair of philosophy at the

[58] Hamilton, 123, 142, 154.
[59] Quoted in John Gray: *The Silence of Animals*, New York 2013, 115, 116.
[60] Robert Jay Lifton: *Witness to an Extreme Century: A Memoir*, New York 2011, 289–290.
[61] Sheratt, 118, 120, 124.

same university and continued to support the regime until it ceased to exist, keeping his Nazi Party membership until the end, that is, 1945.[62]

Heidegger, Schmitt, and the theologian Gerhard Kittel were among the prominent German intellectuals who "never publicly regretted their support for Hitler or their embrace of a doctrine that was not only authoritarian and nationalist but genocidal."[63] Benedetto Croce, the famous Italian philosopher, compared Heidegger's political disposition to Giovanni Gentile's, the major ideologue of fascism and legitimizer of Mussolini whose loyalty never wavered.

According to Wolin, Heidegger, "well after his resignation from the position of rector of Freiburg University ... remained convinced that despite its historical excrescences and transgressions, a philosophically idealized version of National Socialism ... was the potential savior of Western tradition ... capable of redeeming European culture from the dislocations of a rationalistic, modernizing and nihilistic bourgeois *Zivilization*." Wolin also believed that Heidegger aspired to play the role of "philosopher king" in Hitler's state and was convinced that "in its early manifestations National Socialism possessed the capacity to initiate a great spiritual renewal of German Dasein [existence]" as well as "a spiritual renewal of life in its entirety, [and] a reconciliation of social antagonisms."

These observations suggest that Heidegger (among others) was drawn to Nazism largely because of his misgivings about modernity and his mistaken belief that Nazism would alleviate its noxious by-products. Not surprisingly Heidegger also believed that "Hitler and Mussolini ... each in essentially different ways, introduced a counter-movement to nihilism," and for that reason supported them.

Heidegger's exhortations of his students to be loyal to the system and its leader are among the most explicit indicators of his political beliefs: "Let your loyalty and your will ... be daily and hourly strengthened. Let your courage grow ... so that you will be able to make the sacrifices necessary to save the essence of our Volk [nation] and to elevate its innermost strength in the State."[64] Heidegger was especially enthusiastic about the Nazi Labor Service, which enlisted students for manual labor for a few months each year and "brought them into contact with workers and peasants." He "encouraged his students to volunteer, convinced that

62 Koonz, 49, 55.

63 Koonz, 49.

64 Cited in Wolin ed. 1993, 2, 8, 16, 17, 47, 49.

the Labor Service would produce a 'new man,' the intellectual laborer." He wrote: "In the Labor Camps there is a new reality ... Camps and schools intend to gather ... the educational powers of our people in order to obtain that new unity in which the nation will drive towards its destiny under the State." According to Hamilton, Heidegger believed that under Nazism the social roles and ways of life of the warrior, worker, and intellectual would blend harmoniously.[65]

Nazi propaganda explicitly linked manual labor to the improvement of character and the struggle against the "overestimation" of reason, the delusion of "intellectualism." A Nazi newspaper wrote: "Labor service is an excellent defense against the danger of intellectualism. Manual work makes demands not only on one's physical powers but also on one's character and thus brings about a transformation of one's mental attributes."[66]

Strikingly similar ideas – including that of the new politicized renaissance man who transcends the old division of labor – were held by the ideologues and theoreticians of communist systems, including of course Marx himself, especially in his musings in *German Ideology*. Communist states too were eager to introduce programs designed to expose students (sometimes office workers as well) to manual labor, especially in China under Mao and in Cuba under Castro. Similar programs in the Soviet Union and Soviet Bloc countries also existed but were less zealously implemented. Communist ideologues, like the Nazi ones, also believed (or pretended to) that contact between students and manual workers was an important source of political enlightenment and rectitude for the students. The Marxist-Leninist veneration of manual labor, and belief in its redeeming qualities (or the pretense thereof), was part of the doctrinal veneration of the working class, the proletariat, that was absent from Nazi ideology.

The Western intellectuals' apparent reverence for what might be called politically correct manual labor[67] probably had other sources as well, such as an ambivalent sense of identity, the lack of engagement with productive labor, and possibly a lingering unease about and questioning of the authenticity of their own way of life. It is relevant to note here that

65 Quoted in Hamilton, 146, 147, 148.

66 Quoted in Mosse ed., 145–146.

67 It should be recalled here that in the heyday of sympathy for Cuba under Castro, groups of American students volunteered to cut sugarcane in Cuba as a symbolic contribution to building Cuban socialism. In later years other groups, again mostly students, provided similar assistance to various construction projects in Sandinista Nicaragua.

totalitarian ideologues and dictators – both Nazi and communist – had serious reservations about, and often-outright contempt for, intellectuals, deeming them frivolous, undisciplined, individualistic, and incapable of serious political commitment.[68] Western intellectuals seemed unaware of these attitudes and preferred to believe that in these idealized societies (and especially the communist ones) intellectuals would be well integrated, enjoy important social-political roles and recognition, and attain a new sense of identity. Alan Kahan wrote: "It is striking how much abuse intellectuals are willing to accept, and even to inflict upon themselves, while serving the anti-capitalist movement of their choice."[69]

Albert Speer's attitude toward Hitler and Nazism deserves attention as an example of a complicated relationship between an intellectual and a dictator. No other public figure, especially intellectual, German or foreign, had a comparably trusting and intimate relationship with Hitler as Speer. "It remains a mystery how such a rational character," Joachim Fest wrote, "could develop the naive faith that was a prerequisite for belonging to Hitler's inner circle."[70] It has been suggested that Speer and Hitler had in common, among other things, a deeply anti-social disposition, a difficulty in opening up to others. But, as a biographer of Speer, Matthias Schmidt, has written:

> Their mutual enthusiasm for architecture overcame their inhibitions. The two men shared the same dream of going down in history by creating gigantic constructions that would far surpass anything ever done before. Hitler ... a passionate amateur architect, saw Speer as the personification of his life's dream ... [and] saw the possibility of emulating the patrons of earlier centuries and achieving immortality with the help of stone monuments.

Speer was tied to Hitler by an "aura of artistic comradeship,"[71] by an affinity rooted in these supposedly shared artistic interests and impulses,

[68] Hitler was said to harbor a "rancour against the 'intellectual classes'" and in a speech in 1938 said "Unfortunately we need them [i.e., the intellectuals]; otherwise we might one day ... exterminate them ... But unfortunately we need them" (quoted in Fest, 259). Lenin's contempt for, or what Adam Ulam called his "pathological dislike" of, intellectuals might have been even deeper. Ulam wrote: "his hatred of the intelligentsia ... runs like a thread through his personal and public life, and provides much if not most of the emotional intensity behind the revolutionary strivings." At the same time, "Lenin never forgot that the hated intelligentsia were still the key to the success of the revolutionary, or of any political movement in Russia." The latter realization closely resembled Hitler's disposition (Adam Ulam: *Lenin and the Bolsheviks*, London 1965, 148, 210, 213).

[69] Alan S. Kahan: *Mind vs. Money: The War between Intellectuals and Capitalism*, New Brunswick NJ 2010, 181.

[70] Joachim Fest: Speer: *The Final Verdict*, New York 2001, 7.

[71] Schmidt, 42, 73.

and Hitler's belief that his rule represented "the final reconciliation of art and politics."[72] In his memoirs Speer acknowledged: "I too was intoxicated by the idea of using drawings, money and construction firms to create stone witnesses to history, and thus affirm our claim that our works would survive for a thousand years."[73] Speer also shared with Hitler an interest in urban planning.

Fest suggested that "without him [Hitler] this life [Speer's] would not have been what it was. All observers have noticed the strange captivation by the dictator, for which Speer used such helpless terms as 'enthrallment' or 'magic.' ... Hitler fired his [Speer's] ambition [with] dazzling possibilities."[74] Stalin, who shared Hitler's artistic and architectural tastes, was also impressed with Speer's work and invited him to visit Moscow (Hitler disapproved of such a visit and it did not take place).[75]

Speer joined the Nazi Party in 1931, designed the props for the Nuremberg Rally in 1933, and built the new Chancellery in Berlin, as well as other important public buildings. Hitler appointed him in 1938 as General Inspector of Buildings for Berlin and entrusted him with redesigning Berlin as a whole in the grandiose manner he favored. In 1942 he appointed him minister of armaments and war production, a position of huge importance during the last three years of the war. By all accounts Speer performed brilliantly in this role and the level of German military production remained high despite the prolonged aerial bombardments.

Following World War II Speer wrote several largely autobiographical books about Nazi Germany that bolster his status as a reflective intellectual. In these writings, he sought, somewhat paradoxically, to present himself as both a critic of the Nazi regime and one who shared responsibility for its misdeeds. He was the only defendant in the Nuremberg Trials who expressed remorse for his past political beliefs and activities.

It may be argued that Speer was not "a true intellectual" but merely a highly qualified specialist, an architect by training, and that by accepting important positions of power in the Nazi regime he disqualified himself from being considered "a true intellectual." Joachim Fest in his early assessment thought of him as a typical representative of "the narrow specialist and his technocratic immorality," as well as "intelligent, life-oriented [whatever that means – P.H.] ... imbued with the traditional anti-social indifference of the artist and the technologist." But he also

[72] Fest 2001, 64.

[73] Albert Speer: *Inside the Third Reich*, New York 1970, 69.

[74] Fest 2001, 339.

[75] Ibid., 79.

pointed out that Speer "had always preserved an idealistic readiness to place the cause above persons, and his sober, calculating temperament was permeated by a very German, romantically tinged enthusiasm."[76] In his later assessment Fest concluded that "Speer felt that his moral indifference was justified by the prevailing image of the artist. The idea of the artist standing outside society, not subject to any norm and moral law."[77] Needless to say this idea is very different from that of the "public intellectual" who sees himself as an engaged guardian of public interest and rectitude. To be sure, the latter attitude may be compatible with tolerating and endorsing destructive, inhumane policies as long as they are justified by idealistic, long-term goals.

In any event, Speer was not merely an apolitical technocrat, or detached aspiring artist. He had a genuine and deep attachment to and respect for Hitler and the Nazi system, proved by his arduous work, stretching to the very end of the war, devoted to maintaining and increasing the military capabilities of the system. His disposition was further reflected in his occasional exhortations to the troops and subordinates. Last but not least, he harbored aspirations to become a historic figure, "to make history" – aspirations far beyond the technocratic role.[78]

Speer's durable, at times ambivalent, devotion to Hitler is encapsulated in a statement he made after the war: "Adolf Hitler was rooted in the people. His irreproachable life-style and his persevering labor have become widely known, so that his memory cannot be easily wiped away."[79] As Schmidt writes, "throughout his life, Speer could not escape the spell that Hitler had cast upon him."[80] Fest too noted that Speer "declared a residue of loyalty to Hitler, in spite of all the contradictions in their relationship ... and isolated impulses of loyalty remained."[81]

Greatly superior to Hitler, both intellectually and morally, Speer's durable loyalty and devotion to Hitler may seem difficult to fully understand. Speer's recollections help somewhat to do so. Apparently the close personal relationship to Hitler began with the deep impression a speech of his (to students at Berlin University) made on Speer in 1931. As he recalled the occasion:

76 Fest 1970, 199, 205.
77 Fest 2001, 348.
78 Schmidt, 5, 117, 204.
79 Quoted in Schmidt, 146.
80 Ibid., 200.
81 Fest 1970, 201, 207.

Hitler entered and was tempestuously hailed by his numerous followers among the students. This enthusiasm itself made a great impression upon me ... He spoke urgently and with hypnotic persuasiveness ... The mood he cast was much deeper than the speech itself ... I was carried on the wave of enthusiasm which ... bore the speaker along ... It swept away any scepticism, any reservation ... Here, it seemed to me, was hope. Here were new ideals, a new understanding, new tasks ... The following day I applied for membership in the National Socialist Party ... It was an utterly undramatic decision. Then and ever afterward I scarcely felt myself to be a member of a political party. I was not choosing the NSDAP, but becoming a follower of Hitler, whose magnetic force had reached out to me the first time I saw him and had not thereafter, released me.[82]

These feelings and recollections were confirmed in Speer's conversation with Robert Jay Lifton:

He told me how he had heard the Nazi leader speak at his university in Berlin in 1930, [he] was "really spellbound" at the time and remained for the next fifteen years ... Hitler's words were for him transformative, a message of new hope and a promise ... that "all can be changed," and "everything is possible." ... He was in the process of experiencing a secular form of classical religious conversion.[83]

Joachim Fest also wrote about the same speech and its impact on Speer and offered his interpretation:

Hitler did not dwell on the countless problems of everyday life. Instead he mapped out a huge historical panorama, in which he set the present crisis as part of a never-ending struggle of the forces of good against evil. It was the vagueness of the program, delivered with all the authority of the charismatic leader ... that left the strongest impression on Speer ... After the event the group of students went on to a beer hall but Speer did not join them. He later wrote that he left "a changed person" ... Speer's strange need to be alone after a political meeting ... is better explained if one sees that evening as an awakening, with all the pseudo-religious, magical, alarming and sudden insight associated with the concept ... From the moment he met Hitler, he wrote, "everything changed; my whole life was as if under high voltage."[84]

Speer's reservations about the system, such as they had been, "were swept aside by the sense of a new beginning ... which engulfed the country and soon engulfed him too."[85] Such a sense of new beginning was all the more welcome and "transformative" since Speer's (and not only his) "formative experience of his early years had been a general decline in values."[86]

[82] Speer, 16–18.
[83] Lifton, 308–309.
[84] Fest 2001, 28, 42.
[85] Ibid., 43.
[86] Ibid., 8.

Subsequently, and thanks to the numerous commissions Speer received from Nazi authorities and Hitler himself, "he felt energized by the purposeful atmosphere surrounding the Nazi leaders."[87] His support for the regime and loyalty to Hitler opened up otherwise unimaginable career opportunities. Not surprisingly, "the wide acclaim he received for his new tasks made it even more difficult for Speer to be aware of his own errors."[88] As he saw it in retrospect:

> I gave up the real center of my life, my family, completely under the sway of Hitler, I was henceforth possessed by my work ... My position as Hitler's architect had soon become indispensable to me. Not yet thirty, I saw before me the most exciting prospects an architect can dream of ... the intensity with which I went at my work repressed problems that I ought to have faced.[89]

As is often the case, personal and political motives were intertwined. Speer's career allowed him to become both emotionally committed to the political system through the admiration of its leader, and to play a key role in the system's legitimation and survival. Unlike most intellectuals who admired powerful and seemingly idealistic dictators without translating such attitudes into action, Speer was given, and eagerly seized, the opportunity to contribute to the realization of these ideals by using his professional skills. The sense of personal fulfillment was validated and enhanced by working for the Nazi system at the highest level, by contributing to the war effort, and earning the approval of Hitler. This convergence of personal and political motives helps us to understand why and how he managed for over a decade to inhabit Hitler's inner circle, his "entourage," "where a human life meant nothing." He came to realize "that this atmosphere had not left me untouched. I was not just entangled in a thicket of deceptions, intrigues, baseness and killing. I myself had become part of this perverted world. For twelve years ... I had lived thoughtlessly among murderers."[90]

The admiration of Hitler by German intellectuals and other public figures, as the case of Speer suggests, was not a great mystery. These intellectuals witnessed – at least initially – substantial improvements in social and economic conditions that Hitler and his government could be given credit for. Not only did the Nazi regime cope with unemployment and inflation, it restored the collective self-esteem of the nation, helping it to recover from the humiliations and losses of the defeat in World War I and the peace treaty that was imposed. The Nazi regime succeeded in

[87] Evans, 183, 184.
[88] Fest 2001, 46.
[89] Speer, 32.
[90] Speer, 429–430.

reestablishing and reinvigorating the sense of national community sorely missed by much of the population – a development that was eagerly embraced by both intellectuals and the rest of the people. Hitler, given his personal attributes and fervent sense of mission, succeeded in symbolizing the triumphant recovery and new power of Germany, at any rate until the military setbacks suffered in the course of World War II.

THE APPEALS OF NAZISM AND HITLER OUTSIDE GERMANY

For understandable reasons the admiration of Hitler and Nazism among intellectuals outside Germany was far less widespread and durable than comparable attitudes toward communist leaders and systems. Many Western intellectuals and political figures who sympathized with Nazi Germany sometimes justified these sentiments by claiming that Nazi Germany was an essential bulwark against Soviet communism. Concurrently such sentiments were replicated by those on the left who argued that the Soviet Union under Stalin deserved Western support because it was the staunchest adversary of Nazism. Both sets of arguments were dealt a decisive blow by the Soviet–Nazi non-aggression pact of 1939.

Although the phenomenon was limited in duration, it is important to recall that even Hitler and his regime were capable of earning the esteem of some distinguished Western intellectuals and other public figures disenchanted with their own society. It was a similar disenchantment that made other intellectuals susceptible to the putative attractions of the Soviet systems that appeared, and which claimed to be a superior alternative to their own society at the time.

Knut Hamsun, the Norwegian Noble Prize-winning writer, was among the unwavering devotees of Hitler and, throughout World War II, a vocal supporter of Nazi Germany. He met Hitler and gave as a gift to Goebbels his Noble Prize Medal. In May 1945 he wrote the following obituary of Hitler for a Norwegian newspaper:

> I am not worthy to speak for Adolf Hitler ... Hitler was a warrior, a warrior for humankind and a preacher of the gospel of justice for all nations. He was a reforming character of the highest order, and his historical fate was that he functioned in a time of exampleless [unequalled] brutality, which in the end felled him. Thus may the ordinary Western European look at Adolf Hitler. And we, his close followers, bow our heads at his death.[91]

[91] Quoted in Walter Gibbs: "Norwegian Nobel Laureate Once Shunned Is Now Celebrated," *New York Times*, online, February 27, 2009.

Georges Bataille, the French philosopher, given his contempt for democracy, parliamentary government and Western decadence, found much to admire in both Hitler and Mussolini. He saw them as veritable Supermen, impressively different from and superior to democratic politicians, symbolizing a "force that situates them above other men." He revered fascism because – he believed – it allowed these leaders to create an emotional bond with the masses. He admired the same leaders because they promoted "collective solidarity in a society otherwise suffused with anomie and fragmentation ... allow[ing] ... the reprise of an ecstatic politics amid the forlorn and disenchanted landscape of political modernity." Bataille was also preoccupied with renewing "affective energies associated with the communitarian bonds prevalent in premodern societies." These attitudes place him in the forefront of Western intellectuals distressed by and bemoaning modernity.[92]

Largely unknown (or forgotten) were expressions of sympathy for Nazi Germany on numerous American college campuses in the 1930s displayed by administrators, faculty, and students alike. While not as widespread as similar sentiments toward the Soviet Union in the same period, and in similar settings, the phenomenon was quite substantial and exhaustively documented by Stephen Norwood. He wrote:

> the leaders of American universities maintained amicable relations with the Third Reich, sending their students to study at Nazified universities, while welcoming Nazi exchange students ... America's most distinguished university presidents crossed the Atlantic in ships flying the swastika flag, openly defying the anti-Nazi boycott ... By warmly receiving Nazi diplomats and propagandists on campus, they helped Nazi Germany to present itself ... as a civilized nation, unfairly maligned in the press ... many of their professors, college and university students ... adopted a similar outlook.

Harvard University and its president, James Bryant Conant, excelled in displaying friendly attitudes toward Nazi Germany and its universities. Nazi leaders were welcomed on Harvard campus and invited to high-profile social events, ties were cultivated with the Nazified universities. Conant was especially determined to have such ties with the universities of Heidelberg and Goettingen, even though they expelled their Jewish faculty and "thoroughly nazified" their curriculum.[93]

On the occasion of the visit of the German warship *Karlsruhe* to Boston harbor in 1934, arrangements were made to entertain the crew

[92] Cited in Wolin 2004, 173, 174.

[93] Stephen Norwood: *The Third Reich in the Ivory Tower: Complicity and Conflict on American Campuses*, New York 2009, 34, 36, 37.

(these plans were made in 1932 before Hitler came to power) involving the participation of "prominent alumni, student leaders, the *Harvard Crimson* and several Harvard professors." Ernst Hansfstaengl, prominent Nazi official and personal friend of Hitler, was invited to the reunion of his class and welcomed by president Conant at the commencement in May 1934. William L. Langer, a Harvard history professor, defended the German occupation of Rhineland in 1936 and "disputed the charge that Hitler was a militarist." Professor Francis P. Magoun, chairman of the Harvard Modern Languages Division, "urged Houghton Mifflin" to publish *Mein Kampf*. Law School Dean, Roscoe Pound, accepted in 1934 an honorary degree from the University of Berlin in a public ceremony, presented by the German ambassador. On another occasion he claimed that "freedom of speech prevailed in the Third Reich." In April 1935 Conant "personally received Mussolini's ambassador ... and his consul general in Boston ... at his office at Harvard." Harvard also continued student exchanges, even though a German official in charge of them publicly stated in 1936 that the students were sent abroad as "political soldiers of the Reich." Harvard also sent a delegation to celebrate the anniversary of Heidelberg University, a highly politicized event, attended by Goebbels, Alfred Rosenberg (the Nazi theorist), and Heinrich Himmler (head of the SS). The student newspaper, the *Harvard Crimson*, strongly supported participation. Major British universities refused to participate in the same event.

Columbia University was another institution that maintained friendly relations with Nazi academic institutions and representatives of Nazi Germany. Seven months after the notorious book burning in 1933 the German ambassador was invited to give a lecture and "warmly welcomed" by President Nicholas Murray Butler.[94]

Sympathizers with Nazi Germany were particularly numerous in Britain and, in addition to intellectuals, represented other segments of society as well. T.S. Eliot argued that "We cannot condemn Nazi tyranny, brutality and paganism ... because our own society is also infected with tyranny, brutality and paganism."[95] Similarly exaggerated self-critical sentiments were often voiced in the 1960s and 1970s by many American intellectuals in attempts at stifling critiques of the Soviet system and others whose defects greatly exceeded those of the United States or various Western European nations.

[94] Ibid., 37, 41, 42, 44, 49, 56, 57, 59, 63, 65–67, 76.

[95] Eliot quoted in Surette, 251.

Houston Stewart Chamberlain, an English philosopher and admirer of German culture (he took German citizenship), met Hitler in 1923, well before his rise to power, and subsequently wrote in a letter to him:

> You are not as you were described ... you are not a fanatic ... Your eyes ... capture people and hold them in their grip ... And your hands are so expressive ... that they compete with your eyes. Such a man can administer peace to a poor tortured soul. My belief in Germany never wavered but I must confess that my hopes were at a low ebb. You have transformed my state of mind with one stroke.[96]

Another remarkable instance of admiration for Nazism and Hitler was displayed by the prolific and popular British novelist and nature lover, Henry Williamson (1895–1977). In his case there seemed to be a connection between love of nature and farming, on the one hand, and the strongly felt but mistaken idea that Nazi Germany ushered in a return to a more authentic and natural way of life. Reporting of his 1935 visit to Germany, he wrote:

> No beggars in the street: there was work of a kind available to any who applied for it ... Everywhere I saw faces that looked to be breathing extra oxygen; people free from mental fear ... Hitler had freed the farmers from the mortgages ... cleared the slums, inspired work for all the seven million unemployed ... the former pallid leer of hopeless slum youth transformed into sun-tan, the clear eye, the broad and easy rhythm of the poised young human being.[97]

It is noteworthy that time and again sympathetic Western visitors (such as Williamson) to various authoritarian or totalitarian police states were impressed by the absence of beggars on the streets. It did not seem to cross their minds that nothing prevented the authorities from removing beggars from the streets of major cities.

It is also noteworthy that, like Williamson, numerous admirers of the various political systems here discussed often found their benign aspects reflected in the physical features and appearance of their citizens. Remarkably similar sentiments had been expressed by favorably disposed visitors to the Soviet Union, often using identical metaphors about handsome people breathing more freely under the blissful conditions created by the benevolent authorities. It is plausible to attribute these impressions to a combination of selective perception and wishful projection.

[96] Quoted in Hamilton, 109.

[97] Quoted in ibid., 266.

Williamson's grotesque misperceptions included the conviction that Hitler was "the only true pacifist in Europe."[98] Of further interest is that, according to Williamson, who was a friend of T.E. Lawrence, the latter believed that

> "Adolf Hitler was gradually releasing and reaffirming the aspirations of the ordinary man in Germany, and so gradually converting a nation in the image of himself" ... Lawrence saw parallels between himself and Hitler who was "a vegetarian, neither drinking nor smoking ... owning nothing except a small retreat in the mountains – the equivalent of Lawrence's own cottage..." Lawrence, Williamson tells us, was convinced that the press must have misrepresented Hitler ... "He read the speeches of Hitler and was confirmed in his divination. A man who had served in the ranks of the infantry, been wounded ... a man who loved Beethoven and lived only for the resurrection of his country's happiness ... a man who was the ideal of youth, was one who not only knew the truth but could speak it and convey it to the minds of others. He was the corner-stone for the new, the realistic pacification of Europe."[99]

Wyndham Lewis, who sympathized with Italian fascism, was also impressed by Nazi Germany, at any rate in its early incarnation. Following his visit to Germany in early 1930s, he too showed a stellar capacity for wishful misperceptions. He wrote, among other things, that "if Hitler had his way ... he would, I am positive, remain peacefully at home, fully occupied with the internal problems of the *Dritte Reich*. And as regards ... the vexed question of the 'anti-semitic' policy of his party ... I believe that Hitler himself – once he obtained power – would show increasing moderation and tolerance."[100] Richard Griffiths suggests that "Lewis's ascetic disapproval of what he saw as the moral decline of the age was one of the main causes for his sympathy with Hitler ... For Lewis Nazism summed up enthusiasm, asceticism and a non-communist attack on the ... evils of the capitalist system."

Arnold Toynbee, the famous historian, in 1936 "had a long interview with Hitler and returned 'convinced of his sincerity in desiring peace in Europe.'" As these and other examples indicate, the dread of another war, especially for those who witnessed World War I, provided strong motivation for wishful projections upon Hitler and his policies.[101]

98 Quoted in ibid., 267.

99 Richard Griffiths: *Fellow Travellers of the Right: British Enthusiasts for Nazi Germany 1933–1939*, London 1980, 134–135.

100 Lewis quoted in Hamilton, 283.

101 Griffiths, 178, 179, 208.

George Ward Price, author and correspondent of the London *Daily Mail*, "who developed a fairly close relationship with Hitler," wrote of him that "'behind the forceful character which he displays in public' he had 'a human, pleasant personality.' He had 'the artistic, visionary tendencies of the South German type' and there was 'a strong strain of sadness and tenderness in his disposition.' Price found in his 'fondness for children and dogs' an 'evidence of good nature.'"[102] As will be seen later, Stalin too was credited with being an object of affection of dogs.[103]

Lord Allen of Hurtwood, after an interview with Hitler in 1935, wrote that "every word that had been spoken [with Hitler] filled him with hope." As Griffiths commented, "a man of the undoubted moral qualities of Clifford Allen [of Hurtwood] was prepared ... to temper his moral concerns with an apparently more practical commitment to the overriding need for peace." Likewise Lord Noel-Buxton, a former government minister, "showed an awareness of the violence and repressive measures to be found in the new Germany, while producing a series of excuses for these attitudes." He further argued that Allied policy since World War I was "mainly responsible for the abnormal psychology of today." Arthur Headlam, Bishop of Gloucester (subsequently professor of divinity at Oxford), was another prominent figure who, in 1933, averred that "the people were happy in Germany for the first time since the war. Berlin had been cleaned up in a remarkable way. The great body of the young Nazis is the best element in the country, anxious for self-discipline and sacrifice."[104]

Sir Arnold Wilson, conservative member of parliament, colonial administrator and author, was another aristocratic sympathizer with Nazi Germany (as well as Fascist Italy). He made several visits to Germany and

> was impressed by Hitler, who "left on my mind an indelible impression of single-mindedness, with great reserves of strength" ... "Hitler is at heart, like the best Socialists ... profoundly conservative in that he desires to conserve what is best. He trusts the people ... There is in Nazi doctrine and policy much that is true and good, much to inspire hope and confidence in the youth of the world."[105]

Sir Admiral Barry Domville, Director of Naval Intelligence until 1930 and author of several books, also had high hopes about Nazi Germany.

[102] Ibid., 165, 166.

[103] Joseph Davies, US ambassador to the Soviet Union in the 1930s wrote of Stalin that "a child would like to sit on his lap and a dog would sidle up to him" (*Mission to Moscow*, New York 1943, 217).

[104] Griffiths, 149–151, 176.

[105] Ibid., 160–161.

More unusually, he met Himmler (head of the SS and among the most ruthless of Hitler's associates) and found him of

> "a quiet and unassuming disposition", with "a charming personality", who "wears glasses and in appearance might be a benevolent professor" ... He had helped Hitler to raise their fellow-countrymen from despondency to self-respect. The most impressive moment of Domville's stay was his visit to the Adolf Hitler SS Regiment, "the pick of the Army" full of men of "splendid physique".[106]

Sir Neville Henderson (ambassador to Berlin during 1937–1939), in a speech to the German–English Society, sought to correct "the 'entirely erroneous conception' that people of England had of the Nazi regime." He suggested that they should "lay less stress on Nazi dictatorship and much more emphasis on the great social experiment which is being tried in this country ... they might learn some useful lessons."

Lord Tavistock too was among those who asserted that "Hitler is supported with enthusiasm by large sections of the population because he gave German youth faith and hope in the future, restored their self-respect and did much to reduce unemployment."[107]

While some of these observations were correct in the short term, few of these enthusiasts recognized the dark side of Hitler and his regime that foreshadowed his disastrous and destructive policies leading to World War II and the Final Solution.

George Robey, a popular English actor in 1938, observed that "Hitler's done a marvelous job for this country, as well as for Germany. He's woken us up ... Hitler stopped Germany from going Red ... You can't hold down a great nation like the Germans." This was also the theme of "a major article" published in 1936 in the *Saturday Review* entitled "What a Man!" It described Hitler as deliverer of the German nation "from oppression and despair ... He has brought them through fire, beaten them on the anvil of a pure nationalism, enthused them with his vigor and spirit until they stand today, proud of their sacrifices, rejoicing in their new formed strength, a nation in arms, ready to serve whatever their Fatherland requires."

Diana and Unity Mitford were also among admirers of Nazi Germany and became members of Hitler's inner circle. By contrast their sister, Nancy, preferred the Soviet system and became a devoted communist.[108]

106 Ibid., 181–182.

107 Ibid., 281, 351.

108 Ibid., 172–173, 206, 361. On Unity Mitford's enthusiastic involvement with Nazi Germany, see David Pryce-Jones: *Unity Mitford: An Enquiry into Her Life and the Frivolity of Evil*, New York 1977.

Conducted group tours were often used by the German government to solidify, or create, favorable dispositions toward Nazi Germany. Veterans of World War I, belonging to the British Legion, were among the participants in these tour groups. Their hosts counted on a sense of comradeship among the veterans of the two nations that would make the British more susceptible to their political messages. In 1934 one such group was taken to Dachau (one of the first concentration camps) and afterward "treated to a 'quiet family supper with Herr Himmler,' who gave them 'the impression of being an unassuming man anxious to do his best for his country ...'."

Colonel George Crosfield of the British Legion, in an interview with a German newspaper in 1937, said of his impressions that: "'The men and women of the people had been full of enjoyment and good cheer. In their laughter and in their eyes one could read that a strong, new and healthy spirit was growing upon Germany' ... [He] praised highly the compelling sincerity of the Fuhrer's address to the delegates."[109]

Groups and individuals were also taken to the annual Nuremberg Rally, including Sir Harry Brittain, Lord Mount Temple, Admiral Sir Barry Domville, Sir Frank and Lady Newness, and members of parliament such as Lord Apsley, Sir Frank Sanderson, Sir Thomas Moore, Sir Arnold Wilson, and Admiral Sir Murray Sueter. As Griffiths wrote:

> the main effect of the rally was to arouse enormous enthusiasm for things German ... Some British reactions were violently enthusiastic. The ceremony of dedication of the *Arbeitsdienst* [labor service] was, to Sir Arnold Wilson "so simple, so solemn, so moving and so sincere as to merit, better than many customary religious rites, the title of worship ... Such a ceremony would have satisfied the early saints ..." It was not just the ceremonies which impressed ... this had been an opportunity to bring British people (particularly VIPs) in contact with the "New Germany". Everything was done to give them the best impression. And there were numerous affidavits in print to the health, vigour, and peace-loving nature of the German nation.

Lady Snowden (widow of Philip Snowden, Chancellor of the Exchequer) revealed that "This [the Nuremberg Rally] is the most impressive thing I have ever seen in all my experience."[110]

Beverly Nichols, reporting in the *Sunday Chronicle* on what he had seen in Germany, wrote: "Very few people in this country have the faintest conception of the strength of the new Germany. I do not mean the

[109] Griffiths, 128, 131.
[110] Ibid., 225, 269.

military strength but the moral strength. Here is a nation united as no nation has ever been before ... There is so much in the new Germany that is beautiful ... fine and great."[111]

Randolph Hughes, author of book *The New Germany* (1936), felt that he was in

"a country that in the truest sense of the word was a nation; living whole of concordant wills; a people regenerate and restored, physically and morally sound, and set firmly and resolutely on the way towards grandiose masteries and achievements ... Everywhere health, character and order and a virtual absence of the evils that are their negation." This was contrasted with England with its "louts and hooligans and wastrels...".

Norman Hillson, author of *I Speak of Germany* (1937), "appears to have been aware of German internal repression, but basically ... ignored it," although he noted the absence of Jews in Frankfurt. "E. Wait, writing in *The Plebs* in January 1937, declared that what impressed him most about the Nazi attitude was 'its strong equalitarian and socially leveling element,' and called it 'a democracy in personal social relationships ...'."[112] Needless to say, egalitarianism was also among the major attractions of communist societies.

These sympathetic sentiments toward Hitler and the Nazi regime closely resembled those that emerged later (or concurrently) toward Stalin and the Soviet Union. The latter too had been inspired, to a large extent, by the fervent desire to avoid conflict and confrontation that could lead to nuclear war, particularly feared during the Cold War period.

As will be seen later, these impressions and observations of Hitler and Nazi Germany (as well those of Mussolini and Fascist Italy noted earlier) anticipated and resembled those stimulated by the tours of communist states such as the Soviet Union, China, and Cuba. There may be three explanations of these similarities. One is that all these states were in fact similar to one another due to their totalitarian character, or for other reasons. Second, credit (for the favorable impressions) must also be given to what I called elsewhere the "techniques of hospitality."[113] Third, and probably the most important, the visitors to these different countries shared highly patterned positive expectations and dispositions that led to similar projections and uncritical perceptions. Fascist Italy, Nazi Germany, and the Soviet Union were each seen as attractive alternatives

[111] Ibid., 225–227.
[112] Ibid., 227, 268.
[113] See Paul Hollander: *Political Pilgrims*, New York 1981, ch. 8.

to the moral decline, anomie, and the wide variety of social and economic problems Western capitalist systems grappled with at the time (as well as in the second half of the twentieth century).

The favorable attitude of Western intellectuals toward Hitler and his government sampled above may also be better understood by falling back on the general proposition (put forward in Chapter 1) that these sympathizers mistakenly believed that Hitler and his system could repair the damages of modernity, and create, or recreate, a more communitarian and just society, populated by people free of alienation. They believed that this new social system was, or will be, free of the symptoms of the corrosive moral decay or decadence they diagnosed and experienced in their own societies. Many of them also believed that Germany was unjustly penalized after World War I by the Versailles Treaty and they too gave credit to Hitler for coping with the severe economic problems of the period.

There was, in addition, before the outbreak of World War II, an almost total unawareness among the foreign sympathizers of the inhumane policies of the Nazi authorities. But again it is to be emphasized that this ignorance, as well as the numerous misperceptions and idealization, did not endure, especially when compared to the illusions inspired by communist systems. In some instances antisemitism probably added to the attractions of Nazi Germany. An American sympathizer, Congressman Louis T. McFadden of Pennsylvania, was unembarrassed to read, on the floor of the US House of Representatives in May 1933, passages from *The Protocols of the Elders of Zion* in support of his belief in the Jewish world conspiracy.[114]

It is likely that some Western intellectuals outside Germany were initially also impressed by the combination of nationalism and socialism the regime represented. The appeals of socialism, that is, the apparent commitment to social justice and policies aimed at transcending class distinctions, certainly played an important part in the attractions of Nazi Germany. George Watson, the British author, argued that "Hitler was an unorthodox Marxist" and "dissident socialist" and that the "National Socialist vision" was appealing because it was "at once traditional and new."[115]

[114] Oliver Stone and Peter Kuznick: *The Untold Story of the United States*, New York 2012, 52.

[115] George Watson: "Hitler and the Socialist Dream," *The Independent* (London), November 22, 1998.

While Italian Fascism and Nazism were in many ways different ideologies and political systems, presided over by leaders of different personalities, temperaments and agendas, their appeals and attractions for many Western intellectuals were similar.[116] Neither was perceived as dictatorial but rather an embodiment of popular will and engine of progress. Both Mussolini and Hitler were seen by the intellectuals attracted to them (in Germany and Italy as well as outside of the two countries) as powerful and charismatic leaders who used their power wisely and selflessly for the benefit of their people. Their charisma was reflected in, and proved by, their capacity to mobilize the masses and inspire their seemingly unconditional loyalty and support. Both Mussolini and Hitler were believed to be capable of bringing about major, and highly desirable, social transformations, overcoming the stagnation, corruption, and decadence associated with liberalism, capitalism, and modernity. Even more important was the belief that they were "redeemers" – men of strong beliefs able to infuse life with a new meaning in increasingly secular societies. As will be seen later, there was an implausible and temporary convergence of the appeals of fascist, Nazi, *and* communist systems and their leaders. But the appeals of Nazism could not endure given the defeat in World War II and the world learning about the Holocaust.

[116] For a recent study of the similarities and differences between Nazi and communist totalitarianism, see Vladimir Tismaneanu: *The Devil in History: Communism, Fascism and Some Lessons of the Twentieth Century*, Berkeley CA 2012.

4

Stalin, Rakosi, Soviet Communism, and Intellectuals

> This was a man ... dominated by an insatiable vanity and love of power ... an inordinate touchiness, an endless vindictiveness, an inability to forget an insult or a slight ... [who] once observed that there was nothing sweeter in life than to bide the proper moment for revenge, to insert the knife, to turn it around and to go home for a good night's sleep ... a man apparently foreign to the very experience of love, without pity or mercy ... As the outlines of Stalin's personal actions begin to emerge ... we are confronted with a record beside which the wildest murder mystery seems banal.
>
> *George F. Kennan*[1]

> [T]o him [Stalin] will fall the glory of being the greatest criminal in history ... He was one of those rare terrible dogmatists capable of destroying nine tenths of the human race to "make happy" the one tenth.
>
> *Milovan Djilas*[2]

Two general propositions may explain the *durable attraction of communist dictators*, such as Stalin, for many Western intellectuals.[3] The first is the profound ignorance of the personalities, policies, and intentions

[1] George F. Kennan: "Criminality Enthroned," in T.H. Rigby ed.: *Stalin*, Englewood Cliffs, NJ 1966, 168–169, 173, 174.

[2] Milovan Djilas: *Conversations with Stalin*, New York 1962, 187, 190.

[3] We may need a different explanation for the durable affection of non-intellectuals and especially of the people these dictators ruled. For instance in post-communist Russia there remains a great deal of nostalgia and a reservoir of seemingly incomprehensible affection for Stalin. The latter are likely to be associated with the former superpower status of Russia (when it was the dominant part of the USSR), a militant patriotism, and the stability and modest security the Soviet system seemed to guarantee to ordinary people. Thus even in post-communist Russia, the qualities of Stalin described by Kennan and Djilas have been overlooked, and would likely be denied by large portions of the population.

FIGURE 5. Typical symbolic representation of Stalin guiding his people and basking in their admiration; text on poster: "Under the Leadership of the Great Stalin – Forward to Communism!"

FIGURE 6. Acclaimed by joyous children embodying authenticity and purity.

of these dictators. The other is a remarkable capacity for projection and wishful thinking on the part of many intellectuals (of all human beings) for attributing qualities they highly value to individuals they were disposed to admire. Even when such circumstances are taken into account, the gulf between the reality (as summarized, for example, in the assessments of Kennan and Djilas) and the deluded positive views of Stalin (to be sampled below) is so enormous that its satisfactory explanation and understanding requires both considerable effort and imagination.

It is of course easier to account for the reverence and the susceptibility to his cult on the part of the Soviet population, intellectuals included. The Soviet public could not avoid daily exposure to the systematic and thorough bombardment by the deified images of Stalin disseminated by the institutions of propaganda and education. At the same time it could also be argued that the cult might have encountered greater resistance among Soviet citizens who had intimate, daily personal experience of the many discrepancies between the promises of the authorities, Stalin included, and the disillusioning realities of their life – economic as well as political. We can only speculate about the nature of popular sentiments toward Stalin while he was in power since obviously public expression of unfavorable sentiments was (to say the least) discouraged by the authorities and independent opinion research did not exist.

In any event it is important to note that "the development of the popular cult [of Stalin] was permeated, as in [Hitler's] Germany, with metaphors that were unashamedly sacred"[4] – that is to say, the cult tapped into religious traditions and forms of worship including that of the Tsar. Even some intellectuals absorbed the deified image of Stalin, as Soviet writers took the lead in singing his praises. A poignant example is Konstantin Simonov (sometime favorite of Stalin, who late in life renounced his own servile political attitudes). He wrote: "The whole people/Are His friends:/ You cannot count them,/They are like drops of water in the sea."[5] Ilia Ehrenburg, another prominent Soviet author, wrote: "I often think of the man [Stalin], his courage and grandeur, who took upon himself an enormous burden. The wind will always blow, people carry on their daily activities ... nurse children ... or sleep peacefully while He stands at the helm." He further averred that Stalin "suffered with everyone and

[4] Richard Overy: *The Dictators: Hitler's Germany and Stalin's Russia*, New York 2004, 121.

[5] Quoted in David Satter: *It Was a Long Time Ago, and It Never Happened: Russia and the Communist Past*, New Haven CT 2012, 166.

triumphed with everyone."[6] In his memoirs he acknowledged that "he thought of Stalin as a kind of Old Testament God."[7]

Richard Overy provides a broader background for these attitudes: "a tradition of systematic adulation existed long before 1917 ... [this] adulation survived the revolution, transferred to new leaders." In particular the image of the care-giving, tirelessly solicitous leader was time and again projected upon Stalin. A poet honoring him on his birthday in 1939 wrote: "Moscow is asleep ... Stalin is the only one awake/At this late hour/He thinks of us ... He can even hear the song/Which a shepherd sings in the steppe/The little boy will write a letter to Stalin/And will always receive a reply from the Kremlin."[8]

Walter Laqueur suggested that Stalin's cult may better be understood when compared to those of Mussolini and Hitler (as will also be done in this study). Laqueur found numerous similarities between these cults and the particular attributes projected upon the three dictators. The major difference, in his view, was that the Nazi and Italian Fascist systems were far more the creations of their founders and leaders, and far more dependent on them, than was the case with Stalin and the Soviet system.[9] The Soviet system was in existence well over a decade before Stalin became its undisputed leader, whereas the creation of Nazi Germany and Fascist Italy was inseparable from the rise to power of their respective leaders.

Stalin was the first of several communist dictators who inspired the admiration and reverence of many notable Western intellectuals, and for obvious reasons much more was written about him than Lenin. Correspondingly the misperceptions of Stalin have been more striking, more abundant, and enduring. To be sure, Lenin too inspired reverence (except in Bertrand Russell, who met him), but his tenure in power was short whereas Stalin was a living presence for decades and in charge of major social-political transformations that thrilled these intellectuals. Some of them expressed their respect of Lenin posthumously, visiting the mausoleum where his embalmed body was displayed. Among them, Corliss and Margaret Lamont, inspecting his remains, were impressed by "his impersonally beautiful and resolute face." Edmund Wilson also

[6] Quoted from Ilia Ehrenburg: "Nagy Erzesek" [Strong Feelings], *Szabad Nep*, December 20, 1949. The source was the daily newspaper of the Hungarian Communist Party; "Merhetetlen Szeretet" [Boundless Affection], *Szabad Nep*, December 14, 1949 (translation from Hungarian by the author).

[7] Alan Bullock: *Hitler and Stalin: Parallel Lives*, New York 1991, 366.

[8] Overy, 106.

[9] Walter Laqueur: *Stalin: The Glasnost Revelations*, New York 1990, 184–188.

thought that he had "a beautiful face of exquisite firmness" that was "profoundly aristocratic" in a uniquely authentic manner.[10] G.B. Shaw was struck by what he saw as Lenin's aristocratic traits: "A true intellectual type ... that is the true aristocracy."[11] Pablo Neruda discerned Lenin's posthumous "presence" in Soviet life while watching a parade in Moscow's Red Square celebrating the anniversary of the October Revolution: "They marched with sure and firm step ... They were being observed by the sharp eyes of a man dead many years, the founder of this security, this joy, this strength ... immortal Lenin."[12] Neruda was also deeply moved by the passing of Stalin, writing in his obituary that he was an exemplar of "sincere intensity" and advised to "take pride in the title 'Stalinist.'"[13] It was a piece of advice not widely taken.

WESTERN ADMIRERS OF STALIN AND THE SOVIET SYSTEM

Perhaps the most grotesque misconception of Stalin was that he had little interest in power. Emil Ludwig (cited earlier on Mussolini), upon visiting Stalin, "found a lonely man who is not influenced by money or pleasure or even ambition. Though he holds enormous power he takes no pride in its possession." Lion Feuchtwanger, another well-known German writer of the period, considered Stalin "the most unpretentious" of all the men known to him who held power.[14] W.E.B. Du Bois believed that "He [Stalin] asked for neither adulation nor vengeance. He was reasonable and conciliatory."[15] Sidney and Beatrice Webb averred that "Stalin is not a dictator ... he is the duly elected representative of one of the Moscow constituencies to the Supreme Soviet ... [he] has persistently asserted ... that as a member of the Presidium of the Supreme Soviet of the USSR he is merely a colleague of thirty other members."[16]

The Webbs were also impressed by what they saw as Stalin's caring attitude: "As Stalin said 'man must be grown carefully and attentively as a gardener grows his favorite fruit tree.'"[17] Jerome Davis, a professor at

[10] Corliss and Margaret Lamont: *Russia Day by Day*, New York 1933, 63; Edmund Wilson: *Travel in Two Democracies*, New York 1936, 322.

[11] G.B. Shaw: *The Rationalization of Russia*, Bloomington IN 1964 (first published 1931), 18.

[12] Pablo Neruda: *Memoirs*, New York 1977, 250.

[13] Quoted in Robert Conquest: *Reflections on a Ravaged Century*, New York 2000, 138.

[14] Emil Ludwig: *Nine Etched From Life*, Freeport NY 1969, 348 (first published New York 1934); Lion Feuchtwanger: *Moscow 1937*, London 1937, 76.

[15] *The Thought and Writing of W.E.B. Du Bois*, Vol. II, New York 1971, 619.

[16] Sidney and Beatrice Webb: *The Truth about Soviet Russia*, London 1942, 16, 18.

[17] Sidney and Beatrice Webb: *Soviet Communism: A New Civilization?* London 1936, 804.

Yale Divinity School, reached the conclusion that "it would be an error to consider the Soviet leader [Stalin] a willful man who believes in forcing his ideas upon others."[18] J.D. Bernal, the British scientist, believed that Stalin "combined as no man had before his time, a deep theoretical understanding with unfailing mastery of practice ... [and] a deeply scientific approach to all problems with his capacity for feeling."[19] In Neruda's estimation Stalin was "a good natured man of principles, as sober as a hermit, a titanic defender of the Russian Revolution ... [who] had become a giant in wartime."[20]

Shaw's admiration of Stalin was an integral part of his disposition to think well of a variety of dictators of different ideological persuasions: "Mussolini, Kemal, Pilsudski, Hitler and the rest can all depend on me to judge them by their ability to deliver the goods ... Stalin has delivered the goods to an extent that seemed impossible ten years ago; and I take off my hat to him accordingly."[21]

Walter Duranty, who used to be considered "one of the great foreign correspondents of modern times" and won the Pulitzer Prize in 1932 as the best news correspondent, was another influential admirer of Stalin.[22] His reputation as an expert on Soviet affairs was such that F.D. Roosevelt, while campaigning for the presidency as governor of New York, "summoned him to the governor's mansion to talk over the Russian situation." Stalin granted Duranty two interviews and Duranty described him in his dispatches "as a wise and perceptive leader capable of great powers of understanding: 'a quiet, unobtrusive man ... who saw much but said little.' "[23] He believed that "there was an indomitable

[18] Jerome Davis: *Behind Soviet Power: Stalin and the Russians*, New York 1946, 12.

[19] Bernal quoted in Gary Werskey: *The Visible College: The Collective Biography of British Scientific Socialists of the 1930s*, London 1978, 318.

[20] Neruda, 319.

[21] Quoted in G.B. Shaw, J.M. Keynes et al. *Stalin–Wells Talk: The Verbatim Report and Discussion*, London 1934, 47.

[22] In 2004 Mark von Hagen, a historian of Russia and professor at Columbia University in New York, examined and refuted many of Duranty's assertions and distortions about conditions in the Soviet Union and concluded that his Pulitzer Prize "should be rescinded." Bill Keller, executive editor of the *New York Times*, refused to do so (see Anthony DePalma: *The Man Who Invented Fidel: Cuba, Castro and Herbert L. Matthews of the New York Times*, New York 2006, 268). The Pulitzer Prize Committee issued a statement admitting that Duranty's reporting "falls seriously short" but refused to rescind the prize on the ground there was "no clear and convincing evidence of deliberate deception on his part" (*Statement on Walter Duranty*, Columbia University, November 21, 2003).

[23] S.J. Taylor: *Stalin's Apologist: Walter Duranty, the New York Times's Man in Moscow*, New York 1990, 2, 167–168, 182, 184.

purpose in his [Stalin's] heart" as well as a "vindictive willingness to bide his time."[24]

Stalin appreciated the favorable publicity Duranty provided. He wrote to him: "You have done a good job reporting the USSR ... because you try to tell the truth about our country and to understand it and explain it to your readers ... you bet on our horse to win when others thought it had no chance."[25]

Duranty's reverence for Stalin was closely linked to his sanguine assessments of the progress made under his leadership that overshadowed the great human costs that Duranty was well aware of:

> In a bare quarter century the USSR has accomplished ages of growth. The most ignorant and backward of all the white nations has moved into the forefront of social, economic and political consciousness. Its obsolete agricultural system has been modernized ... its small ... industry has become gigantic and self-supporting; its illiterate masses have been educated and disciplined to appreciate and enjoy the benefits of collective effort.[26]

Far more recently (and overlooking, or dismissing, vast amounts of disconfirming evidence), Fredric Jameson, the American literary critic, concurred with Duranty as he claimed that "Stalinism was a 'success,' having 'fulfilled its historical mission to force rapid industrialization of an underdeveloped country.' "[27]

Of the collectivization of agriculture (one of the most brutal and destructive chapters in Soviet history), Duranty wrote:

> Future historians ... may well regard the Russian struggle for collectivization as a heroic period in human progress ... The most backward section of the population would have the chance to obtain what it most needed, namely education ... women would have the chance for leisure and freedom as well ... whether the villages preferred their dirt and ignorance to Progress or not, Progress would be thrust upon them.[28]

Duranty also believed in the necessity of the purges and the Moscow Trials, justifying them as essential for defeating traitors and saboteurs and "taking at face value the government's contention of actual widespread conspiracy which involved many men in the highest echelons of government," his biographer wrote.[29] He pleaded for understanding the

[24] Walter Duranty: *I Write as I Please*, New York 1935, 180, 181.
[25] Taylor, 192.
[26] Quoted in Taylor, 305.
[27] Quoted in Conquest, 149.
[28] Duranty 1935, 286–287.
[29] Taylor, 270.

Soviet judicial system as one very different from the Western kind, and professed to believe that the confessions at these trials were genuine:

> No one who heard Piatakof or Muralov could doubt for a moment that what they said was true ... Their words rang true, and it is absurd to suggest or imagine that men like this could yield to any influence against their own strong hearts ... It is unthinkable that Stalin and Voroshilov and Budenny and the Court Marshall could have sentenced their friends to death unless the proofs of guilt were overwhelming.[30]

It is conceivable, even likely, that at the time Duranty believed what he wrote, given the novelty of the staged confessions and unfamiliarity with the ways they were obtained. In doing so he had to choose between two scenarios: one was that the old revolutionaries, with a lifelong commitment to the Party and the Soviet system, actually became traitors (or managed to conceal their treacherousness for decades); the second possibility to consider was that Stalin ruthlessly and deceitfully framed and destroyed loyal fighters for the same cause, for no comprehensible reason, other than his overwhelming personal ambition and seemingly unquenchable thirst for power. Duranty was constrained to believe that if Stalin was willing to sacrifice high-ranking, time-tested members of the political elite, they had to be guilty of the most heinous crimes. Had he not been sympathetic toward the regime and Stalin to begin with, he would not have been able to accept that these deeply committed members of the highest echelons were determined to undermine and sabotage the system.

It would be interesting to know whether or not Duranty ever read (or heard of) Arthur Koestler's *Darkness at Noon*, which provided the most plausible theory of the motivation of the highly placed, former revolutionaries who made the staged confessions, and if he had, would it have made a dent in his belief in the authenticity of the confessions? In any event Duranty was firmly and explicitly committed to the idea that great ends justify sordid means, encapsulated in his infamous omelette-making metaphor: "to put it brutally – you can't make an omelette without breaking eggs and the Bolshevik leaders are just as indifferent to the casualties ... involved in the drive toward socialism as any General during the World War who ordered a costly attack." Elsewhere (in a poem) he wrote: "Russians may be hungry and short of clothes and comfort, But you can't make an omelette without breaking eggs." This attitude explains his indifference to the sufferings brought about by the forcible collectivization of agriculture. A trainload of

30 Walter Duranty: *The Kremlin and the People*, New York 1941, 49, 65.

starved people being deported that he saw were, in his own words, "more like caged animals than human beings" – they were "victims of the March of Progress." This was not an ironic and critical comment. He "dismissed their suffering, noting that he had 'seen worse debris than that, trains full of wounded from the Front in France'."[31]

According to his biographer,

> Duranty consistently discarded "moral issues" believing them to be irrelevant to the job of a reporter ... [he] affected immunity from any kind of morality ... The deeply held moral convictions of other men served only to make Duranty uncomfortable, and he liked to believe that he was better than they were because he was free from the bonds that tied their hands.[32]

Duranty himself informed his readers that he "pride[d] himself on having no bowels of compassion to weep over ruined homes and broken hearts." Accordingly he asserted that industrialization and collectivization were successful, but admitted that "their cost in blood and tears and ... human suffering has been prodigious ... In a world where there is so much waste and muddle it may perhaps be true that any plan, however rigid, is better than no plan at all and that any altruistic end, however remote, may justify any means, however cruel."[33]

His overall assessment of the Soviet system remained positive and he concluded his book by averring that

> In the USSR ... there is full real Socialism, in that all the dynamic forces of the country ... are applied for and by the community instead of for and by individuals ... Looking backwards over the fourteen years I have spent in Russia, I cannot escape the conclusion that this period has been a heroic chapter in the life of Humanity. During these years the first true Socialist State ... was constructed ... I am profoundly convinced that the USSR is only just beginning to exercise its tremendous potentialities ... This progress ... has been paralleled by a remarkable advance of the Soviet leaders in knowledge and wisdom.[34]

He kept returning to the issue of ends and means:

> I suppose that the real answer to the problem of end [*sic*] and means is belief, and passionate single-minded earnestness ... Whether one approves of the Bolsheviks and their methods or not, the fact remains that they have applied, developed and set going ... the only form of complete national collectivism which the world has known since the Inca civilization.

[31] Quoted in Taylor, 164, 185, 207.
[32] Ibid., 232.
[33] Duranty 1935, 301–302.
[34] Ibid., 339–340.

Duranty's awareness of the costs of "the Soviet experiment" set him apart from many of the other admirers of Stalin and the Soviet system, who were similarly infused with moral impulses and ideals and dreamed of a social system morally superior to their own but knew little of the human costs of the attempt to create such a system.

It should also be pointed out that Duranty's positive views of Stalin and the Soviet system were intertwined with his personal and professional interests, opportunities, and well-being. As the long-term resident correspondent of the *New York Times* in Moscow, with access to Stalin and other major political figures, he led a privileged life that conveniently dovetailed with his favorable assessments of the social-political system that enabled him to lead this charmed existence. His household in Moscow included a "chauffeur, a charlady, his cook and mistress Katya." He had access to the State-run Commission shops "where foreigners could pick up amazing bargains for foreign currency." He came to view himself as "the intimate of presidents and dictators, the matchmaker for the marriage of convenience between two superpowers ... and a world figure of sufficient importance to influence the outcome of major social and economic issues." He became an especially valuable and favored source of information for those on the left, as he "told them what they wanted to hear ... Everybody quoted Duranty – Edmund Wilson, Beatrice Webb, the entire group of intellectuals who admired the Soviet experiment."[35]

Duranty also differed from other favorably disposed intellectuals because he spent many years in the Soviet Union and was bound to learn something about the human costs of the "Soviet experiment." He did not seem particularly idealistic but nonetheless his moral calculus – if that is what it was – reflected an unshaken conviction that the ends justified the means. The rare privilege to interview Stalin on two occasions is likely to be among the circumstances that had a major influence on his views of him and the system he presided over.

Joseph E. Davies, US ambassador to the Soviet Union 1936–1938, was another prominent public figure (if not an intellectual) who, despite an extended period of living in the Soviet Union, managed to remain impressively uninformed about the nature of the Soviet system and Stalin, both of which he admired. He wrote of his meeting him:

> He greeted me cordially with a smile and with great simplicity but also with a real dignity. He gives the impression of a strong mind which is composed and

[35] Quoted in Taylor, 176, 190, 224, 249.

wise. His brown eye is exceedingly kindly and gentle. A child would like to sit in his lap and a dog would sidle up to him ... [the meeting] was really an intellectual feast ... Throughout it we joked and laughed at times. He has a sly humor. He has a very great mentality [*sic*]. It is sharp, shrewd, and, above all things else, wise.[36]

Davies also believed that Stalin was a democrat at heart for whom autocratic ways of governing were distasteful: "Stalin, it was reported, insisted upon liberalism of the constitution even though it hazarded his power and party control ... It is stated that Stalin himself decided the issue of projecting actual secret and universal suffrage which the new constitution calls for." Evidently it did not occur to Davies that "secret and universal suffrage" had little meaning and made little difference in a one-party system. The reader is not informed where or when "it was stated" that Stalin made the alleged decisions about voting. Given these groundless beliefs about Stalin and his system, it was not altogether surprising that Davies had no doubts about the authenticity of the Moscow Trials taking place while he was ambassador:

To assume that this proceeding was invented and staged ... would be to presuppose the creative genius of Shakespeare and the genius of Belasco in stage production ... There can be no doubt that the Kremlin authorities were greatly alarmed by these disclosures and confessions of the defendants ... The attorney general [Andrei Vyshinski] is calm, dispassionate, intellectual, able and wise. He conducted the treason trial in a manner that won my respect and admiration as a lawyer ... [his attitude] was entirely free of brow-beating ... [he] conducted the case with admirable moderation.[37]

This delusional characterization of Vyshinski set a new record in misperception and projection. It was intended to describe a man who in court routinely denounced the defendants as dogs, rats, snakes, brigands, degenerates, and vermin.

Similarly remarkable was the assessment of these trials by John Strachey, the influential British author and Labour Party politician: "I believe that no one who had not unalterably fixed his mind on the contrary opinion could read the verbatim reports of these trials without being wholly convinced of the authenticity of the confessions ... I can only say that no man can advance his political education more than by studying this supreme historical document of our time."[38]

[36] Joseph E. Davis: *Mission to Moscow*, New York 1943, 8, 72.

[37] Ibid., 25, 26, 29, 46, 168, 169.

[38] Strachey quoted in Conquest, 129.

Misapprehensions of Soviet-style show trials persisted after World War II when Julian Benda (of all people) "approved of the death sentence passed on Rajk," the key figure in the 1949 Hungarian show trial, modeled on the Soviet ones. He wrote in a French publication: "Voltaire was true to his role when he took up the Calais affair. So was Zola in the Dreyfus scandal. I claim to be like them when I defend the Hungarian verdict, whose justice only the prejudiced seem to deny."[39]

Lilian Hellman was among the American fellow travelers whose support of the Soviet system extended to the acceptance and justification of the Moscow show trials: "along with 150 other artists, writers and scientists, [she] signed a letter declaring their faith in the guilt of the defendants and accepting the trials as necessary to preserve progressive democracy in the Soviet Union." The letter was published in the *New Masses* on April 3, 1938. Even in the wake of the Soviet–Nazi Pact of 1939, "Hellman sided with the Soviets ... she did not withdraw from the Communist Party ... she did not condemn the Soviet Union's ruthless betrayal of its own principles and its callous division of Polish territory with the Germans." She was one of many on the left who "clung to the idea that, whatever the defects of the Soviet Union, the idea of communism remained the last, best hope for a socialist nirvana."[40]

Apparently Hellman was attracted to the Soviet system because of a desire to "claim the moral high ground" that entailed commitment to social justice and fierce opposition to what she considered the grave moral defects of American society. She joined the Communist Party of the United States (it is not clear how long she stayed in it), visited the Soviet Union in 1944, was a major organizer of and speaker at the pro-Soviet 1949 Waldorf-Astoria conference, which, in the words of the historian John Diggins, brought "communist cultural celebrities together to defend the USSR." She was also a prominent supporter of Henry Wallace when he was running for president. As she and other fellow travelers of the period saw it, "only the Soviet Union provided a living example of this idea," that is to say, of the striving for social justice and equality.

In 1944 she was invited by the Soviet embassy in Washington to visit the Soviet Union and "accepted the invitation with alacrity." Her impressions

[39] Benda quoted in Arpad Kadarkay: *Georg Lukacs: Life, Thought, and Politics*, Cambridge MA 1991, 404.

[40] Alice Kessler-Harris: *A Difficult Woman: The Challenging Life and Times of Lillian Hellman*, New York 2012, 123, 126, 234. For a critical assessment of Hellman's politics, see Sidney Hook: "The Scoundrel in the Looking Glass," in his *Philosophy and Public Policy*, Carbondale IL 1980.

were predictably favorable and similar to those of other favorably disposed visitors. Of those she met, or observed, she wrote: "these are warm, strong men ... who know they are men and act with simplicity and tenderness ... Russians have the best natural manners in the world ... All Russians have a sense of humor." After being taken for a visit to the front lines she was ready to project upon the Russian soldiers her imaginary positive stereotypes: they were "open and informed about 'political issues at home and abroad.' They speak 'without self-consciousness and without fake toughness; they speak simply, like healthy people who have never ... learned to be ashamed of emotion.' "[41]

Like other sympathetic visitors she was in search of authenticity and succeeded in finding it, conflating fantasy with reality. She was also among numerous American intellectuals whose personal success was irrelevant to their profound dissatisfaction with American society and who believed that the Soviet Union even under Stalin offered an inspiring model to be emulated.

Henry Barbusse (1873–1935), the famous French writer, provides another example of the close connection between the veneration of a dictator and the admiration of the political system he symbolized. Barbusse was among many Western intellectuals whose rejection of capitalism, intensified by the economic crisis of the late 1920s and early 1930s, led them to embrace the Soviet system, the apparent, superior alternative. He was outraged, among other things, by the spectacle of farmers in capitalist countries destroying the food they could not sell:

> carefully arranged catastrophes ... are taking place at a time when there is a serious shortage of these destroyed commodities ... whilst famines are decimating crowds of people, whilst in China and India hundreds of millions of human beings are eating grass and tree bark, and whilst the unemployed and undernourished swarm over the very land where these murders of commodities ... take place.

There was more to blame capitalism for: "Who knows what goes on in all the capitalist gaols of the universe, and who can give us insight into the thousands and thousands of hellish and bestial scenes for which the guardians of class order and their sadistic genius for human suffering are responsible!"

As Barbusse saw it, in the Western world, "for reasons which a child could understand, ... there is nothing but disorder and decline ... [whereas] Over there [in the Soviet Union, that is] everything is order and progress."

[41] Quoted in Kessler-Harris, 10, 48, 109, 132, 135.

In the latter, Barbusse firmly believed, the planned economy was triumphant: "Every detail of execution and every wheel in the machinery fit together. The single centralized management never loses sight of the nation as a whole." Under these blissful conditions, "the look of pride and happiness ... shines from the faces of Soviet workers," Barbusse testified following a visit. Most important, in "Soviet society ... everyone looks after everyone else." Barbusse came to the conclusion that "The October Revolution really did bring about a purification of morals and of the public spirit, which no other religious or political reform ever before succeeded in doing."[42]

Barbusse entertained these delusional views in the early and mid-1930s, at a time when some of the most violent and destructive chapters in Soviet history were unfolding. They included the coercive collectivization of agriculture and the attendant famines, the beginnings of the Great Purges, the Moscow Trials, the growing power of the agencies of repression as well as the overall totalitarian regimentation of Soviet society. It was an invincible combination of wishful thinking and profound ignorance of existing conditions that enabled Barbusse to entertain unhesitatingly his illusions.

He gave full credit to Stalin, "the man at the wheel," for the wondrous conditions and transformations he observed:

> He is as strong and yet as flexible as steel. His power lies in his formidable intelligence, the breadth of his knowledge, the amazing orderliness of his mind, his passion for precision, his inexorable spirit of progress, the rapidity, sureness and intensity of his decisions, and his constant care to choose the right men ... This frank and brilliant man is ... a simple man ... He laughs like a child ... People who laugh like children love children ... One of his main objects seems to be never try to shine, and never make himself conspicuous.

Barbusse also believed that Stalin "looks after everything and everybody ... He has saved Russia in the past and he will save it in the future."[43]

We do not know how Barbusse came to attribute modesty (among other things) to Stalin nor how he succeeded in overlooking the immense official cult that surrounded him, his virtual deification. He might have believed that Stalin objected to the cult but resigned himself to it since

[42] Henry Barbusse: *Stalin: A New World Seen Through One Man*, New York 1935, 197, 212, 232, 233, 269, 272, 325.

[43] Ibid., 75, 280, 291.

it reflected the outpourings of the love of his people.[44] More plausibly Walter Laqueur suggested that

gradually their innate megalomania [that is, of dictators including Stalin – P.H.], reinforced by their political victories, seems to have persuaded them that the cult was not just a political-educational necessity but a natural expression of the true state of affairs. Constant repetition of their greatness came to persuade them that they were all that their lackeys proclaimed them to be.[45]

In the concluding, effusive lines of the book, Barbusse expressed his veneration of both Lenin and Stalin in words that are redolent with quasi-religious sentiments:

When one passes at night through the Red Square … it seems as though the man who lies in the tomb [i.e., Lenin], in the center of that nocturnal, deserted square, is the only person in the world who is not asleep, and who watches over everything around him, in the towns and fields … he is the paternal brother who is really watching over everyone. Although you don't know him, he knows you and is thinking of you … Whoever you may be, the finest part of your destiny is in the hands of that other man [presumably that is Stalin] who also watches over you and who works for you – the man with a scholar's mind, a workman's face and the dress of a private soldier.[46]

As these words suggest, Barbusse at last succumbed to his religious yearnings as he transformed, in his imagination, these mortal leaders into omniscient, omnipresent deities.

It is not easy to reconcile the impressions Victor Serge (a supporter and later critic of the Soviet Union) had of Barbusse with the idealistic image Barbusse projected of himself. Serge met him when he was touring the Soviet Union. Serge wrote:

Right from the first I saw him as a … person concerned above all not to be involved … concerned above all to disguise opinions he could no longer express openly, sliding past any direct questioning … and all with the real aim of making himself the accomplice of the winning side! Since it was not yet known whether

[44] Martin Amis wrote that Stalin "always said that the cult of personality, while useful politically, was distasteful to him." He also quoted Robert Conquest, who observed that Stalin's "sporadic and ineffectual criticism of the cult may be seen as a ploy to add modesty to the rest of the panoply of his virtues" (*Koba the Dread: Laughter and the Twenty Million*, New York 2002, 136).

[45] Laqueur 1990, 185. Louis Fisher, who became disillusioned with the Soviet Union, also questioned Stalin's modesty: "From being the modest, retiring leader … he has in recent months stepped forth into the brightest limelight and seems to enjoy it. He has become the object of thickly smeared praise, fawning adulation" (see "Why Stalin Won," *Nation*, August 13, 1930, 176).

[46] Barbusse, 282–283.

the struggle had been definitely settled, he had just dedicated a book, at great length to Trotsky, whom he did not dare to visit for fear of compromising himself. When I told him about the persecution, he pretended to have a headache or not to hear ... "Tragic destiny of revolutions ... yes ... Ah, my friend!" My jaws shuddered as I realized that I was face to face with hypocrisy itself.[47]

Romain Rolland (1866–1944), another well-known French writer of the same period, also admired Stalin, at any rate as far as his public statements indicate. On his 1935 visit to the Soviet Union, he too was granted the privilege of meeting him:

Rolland was received like royalty, bombarded with kindness, and assailed by delegations of flatterers staggering under fabricated laudatory speeches, which nonetheless tickled his vanity. The high point of the visit was a two-hour tete-a-tete with Stalin, who also spared no effort and greeted his visitor with the words, "I am happy to chat with the greatest writer in the world."[48]

Stalin's tribute to Rolland suggests another explanation of, or contributing factor to, the favorable assessment of the dictators and their system by many intellectuals – namely, the flattering treatment they received during their visits to the countries concerned. I called these treatments "the techniques of hospitality."[49] Meeting Stalin and being complimented by him was a rare privilege, but, more generally speaking, being "bombarded with kindness" (as Furet put it) was an essential part of the hospitality. Although most of the intellectuals here discussed were, to begin with, favorably disposed toward the system and its leader, the flattery and carefully devised itineraries confirmed and deepened the favorable predisposition.

During his four-week visit Rolland stayed with Maxim Gorky, the most famous and officially celebrated Soviet writer of the period, and he met, in addition to Stalin, numerous high-level officials including members of the Central Committee of the Communist Party.

Rolland was better informed than most pro-Soviet intellectuals about Soviet political realities and at times privately agonized over them but refused to be critical in public.[50] He did, however, intervene with the

[47] Victor Serge: *Memoirs of a Revolutionary*, London 1984, 328.

[48] Francois Furet: *The Passing of an Illusion: The Idea of Communism in the Twentieth Century*, Chicago 1999, 276.

[49] See *Political Pilgrims*, ch. 8, 347–399.

[50] Richard Wolin wrote: "he [Rolland] was silent about the distortions of Soviet communism. To have publicly condemned the internal or foreign policies of the Soviet Union would inevitably have weakened the antifascist cause," Rolland believed (*The Seduction of Unreason: The Intellectual Romance with Fascism from Nietzsche to Postmodernism*, Princeton NJ 2004, 266).

Soviet authorities on behalf of Victor Serge, although "'not from humanitarian convictions' he said, 'but under pressure from his many friends in the West.'"[51] Not as blinkered and rigidly loyal to the Soviet system as Barbusse, he nonetheless also took every opportunity to defend it in public, express support of its policies, and find excuses for its misdeeds in the glorious objectives pursued. His biographer wrote:

> Romain Rolland viewed political repression in fascist regimes as typical of both the ideology and politics of fascism ... Yet as a fellow traveler, he separated Soviet abuses from Soviet construction acknowledging acts of cruelty but seeing them as oversights, not representative policy ... In the Soviet Union, the whole was considerably greater than the parts, the socialist humanist core compensating for the internal errors, violence and deformations ... The Gandhian Romain Rolland was less easily disgusted by the role of expediency and less moralistic about the role of compromise and coercion in the work of social reconstruction. "One has no right to be squeamish because the builders had to soil their hands."

He also believed that "the Soviet Union was an open-ended experiment capable of rectifying itself." His credulousness went so far that after studying the French translation of the court proceedings of the Moscow Trials (of the alleged Trotskyite conspirators), "he accepted the theory that a real conspiracy existed against the Soviet system ... [and] was convinced that the accused had committed villainous acts."[52]

Like many other intellectuals supportive of ostensibly idealistic political systems using dubious means in pursuit of their lofty goals, Rolland too found it morally unproblematic – at any rate in his public statements – to separate idealistic ends from reprehensible means, and he succeeded in avoiding doubts about goals that required such profoundly tainted means to accomplish. Even his sympathetic political biographer pointed out that "his idea of the USSR remained mythical: a society founded on socialist humanist principles." Projecting attributes he cherished upon Soviet society was an essential component of his admiration, as for example the quaint belief that the Soviet Union "fortified the intellectual capacities and nourished the emotional needs of its citizens," as opposed to corresponding conditions in "decadent Europe."

Rolland was also among the Western intellectuals who believed that intellectuals in the Soviet Union enjoyed an enviable and important position: "By forging a community of mental and manual labor, the Soviets

[51] Quoted in Maurice Nadeau: "Romain Rolland," in Walter Laqueur and George L. Mosse eds.: *Literature and Politics in the Twentieth Century*, New York 1967, 209.

[52] David James Fisher: *Romain Rolland and the Politics of Intellectual Engagement*, Berkeley CA 1988, 217, 220, 240, 274.

showed their understanding of the seminal role of the politically active writer, those '*engineers of souls*' who helped to 'inaugurate a more just, freer, better ordered humanity.' "[53]

While he expressed reservations about Stalin in his journal, for public consumption he had only good things to say about him and his associates:

> Stalin and his "great Bolshevik companions" were ... fearless optimists, without illusions. Orienting themselves to the future, they anchored their social construction to the "Marxist Gospel" ... If they were "realists," the Soviet leaders were also motivated by a "social idea of justice and panhumanism that is more idealist than human dreams." ... Soviet success was bound up with the "best hopes of the world."

Rolland vigorously disputed Andre Gide's critique of the Soviet system, including his assessments of Stalin. Unlike Gide, Rolland found Stalin "accessible and unpretentious" and "quoted Stalin's phrase 'Modesty is the ornament of the true Bolshevik' " as he sought to refute Gide's observations about the cult of personality.

While his private correspondence made clear that he "knew much more about deformations of the Russian Revolution under Stalin than he stated in public" and that he privately entertained occasional doubts and reservations about the system, "regardless of Moscow's treatment of individuals ... [he] remained convinced that the general cause transcended specific injustices."[54]

H.G. Wells was also among those granted the privilege of meeting Stalin, as well as Lenin, and he too appreciated the "ego massage" conferred by such meetings. As Furet put it, "Wells was no stranger to the kind of status seeking that drew certain men of letters to heads of state so that they might bring home the photograph that would broadcast their rank."[55]

After his audience with Stalin, Wells said that he had "never met a man more candid, fair and honest," attributes accounting for "his remarkable ascendancy over the country since no one is afraid of him and everybody trusts him"[56] – an observation so profoundly mistaken in every one of its particulars that it deserves to be preserved for posterity as a reminder of the ability of some intellectuals to radically misread the nature of other human beings.

[53] Ibid., 221–222, 223, 252.
[54] Ibid., 249–250, 270, 276, 278.
[55] Furet, 151.
[56] Quoted in Conquest, 21.

In the course of an earlier (1920) visit, Wells came to the conclusion that the Red Terror, although "fanatical," was "honest" and "apart from individual atrocities it did on the whole kill for a reason and to an end", that is to say, good intentions redeemed it. He found the Bolsheviks authentic, that is, "very much of what they profess to be ... straightforward people," "essentially ... honest," and capable of "recivilising Russia." He understood and respected their spirit while rejecting their Marxist beliefs – an unusual position among Western intellectuals. Wells considered himself "neither Marxist nor Communist but a Collectivist." Also unlike most intellectuals sympathetic toward the Soviet system, he expressed a dim view of Russian peasants: "absolutely illiterate and collectively stupid ... incapable of comprehensive foresight and organization. They will become a sort of human swamp."[57]

Emil Ludwig's views of Stalin (based largely on his conversation with him) are a blend of ludicrous misperceptions and some insightful observations. His peculiar characterizations (in addition to Stalin's alleged lack of interest in power, noted earlier) included the idea that Stalin found his official worship (later called the "cult of personality" by Khrushchev) distasteful and it had nothing to do with his real personality, or his own intentions. Ludwig believed that Stalin was "a particular victim of public craze," of "public hero worship," and Soviet journalists gave the wrong impression of him that was "unreal and untrue."

Ludwig further revealed that, contrary to his own expectations to "meet a Grand Duke of the old regime," he found himself "face to face with a dictator to whose care I would readily confide the education of *my* children." It was his "intuition" that "Stalin is naturally good-hearted. But his position has made him hard and unyielding ... He is not ambitious but he is ruthless toward his opponents." Stalin was certainly ruthless, but the attribution of "good-heartedness" is grotesque unless Ludwig had a rather unusual notion of what it meant. But he was on target in judging Stalin to be supremely patient and "innately" mistrustful of everybody. More questionable, though perhaps partly true, was that "the mission to which he has devoted his life has made him cold and reserved." Likewise, "absolute severity and intransigence" – intolerance might have been a better word – were essential "to get ahead," as Ludwig put it, given the ideologically inspired goals he sought to achieve.[58] It remains hard to determine to what degree ruthlessness and intolerance were essential

[57] H.G. Wells: *Russia in the Shadows*, London 1920, 64, 66, 75, 117, 146.

[58] Ludwig, 346, 346–347, 348, 349.

or innate parts of his personality, or traits he gradually acquired in the course of pursuing his over-ambitious political objectives.

It is likely that Ludwig's assessments of Stalin's personality were influenced by his limited grasp of the nature of the Soviet system Stalin created and molded. Thus, in such a system there could not have been any public worship of Stalin if it had truly displeased him. Democratic, pluralistic decision-making procedures, such as Stalin claimed to characterize the Soviet system in his conversation with Ludwig, did not exist. Ludwig was in no position to know how political decisions or policies were made and evinced no skepticism about Stalin's assertion that 85 percent of the population not only wholeheartedly supported him but favored even more radical policies. Ludwig did not wonder, or ask Stalin, about the validity of one-party elections either, in which 99 percent of the voters chose the official candidates. He also seemed to accept Stalin's insistence that the population was not intimidated and it was impossible to intimidate the Russian masses!

Clearly, Ludwig was unaware of, and evidently not alerted by anyone to, Stalin's superb ability to deceive and put on airs calculated to make the appropriate impression on his interlocutor. This may also explain his peculiar belief that Stalin was easily embarrassed. He wrote: "A certain degree of embarrassment is as graceful in a man of power as it is in a beautiful woman. In the case of Stalin it did not surprise me at all because he scarcely ever sees people from the West." We do not know if Stalin showed any sign of embarrassment upon meeting Ludwig (as Ludwig alleged, see 367), or if he put on an overly courteous demeanor that Ludwig misinterpreted as embarrassment.

There is at last a curious claim Ludwig made about the ease with which he could enter the Kremlin: "It seemed to me that almost anybody who had laid a plan for the assassination of the chief personalities in the Kremlin could very simply gain entrance."[59] This comment was based on the fact that the guard only asked for his name and not his passport.

Of more recent vintage, Theodore Von Laue's perceptions and assessments of the Soviet system and Stalin are among the most explicit and unembarrassed attempts to lift the burden of moral responsibility from the system and its leaders. This is all the more unusual since they were made well after Stalin's death and the dissolution of the Soviet Union, at a time when huge amounts of data became available for the evaluation of Stalin's rule, eroding the basis of apologetics.

[59] Ibid., 366–368, 372–375.

Unlike many other sympathizers, Von Laue was a historian knowledgeable of Soviet-Russian realities. He was not unaware of, and did not dispute, the atrocities and moral outrages that took place under Stalin, although he preferred not to dwell on them: "There is no need here to go into detail on this subject [terror] as it has been highly dramatized," he remarks. Apparently he felt that dwelling on or detailing the terror was unnecessary and its extent or impact was exaggerated. Designating such discussions as "dramatized" reveals his disapproval of dwelling on and deploring Soviet terror.

As the rest of his article makes clear, Von Laue regarded the Soviet terror as both inevitable and essential for the survival of the system and no more deplorable than other instances of political bloodletting in modern history. An unmistakable determination to mitigate and morally neutralize the outrages of the Soviet system permeates his attempt to "reconsider" Soviet history.[60]

To start with, Von Laue questions the right and the capability of (non-Soviet) outsiders to make moral judgments about matters that were totally outside the scope of their own experiences and alien to their own (Western) societies. Second, he insistently argues that the Soviet leaders, Lenin and Stalin in particular, had no choice but to act in the way they did under the circumstances – making autonomous moral choices was not an option. Pursuing these points with fervor and conviction, Von Laue emerges as an unrestrained believer in historical determinism and the inevitability of reprehensible and destructive policies (inspired by desirable goals) for which no human beings ought to be held responsible.

The point of departure for his plea for a major reconsideration of the Soviet system is the following:

> Proper evaluation of the Soviet experiment ... requires that it be set into the broad context of the twentieth century, a century of unprecedented bloodshed. Such an evaluation reveals that far from being the monsters they are often portrayed as, Soviet leaders such as Vladimir Lenin and Josef Stalin followed the only practical course of action to ensure the survival of their country.

This sweeping relativization of the misdeeds of the Soviet rulers is thus accomplished by placing them in the context of the "unprecedented bloodshed" of their times and, again, by designating Lenin's terror as "a minor cruelty amidst the continuing battles of war." In the same spirit, moral indignation about the Holocaust can be tempered by reminding

[60] Theodore von Laue: "A Perspective on History: The Soviet System Reconsidered," *Historian*, Vol. 61, Winter 1999, 388.

ourselves that on the battlefields of World War II (another period of "unprecedented bloodshed") far more people were killed than in the Nazi death camps.

Von Laue proffers an impressive list of circumstances that are intended to exculpate the Soviet leaders: "Catastrophic mistakes and chaotic mismanagement were *inevitable* given the urgency of the change, the total lack of experience, and the *vindictive temper of the times*." Especially intriguing here is the reference to the "vindictive temper of the times" – a rather elusive concept ("the times") that he adds to the other circumstances that absolve the actual human beings of responsibility for their murderous policies. Elsewhere, commenting in the same spirit on Stalin's "assistants in his campaigns of terror," Von Laue suggests that their "wolfish brutality was rooted in Russian life." What precisely he means by "Russian life" we do not learn, nor of the way it *compelled* [my emphasis] "wolfish brutality." The most important reason for suspending moral judgment, Von Laue argues (as did other apologists), is that "Western experience ... is inapplicable to the Soviet Union. No European country had suffered as much as Russia in the First World War; Soviet leaders were fighting to save their country from utter collapse ... In Russia necessary changes could be accomplished only by a highly centralized dictatorship"[61] – the latter an especially unverifiable assertion.

Von Laue never tires of telling his readers that moral judgments cannot be made, or must be suspended, when a country, a group, a political movement, or an individual is victimized – that once human beings have been victimized they are automatically and decisively absolved of the responsibility and capacity of making moral choices.

Chaos and feeling threatened are added to the circumstances that legitimate political repression. Thus, "the Leninist model offered the only rational alternative to chaos." He further raises the rhetorical question: "given the threat to the country's survival, how much of the anachronistic and individualistic tradition was worth preserving in this backward country threatened with political destruction?"

Von Laue was assured that the "inevitably" harsh policies and human sacrifices were balanced by the benefits brought by the regime: "Soviet citizens had access to music, ballet and theater. Physicists and engineers were trained for the future glory of the Soviet Union, and all citizens enjoyed a degree of economic security." He detected no moral problems balancing ends and means: "although the price was brutal, Stalin had

[61] Ibid., 383, 385, 387, 388.

opened to them [the Soviet people] a source of confidence and patriotic pride ... Though his achievements were at the cost of exorbitant sacrifice of human beings and natural resources, they were on a scale commensurate with the cruelty of two world wars." The readers are not informed how this moral calculus was made.

Soviet policies are further excused by the leaders' alleged efforts to emulate Western models and ideas "under non-Western conditions in perilously critical times." He does not explain, or specify, in what way the West was "the proud source of Stalin's model."[62]

Von Laue even rebukes Soviet dissidents for their critique of the Soviet system under Stalin, although he cannot disqualify them as outsiders (ignorant, judgmental Westerners) unfamiliar with Soviet-Russian conditions:

> Modern Russian intellectuals' blindness about world affairs is appalling; none of the ... intellectuals who condemn Stalin's policies – Alexander Solzhenitsyn foremost – have shown any sensibility about their country's external insecurity at that time ... [By contrast] In his grasp of global realities, Stalin clearly outshone all his contemporaries. Carrying Lenin's prescription to its extreme, he aimed at total control not for his own ego but to guide his ignorant country firmly through a necessary cultural transformation.

Evidently Von Laue had no difficulty reading Stalin's mind and reaching the conclusion that his ego played no part in his thirst for "total control." Equally remarkable is his dismissal of the rest of Russia as an "ignorant country" in no position to offer any alternative to Stalin's policies.

Stalin's liquidation of his former comrades-in-arms is written off by the proposition that "Remembering his adversaries in the early days of Soviet rule, Stalin had reason to distrust his comrades especially in this time of perilous change." Apparently only Stalin and Von Laue were qualified to determine what were the reasons for such a distrust, what threatened the survival of the country, and what measures would forestall the threat.

Von Laue never tires of reminding his readers of the irrelevance of "Western standards" for judging anything Soviet, including Stalin himself: "Stalin's style of leadership although crude by Western standards, was persuasive among his disoriented people ... However brutal, it was a remarkable human achievement despite its flaws." Not only was Von Laue assured that this style of leadership met the needs and approval of his people, but he also offers even more startling and implausible conjectures about Stalin's self-conception: "though he knew how to act his public

[62] Ibid., 386, 387, 388, 389, 390.

role, Stalin himself retained a sense of fallibility and imperfection, remaining remarkably humble."

These bewildering and misguided exertions on behalf of Stalin and his system conclude with a sentence that may shed some light on the roots of Von Laue's seemingly inexplicable uncritical disposition: "We need first of all to let a loving compassion open our eyes to the alien realities in Russian Eurasia and to the helplessness of its people, just as Goethe advised 200 years ago."[63]

It appears that the "loving compassion" here advocated was, for the most part, reserved for Stalin and Lenin and their functionaries rather than the people they dominated and brutalized, whom Von Laue often characterized as benighted, backward, ignorant, helpless, and unaware of their true interests. Von Laue thus emerges as embodying what might be called an elitist idealism that is compatible with sympathy for ruthless dictators and condescension for the masses they dominate. This outlook seems rooted in an unfathomable incomprehension of the way sordid means discredit even the loftiest ends, let alone the questionable ones that were pursued by the Soviet leaders.

Noel Field – a far from well-known figure with an unusual career – shared what might be called an "elitist idealism" and a Quaker background with Von Laue, but in other respects he personifies a far more unusual expression of idealism. Field's career began as an employee of the State Department who became a friend of Alger Hiss, his colleague, a more important and better-known agent of the Soviet intelligence services.[64] Following his work at the State Department, Field had a job at the League of Nations in Geneva and later worked for the Unitarian Service Committee, helping refugees in Europe during and after World War II. After losing the latter job he sought employment in Eastern Europe, a quest that took him to Prague in 1949. In doing so he was also motivated by the desire to remove himself from the United States where the trial of Alger Hiss was taking place and might have implicated him. He disappeared from Prague in May 1949 – abducted by Soviet and Hungarian agents and taken to Hungary, destined to play an important part in the forthcoming show trial of Laszlo Rajk, a high-ranking communist

[63] Ibid., 386, 386–387, 387, 391. For a lengthier exposition of similar views, see his *Why Lenin? Why Stalin? A Reappraisal of the Russian Revolution 1900–1930*, Philadelphia 1964.

[64] On the Hiss–Field connection, see Maria Schmidt: "The Hiss Dossier," *New Republic*, November 8, 1993; see also Flora Lewis: *Red Pawn*, New York 1965, 7–58, 74–75, 194–195, 257–258.

functionary. Although never brought to court, Field was forced to act as witness against several of the accused. He spent five years in prison in Hungary (as did his wife) and in 1954 was released and "rehabilitated" and given a comfortable job at a Hungarian state foreign language publishing house. He spent the rest of his life in Hungary, unwavering in his political beliefs and commitments. The authorities, in appreciation of his services, provided him with "an elegantly furnished villa, 100,000 forint in one-time compensation and 10,000 forint monthly salary," later reduced to 7,500 at his request. In 1954, 1,080 forint was the average monthly income in Hungary.[65] Upon his release he was "shaken by sobs" when he learned about the passing of Stalin.[66]

Unlike most of those dealt with in this volume, Field sought to serve actively the idealized political system by becoming its clandestine agent.[67] Coming from a Quaker family that "had always prided itself on being liberal, open-minded people who would never condemn ... an idea that seemed to stem from aspirations to goodness," Field was determined to dedicate his life to such "aspirations to goodness." In his college days he labeled himself a "pacifist idealist" while at the same time "he had growing doubts that peace could be achieved without some form of revolution."[68]

Also characteristic of Field's disposition and especially his thirst for community – and reminiscent of similar sentiments expressed by Eric

[65] Maria Schmidt: *A Titkosszolgalatok Kulisszai Mogott* [Behind the Props of the Intelligence Services], Budapest 2006, 200. The author of this book is probably the only person (other than former employees of the Hungarian political police and some high-level party functionaries) who had access to the archives of the defunct Hungarian political police (AVO, AVH), sometimes erroneously called "secret police." There was nothing "secret" about it, its personnel had a distinctive uniform, the location of its headquarters and local detachments were not concealed and were well-known, and the official media of communications often referred to it.

[66] Noel Field: "Hitching Our Wagon to a Star," *Mainstream*, January 1961, 9.

[67] Stephen Koch suggested that this was a broader phenomenon, that there was a connection between alienation, the adversarial disposition, idealism, and spying. He wrote: "Precisely the same people who instituted the Cambridge penetrations (Kim Philby et al.) supervised parallel operations in New York and Washington, in the Ivy League and at the *Ecole Normale Superiour* ... behind all such operations was the simple recognition of an essential bond between the so-called 'establishment' ... and what Lionel Trilling called the 'adversary culture' ... The recruitment of the Cambridge spies and similar agents in all the democracies was based on this simple insight: The adversary culture is an elite ... to organize the elite meant organizing on the assumption that artistic and political radicalism were really the same things" (Stephen Koch: *Double Lives: Spies and Writers in the Secret Soviet War of Ideas Against the West*, New York 1994, 154, 229).

[68] Lewis, 36, 41.

Hobsbawm[69] – was that as a young man he relished participation in a protest march of unemployed veterans in Washington DC in 1932: "His eyes shining with excitement ... He was immensely proud of what he had done. Joining the marchers gave him sense of pitching in, of striking a blow for his ideals."[70]

Like other true believers, Field easily transcended the problem of ends and means:

> When he found somebody who would listen he argued endlessly about the ideals of communism and the fine things it would bring to the world when the war was over. He called himself a communist, even a Stalinist and huffily rejected as hopelessly naive any protests that the communists who had hurt so many people had gravely impaired their claim to discovery of the formula for a perfect society.[71]

Arthur Schlesinger Jr., upon meeting him, was struck by "his self-righteous stupidity ... [and] 'arrogance of humility.' He was a Quaker Communist filled with smugness and sacrifice."[72]

The Sacco–Vanzetti case made a huge impact on Field's social-political outlook and contributed to his identification with the left. His biographer wrote:

> The night that Sacco and Vanzetti were executed, Noel sat by the radio in a state of shock. He never forgot the date, even remembering a quarter century later ... in his own prison cell. The two Italians became ... his personal martyred saints, and he felt a tremendous urge to pattern his life so as to be worthy of them.

The execution strengthened his growing political commitments since he "had always felt a moral obligation to be involved if he passed by and saw the devil grappling with angels, and a revulsion of mere spectatorship."[73]

In becoming a Soviet agent propelled by lofty ideals, Field followed in the footsteps of better-known "idealists" of this type who became spies, such as the British Kim Philby and his fellow graduates of Cambridge University. In the course of his work for the League of Nations (preceded by his years in the State Department), Field's political beliefs solidified.

[69] Hobsbawm wrote: "Next to sex, the activity combining bodily experience and intense emotion to the highest degree is the participation in a mass demonstration at a time of great public exaltation ... It implies some physical action – marching, chanting slogans, singing – through which the merger of the individual in the mass ... finds expression. The occasion has remained unforgettable" (*Interesting Times: A Twentieth Century Life*, New York 2002, 73).

[70] Lewis, 46.

[71] Ibid., 130.

[72] Arthur Schlesinger Jr.: "Left Field," *New York Review of Books*, February 11, 1965.

[73] Lewis, 36–37, 37.

Flora Lewis wrote: "for Noel, though the misery and brutality he saw [in Spain – P.H.] filled him with compassion, it was an exhilarating relief to be involved. From then on, any lingering emotional doubts or ties of nation and family were overwhelmed by a sense of total commitment. To a cause. In Spain he completed his full dedication to communism."[74] Many years later Field wrote that his months in Spain "resolved my wife's and my lingering hesitations, and by the time the Second World War broke out, we had advanced from emotional anti-fascists to communists in thought and action." Later, while working for the Unitarian Service Commission in Europe, he reached the conclusion that "communists ... [were] the truest humanitarians of our age."[75]

A more unusual part of Field's story is that for several years he was treated by the communist authorities as an enemy of the political system he admired and tried to serve. His 1949 abduction from Prague was followed by imprisonment (without trial or conviction) for five years in Hungary. He was assigned the role of an alleged "master spy" of the United States. His loyalty to the Soviet Union did not save him from being used as a (false) witness to incriminate defendants in the post-World War II show trials in Eastern Europe. Lewis wrote: "His interrogations were the longest and most intensive, for he was the vital hub to hold together a thousand wild stories."[76]

Unlike many Western idealists whose admiration rested on profound ignorance of the nature of communist states and their methods, Noel Field had insider knowledge of the system he sought to serve, being involuntarily enlightened in the course of his prolonged imprisonment and interrogations. Despite these experiences Field preserved intact his beliefs and commitments for the rest of his life, personifying the purest incarnation of the true believer. He also excelled in handling cognitive dissonance, that is to say, "occasions when actual events ... [the true believers] experience contradict their beliefs and view of the world."[77] As Field explained later: "My accusers have the same conviction that I do, they hate the same things and the same people I hate – the conscious enemies

74 Quoted in Lewis, 105.

75 Field, 6.

76 Lewis, 204–205.

77 John Gray offers a persuasive explanation of the way such dissonance is handled: "Human beings do not deal with conflicting beliefs and perceptions by testing them against facts. They reduce the conflict by reinterpreting facts that challenge the beliefs they are most attached to ... The confounding of all their expectations only led them to cling more tightly to their faiths" (John Gray: *The Silence of Animals*, New York 2013, 72–73).

of socialism, the fascists, the renegades, the traitors. Given their belief in my guilt, I cannot blame them." Moreover, he wrote, "the wrongs we had undergone had been righted, the wrongdoers punished, our innocence recognized."[78]

Not even the post-Stalin revelations made a dent in Field's faith. The new evidence of the human costs of the policies he had zealously supported registered mainly as "openings for the poison of a skillful enemy! For a short time ... the eyes of many have become riveted to what was evil and have lost sight of the good. The former was sick excrescence, tragic but curable. The latter intrinsic. Of this I am sure." He was assured of "the regenerative power of essential health within the socialist body."[79]

Field discussed his political motives and career with his interrogators during his imprisonment in Hungary:

> Beginning in 1927 besides my official life I also led a separate, illegal life ... Gathering information amounted to spying. At the time I did not realize that my confidential activities on behalf of the Soviet Union should have been evaluated by political criteria ... At last I succeeded in overcoming my inhibitions and undertook the information gathering task for the Soviet intelligence service. My wife was also present when I agreed to engage in these activities ... Even earlier I recognized that this was honorable work.[80]

As Stephen Koch wrote:

> [Field] never looked back. One might suppose that the experience (of being used in the preparation of the trials and jailed for five years) could have left an "idealist" like Noel Field with a second thought or two about Stalin's justice. Not at all. While Hungary slowly de-Stalinized, Noel lived on in Budapest, more loyal than the regime. He never returned to the West, even when it would have been perfectly safe or him to do so. He never gave any historian or journalist an interview about his life.[81]

In 1960 Field refused to meet Flora Lewis, who waited outside his villa in Budapest intent on interviewing him for the book she was writing.[82]

Apparently it was an easy decision for Field and his wife to stay in communist Hungary, having been assured by their "new friends" (erstwhile captors) that they would be welcome to do so: "Our first spontaneous reaction is: Let us stay here!" He insisted that it was a decision they "have not, for one moment, regretted" and he also averred, more

[78] Field, 4, 14.
[79] Ibid., 12.
[80] Ibid., 9, 14, 15, 16.
[81] Koch, 172.
[82] Lewis, 264.

implausibly, that "to the depths of our being we have the sense of 'belonging'." As to the 1956 Revolution, Field sincerely believed that "the Soviet troops came in defense of socialism ... They – and not those poor misled youngsters ... – are the real 'freedom fighters.'" As of 1961 he insisted that

> it is here [in Hungary] that we have witnessed the marvelous years of consolidation and then of constant advance, of promises held, of plans fulfilled, of doubt converted into confidence all around us ... Each day brings new achievements that make us want to live to be a hundred, so that we too may continue to delight in the fruits of peaceful socialist labor.

Field favorably contrasted Hungary under Kadar with the United States: "most important of all, the sense of insecurity, so characteristic of the lives of millions in America, has been converted [in Hungary] into a priceless sense of security for the individual and his family."[83]

These statements show how profoundly Field was insulated from Hungarian realities while living in the country. There is no doubt that Field believed what he said, seeking and finding vindication for his life-long commitments, sufferings in jail, and decision to stay in Hungary.

Maria Schmidt, a Hungarian historian, too concluded that Field was

> a communist true believer. He took pride in the fact that despite his middle class background he became a loyal fighter of the party ... His faith was not shaken by being treated as an agent of imperialism, imprisoned for five years without trial and held in solitary confinement ... He believed that questionable means served lofty ends ... He kept his faith until his death ... Only those were capable of such persistence who had a singular focus on the future and paid no attention to present day reality.[84]

Field himself confirmed these assessments as he wrote (while in jail):

> in my own smaller ... way I have remained true to the beliefs that began to take shape ... [following the execution of Sacco and Vanzetti – P.H.] It took a decade for those views to ripen into conviction and further years for them to result in consistent action. Many an inner conflict had to be fought out and overcome before the pacifist idealist – a typical middle class intellectual and son of a middle class intellectual – could become the militant communist of later years and of the present.

While in prison he expressed fleeting bewilderment about his fate, quickly followed by the successful effort to banish doubts:

[83] Field, 9, 13–16.

[84] Schmidt 2006 [in Hungarian], 117–119. Quotations translated by author.

Did I, perchance, enter a fool's paradise? Before my mental eyes pass the wonderful men and women – comrades ... who were my friends and with whom I worked for a better world. No, they cannot have been wrong [i.e., *he* could not have been wrong – P.H.]. Steadfast, clear-sighted, they were my guides and mentors. I revere them still. And the Marxist works, the Soviet novels I am privileged to read in my cell – are they not even more convincing, more inspiring than when I read them as a free man? Whatever mistakes, whatever crimes have been committed, they cannot affect the fundamental truths that began to dawn on me a quarter of a century ago. These truths will inevitably win out over temporary aberrations.

After his (and his wife's) release from prison, Field wrote:

A new life is about to begin for us, right here in this land ... we shall study and revalue the past ... We shall be wiser than we were, discard beliefs that have proved to be fallible, replace them by knowledge more solidly founded. But *fundamentally we shall find our convictions justified, strengthened, unchallengeable* ... And once more we shall contribute our mite, however small, towards a happier future for all mankind.[85]

GEORG LUKACS AND OTHER EAST EUROPEAN INTELLECTUALS

The life and beliefs of Georg Lukacs, the Hungarian philosopher and literary historian, provide one of the most remarkable examples of the complex and lifelong bond between some twentieth-century intellectuals and what they believed to be an idealistic dictatorship devoted to both the eradication of social injustices and the transformation of human nature. Lukacs joined the Hungarian Communist Party after World War I and was deputy commissioner of education in the short-lived Hungarian Communist government in 1919. Subsequently he went into exile in Austria, Germany, and finally the Soviet Union, where he lived between 1930 and 1945. He returned to Hungary from the Soviet Union in 1945 with other communist exiles and was appointed to the chair of aesthetics and cultural policy at the University of Budapest. During the 1956 Hungarian Revolution he briefly joined the revolutionary government as minister of education and was subsequently detained in Romania for six months.

Although a lifelong, committed supporter of the Soviet Union and the Hungarian Communist Party, he was forced on several occasions to engage in self-criticism on account of his allegedly deviant ideological

[85] Field, 4, 6, 7, 11 (emphasis added).

positions that included "idealism," "cosmopolitanism," "revisionism," and insufficient appreciation of Soviet socialist realist literature. After 1956, resulting from his short-lived participation in the revolutionary government, he was expelled from the party and "in effect excommunicated, [yet] remained a believer with faith." Arpad Kadarkay, his biographer, further wrote that "It is a testimony to Lukacs's duality that he could convert his dissatisfaction with communist realities ... into a conviction that a 'renaissance of Marxism' was forthcoming ... [he] had an unshakeable faith in Marxism."

Lukacs came from a wealthy Jewish family and was from an early age profoundly alienated from it and the social class it represented. As Kadarkay put it: "Lukacs incarnated alienation in its deepest and broadest sense ... [his] moral vocabulary expanded ... early on with savage parodies, indignation and resentment at unmerited privilege and wealth ... Born with an existential discontent, he hardly needed Marx's evidence in order to feel the need to 'change' the world."[86]

In 1969 Lukacs wrote:

> It is well known that I come from a capitalist, Lipotvaros [a district of Budapest] family ... ever since my childhood, I was profoundly dissatisfied with this "Lipotvaros" way of life. Resulting from my father's economic activities we were in regular contact with the urban patrician and bureaucratic elements and my rejection [of our way of life] extended to them.[87]

As Kadarkay wrote, at an early age he rebelled against the prevailing "social norms and conventions." As a young man "disgusted with the chaotic, prosaic and life-denying bourgeois world, he domiciled himself in philosophy and sought refuge in pure spirit." Later in life he "considered his earlier life, his pre-Marxist stage, of no value, better buried and forgotten."[88]

World War I played an important part in his evolving attraction to the communist movement and Marxism–Leninism. He recalled:

> The imperialist war elicited a profound crisis in my world view; the latter had earlier manifested itself in disavowing the pacifist-bourgeois rejection of the war and in the pessimistic critique of bourgeois culture. Only in the second half of the war did these attitudes acquire a political character under the impact of the

[86] Arpad Kadarkay: *Georg Lukacs: Life, Thought, and Politics*, Cambridge MA 1991, 3, 11, 340, 441, 461.

[87] Georg Lukacs: *Curriculum Vitae* [in Hungarian], Budapest 1982, 380–381. Quotations translated by author.

[88] Arpad Kadarkay ed.: "Introduction," in *The Lukacs Reader*, Cambridge MA 1995, 3, 4–5, 5.

Russian Revolution and the writings of Rosa Luxemburg. My opposition to the ruling order intensified and I began to seek connections with leftist radical circles.[89]

Reading Lenin's *State and Revolution* and various communist publications led him "to the realization that only the communists have the solution for the situation and only they possess the determination to proceed." In the last year of his life, when he began to work on his memoirs, he averred that "there is no doubt that becoming a communist was the most significant turning point of my life."[90] His praise of Jeno Landler, a fellow activist in the communist movement, provides a revealing summary of Lukacs' conception of the ideal human being and his way of life:

His [Landler's] capacity to seamlessly become one with the movement relegating private matters to lesser importance did not make him an ascetic. He loved life, his family and friends but this love was an integral part of the single greatest devotion of his life: the devotion to the working class and his fanatical commitment to its liberation and a fierce hatred of the obstacles to this liberation. A few days before he died he said to his wife that she should join the party and work in the party. He could not think of a more precious advice to bequeath to his widowed partner in life.[91]

Lukacs himself did not quite live up to this ideal of the total subordination of the private to the political realm, but evidently admired those who were capable of it. In any event he did profess to place political or public concerns above personal ones. Thus he wrote that, in light of the rise of Nazism, all personal decisions "had to be subordinated" to these grave conditions and "I considered the central task of my life to apply properly the Marxist-Leninist worldview to areas of life I was familiar with."[92] More generally, he used his professional standing and reputation "not only to promote an ideal he believed in, but also to cover up terrible crimes ... he kept silent about obvious lies and repeated empty slogans."[93]

As early as in 1921 Lukacs settled the issue of ends and means, as reflected in his response to the question of an interviewer about the propriety of lying and cheating by the party leaders: "Communist ethics make it the highest duty to accept the necessity of acting wickedly. This, he [Lukacs] said, was the greatest sacrifice the revolution demanded from us."[94]

[89] Lukacs, 463.
[90] Ibid., 464, 27.
[91] Kadarkay 1991, 92–93.
[92] Lukacs, 228.
[93] Tamas Aczel and Tibor Meray: *Tisztito Vihar: Adalekok egy korszak tortenetehez* [Cleansing Storm: Data for the History of an Era], Munich 1978, 63–64.
[94] Quoted in George Lichtheim: *George Lukacs*, New York 1970, 46.

A key to Lukacs' lifelong loyalty to the Soviet system and its founding ideals was his remarkable capacity to overlook, or altogether ignore, the moral significance of actual events or political developments, and the manifestations of human suffering associated with them.[95] He was enabled to do so by a blinding idealism, a devotion to ends pursued by sordid means whose moral or ethical importance he seemed able to dismiss. As Kadarkay puts it, "common sense was not one of Lukacs's virtues. He considered empirical reality an impediment to the aesthetics of totality."[96] "Totality" (an obscure concept, favored by Marxist intellectuals) was the sum total of the original ideals and conceptions of the superior social system to be built. Kadarkay believes that "Lukacs ... craved 'totality' and accepted with a good conscience the sacrifices he felt it demanded."

He venerated "the actual and attempted moral justification of historical necessity," which is another way of saying that *perceived* historical necessity justified everything. Lukacs mystified historical necessity and the historical process: "the absoluteness of the party's political power, embodied in Stalin, could not be impugned without impugning the 'rightness' of the historical process." Kadarkay sums it up: "faith replaced reason."[97]

Once more Orwell's observation comes to mind, namely, that one had to be an intellectual to believe all this ("historical necessity" in particular) and utilize highly abstract concepts to justify concrete and tangible realities that otherwise would be deemed morally intolerable and impermissible. It is unlikely that Lukacs ever had a conversation with a real worker or peasant, or had any specific knowledge or experience of how such people lived, either in the Soviet Union or Hungary.

The true believers' thinking – such as that of Lukacs – about historical necessities was circular: the party and its leader were the best, indeed the only infallible judges of what constituted historical necessity, while at the same time "historical necessity" created the party and placed its leader into the position he occupied.

Late in life Lukacs made an attempt to better explain his lifelong political subservience: "Inasmuch as my activity coincided with the world

[95] Or, as Roger Scruton put it, once his political commitment took "the form of an immovable religion ... the surrounding world lost all claim over Lukacs's conscience. All was to be swept away in the refining fire of revolution" (see *Fools, Frauds and Firebrands*, London 2015, 119). For further incisive comments on Lukacs's detestation of capitalism and quasi-religious worldview, see also ibid., 118–120).

[96] Kadarkay 1991, 304.

[97] Ibid., 312.

historical significance of socialism in one country [i.e., the Soviet system], and the struggle for its interest, it is natural that all my concerns, including those of my work, were subordinate to this consideration." As his biographer writes: "Lukacs found the 'moral necessity' to suspend all criticism of the Soviet Union. Even when Stalin's crimes were exposed by the Party itself, Lukacs wrote, 'It is my long-held position that even at its worst, it is better to live under socialism than under the best of capitalism.' "[98] The latter affirmation brings to mind another of his remarks (made in 1967), namely that "even if every empirical prediction of Marxism were invalidated, he would still hold Marxism to be true."[99]

Lukacs' subservience to party doctrine was also reflected in his repeated insistence that Soviet socialist realist fiction was "essentially" superior to Western classics – a position all the more striking since he was intimately familiar with and appreciative of Western literature. In 1950 he engaged in self-criticism for insufficiently emphasizing the superiority of Soviet literature over the bourgeois classics: "The superiority of socialist realism over all older forms of realism ... pertains to the totality of literature ... This superiority follows from the higher accomplishments of socialism."[100]

This assertion was part of the dubious logic Lukacs employed: since socialism is superior to capitalism (a dubious premise to start with), it follows that socialist realist literature, that is, an integral part and product of socialism, is also bound to be superior to capitalist literature.

Leszek Kolakowski offered a penetrating critical assessment of the political disposition of Lukacs:

> [he] accepted Communism whole-heartedly as a moral, intellectual and political solution. Despite various philosophical adventures, he completely identified himself with the Communist movement for the rest of his life. He believed that Marxism was the final answer to the problem of history, that Communism guaranteed the final reconciliation of all human forces and the free play on all human possibilities; that the conflict between the individual and society ... had in principle been resolved.[101]

These basic commitments and beliefs account for the willed, voluntary politicization of his personality and way of life and his willingness to suspend, or suppress, on many occasions, his capacity for critical thinking.

[98] Quoted in Kadarkay 1991, 326, 327.

[99] Quoted in Conquest 2000, 44.

[100] Ibid., 144.

[101] Leszek Kolakowski: *Main Currents of Marxism*, New York 2005, 993.

For example, he claimed that he "considered every engagement abroad [that is, in the West] an opportunity to participate in the class struggle and fight the class enemy." Until the beginning of the official Soviet de-Stalinization campaign in 1956, he displayed abject loyalty to Stalin and his policies. Writing about Stalin's book, *The Foundations of Leninism*, in 1930 he proposed that the book "showed us the self-evident truth that the teachings of Lenin constitute a total system ... providing a method to find concrete *answers to all questions of life* ... [my emphasis – P.H.] Our entire Marxist thinking has been resting on these foundations Stalin broadened and deepened."

Seeking to explain in the summer of 1956 his past support of Stalin's policies and his silence during the campaign of extermination of alleged Trotskyites, Lukacs said (at a meeting of the Hungarian Institute of Party History):

> the Soviet Union was, at the time, directly anticipating a life and death struggle with fascism. Therefore a communist of strong commitments could only say "Right or Wrong my party." [English in the original] Whatever the Party, led by Stalin, did under these circumstances ... we had to display unconditional solidarity in this struggle and rank this solidarity above everything else.

He offered a similar justification for his unwillingness to question the Moscow (Show) Trials that coincided with the VIIth Congress of the Communist International and its advocacy of a broad popular front against fascism:

> Like many others in that period I also considered it my sacred [*sic*] duty to abstain from making any statement that could have been viewed in the West as advising patience towards Hitler. I evaluated the (Moscow) Trials in this light: as revolutionary retribution against the active opponents of existing socialism. That the means used in this process were in many ways rather problematic [*sic*!] could not shake the fundamentals of my disposition at the time.

Lukacs further proposed that while the intensification of Stalin's campaign against Trotskyism stimulated an internal moral and intellectual critique, "as far as its public expression was concerned it was mandatory to remain silent since the struggle against Hitler was the most important."[102] While it is understandable that as a resident in the Soviet Union at the time it would have been suicidal for Lukacs to question the Moscow Trials or the persecution of Trotskyites, he was far from

[102] Lukacs, 117–118, 147.

persuasive in implying that a critique of Stalin would have been incompatible with opposing fascism on *moral grounds*.

Furet suggests that for Lukacs "Stalin incarnated world-historical reason, which the philosopher had adopted as his own principle ... Lukacs was a Stalinist not out of cynicism but out of wisdom – not the wisdom of resignation but that of philosophy." Furet further argues that Lukacs, as other true believers, made his huge and durable "psychological investment" in communism (that is, Marxism-Leninism) because "it appeared to unite science and morals – a miraculous combination."[103]

While Lukacs somewhat modified his views of Stalin over time, his admiration of Lenin remained unshakeable. As of 1967 he wrote: "Lenin, as the embodiment of a permanent readiness to take action represents an indestructible value: Lenin's disposition typifies a new and exemplary relationship between action and reality."

Late in life, Lukacs made clear that notwithstanding his acknowledged political illusions and errors of the past, he would refuse "to choose the path of Koestler. I could never accept critiques [such as those of Koestler – P.H.] which combined the rejection of the methods of Stalin with that of socialism." This remark, as other expressions of his deepest beliefs, reflects how Lukacs (as other true believers) handled the dissonance between ends and means. He would not allow sordid means to discredit the glorious ends, even when their attainment kept being postponed.

Following Khrushchev's famous speech at the 20th Party Congress in 1956, Lukacs shifted gear. But instead of expressing distress over the horrors of Stalin's policies and abuses of power revealed by Khrushchev, he averred that the Congress opened up new "prospects for the triumphs of Marxism-Leninism," especially for the younger generations.[104] As Kadarkay pointed out, Lukacs "could convert his dissatisfaction with communist realities ... into a conviction that a 'renaissance of Marxism' was forthcoming."[105] In Kolakowski's words, "He maintained the belief that socialism ... would liberate itself from the aftermath of Stalinist 'distortions' and return to the path of 'true' Marxism. He stated in an interview that the worst socialism was better than the best capitalism."[106]

Another reflection of his political disposition, Lukacs, rather implausibly, became a defender of Angela Davis, insisting that her case was comparable to those of Dreyfus and Sacco and Vanzetti, and expressed alarm

[103] Furet, 121.
[104] Lukacs, 159, 346, 378.
[105] Kadarkay 1991, 461.
[106] Kolakowski, 997.

that her "judicial murder" was imminent. Confusing American judicial-political practices with those in the Soviet Union he was familiar with, he believed that "the verdict is predictable"[107] and politically ordained and that only worldwide protest would save the life of Angela Davis. We do not know what he thought when she was acquitted of all charges by a friendly jury.

In the final analysis it becomes clear that Lukacs was a highly sophisticated "true believer" fixated on the idealized ends, who always found ways to avoid disillusionment with or questioning the ends by resolutely and rigidly overlooking the practices they inspired and legitimated. Furet wrote:

> he never wavered from the conviction that he would reaffirm on his deathbed: "I have always thought that the worst form of socialism was better to live in than the best form of capitalism" ... Lukacs thus presents a prime example of a political belief that would survive more than a half-century of observation and even experience ... He never stopped digging for the meaning of Marxism, without ever questioning Bolshevism ... he was never tempted to renounce the idea of the *essential superiority* of Stalinist socialism over liberal democracy, or to question the ideological foundations of Bolshevism ... The end of his life revealed the internal captivity that bound him to an idea of the Soviet Union so potent that it had annulled his knowledge of history.[108]

Kolakowski persuasively identified the motives and thought processes that enabled Lukacs to persist in his beliefs: "As long as the world is torn by the struggle between capitalism and socialism, and if socialism is assumed on philosophical grounds to be an essentially superior system irrespective of any empirical facts, then clearly any internal opposition to socialism as it exists at any given time is a blow struck in favor of the enemy." Kolakowski, a former Marxist, also recognized that Lukacs, as other true believers, could also fall back on the conviction that "Marxism ... is an understanding of the world that can only be enjoyed within that movement and in political commitment to it. Marxism in this sense is invulnerable to rational argument [as all religious beliefs are – P.H.]: outsiders cannot understand it correctly, and therefore cannot criticize it."[109]

[107] Quoted in Kadarkay 1991, 367.

[108] Furet, 117, 122, 123 (emphasis added). Daniel Bell also believed that Lukacs was "in the grip of 'messianic utopianism'" motivated by unshakeable quasi- or secular-religious convictions and commitments (quoted in George Urban: "A Conversation with Daniel Bell," *Encounter*, February 1983, 20–21).

[109] Kolakowski, 1025, 1029.

The entire life, political beliefs, and political behavior of Lukacs prove conclusively that a refined intellect, an exceptional knowledge of literature, philosophy and modern history, as well as a capacity for critical thinking are compatible with deep-seated, unshakeable, and irrational ideological convictions unsupported by empirical realities or evidence.

Lukacs was by no means the only Hungarian intellectual who admired Stalin and his system. Between the late 1940s and mid 1950s many Hungarian intellectuals and especially writers rallied around the party and displayed worshipful attitudes toward Stalin, modeled on, and virtually identical with, those of their Soviet counterparts. Most well-known Hungarian writers were enthusiastic supporters of the communist government, and its policies, until disillusionment set in following Stalin's death and the more permissive policies which allowed the expression of doubts about prevailing conditions. In evaluating these attitudes we must keep in mind that, as in Nazi Germany and Fascist Italy, in the communist countries too it was difficult to differentiate committed, idealistic support from careerism or opportunism. Unlike in pluralistic Western societies where political sympathies or affiliations had little if any bearing on one's professional life, in communist countries vocal support of the authorities was an essential precondition of getting published and gaining access to desirable positions in academic institutions, publishing houses, journals, or cultural organizations affiliated with the state or the party.

In addition to the influence of access to such privileges, there was also an element of idealism motivating prominent Hungarian writers in their vocal support of the communist government. This idealism found expression in the fact that many of them, disregarding and endangering their privileged positions, became outspoken critics of the system and subsequently supporters of the 1956 Revolution. Thomas Aczel and Tibor Meray wrote:

> As they looked back on past years, they were horrified to realize that they not merely approved of all that happened but were helpers, promoters, propagandist for all that took place ... They came to hate themselves, as feelings of guilt and shame converged ... the trouble was not merely that they believed ... But that they believed blindly ... suddenly it became clear what transpired with their help ... The process that altered ... the psychology of the Hungarian communist writers took little time.

What made them true believers, for a period of time, in the first place? Aczel and Meray suggest that it had to do with "the longing of the lonely human being for an imagined community ... [and] with a religious yearning for a universalistic view of the world that had answers for every question."[110]

One of the best-known among these intellectuals, the writer Tibor Dery, longtime supporter of the communist movement and party member, provided a remarkable example of such dramatic reversal of attitudes. A major voice for reform after the death of Stalin, and, later, supporter of the 1956 Revolution, he was imprisoned for four years after 1956. A few years earlier he was among the sycophantic worshippers, deifiers, of Stalin as he wrote: "We celebrate a man who destroys with one hand to build with the other; who recognizes and demolishes that which is disintegrating, who makes the perishable perish ... We celebrate the man who built himself so that he could build later a whole world."[111]

A volume of Hungarian writers celebrating Stalin's seventieth birthday[112] was an authentic product of the official cult as originally conceived in the Soviet Union. These poems, by authors largely forgotten in Hungary and unknown outside of it, include such lines, reminiscent of prayers:

> Your steadfast hand remolded old earth ... You hand planted trees in the desert, harnessed wild rivers with dams, your hand supports and protects us, at waving your finger light and abundance burst forth ... In Stalin's name rejoices the Earth and its wide spaces thunder and tremble ... Every city, village the land and the factory salutes Stalin, the machines are throbbing with his name ... Stalin's name is burning in our soul ... That I exist, that I write my poems, that I can breathe today ... it is your work Stalin!
>
> All nations praise you ... Look at your eternal work ... Unfailing you point the direction.

Another poem in the same volume describes "a thoughtful mother, studying the life of Comrade Stalin and holding her little son on her lap telling a story of the Soviets ... My dear son you can smile, your mother can tell you stories, the battle was fought for us at Caricin and Stalingrad."[113]

[110] Aczel and Meray, 229–230, 235, 237, 295.

[111] Tibor Dery: "Unnep" [Celebration], *Csillag* [Star, a literary journal], January 1953, Budapest.

[112] *Stalint Koszontjuk – Magyar Koltok Versei a Hetven Eves Sztalinhoz* [We Salute Stalin: Hungarian Poets Addressing Stalin], Budapest 1949.

[113] Ibid., 7, 14, 33, 36, 45–46. In the Hungarian original these poems are not quite as bad as they are in the English translation I provided. Since I am not a poet my translations tend to be more literal than poetic and cannot do justice to the original. At the same time it is difficult to separate the literary qualities of these poems from their intended message: the glorification of one of the most unscrupulous and ruthless dictators.

The case of Maxim Gorky, the Russian writer, an old revolutionary and opponent of the Tsarist system, has some similarities with that of Lukacs. He too was, in more than one way, a captive of the system and its lifelong supporter with some reservations. He was, according to Stephen Koch, "the house humanist among the Bolsheviks."[114] He lived abroad until 1932, when he returned responding to Stalin's warm personal invitation. On one of his visits to the Soviet Union in 1929 he was taken on a conducted tour of the first Gulag, established in the Solovki Islands. He wrote in the Visitor's Book:

> I am not in a state of mind to express my impressions in just a few words. I wouldn't want ... to permit myself banal praise of the remarkable energy of people who, while remaining vigilant and tireless sentinels of the Revolution [members of the NKVD guarding the inmates – P.H.], are able, at the same time, to be remarkably bold creators of culture.

These comments were preceded by a conversation he had with a fourteen-year-old boy in the Children's Colony who told him about the stage-managed aspects of his visit ("Everything you see here is false").[115]

Gorky was also the co-editor of and contributor to the volume entitled *The White Sea–Baltic Canal* published in 1934 that contained the writings of thirty-six Soviet authors who had visited the canal built by slave labor in 1933. In their writings they testified to the miraculous transformation of the prisoners who built it into upright Soviet citizens. Gorky also seized this opportunity to praise the GPU for "reeducat[ing] people."[116]

We do not know what, late in his life, Gorky thought of Stalin following his return and of the accelerating deformation of the Soviet system, or to what degree his views were influenced by his new eminence in the Soviet Union following his return. In any event,

> Stalin lavished on [him] everything the Soviet world could offer any writer ... he became the object of ... a kind of literary "cult of personality" ... and lived with every privilege the regime had to offer ... He was supplied with a palatial country estate and a town house in Moscow. His books were published in huge editions ... Cities, streets and squares began to be named after him ... Gorky's original vision of his role reached a kind of grotesque fulfillment.[117]

[114] Koch, 249.

[115] Quoted in Aleksandr Solzhenitsyn: *The Gulag Archipelago*, Vol. II, New York 1975, 62–63, 62.

[116] Ibid., 81, 85. The English translation of the book edited by Amabel Williams-Ellis was entitled *Belomor: An Account of the Construction of the New Canal Between the White Sea and the Baltic Sea*, New York 1935.

[117] Koch, 250.

THE CULT OF MATHIAS RAKOSI IN HUNGARY

It is of some historical significance that the Stalin cult was replicated in the cults of lesser communist leaders in Eastern Europe, such as Nicolae Ceausescu of Romania, Vulko Chervenko of Bulgaria, Klement Gottwald of Czechoslovakia, Enver Hodza of Albania, Mathias Rakosi of Hungary, and Walter Ulbricht of East Germany. In all these countries the politicized intellectuals made substantial contributions to these cults. In the following I will only discuss the cult of Mathias Rakosi, head of the Hungarian Communist Party, described by a historian as "the Hungarian Stalin."[118]

A faithful reflection of the similarities between Rakosi's cult and that of Stalin can be found in a collection of writings produced by Hungarian writers to honor Rakosi on his sixtieth birthday.[119] As will be seen below, his attributes bear striking resemblance to those projected onto Stalin by the Soviet writers. I translated these poetic effusions from Hungarian and, arguably, the original may sound somewhat better. Here are some samples:

> In his hands a lovely stalk of wheat: the radiant fate of the nation. He is never frightened and confronts storms with courage. He takes to his heart the troubles of millions.
>
> Today Rakosi speaks on the radio ... The wind subsides, and the heart of the country is throbbing in the palm of his hand ...
>
> [Y]ou are watching over me, brother, father, my lucky star ... Only now do I have a true father! Adopt me as your faithful son, you who feed me and take care of us ... I love you. You gave your sixty years – what shall I give?
>
> [W]hen ... he returned to his country, his people, clutched his strong hand like a small child does his father's. The gentle strictness of teachers radiated from him ... When we rejoiced, he rejoiced with us, when we suffered he suffered with us.
>
> Miraculously I talked to him so calmly as I did with my father. He exuded tranquility. I was tired and gained strength.

In another poem Rakosi stands by the bed of an orphaned North Korean child, who is asleep, and covers her up, caressing her and telling her fairy tales.[120] (During the Korean War Hungary had many North Korean refugees.)

The adulation of Rakosi was not limited to literary projects. At official functions and celebrations the admiration expressed by those attending

[118] Peter Kenez: *Hungary from the Nazis to the Soviets: The Establishment of the Communist Regime in Hungary, 1944–1948*, New York 2006, 20.

[119] *Magyar Irok Rakosi Matyasrol* [Hungarian Writers on Mathias Rakosi], Budapest 1952.

[120] Ibid., 52, 139, 175, 255, 266, 321.

approximated the kind of adulation genuinely charismatic leaders received from larger crowds of more diverse composition. Those here described were mostly party functionaries, government officials, and members of other privileged groups, including intellectuals loyal to the party. Thomas Aczel and Tibor Meray[121] described one such highly orchestrated celebration of Rakosi at the opera house in Budapest:

> It was an expression of a kind of religious fervor that converted obligatory respect into a delirious rapture, [it was] the bliss of the crowd, its gratitude toward the leader who lifted the burden of thinking and provided clear channels for action, who undertook to redeem their lives and whose strength, knowledge and power was far superior to those of ordinary mortals, and who personified intelligence, toughness, superiority as well as humility, unwavering faith and perfect certitude.[122]

Rakosi's designation as Stalin's foremost Hungarian disciple and recipient of his alleged unconditional trust was integral to his cult, as were the numerous attributions of genius. Aczel and Meray wrote: "It would not have been surprising if it turned out that, even biologically speaking, comrade Rakosi had a life different from those of ordinary mortals ... The true believers were tremendously proud that the country was blessed by a leader such as Mathias Rakosi." Rakosi, like Stalin, was credited with being omniscient, omnipresent, powerful, just, kind, and caring. He too got by with minimal sleep; stayed in his office from early morning until late night; managed to read several hundred pages a day, which included politics, history, science, and fiction, including poetry; he perused early in the morning not only *Pravda* and *Szabad Nep* (official daily newspapers of the Soviet and Hungarian communist parties respectively) but also the *Manchester Guardian*, *New York Times*, *Le Monde*, and *Unita*.[123]

In conclusion, it is should be emphasized that admiration of Stalin was not stimulated by his charisma, such as that possessed by Mussolini, Hitler, and Castro. Unlike them he rarely spoke to crowds, and when did he was by no means an electrifying speaker. Nor did he project a heroic, dynamic demeanor. Charisma, as generally understood, played

[121] Like Dery, both Aczel and Meray used to be devoted supporters of the regime and party members until the early 1950s. Aczel was the only Hungarian writer who was awarded the Stalin prize. Meray, a journalist, was distinguished by reporting at great length on the biological warfare – an invention of communist propaganda – supposedly engaged in by the United States during the Korean war.

[122] Aczel and Meray, 152.

[123] Ibid., 157, 159, 160.

little if any part in his rise to power and worship. Rather, it was a deified image, part father figure, that was the source of his attraction. The central themes of the official cult are reflected in the following statement of the Central Committee of the Party:

> You, Comrade Stalin were, with Lenin the inspiring leader of the great socialist revolution of October ... Your wisdom, boundless energy and iron will contributed to each and every step ... that made our country more powerful ... Under your leadership ... the Soviet Union has become an enormous, invincible force ... Every honest individual and generation all over the world will praise the Soviet Union and your name, as the man who rescued world civilization from the fascist warlords ... your name is the most precious for our people and for all the ordinary people of the world.[124]

While the misconceptions and idealization of Stalin here sampled were largely products of predisposition and ignorance, Stalin's remarkable capacity to deceive those whom he met also played a part. Maria Joffe, widow of Adolf Joffe, the prominent Soviet diplomat and former revolutionary who met Stalin on numerous occasions, recalled: "Stalin was an actor of rare talent. Capable of changing his mask to suit any circumstance. And one of his favorite masks was ... the simple, ordinary, good fellow wearing his heart on his sleeve."[125] A Soviet historian and former Gulag inmate, Anton Antonov-Ovseyenko, wrote:

> With time, hypocrisy and dissembling became second nature to him. Whether he was playing the role of the straightforward, good-hearted fellow, or the strict and serious enforcer of party rules, or the omnipotent leader, Stalin entered into each part so thoroughly that he sincerely began to believe it. Nature itself blessed him with this unusual capacity to assume many roles.[126]

Milovan Djilas, who met Stalin on several occasions, came to the conclusion that "with him, pretense was so spontaneous that it seemed he himself became convinced of the truth and sincerity of what he was saying. He very easily adapted himself to every turn in the discussion of any new topic, and even to every new personality."[127]

[124] The Central Committee of the Soviet Communist Party and the Council of Ministers of the Soviet Union on the occasion of Stalin's 70th Birthday. Quoted in Dmitrij Volkogonov: *Gyozelem es Tragedia: Stalin Politikai Arckepe* [Victory and Tragedy: The Political Portrait of Stalin], Budapest 1990, 8.

[125] Quoted in Anton Antonov-Ovseyenko: *The Time of Stalin: Portrait of a Tyranny*, New York 1980, 245.

[126] Ibid., 45.

[127] Djilas, 97.

It also needs to be emphasized once more that the admiration of Stalin on the part of Western intellectuals, while inseparable from their support for the system he symbolized, was strengthened by their readiness to embrace a political leader whose accomplishments and personal qualities appeared to be greatly superior to the familiar political leaders of their own countries. It is of further importance that the favorable predispositions and sentiments regarding Stalin (as well as the other dictators here considered) were hardly ever challenged by knowledge of social and political realities. The intellectuals here discussed were isolated from dissonant experiences that could have prompted them to reexamine and reevaluate their beliefs or disposition. Last but not least, they were not anxious to gain access to information that would have undermined their beliefs.

Finally, it is important to reemphasize the religious affinities and undercurrents of these political cults, including that of Stalin. Richard Overy wrote:

> Cults are conventionally religious rather than political phenomena. In both Germany and the Soviet Union the distinction between the two became blurred ... In the Soviet Union direct reference to Christian imagery was more difficult in a state that was at least officially atheist. Nevertheless the development of the popular [Stalin] cult was permeated, as in Germany, with metaphors that were unashamedly sacred. The ideas of Stalin as savior, as the source of a supernatural power, as prophet or redeemer, were borrowed from traditions in Russian popular religion.[128]

[128] Overy, 120–121.

5

Western Intellectuals, Mao's China, and Cambodia under Pol Pot

The people seem happy and well fed ... the change in the countryside is miraculous ... The stress and even violence of 1966–69 have now been succeeded ... by a sense of relaxation and euphoria that makes 1972 a happy time to be in China ... The Maoist revolution is on the whole the best thing that happened to the Chinese people in centuries.

John K. Fairbank[1]

[Here is] a people marching with light step and with fervor toward the future. This people may be the incarnation of the new civilization of the world. China has made an unprecedented leap into history ... Mao is essentially antidogmatic and antiauthoritarian. He prizes the initiative of the masses.

Maria Macciocchi[2]

[Mao] seldom seemed moved by the suffering of lovers, children, and friends any more than he flinched from imposing misery on millions of faceless "masses" in pursuit of his economic and political schemes ... he ignored realities that contradicted his vision ... Mao was devoid of human feeling, incapable of love, friendship or warmth ... he had become inured to human suffering ... Morality had no place in Mao's politics.

Li Zhisui[3]

[1] John K. Fairbank: "The New China and the American Connection," *Foreign Affairs*, October 1972, 36.

[2] Macciocchi quoted in Richard Wolin: *The Wind from the East: French Intellectuals, the Cultural Revolution and the Legacy of the 1960s*, Princeton NJ 2010, 124.

[3] Dr. Li Zhisui: *The Private Life of Chairman Mao: The Memoirs of Mao's Personal Physician*, New York 1994, viii, x, 120–121, 122.

FIGURE 7. Towering over the masses, acclaimed by his people. Text on poster: "Long live the victory of Chairman Mao's revolutionary line."

FIGURE 8. Leading smiling, joyful peasants during the Cultural Revolution.

Once more it has to be emphasized that it is difficult to separate the favorable attitudes toward the leaders here examined from similar attitudes toward the political system they represented. The admiration of the supreme leaders was an integral part of the wholehearted endorsement of the political-social system they created and presided over. It was the leaders who were credited with, and praised for, all the perceived accomplishments of the systems concerned. But readers also need to be reminded that, for the most part, the sanguine assessments of China under Mao belong to the past, as reflected in the conclusion reached by the University of Hong Kong historian, Frank Dikotter: "in China the story of liberation and the revolution that followed is not one of peace, liberty and justice. It is first and foremost a history of calculated terror and systematic violence." Andrew Walder, an American sinologist and political sociologist, came to similar conclusions about "the human costs of Maoism," pointing out that

> modest accomplishments were offset by enormous human costs. The largest of such costs was the death through starvation of 30 million people in the famine created by the Great Leap Forward ... a significant portion of this number were in fact executed or beaten to death during regional campaigns ... The one modern event that is directly analogous to China's Great Leap famine is the starvation caused by forced collectivization in [Soviet] Russia.

He further observed that "almost none of Mao's initiatives led to outcomes that he and his supporters fully anticipated, foresaw, or welcomed."[4]

Sympathy for communist China and its supreme leader during the 1960s and 1970s was particularly strong among American academics and it coalesced in an organization that called itself the Committee of Concerned Asian Scholars.[5] Its members were among the most ardent admirers of Chinese communism and Mao and, as is often the case, also among the fiercest critics of their own society. It was their proclaimed intention "to change America's mind about Asia," meaning for the most part China. Steven W. Mosher wrote about this organization:

[4] Frank Dikotter: *The Tragedy of Liberation: A History of the Chinese Revolution, 1945–57*, New York 2013, ix; Andrew G. Walder: *China under Mao: A Revolution Derailed*, Cambridge MA 2015, 333–334, xi.

[5] Simon Leys believed that these scholars "failed most scandalously in their moral responsibilities toward China and the Chinese people during the Mao era" (*The Burning Forest: Essays on Chinese Culture and Politics*, New York 1985, 99).

In their most expansive moods, the concerned scholars imagined that Chairman Mao and the Chinese Communist party had invented a solution to the problems of mankind. "How can people break the shackles of oppression, poverty and fear...?" asked Professor Mark Selden, one of the founding fathers of the Committee ... His answer: "The Chinese revolution offers inspiration not only to those who would expel colonial oppressors. Nor is its message limited to new nations ... It addresses men and women everywhere who seek to create a society free from stifling oppression, arbitrary state power, and enslaving technology."[6]

Michael Oksenberg, a political scientist, as of 1973, shared these sanguine expectations, and suggested that "America's 'dreary list of domestic problems: racism, bureaucratism, urban decay' etc. might be solved by adopting the Chinese model." In the same spirit John K. Fairbank, the widely respected China scholar, wrote in 1972 that "Americans may find in China's collective life today an ingredient of personal moral concern for one's neighbor that has a lesson for us all."[7]

Richard Madsen, another China scholar, offered a critical summary of these attitudes prevalent in the same period:

The story that developed in the late 1960s on the left was that China was ... the redeemer revolution. There was a profound impulse to idealize it, to say that everything about it was progressive and perfect. The revolutionary redeemer nation was the leader in the struggles of the world's poor and oppressed against US imperialism and monopoly capitalism. The Cultural Revolution was a grand experiment in creating a more just society, that eliminated inequality and achieved authentic participatory democracy, a society in which the aspirations of the masses and leaders were united under the charismatic leadership of Mao Zedong ... From what we know about life in China during the Cultural Revolution, it is clear that the China story told by the American new left in the 1960s was a fiction.[8]

It is of some interest that some of the admirers of Mao and his system had earlier also been attracted to the Soviet Union under Stalin and Stalin himself, suggesting that these skewed perceptions and questionable judgments were rooted in a long-standing disposition to project hopes and wishes onto different plausible subjects. As Simon Leys wrote: "Karl Marx remarked that some historical phenomena happen twice, the first time as tragedy, the second as farce. The way some sections of the Western

[6] Stephen Mosher: *China Misperceived: American Illusions and Chinese Reality*, New York 1990, 129–130.

[7] Oksenberg and Fairbank quoted in Jonathan Mirsky: "The Myth of Mao's China," *New York Review of Books*, May 30, 1991, 16.

[8] Richard Madsen: *China and the American Dream: A Moral Inquiry*, Berkeley CA 1995, 52, 565.

intelligentsia have prostrated themselves, first before Stalin's Soviet Union and then before Mao's China, is a striking verification of this."[9] Scott Nearing, the American writer, was one of these "recidivists." Visiting China in 1957, at the beginning of the disastrous "Great Leap Forward," he found that "The Communists had eliminated the scourges that were rife thirty years earlier ... Cooperatives in agriculture, in trade and handicrafts had become a prominent feature of Chinese economy ... A flood of energy, dealism and high striving marked the mood of China."[10] Joseph Needham, a British scientist who extolled Stalin and the Soviet system in the 1903s, "in 1952 endorsed without question the Chinese-North Korean charges that the United States had practised bacteriological warfare" in the Korean War.[11] Hewlett Johnson (Dean of Canterbury) and Anna Louise Strong were drawn to both the Soviet and Chinese systems under Stalin and Mao respectively. Jean-Paul Sartre and Simone de Beauvoir admired both Mao and Castro and their respective systems and for a period of time also sympathized with the Soviet system.

It is to be pointed out that admiration on the part of intellectuals was almost entirely one-sided, as Mao (like the other dictators here considered) had little appreciation of intellectuals.[12]

IMAGE AND REALITY

None of the dictators featured in this volume presents a more striking contrast between public image and personal qualities than Mao. Arguably, he might well have been the least deserving of the accolades he received, both on account of his policies and his personality. The reverence shown toward him by some Western intellectuals (and others) was probably the most misplaced and perplexing of all the worshipful political attitudes here examined.

Mao's defining personal characteristics contrasted spectacularly with those projected upon him according to two biographers and his physician. Chang and Halliday believed that his negative personal characteristics defined his personality and ways of exercising power for his entire

[9] Simon Leys: *Broken Images: Essays on Chinese Culture and Politics*, New York 1979, 129.

[10] Nearing quoted in Mosher, 100.

[11] Lewis S. Feuer: "The Fellow Traveller," *Survey* (London), Spring–Summer 1974, 210.

[12] Jung Chang and Jon Halliday: *Mao: The Unknown Story*, New York 2005, 419. Ross Terrill also noted that "Such an actor-thinker [i.e., Mao] is out of sympathy with the abstract intellectual. He is military-minded; the sword lies by the history book" (*Mao: A Biography*, Stanford CA 1999, 462).

life.[13] His unattractive traits of character were not widely, if at all, known by his Western admirers.

Simon Leys too was judgmental:

> In three disasters of genius, the Hundred Flowers, the Great Leap Forward and the "Cultural Revolution," Mao managed first to strangle intellectual creativity ... then to break the impetus of the national economy ... by plunging the countryside into famine ... and finally to throw the whole country into a bloody, monstrous chaos which was to cause suffering to millions of innocent people.[14]

Over time Mao's policies led to tens of millions of unnatural deaths, putting him at the top of the list of ideologically inspired mass murderers of all times, considerably exceeding the death toll exacted by Hitler and Stalin respectively. Mao's personal attributes were also highly unappealing, even by the standards of dictators such as Hitler, Stalin, or Pol Pot. He was not only power-hungry, ruthless, and duplicitous, but lecherous and self-indulgent as well. Unlike Hitler, Stalin, Castro, and Che Guevara, and some other powerful leaders,[15] Mao had no discernible puritanical traits and displayed monumental self-indulgence: "When it came to personal lifestyle ... [he] indulged every whim in his daily life ... He was a gourmet, and had his favourite foods shipped in from all over the country." He had numerous lavish villas on scenic spots all over the country, and had swimming pools built if they didn't have one. Since he didn't like taking baths he had his servants rub him daily with a hot towel. He was also a voracious and promiscuous sexual predator (unlike the other dictators mentioned), surrounding himself with young

[13] Chang and Halliday, 13–14. However, Richard Baum (not an admirer of Mao) believed that their book offered a "starkly negative portrait of Mao" and "its prevailing narrative tone was polemical and tendentious." But he also noted that the book "presented a good deal of important and new factual material about Mao" (*China Watcher: Confessions of a Peking Tom*, Seattle 2010, 222).

[14] Leys 1979, 55.

[15] A lesser-known figure, Ferenc Szalasi, the Hungarian Nazi leader who briefly ruled and terrorized the country during the last six months of World War II, also displayed some puritanical inclinations. He averred, "I did not want to have a child to avoid the possibility that some day my wife would say: 'please consider your son, take a different path!' I did not want to have a child to restrain me from anything." He also shared with other dictators a difficulty expressing his feelings. He wrote in his diary: "My moods fluctuate. I have a vigorous inner life. But it is very difficult to express my feelings. It took years before I could say to my wife: 'I love you.' I was always afraid that the feeling would be expressed in a distorted way and therefore I preferred to stifle it" (quoted in Bela Vinceller: *Szalasi Hat Honapja: 1944. Oktober – 1946. Majus* [The Six Months of Szalasi: 1944 October–1945 May], Budapest 1996, 47, 48. Translated by the author.

women and using the "army entertainment groups [as] procurement agencies."[16]

According to his doctor, "he was happiest and most satisfied with several young women simultaneously sharing his bed. He encouraged his sexual partners to introduce him to others for shared orgies." He was always surrounded by young women and, given the high volume of promiscuous sexual activities, venereal disease was frequent. However, "the young women were proud to be infected. The illness, transmitted by Mao, was a badge of honor, testimony to their close relationship with the Chairman."[17]

These personal proclivities were not incompatible with favoring and promoting puritanical policies and behavior for the masses, and with seeking to eliminate any reference to matters sexual from literary works.[18] Mao, like Stalin, was "determined to play a leading role as a cultural critic and arbiter ... [and] often intervened in discussions on film, literature and philosophy."[19]

The highly critical portrayal of Mao by the biographers Chang and Halliday quoted above was challenged and questioned by a group of China scholars, who favored what they considered to be a more balanced and favorable judgment of Mao's historical record.[20] The volume expressing these sentiments contains, in addition to the editors' introduction, twelve critical reviews of the biography and two positive ones.

There were several objections voiced by the critics. In the first place they argued that Mao's personality as portrayed in this biography is oversimplified, one-dimensional, and distorted, and that the authors greatly overstate the impact of his negative personality traits on his policies. They concurred that Chang and Halliday exaggerated the importance

[16] Chang and Halliday, 329, 330–331, 331, 332, 333.

[17] Zhisui, 358, 363, 407.

[18] Bruce Mazlish wrote: "Mao tightened the screw on the repression of sexual feelings, even seeking to eliminate its [*sic*] presence in literary works" (*The Revolutionary Ascetic: Evolution of a Political Type*, New York 1976, 210). All totalitarian systems favored such puritanical policies. The so-called positive heroes in Soviet (and other communist) novels were invariably indifferent to carnal pleasure, immune to romantic involvements. They preferred to invest their emotional energies in collective, political goals and gratifications. Nazi authorities promoted sex as procreation and disapproved of hedonistic promiscuity.

[19] Jonathan Spence: *Mao Zedong*, New York 1999, 128.

[20] Gregor Benton and Lin Chun eds.: *Was Mao Really a Monster? The Academic Response to Chang and Halliday's Mao: The Unknown Story*, London 2010. The editors admitted (in the introduction) that "for the most part" the critics "confine[d] themselves to questioning Chang and Halliday's methods and approaches" rather than the overall assessment of the system under Mao.

of Mao's personality at the expense of the historical, social, cultural, and political variables and circumstances that influenced and shaped conditions in China while he was in power. David Goodman, one of the critics, called the book "demonography."

Second, the critics charged that Chang and Halliday ignored the ideological determinants of Mao's policies, due to their focus on his vileness and power-hunger. Andrew Nathan suggested that these authors lost sight of "the larger forces of history that some might think explain the violence ... [as well as] the sociological or institutional explanations." Likewise it is difficult to dispute Jonathan Spence's point that "by focusing so tightly on Mao's vileness – to the exclusion of all other factors – the authors undermine much of the power their story might have had. By seeking to demonstrate that Mao started out as a vile person and stayed vile throughout his life, the authors deny any room for change, whether growth or degeneration." Gregor Benton and Steve Tsang argued that "Chang and Halliday merely invert the error of Mao worshipers. Where the worshipers imply that Mao sprang from the womb a Marxist, Chang and Halliday argue that Mao sprang from the womb a monster." Even Arthur Waldron, author of the only overwhelmingly positive review in the volume, observed that there is

> no real discussion of social or cultural forces. Instead, the human actor is everything ... The stress on conspiracy and personal politics to the exclusion of nearly everything else is a weakness, perhaps the greatest weakness of Chang and Halliday's account ... [They] describe the evil man, but never attempt to probe the origins of his evil or to explain why it spread through Chinese society.[21]

Third, the critics claimed that the book's methodology is flawed, that the authors misuse and misinterpret source materials, quote out of context, and ignore sources that do not support their biased predisposition. At the same time, most of these critics suggested or implied that they too have been critical of Mao's destructive policies yet found the portrait drawn by Chang and Halliday incomplete and misleading. Finally, the critics deplored the absence of any reference to other available Western scholarly works on the subject.

Several of these critics insisted that a more balanced view of Mao and China under his control ought to take into account external circumstances that would help to explain his harsh domestic policies. Thus the editors wrote that "a balanced view of China ... after 1949 would also give full

[21] Ibid., 22, 39, 43, 92, 171, 172.

weight to the international environment. Blockades and threats by foreign powers created a fear of subversion that degenerated ... into cruel hysteria. Political controls tightened ever further." Delia Davin argued in a similar spirit that Mao's "preoccupation with military development must be understood against both the humiliation and military defeat by the British, French, Russians and Japanese suffered by China in the nineteenth century and the vulnerability of the People's Republic in its early years to the hostility of the West, in particular the United States." These points are reminiscent of the alleged mitigating circumstances invoked by Western defenders of Stalin's repressive policies in the 1930s.

The balanced view of Mao these authors advocated should also have included discussion of his alleged accomplishments. The editors believe that "Mao is inseparable from China's national and social progress." Delia Davin suggested that "although he [Mao] was responsible for millions of deaths, his regime also brought about huge improvements in the lives of his fellow countrymen." Mao also gets points for "reuni[fying] China" and making it "a force to be reckoned with."[22]

The editors, and several contributors to the volume, were particularly incensed by Chang and Halliday comparing Mao to Hitler and Stalin. They found it "unacceptable to put Mao at the top of a league of modern atrocities without due regard for historical perspective, given that the twentieth century is littered with such tragedies and evils." Such pleading overlooked the fact that all moral outrages, evils, and atrocities had, and have, a historical context and counterparts that can be used to caution against being unduly judgmental; the abundance of such outrages lends itself to relativize any particular atrocity or outrage. Along these lines, the editors also claimed – without quantitative substantiation – that the death toll of the British Empire "is at least as deplorable as China's." It was further proposed by Jin Xiaoding that, unlike Hitler, Mao did not deliberately kill people, the deaths caused by the famine were due to "mismanagement" – "there is no proof that he *intended* to let people to die or was indifferent to their deaths." This is a flimsy argument from the moral point of view since decision-makers and power-holders (and human beings in general) are generally held accountable for the results or consequences of their actions, and not for their putative intentions, however lofty they might have been. Time and again defenders of Mao in this volume (and elsewhere) fall back on alluding to his good intentions.

[22] Ibid., 2, 8, 17–18, 20.

Of all the contributors to the volume, only Arthur Waldron pointed out that there has been a long-standing reluctance to recognize, let alone condemn, the mass murders of communist regimes and that "only the Nazi horror is regularly acknowledged and truly well known," presumably because it would have been difficult to credit the Nazis with good intentions. Unlike all the other contributors Waldron did not hesitate to assert that "Mao was the greatest mass murderer of the twentieth century ... Mao set his numerical targets openly and stressed the 'revolutionary' importance of killing."[23]

While some of the critiques of Chang and Halliday were reasonable – especially of the over-emphasis on personality at the expense of other factors and the neglect of competing scholarly sources – the vehemence of the critics' indignation calls into question their scholarly impartiality. It is also noteworthy that almost every reviewer began by pointing out, with apparent irritation, that the book was a widely publicized best-seller, favorably reviewed in non-scholarly publications by writers without scholarly credentials. It cannot be ruled out that the great commercial success of such a supposedly flawed book also interfered with its dispassionate evaluation by some of these authors. Most difficult to determine is the influence of the political position of the critics, that is to say, to what, if any, degree the far more favorable view held by some of them of Mao contributed to their fierce reaction to the negative portrait Chang and Halliday presented.

Most problematic has been the argument repeatedly made (in this book and elsewhere) that Mao's defects, or crimes, must be weighed against his accomplishments, that is to say, these accomplishments ought to make us less judgmental of him. In the first place it remains a matter of dispute what, and how enduring, his true accomplishments were. Even if we grant that they include unifying China, equalizing the status of women, reducing socio-economic inequalities, improving health care and access to education (all of these to a debatable degree), it may be asked how such accomplishments could *morally* neutralize or balance the imposition of an exceptionally repressive and intolerant system of government and the attendant severe deprivations inflicted on the entire population? Can they balance the loss of millions of lives as a result of profoundly wrongheaded policies (such as the Great Leap Forward and the Cultural Revolution), regardless of their supposed objectives?

[23] Ibid., 9, 10, 158, 165, 170.

It is to be noted here that Jonathan Mirsky, well-known and widely recognized longtime observer of China, had a positive response to *Mao: The Unknown Story* and its emphasis on the inhumane policies of Mao. He wrote:

> Only now [in this book, that is] has Mao received the historical coup de grace. No one argues any more that even though Hitler, Stalin or Pol Pot did terrible things, they were somehow "great." ... But ... Mao is often praised, after his brutality has been acknowledged, as a visionary, poet, calligrapher, guerilla chieftain, military genius, unifier ... The central thesis of this biography is that Mao was as evil as Hitler and Stalin. Some will dismiss this as a hatchet job, meaning that Mao cannot have been that bad. He was ... Chang is right to claim that Mao "was as evil as Hitler or Stalin, and did as much damage to mankind as they did." ... [W]hat Chang and Halliday have done is immense and surpasses, as a biography, all that has gone before.[24]

In the final analysis it is very likely that the moral balance sheet of Mao would not be significantly more favorable even if Chang and Halliday had paid more attention to the larger context and all the relevant historical, social, and political variables, and less attention to his personality.

MAO AND POLITICAL VIOLENCE

Mao's attitude toward political violence (and its impact on his image) deserves special attention as it was not fully defined and encompassed by the ruthlessness and taken-for-granted subordination of means to ends characteristic of all dictators. According to several reports there was an additional element of cruelty and apparent pleasure taken in witnessing and initiating the mistreatment of human beings. Ross Terrill (another biographer) noted that "it was Mao's dirty secret that he saw the necessity of – indeed he exulted in – violence. He forged ahead of others in the CCP [the Chinese Communist Party] by leaving them in Shanghai and taking a gun to the countryside."[25] According to Chang and Halliday, in the early days of the revolution "public execution rallies had become a feature of local life since Mao's arrival and he had demonstrated a penchant for slow killing ... he did not invent public executions, but added to this ghastly tradition ... organized rallies, and in this way made killing compulsory viewing for a large part of the population." He expressed "a special fondness" for using wooden spears for the execution of a particular

[24] Jonathan Mirsky: "The Truth About Mao," *The Independent* (London), May 29, 2005.
[25] Terrill, 460.

county chief and allegedly observed the actual procedure. Chang and Halliday further noted that as regards his "affinity" with "Leninist violence," Mao did not come to violence via theory. The propensity sprang from his character, and was to have a profound impact on his future methods of rule." Ian Buruma (not considered an inveterate Mao hater) made a similar point: "Since the 1920s Mao had reveled in violence for its own sake, as a cleansing expression of revolutionary zeal. As was true in fascism, collective brutality had an aesthetic appeal."[26]

Richard Solomon concurred: "it was Mao above all others who perceived the absolute necessity of conflict and hostility for social change ... and vehemently encouraged the display of aggressive feelings among the broad masses of Chinese people." In turn Andrew Walder wrote that "Mao's conviction that only violent conflict could bring about genuine social change and liberate the oppressed" was one of his "core ideas ... The young Mao insisted that violence in the course of rebellion was an inevitable by-product of social change and it should never be considered as deplorable 'excesses.' "

Mao shared Stalin's idea that the class struggle intensifies "as the final push to socialism approaches."[27] On a particular occasion, "he invoked the will of the people to justify more shootings: 'The people say that killing counter-revolutionaries is even more joyful than a good downpour.' "[28] Bertrand Russell's observation about such attitudes may here be recalled: "The infliction of cruelty with a good conscience is a delight to the moralists."[29] Or, as Lifton wrote: "Any violation of the individual becomes acceptable if in the service of the larger vision. As a Red Guard was once quoted as saying: 'So long as it is revolutionary, no action is a crime.' The goal of each person, the Chinese press made clear, was to become a 'stainless screw' in the 'locomotive of revolution.' "[30]

As in the Soviet Union during the 1930s, in China too quotas were used

> to eliminate all the enemies of the party. Mao handed down a killing quota ... By the end of 1951 close to 2 million people had been murdered, sometimes during public rallies in stadiums ... the first decade of Maoism was one of the worst

[26] Chang and Halliday, 41–42, 54, 317; Ian Buruma: "China: Reeducation Through Horror," *New York Review of Books*, January 9, 2014, 39.

[27] Solomon quoted in Mazlish, 162; Walder, 336–337.

[28] Dikotter, 94.

[29] Russell quoted in Steven Pinker: *The Blank Slate: The Modern Denial of Human Nature*, New York 2002, 270.

[30] Robert Jay Lifton: *Revolutionary Immortality: Mao Tse-Tung and the Chinese Cultural Revolution*, New York 1968, 59–60.

tyrannies in the history of the twentieth century, sending to an early grave at least 5 million civilians.

Dikotter further wrote that

Mao handed down a killing quota as a rough guide to action ... His subordinates kept track of local killing rates ... occasionally negotiating for a higher quota ... As with land reform, leaders everywhere were afraid of falling behind, comparing their performance with that of others. Villages, counties and provinces emulated each other, preferring to kill too many rather than too few ... [Likewise during the Cultural Revolution – P.H.] Mao had set a quota on the number of rightists and every unit in the country had to meet it. The criteria for identifying a rightist were so vague that they could potentially include almost everyone who had ever voiced an opinion.[31]

During the Cultural Revolution in the mid and late 1960s Mao explicitly encouraged the Red Guards to take violent action. Summarizing these and other events, Chang and Halliday concluded that "in the years from when Mao started the Purge [the Cultural Revolution – P.H.] until his death in 1976, at least 3 million people died violent death ... The killings were ... the direct work of Mao's reconstructed regime." In the late 1960s "'model demonstrations of killing' were staged by the authorities to show people how to apply maximum cruelty, and in some cases police supervised the killings"[32] According to Chinese estimates "nearly *a hundred million* people were ... involved in the violence of the 'Cultural Revolution' – either as active participants or victims."[33]

Fairbank, ruefully reassessing the implications of his earlier upbeat views of Mao's system (quoted earlier), wrote in his memoirs:

The extensive record of such savagery in the Cultural Revolution brings us to the rim of an abyss of incomprehension. Beating to death is not as simple as trigger pulling ... For Chinese youths to beat to death innocent people simply because they were educated poses a problem like that of the holocaust. When the Nazis lit their gas ovens for the Final Solution, where was the influence of Christianity? In the country best known for its esteem and pursuit of education, when Chinese levelers vented their fury upon the educated, where was the

[31] Dikotter, x, xiii, 87, 90, 293.

[32] Chang and Halliday, 517, 544, 547.

[33] Leys 1985, 166–167. For further assessments of other disastrous policies of Mao, see Yang Jisheng: "China's Great Shame," *New York Times*, November 14, 2012; Arthur Waldron: "Starving in China," *New Criterion*, May, 2013; Ian Johnson: "China: More Than You Ever Imagined," review of Yang Jisheng's book *The Great Chinese Famine*, *New York Review of Books*, November 22, 2012. Johnson wrote: "The famine grew out of Mao's desire to speed up China's development and force it into a utopian Communist vision" (ibid., 30).

influence of Confucianism? There was some explanation to do. Understanding China did not seem to become easier as history unfolded.[34]

But in the same memoirs Fairbank also wrote that "to respond to China's revolution with understanding, not with warfare or hysteria, was a national task." To be sure, he voiced these sentiments in a section of the book dealing with the late 1950s, before the Cultural Revolution erupted and its destructiveness came to be widely recognized in the Western world. Similar sentiments apparently persisted throughout his life, as reflected in the concluding passages of his memoirs: "Yet the final message, I think, is positive. The Chinese revolution is much more our friend than our enemy. It is peculiarly self-absorbed and nonaggressive abroad. As we grow closer we can help each other."[35] Some of these sentiments could be considered wishful thinking, others were plainly wrong, as has become clear in the twenty-first century.

In a 1973 review of Bao Ruo-wang's *Prisoner of Mao* (a Chinese Gulag account that earned Fairbank the displeasure of the Chinese authorities and a temporary refusal of a visa), he came to the peculiar conclusion that the Chinese Gulag was more humane than the Soviet.[36] This puzzling assessment reflects his generally favorable disposition (punctuated by occasional criticisms and reservations) about China under Mao. Presumably he felt that the good intentions of the authorities were the basis of their moral superiority over corresponding Soviet penal policies.

Less surprisingly, Edgar Snow, a lifelong admirer and supporter of Mao's China, also compared the Chinese Gulag favorably to its Soviet counterpart, offering as proof that he "*did not see* anything [in China] that looked like the barbed-wire-enclosed concentration camps I frequently saw in Stalin's Russia, guarded by high towers with machine guns." As to forced labor, Snow offered a convoluted comment that seemed to acknowledge its existence: "whether it was voluntary or involuntary [the labor, that is – P.H.] depended somewhat on the person's state of mind ... there was an unknown number of 'irregular' persons who, although they might never have been convicted of a political offense or a criminal felony, were doing full-time compulsory 'education through labor.'"[37]

34 John K. Fairbank: *Chinabound: A Fifty Year Memoir*, New York 1982, 445.

35 Ibid., 366, 458.

36 Ibid., 437–438. See also Leys 1979, 143.

37 Edgar Snow: *Red China Today*, New York 1971, 352–353 (emphasis added).

Mao's affinity with the violent solution of political problems also led him to propose a simple way to deal with the post-Stalin political unrest in the Soviet Bloc countries: "The basic problem with some Eastern European countries ... is that they didn't eliminate all those counter-revolutionaries ... Eastern Europe just didn't kill on a grand scale." This was not a failing of Pol Pot of Cambodia ("a soul-mate of Mao"), who favorably impressed him. After Pol Pot seized power "Mao congratulated him face to face ... 'you have scored a splendid victory. Just a single blow and no more classes.' "[38]

Che Guevara was another political figure Mao was fond of and with whom he shared an ideologically motivated ruthlessness and an easygoing attitude about nuclear war (see also pp. 242–243 re. Che). On Guevara's first visit to China in 1960, "Mao demonstrated uncommon intimacy with him, holding his hand while talking eagerly to him ... Guevara reciprocated, recommending copying Mao's methods in Cuba."[39]

The famine, a direct result of Mao's policies, specifically the so-called Great Leap Forward,[40] inspired little compassion in him toward the victims. Fairbank wrote: "In 1958–1960 some 20 to 30 million people lost their lives through malnutrition and famine because of the policies imposed upon them by the Chinese Communist Party ... this was one of the greatest of human disasters."[41] Mao – unlikely to be unaware of the magnitude of the disaster – reportedly advised the peasants to eat less: "Mao's answer to the peasants' plight was pitiless. They should eat sweet potato leaves, which were traditionally used only to feed pigs. 'Educate peasants to eat less, and have more thin gruel,' he instructed. 'The State should try its hardest ... to prevent peasants eating too much.' "[42]

Li Zhisui, Mao's physician, recalled that Mao "was immune to the tribulations of famine ... He seemed psychologically incapable of confronting the effects of the famine."[43] The same could be said of several sympathetic Western visitors, who either outright denied or minimized the famine. They included Francois Mitterrand, former president of France,

[38] Quoted in Chang and Halliday, 416, 626.

[39] Ibid., 572.

[40] The famine began in 1958 and peaked in 1960. In that year, according to official statistics, the "average daily calorie intake fell to 1534 ... At Auschwitz, slave laborers got between 1300 and 1700 calories per day" (Chang and Halliday, 437).

[41] John K. Fairbank and Merle Goldman: *China: A New History*, Cambridge MA 1992, 368.

[42] Quoted in Chang and Halliday, 392.

[43] Zhisui, 339.

Pierre Trudeau (future prime minister of Canada), Field Marshal Montgomery of Britain, and even Lord Boyd-Orr, the former chief of the United Nations' Food and Agricultural organization.[44] Harrison Salisbury, the well-known *New York Times* correspondent, made no mention of the famine in his 1973 travelogue (dedicated to Edgar Snow); Maurice Meisner, a historian, averred that "massive famine was avoided ... through the institution of a highly efficient system of rationing"; and Dr. Joe de Castro (another former president of the Food and Agriculture Organization of the United Nations) wrote in the fall of 1959: "New China's victory over the eternal plague of hunger is as startling an event as the conquest of interplanetary space." Edgar Snow asserted that "one of the few things I can say with certainty is that mass starvation ... no longer occurs ... I diligently searched, without success, for starving people or beggars to photograph." A "Concerned Asian Scholar," Benedict Stavis, wrote that "China is almost unique in Asia as a land free of widespread hunger, malnutrition and famine ... China is especially successful in distributing food fairly over time, space and social standing."[45]

Mao's apparent indifference to the loss of human lives in the pursuit of political objectives was further and rather strikingly demonstrated in his cost–benefit analysis of a possible nuclear war:

> Let's contemplate ... how many people would die if war breaks out ... One third could be lost; or a little more, it could be half [of the total world population, that is – P.H.] ... but imperialism would be razed to the ground and the whole world would become socialist ... We are prepared to sacrifice 300 million Chinese for the victory of world revolution.[46]

THE CULT OF MAO

Mao was further distinguished from the other dictators here considered by the nature of his cult that was, arguably, the most extreme and irrational, and the closest approximation of religious worship. Daniel Leese, a German Sinologist, wrote: "The cult of Mao was to replace all previous loyalties and belief systems ... Mao's revolutionary credentials and media campaigns resulted in a thorough sacralization of Mao." His cult, at any rate at its peak during the Cultural Revolution, "by

[44] Chang and Halliday, 460.

[45] Quoted in Mosher, 112–113, 114, 129.

[46] Quoted in Chang and Halliday, 410, 430.

its sheer extent surpassed every other twentieth-century leader cult."[47] Robert Jay Lifton concurred: "This is by no means the first time that a political leader has been made into a divinity. But few in the past could have matched Mao in the superlatives used, the number of celebrants, or the thoroughness with which the message of glory has been disseminated."[48]

Mao's megalomania found full and authentic expression in his cult, which he encouraged and apparently enjoyed. Leys suggested that "he was ... the main organizer of his own cult."[49] According to Lifton, "he actively participated in the creation of his own cult," motivated by what Lifton called the pursuit of "revolutionary immortality," by which he meant "a shared sense of participating in permanent revolutionary fermentation and transcending individual death by 'living on' indefinitely within this continuing revolution."[50] Fairbank believed that he was "entranced with himself" and "was in such a unique position of acknowledged power that he could do practically anything he wanted to."[51]

The nature of the political system in communist China has made it difficult to determine to what degree Mao's cult was a product of expedient high-level policy, or a reflection of genuine popularity, or a mixture of both. Likewise it is difficult to estimate the approximate portion of the population that worshiped Mao in the spirit promoted and depicted by the official propaganda, and how these attitudes might have fluctuated over time. Chang and Halliday believed that his deification and worship "had nothing to do with genuine popularity ... Every step in the construction of his cult was choreographed by Mao himself." They wrote that "exaltations of Mao in the press were ... force-fed the entire population, the illiterate as well as the literate, at newspaper-study sessions that were a permanent fixture of life under Mao."[52] Nonetheless it cannot be ruled out that in the earlier years of his rule and during the Cultural Revolution he enjoyed genuine popularity among undetermined portions of the population, as his physician too believed.

[47] Daniel Leese: *Mao Cult: Rhetoric and Ritual in China's Cultural Revolution*, New York 2011, 13, 260.

[48] Lifton, 63.

[49] Leys 1979, 64.

[50] Lifton, 7, 91.

[51] Fairbank and Goldman, 386.

[52] Chang and Halliday, 268, 424.

His doctor (like Chang and Halliday) was convinced that Mao's "life depended on the admiration of others. He craved affection and acclaim" and succeeded in getting it:

> For most Chinese, a mere glimpse of Mao standing impassively atop Tiananmen was a coveted opportunity ... The privileged few who actually got to shake his hand would go for weeks without washing, as friends and acquaintances came ... to touch the hand that touched the hand of Mao ... During the Cultural Revolution even the mango Mao presented to the workers became sacred objects, worshiped on altars.[53]

In the same period the party newspaper ran a quotation by him every day, 4.8 billion badges (to be worn by all citizens) featuring his head were manufactured, and 1.2 billion copies of his *Selected Works* and portraits of him were printed, exceeding the number of China's population at the time.[54] By the end of the twentieth century five billion copies of *The Little Red Book* (a collection of Mao quotations) were printed in fifty-two languages as well as in a Braille edition.[55]

Another remarkable manifestation of his cult was the practice of assembling workers "at the start of the shift ... facing a large portrait of Chairman Mao ... [who] 'asked for instructions' that would guide their conduct for the day; during the shift they would read Mao quotations posted on the walls in order to boost their enthusiasm for work." There were also "quasi-religious confessions before Mao's portrait ... turned into divine worship." In rural areas he replaced "other deities on the house altar." There were also "loyalty chambers" or "loyalty halls" and "precious red book shrines." During the Cultural Revolution various "factions started to build large-scale Mao statues ... to demonstrate their revolutionary credentials ... The use of statues to demonstrate loyalty spread rapidly among ... universities. The already existing statues provided models that were scrutinized in great detail by special delegations." The standard height of most statues was 12.26 meters.[56]

"Quotation gymnastics" was another unusual expression of the Mao cult and the effort to integrate it, in a truly totalitarian fashion, into the non-political spheres of life, in this case the daily morning gymnastics. The goal was "to develop the daily gymnastics into an occasion for praising Chairman Mao" and "to establish a revolutionary Mao Zedong Thought

[53] Zhisui, 357, 381. On the "sacralization" of mangoes, see also Leese, 219–223.

[54] Chang and Halliday, 268, 514.

[55] William Grimes: "Mandated to Be a Best Seller," *New York Times*, November 14, 2014.

[56] Walder, 278; Leese, 156–157, 210.

sports line." Specific exercises were accompanied by shouted quotes such as "political power grows from the barrel of the gun."[57]

A congratulatory telegram in 1967 from a group devoted to studying and applying his thought captures the bizarre quasi-religious flavor of this cult:

> Chairman Mao ... You are the greatest leader of the whole party, the whole army and all of our people. You are the most preeminent leader of the international proletariat. You are the reddest ... sun in our hearts! ... your compassion is deeper than the ocean and we are filled with boundless hot love for you. Thousand songs, ten thousand melodies cannot express our boundless hot love for you ... The unrestrained sea and empty sky are not enough to contain our boundless belief in you.

The president of the Chinese Academy of Sciences also had some poetic thoughts about Mao, rivaling the above:

> Mao Zedong Thought [MZT below] is rain and dew, is air and sunshine. Only with the moisture and nourishment of MZT [can we] look upon thousands of doubling waves of rice and beans. MZT is the soul, is wisdom and is strength. Only [if we are] armed with MZT will there be heroes arising without cessation. This is the new heaven and new earth of the MZT.[58]

As these quotations suggest, the Cultural Revolution probably was the period in twentieth-century history during which "language was most separated from meaning."[59] In other words, these implausible superlatives did not necessarily reflect genuine sentiments.

Mao's increasingly grotesque and irrational cult also found expression in numerous "miracles" attributed to him, including medical surgeries allegedly guided by his thought.[60] In a widely publicized case, People's Liberation Army (PLA) surgeons removed a ninety-pound tumor in a ten-hour operation from the belly of a 214-pound woman whom specialists, trained in conventional ways, were unable to help. The patient, "muttering Mao quotations," entered the operating room, the walls of which "were covered with Chairman Mao posters and quotations, thus destroying the old regulations of capitalist medical health work line."[61]

During the same period when Mao's cult was at its peak,

> All China was wearing Mao buttons and carrying his little red book and reciting his quotations, and even the simplest transactions in a shop had to include a

[57] Quoted in Leese, 202.

[58] Quoted in Leese, 184, 185.

[59] Rana Mitter, quoted in Leese, 181.

[60] For a comprehensive survey of the miracles credited to Mao, see George Urban ed.: *The Miracles of Chairman Mao: A Compendium of Devotional Literature 1966–1970*, London 1971.

[61] Leese, 193.

recitation from Mao's words ... Tens of millions of people throughout the country began each day by bowing before a picture of Mao and asking it for their day's instructions. They ended the day by bowing again, reporting to Mao and confessing their mistakes.[62]

Lin Biao (former minister of defense, vice-president of the Communist Party) averred that "The best weapon of our troops is not the airplane, cannon, tank or atomic bomb, but the thought of Mao Tse-tung; the greatest fighting force is man armed with the thought of Mao Tse-tung, daring, not afraid of death."[63]

It remains difficult to ascertain in what manner Mao's motivation combined megalomania with political expediency.[64] As to the circumstances encouraging this megalomania and its consequences, Jonathan Spence wrote:

Both the Hundred Flowers movement and the launching of the Great Leap show Mao more and more divorced from any true reality check. His scientific speculations, philosophical musings, and economic projections ... [were] extremely simple, if not simple-minded. And he himself seemed to care less and less for the consequences that might spring from his own erratic utterances.[65]

WESTERN MISCONCEPTIONS OF MAO

Once more we must ask what prompted and enabled many Western intellectuals to admire or revere a human being such as Mao, and to project upon him an abundance of appealing traits of character he did not possess? What combination of ignorance, wishful thinking, and projection made possible this reverence and the attendant misreading of character? Jonathan Mirsky asked the related question: "How was it possible to overlook the reality of the Chinese Communists, a reality that should have been apparent from their own statements? ... It is painful to recall how many China specialists resisted allegations like Mosher's – and Wei Jingsheng's – that millions had died of hunger in China, or been tortured and killed, or forcibly aborted."[66]

Mirsky's answer was that the true believers and sympathizers were willing to overlook, or excuse, the atrocities and the disastrous policies of Mao and his regime because they projected on him and his system

[62] Zhisui, 507.
[63] Quoted in Lifton, 51.
[64] See also Leese, 14.
[65] Spence, 135.
[66] Mirsky 1991, 7, 15 [from printout].

an invincible idealism, "purity," and the best of all possible intentions. Mirsky wrote: "What initially bowled over many followers was the illusion that they had seen something pure." John Service (of the US Foreign Service), who visited Mao's headquarters in Yenan in 1948, told Mirsky that "the place seemed like the Christian summer camps he had experienced in his missionary youth." Sidney Rittenberg, an American true believer (until his final disillusionment after spending thirty-five years of his life in China, fifteen of them in prison), had similar impressions of the same headquarters in Yenan: "I felt a strange exultation. Everything around me seemed clean and pure. The people. Their clothes. The building. Music. Even the fierce winds and bleak landscape ... seemed unsullied to me."[67]

Edgar Snow, probably the first major Western figure to meet and admire Mao, might have had better reasons for his reverence than most of the foreigners who became Mao's admirers in later years. The roots of Snow's sympathy toward Mao and his system date back to the 1920s when he lived in China as a journalist and came to feel that "socialism [was] the logical answer to poverty and oppression." Already in 1929 he felt that "what China needed was a 'crusader, a towering pillar of strength, a practical idealist who can lead his people, out of the stench and decay'."[68] He found that "practical idealist" in Mao. In 1936 in his Yenan cave, he still seemed largely free of the corruptions of power and its perks. The somewhat romantic setting of Snow's extensive interviews with Mao was also conducive to favorable impressions that endured for the rest of his life: "During the several nightly interviews ... we were like conspirators ... huddled in that cave over that red-covered table, with sputtering candles between us – I wrote until I was ready to fall asleep." (An interpreter was provided.) As the interviews proceeded, "it was no longer 'I' but 'we' ... no longer a subjective impression of the experiences of a single life, but an objective record by a bystander concerned with the mutations of human destiny."[69]

It was in those days and weeks that Snow's lifelong commitment to Mao's China originated, subsequently fortified by more visits and his official designation as the best "friend of China" and by the privileged

[67] Quoted in Jonathan Mirsky: "Deifying Chairman Mao," *Wall Street Journal*, June 21, 2010. For a detailed discussion of Rittenberg, see Paul Hollander: *The End of Commitment*, Chicago 2006, 125–136.

[68] Quoted in J. Mirsky: "Message from Mao," *New York Review of Books*, February 16, 1989, 3, 4 [printout].

[69] Edgar Snow: *Red Star over China*, New York 1938, 123, 175.

treatment he received from the authorities.[70] Some of the impressions Mao made on Snow in the course of their numerous meetings could be generalized to the impressions that other leaders dealt with in this study made on their admirers. Most important, Snow tells us, "the role of his personality in the movement was clearly immense." More specifically,

> you feel a certain force of destiny in him ... a kind of solid elemental vitality. You feel that whatever there is extraordinary in this man grows out of the uncanny degree to which he synthesizes and expresses the urgent demands of millions of Chinese ... He appears to be quite free from symptoms of megalomania, but he has a deep sense of personal dignity.[71]

It is quite possible that in those early years the symptoms of megalomania were absent, or found limited expression (deferred until Mao came to enjoy uncontested power), or that Snow overlooked these symptoms, given his favorable disposition. At the time of his first visit, Snow found that there was "no ritual of hero-worship built up around him." If so, that too awaited the consolidation and expansion of his power. Snow also came to the conclusion that "his judgments were reached ... on the basis of reason and necessity ... He seemed to me sincere, honest and truthful in his statements." Last but not least, "Mao impressed me as a man of considerable feeling."[72]

There is no indication that in later years Snow had any second thoughts about these characterizations in light of Mao's policies such as the Great Leap Forward and the Cultural Revolution. Snow also persisted in denying the famine, writing that "there was a severe food shortage ... but 'no visible starvation and the population was in good health, as far as anyone could see.' "[73]

Another early supporter of the Chinese Revolution (and close friend of Snow) was Agnes Smedley, a radical leftist and feminist. According to her biographers, "At the peak of her fame in the later 1930s and early 1940s, Agnes Smedley was considered the John Reed of the Chinese revolution for her tireless advocacy of the Chinese Communist cause."[74] She was more deeply alienated from American society than Snow, more

[70] For example, on his 1960 visit he traveled with premier Cho En-la in his luxurious "special train," invited to accompany him on a tour of inspection of a newly built dam and reservoir (see Snow 1971, ch. 10: "Aboard the Premier's Special Train," 102–106).

[71] Snow 1938, 71, 74, 76.

[72] Ibid., 74, 77–79.

[73] Quoted in Mirsky 1989, 6 [printout].

[74] Janice and Stephen R. Mackinnon: *Agnes Smedley: The Life and Times of an American Radical*, Berkeley CA 1988, 1.

of a loner, angrier, and a genuine "maverick." She was not particularly enamored with Mao, whom she met a number of times. In this regard she differed from most admirers of communist (and other dictatorial) states whose admiration of the system and its leader was seamlessly integrated.

She was described as "impetuous, often tactless, and always restless, her behavior bordered on the melodramatic ... a self-appointed warrior." Malcolm Cowley (a more moderate leftist journalist) characterized her in 1934 as both "a dedicated working-class revolutionary" and a fanatic. An American friend "saw in her a Christian vocation of self-sacrifice" and another one described her as "a radical with a great heart, she refused to submit to any form of discipline and distrusted all political leaders." Freda Utley, a British communist (subsequently disillusioned), wrote in her 1970 memoirs:

> [Smedley was] one of the few spiritually great people I have ever met, [with] that burning sympathy for the misery and wrongs of mankind which some of the saints and some of the revolutionaries have possessed ... Unlike those doctrinaire revolutionaries who love the masses in the abstract but are cold to the sufferings of individuals, Agnes Smedley spent much of her time, energy and scant earnings in helping a multitude of individuals.

As a free-wheeling, freelance journalist Smedley spent long periods of her life in China, reporting from the front lines during the war against Japan, interviewing prominent leaders (Mao included), and organizing medical supplies for the communist forces. In 1937 she applied for membership in the Chinese Communist Party but was turned down, probably on account of her "unbridled individualism" and doubts about "her ability to accept party discipline." She was nonetheless considered "as one of the few foreign friends of the Chinese Communist movement" in the 1930s and 1940s. She spent several months in Yan'an in 1937 and conducted lengthy interviews with Mao and other leaders, staying close to his cave quarters. Given the physical proximity, she witnessed a revealing incident one night when Mao was caught, berated, and physically assaulted by his wife when he visited another woman in a nearby cave. We do not learn from Smedley's biography what impact the incident had on her overall assessment of Mao, but according to the biographers "she had grown bitter toward Mao Zedong, perhaps seeing him as the cause of her rejection" of her application to join the party. This setback notwithstanding, "she was determined to fight on for the Chinese revolution. But her mission would remain only a self-appointed one."

Despite this incident she wrote in a letter to a friend that "I've a calmer, more marvelous life [referring to her stay in Yan'an – P.H.] than I ever dreamed of. Neither in Shanghai nor America could I live so freely or so happily." But she was aware of her being an outsider, an "onlooker," as, for example, when she contemplated communist troops marching: "[I] realized that I can never know fully the meaning, the essence of the Chinese struggle for liberation ... I am still an onlooker ... And I hunger for a spark of vision that would enable me to see into their minds and hearts and picture their convictions about the great struggle."[75]

Smedley was different in many ways from the more recent generation of Western supporters of communist China (most of whom were academics) as regards her personality, unstable way of life, fierce idealism, and uncompromising commitment. But she shared with them a profound conviction about the evils and injustices of her own society and the part played by the global villain, capitalism. She was eager to discover and fight for alternative social-political visions and ways of organizing society.

An important part of Mao's image was that of the brilliant philosopher-king, a renaissance man (poet, theoretician, swimmer, etc.) whose thoughts "held China together," according to Jan Myrdal, the Swedish author. Dick Wilson, a British Sinologist, was certain that Mao "wanted to be remembered, above all, as a teacher." Michael Oksenberg saw him as "both a philosopher and politician ... he combined qualities which rarely coexist in one being ... He was an inquisitive thinker who savored power, a visionary who remained an activist."[76] C.P. Fitzgerald, an English historian of China, opened his book with the statement: "*The Thoughts of Mao Tsetung* have become to his own people ... what the Sayings of Confucius were to the Chinese people for the past two thousand years: the source of inspiration and guidance in matters social, political and moral."[77] Edgar Snow too believed that Mao's thoughts were the foundations of the beneficial transformations China had undergone and that they would continue to guide these processes: "A China without the corporeal Mao was an inescapable fact of the relatively near future, but Maoism was larger than Mao and would survive him."[78] That has not

[75] Ibid., 161, 186–187, 190–191, 193, 194, 197, 207, 350–351.

[76] Jan Myrdal and Gun Kessle: *The Revolution Continued*, New York 1970, 191; Dick Wilson ed.: *Mao Tse Tung in the Scales of History*, Cambridge UK 1977, 8; Michael Oksenberg in ibid., 70.

[77] C.P. Fitzgerald: *Mao Tse-tung and China*, New York 1976, 1.

[78] Snow 1971, 40.

been the case, as indicated, among other things, by the policies of the Chinese government during the decades that followed his passing.

Such reverence for Mao's ideas was somewhat surprising since, on closer inspection, they often turned out to be platitudinous or commonsensical.[79] A. James Gregor's observation is relevant here:

> Always more attractive to Western intellectuals at a distance than to any intellectuals at home, Chinese Communism reveals itself to be more shallow than that of the Soviet Union. Those Western academics who counseled us to learn penology, developmental economics, true democracy, education and the schooling of bureaucrats from Mao's Great Proletarian Cultural Revolution have long since fallen mute.[80]

Felix Greene, the British journalist, also had an exalted vision of Mao and his associates, proposing that "China is not being led by a group of men hungry for personal power ... It is, rather a leadership that has shown itself genuinely concerned with the welfare of the people ... there is no evidence of jockeying for power or of the personal rivalry." In the same spirit Fairbank dismissed the idea of a power struggle following Mao's death, suggesting that "Ford vs. Carter is a more naked power struggle than anything going on in Peking."[81] Fairbank implied that in such a comparison of American and Chinese political practices, the Chinese ones were superior.

Orville Schell, the American author and journalist, took a startlingly religious view of Mao replete with Christian imagery:

> It often seemed that Mao had become China ... China might be ... so firmly anchored by one charismatic personality that it might never survive his demise ... even prior to his death, Mao had *transcended his own personality* ... Mao was a thinker as well as a doer. He conceived of the Chinese revolution and then helped it to happen. And, in the process, the *thought of Chairman Mao became inculcated in almost every Chinese. The word almost literally became*

[79] Snow cited with apparent admiration the following pearls of Mao's wisdom in his introduction to Part II of his 1971 book: "Of all things in the world people are the most important. We believe that revolution can change everything ... 'Grasp firmly.' One cannot get a grip on something with an open hand. When the hand is clenched as if grasping something but it is not clenched tightly, there is still no grip ... Guard against arrogance. For anyone in a leading position this is a matter of principle and an important condition for maintaining unity ... We must firmly uphold the truth and truth requires a clear-cut stand. A blunt knife draws no blood" (cited in Snow 1971, 133–134).

[80] A. James Gregor: *A Place in the Sun: Marxism and Fascism in China's Long Revolution*, Boulder CO 2000, xii–xiii.

[81] Felix Greene: *China: The Country Americans Are Not Allowed to Know*, New York 1961, 143–144; John K. Fairbank, "On the Death of Mao," *New York Review of Books*, October 13, 1976, 3.

flesh. And it seemed clear, even before Mao died, that his death could not erase the way in which *he had almost become transubstantiated in his people*.[82]

Jan Myrdal was assured that Mao's legacy would endure since he "solved the problem how ... the revolution can be prevented from degenerating." Myrdal shared a deep-seated, optimistic future orientation with Edgar Snow, who concluded his book on a similarly optimistic note: "The movement for social revolution in China may suffer defeats, may temporarily retreat ... may even for a period be submerged ... but it will not only continue to mature ... it will eventually win simply because ... the basic conditions which have given it birth carry within themselves the dynamic necessity for triumph."[83]

Hewlett Johnson (dean of Canterbury), who admired both Stalin and Mao, replicated his spectacular misconceptions of Stalin in his views of Mao. What struck him most about Mao "was something no picture had ever caught, an inexpressible look of kindness and sympathy, an obvious preoccupation with the needs of others." He was convinced that his views of the great leader coincided with those of his subjects: "All men ... regard Mao as the symbol of their deliverance, the man who shared their troubles and has raised their burdens."[84]

Similarly reminiscent of the misreading of Stalin's personality was the belief Dick Wilson shared with some other visiting intellectuals, namely, that Mao "often exhibited a refreshing personal humility" and disapproved of his own veneration.[85] The English literary scholar, A.L. Rowse (no China expert), also believed that "an endearing feature of the man [Mao] is that he would refuse to accept the tribute 'superman'." Rowse himself had no doubt that "Mao is by far the greatest man in the world today – probably the greatest of this century." These startling judgments included the claim that he was "pragmatic and human" and that "his superhuman achievement [was] ... the capacity to compromise."[86]

Such attributions of humility and modesty were not limited to Mao. Sympathizers with various dictators, if they acknowledged that they were subject of a cult, insisted that it was a genuine reflection of the dictators' popularity and they discouraged it. In fact there is evidence to suggest that most of the dictators here considered endorsed and encouraged their

[82] Orville Schell: *In the People's Republic: An American's Firsthand View of Living and Working in China*, New York 1977, vii–viii (emphasis added).

[83] Myrdal and Kessle, 187; Snow 1938, 494–495.

[84] Hewlett Johnson: *China's New Creative Age*, London 1953, 153.

[85] Wilson, 2; see also Concerned Asian Scholars: *China!* New York 1972, 46.

[86] A.L. Rowse: "Foreword," in Fitzgerald, v, vi.

own cult and often assisted the propaganda apparatus in creating and perpetuating it.[87]

Richard Wolin's observation about French college students of the late 1960s helps to understand the political sympathies and misjudgments of the more recent generation of Western intellectuals (or aspiring intellectuals) similarly uninformed about the realities of life under Mao, including the Cultural Revolution:

> the less information the students possessed concerning the People's Republic [of China] ... the more leeway they had to project their own utopian hopes and dreams ... Cultural Revolutionary China became a projection screen ... for their innermost radical political hopes and fantasies ... China became the embodiment of a "radiant utopian future." ... Maoism seemed the last best hope for a utopian alternative to the dislocations and disappointments of "really existing democracy."[88]

Leftist students at the University of California, Berkeley, displayed similar sentiments. Richard Baum wrote: "for some of my Berkeley classmates – the left-wing *philosophes sois-disants* and radical acolytes of Herbert Marcuse, Che Guevara and Franz Fanon – the Maoist vision of an egalitarian future free from egoism, greed and the 'revisionist' pursuit of material self-interest trumped all considerations of human cost and collateral damage." More generally speaking (and transcending the radical student attitudes at Berkeley), "because the Cultural Revolution coincided with rising popular backlash against US participation in the Vietnam war, there was a tendency in some left-wing academic circles *to suspend disbelief* and embrace the Maoist model as an alternative to American capitalism."[89]

Even after the heady days of the late 1960s and early 1970s when the ravages of the Cultural Revolution could no longer be ignored, denied,

[87] The roots of Mao's cult go back to 1943 when his "senior colleagues began to rewrite Chinese Party history so that Mao would be forever at the center." The new 1945 preamble to the Party Constitution stated that the Party "takes Mao Zedong's thought ... as the guide for all this work" (Quoted in Spence, 101). Similarly Stalin's cult was enshrined in a new version of the Party history that elevated Stalin's role over all others. Stalin himself wrote or edited passages that glorified him. (On Stalin's encouraging his own cult, see Jan Plamper: *The Stalin Cult*, New Haven CT 2012, esp. 120–135.) There is no evidence whatsoever that Mussolini and Hitler were averse to their veneration.

[88] Wolin 2010, 3, 125, 155. Ian Buruma too noted the same phenomenon: "One conspicuous feature of the European Maoists in the 1970s was their obliviousness to actual conditions in China" ("The Man Who Got It Right," *New York Review of Books*, August 15, 2013, 68).

[89] Baum, 10, 11 (emphasis added).

or minimized, some American academic intellectuals continued to harbor positive feelings about Mao and his system because of the enduring appeal of his ideals and intentions. Thus it was a matter of great concern for Arif Dirlik and Maurice Meisner (and a threat to their deepest beliefs) that a harsh critique of the Cultural Revolution could lead to the wholesale rejection of the ideals these dubious policies were supposed to serve:

> A further and more serious difficulty with contemporary criticism of the Cultural Revolution is that for many it provides an occasion for the wholesale repudiation of the history of the socialist revolution in China and, along with it, socialism in general ... It is ... nearly impossible to dismiss the Cultural Revolution as an historical aberration without casting doubts about the validity and utility of China's socialist revolution as a whole ... there is an intimate connection between the legitimacy of the Cultural Revolution and the legitimacy of China's socialist revolution as a whole, and what is at stake ... is not merely a repudiation of the Cultural Revolution but a break with China's socialist revolutionary tradition, perhaps the most heroic revolutionary heritage in our century.[90]

There was indeed a close connection between the Cultural Revolution and the nature of the Chinese political system under Mao as a whole, but its implications were unacceptable for these authors, fixated as they were on the underlying good intentions and ideals that somehow sanitized (in their eyes) the aberrations they acknowledged and deplored. Dirlik also wrote: "It has become fashionable in recent years to portray the Cultural Revolution as an aberration in the history of Chinese socialism. The Cultural Revolution was to end up as an aberration, a parody of its own aspirations; *but* that is no reason to deny the reality of the problems it sought to resolve or *the seriousness of its intentions*." Those good intentions mattered most for these and other sympathizers (of other similar systems as well). The appeal of the lofty ideals best explain why, time and again, they were drawn to, and willing to suspend critiques of these repressive political systems.

Meisner further suggested that "What distinguished Mao's Marxism was a unique attempt, however flawed in practice, to reconcile the means of modern economic development with the ends of socialism."[91] Apparently the deeply flawed practice he acknowledged raised no troubling questions for Meisner about the nature of the ends that inspired, or invited, these practices, or about the recurring difficulty to reconcile ends and means, and about the proliferation of the unintended consequences

[90] Arif Dirlik and Maurice Meisner eds.: *Marxism and the Chinese Experience*, Armonk NY 1989, 12, 14.

[91] Ibid., 29, 106 (emphasis added).

of the pursuit of highly ambitious social-political agendas. As Dikotter wrote: "there was no end to statements of good intent accompanied by ever more decrees, rules and regulations that would nudge China forward to the road to communism. It was all about the world in the making, not the world as it was."[92]

American sympathizers were not in a position to confront and evaluate the conflict between ends and means, ideals and realities, unlike the early generation of idealistic Chinese intellectuals who could, Dikotter wrote,

> see revolution in action. Few were prepared for the sheer violence of land distribution, as victims were beaten, tortured, hanged and sometimes shot. All had to reconcile the huge gap between the propaganda, on the one hand, and the reality of the revolution, on the other. They had to steel themselves, silencing the doubts that welled up when they witnessed physical abuse, constantly reciting the vocabulary of class struggle to justify the violence. A vision of communist plenty for all had to be conjured up to see past the squalor of denunciation rallies and organized plunder.[93]

While it would be unfair to suggest that Meisner and those who shared his outlook were totally unconcerned with the relationship between ends and means, it seems safe to say that in their eyes the appealing aspects of the ends overshadowed the failings of the means. Meisner's positive estimate of the accomplishments of "Chinese socialism" apparently extended to the Soviet case, as he reminded (approvingly) the reader of the warnings of E.H. Carr, "issued upon completing his monumental history of Soviet Russia." Carr wrote: "The danger is not that we shall draw a veil over the enormous blots on the record of the Revolution, over the cost in human suffering, over the crimes committed in its name. The danger is that we shall be tempted to forget altogether, and to pass over in silence, its immense achievements."[94] This was, it seems, exactly what Meisner too thought about the Chinese revolution. It is difficult to avoid the impression that deep down Meisner felt (like Carr about the Soviet system) that Mao's accomplishments outweighed their human costs, that in the final analysis the violence and suffering, occasioned by, among other things, the Cultural Revolution, did *not* discredit "Chinese socialism," or compel a far-reaching rethinking of its goals and ideals. In fewer words, Edgar Snow took the same position: "they [the Chinese communists – P.H.] had

[92] Dikotter, 259.
[93] Ibid., 178.
[94] Quoted in Dirlik and Meisner, 18–19.

evolved a domestic program based on Marxism – a harsh and relentless program but workable."[95]

The importance of good intentions, of lofty purposes, was also apparent in a defense of the Great Leap Forward put forward by Gregor Benton and Lin Chun. While they admitted that "it went catastrophically wrong due to the manner of its implementation," it was nonetheless "a fundamentally rational scheme to mobilize surplus rural labor ... to create local industry, improve rural infrastructure and achieve national self-sufficiency."

These authors felt strongly that any comparison of the victims of the Chinese famine with those of the Holocaust was inappropriate since the *goal* of the Holocaust was obviously evil – mass murder – whereas the adverse effects of the Great Leap Forward were wholly unintended. While this was literally true, the comparison raises the important question of what moral weight should be attached to well-intended actions or policies that have disastrous consequences? The same authors acknowledged both "the disastrous outcome of the Great Leap Forward and the excesses of the Cultural Revolution," but nonetheless believed that "the CCP's achievements outweighed its failures."[96]

According to Bill Martin (co-author of Bob Avakian, perhaps the most ardent American Maoist), the Cultural Revolution was guided by the principle (enshrined in an official document of the period, the "Sixteen Point Decision") that "where there is debate, it should be conducted by reasoning not by force" – a proposition that clearly failed to inform the conduct of the Red Guards. Martin insisted that the Cultural Revolution was not defined by "violence and excess," it was "overwhelmingly a mass political and ideological movement and struggle ... not a plot, purge, or orgy of violence. The violence that did occur was sporadic and limited ... it was a real social revolution. Hundreds of millions were inspired by its egalitarian objectives and values."[97] As to Bob Avakian, he was

"a veteran of the Berkeley Free Speech Movement," chairman of the Revolutionary Communist Party USA and author of *Mao Tsetung's Immortal Contributions*. He was one of the hardcore radicals who persevered in "celebrat[ing] the virtues of Maoism."[98]

[95] Snow 1971, 675.
[96] Benton and Chun, 6–7, 9 [printout].
[97] Bill Martin: "Introduction," in Bob Avakian and Bill Martin: *Marxism and the Call of the Future*, Chicago 2005, xxxv, xxxvi–xxxvii.
[98] Baum, 41.

He was also described as "a visionary leader of a Maoist vanguard party" who "has written the most comprehensive account of Mao's theoretical contribution to Marxism."[99]

Another revealing illustration of deep-seated beliefs seemingly invulnerable to objective realities is provided by Joan Hinton,[100] an American physicist who worked on the Manhattan Project and moved to China in 1948 as a protest against what she considered her own country's profound social, political, and moral failings. A prototypical true believer, she spent the rest of her life in China toiling in an agricultural commune. Thirty years after the Cultural Revolution she still clung to beliefs most Chinese had abandoned (if they ever held them). She remained unwavering in her "devotion to Maoist ideals" and averred that "Mao started the Cultural Revolution to cure the disparity between the few and the many ... How could that be wrong?"[101] She also said: "Of course I was 100% behind everything that happened in the Cultural Revolution – it was a terrific experience."[102] Slavoj Zizek shared these sentiments: "Along with [Alain] Badiou, Zizek celebrates Mao's Cultural Revolution as 'the last truly great revolutionary explosion of the twentieth century.' "[103]

In light of these and other misapprehensions and glorifications of the Cultural Revolution, the reader may be reminded that, in the words of Fairbank,

> whatever may have been Mao's romantic intentions [regarding the Cultural Revolution – P.H.], the Red Guards turned to destructive activities that became a brutal reign of terror, breaking into homes ... destroying books and manuscripts, humiliating, beating and even killing the occupants ... [they] roamed through the streets ... accosting and dealing their kind of moral justice to people with any touch of foreignism [*sic*] or intellectualism ... as evidence has piled up, the Cultural Revolution is now understood not as a pursuit of abstract ideals but as "an unprecedented wave of state-instigated persecution, torture, gang warfare and mindless violence".[104]

99 Raymond Lotta: "Preface," to Avakian and Martin, xi, xiii.

100 She was the sister of William Hinton, also an admirer of Mao's China known for his book (*Fanshen*, 1966) that chronicled what he considered the inspiring transformation of a Chinese village under the communist authorities.

101 Seth Faison: "History's Fellow Travelers Cling to Mao's Road," *New York Times*, August 28, 1996.

102 Cited in Mirsky 2010.

103 Zizek quoted in John Gray: "The Violent Visions of Slavoj Zizek," *New York Review of Books*, July 12, 2012, 23.

104 Fairbank and Goldman, 393, 402.

As these remarks suggest (and as was noted earlier), Fairbank's sentiments about Mao's China fluctuated. Nonetheless, he remained, on the whole, positively disposed. His biographer wrote:

> In May 1975 he referred to Mao as "the greatest emancipator of all times." ... The closest he came to sentimental adulation was in an essay written for the *New York Review of Books* at the time of Mao's death. He reminded his readers that ... China "has no crisis of inflation, unemployment, crime or corruption," adding that the leadership of the CCP consisted of revolutionaries, rather than ambitious individualists ... "Mao and Chou with all their faults" he concluded "may look better and better as time goes by."[105]

Few would agree today that this was a correct prediction, especially as regards Mao.

Fairbank's biographer, Paul M. Evans, was also well aware of his conflicting, or alternating, views of the nature of communist China. Evans wrote: "His views had something of a chameleon-like quality, usually close to, but never in complete harmony with, the prevailing opinion of the day ... the overall image of contemporary China that Fairbank projected in the 1970s was mixed and far from roseate." But he also pointed out that Fairbank "knew more than he was willing to say ... there was little question that his commitment to Sino-American rapprochement influenced the way in which he interpreted the evidence to his large audience."[106]

A possible key to understanding Fairbank's various assessments of communist China may be found in the last sentence of his history of China: "We outsiders can offer China advice about the overriding need for human rights, but until we set an example by properly curbing our media violence and the drug and gun industries, we can hardly urge China to be more like us. Instead we must scrutinize the adequacy of our basic assumptions about the Chinese scene."[107] These remarks are strikingly reminiscent of the sentiments of George Kennan about his own country. Kennan was another great American intellectual burdened by an oppressive awareness of the flaws of his society. He too sternly warned against being self-righteously judgmental of the Soviet system while the United States could not overcome its own grave social and moral defects.[108]

[105] Paul M. Evans: *John Fairbank and the American Understanding of Modern China*, New York 1988, 304–305.

[106] Evans, 325, 327.

[107] John K. Fairbank: *China: A New History*, Cambridge MA 1992, 423.

[108] Kennan wrote: "Show me first an America which has successfully coped with ... crime, drugs, deteriorating educational standards, urban decay, pornography and decadence of one sort or another – show me an America that ... is what it ought to be, then I will tell

Many of the appealing qualities projected upon Mao closely resembled those attributed to Stalin, including the curious belief that both of them exercised power in a new and benevolent way. John S. Service, the State Department expert on China (quoted earlier), not only believed that nobody starved in China but also discerned (rather imaginatively) a "new civility [that] may owe something to the example of a state and party that seem to prefer governing by persuasion and propaganda rather than by command and force."[109] By contrast Sartre was enamored not by civility but by "revolutionary ardor," "insurrectionary elan," and Mao's "unbending commitment to revolutionary struggle."

Sartre (like Norman Mailer) was irresistibly drawn to what he conceived of as authentic, purifying revolutionary violence that he identified with Mao and his political system (as he did with Castro). He declared that this kind of violence had a distinctly moral character: "For the Maoists ... everywhere that revolutionary violence is born among the masses it is immediately and profoundly *moral*." In Wolin's words, Sartre believed that this type of violence was "regenerative, and as such, a precondition for a reborn humanity." These sentiments also found expression in Sartre's preface to Fanon's *Wretched of The Earth* proclaiming "violence as a pivotal act of anticolonial self-affirmation."

In Sartre's view, "negotiations and compromise were distasteful atavisms of bourgeois parliamentarianism." He was especially attracted to Mao's (and Castro's) revolutionary violence because their "revolution depended not on objective conditions but on heroic acts of will," or so it seemed to him.[110] The *heroic self-assertion* that these leaders seemed to embody, and which Sartre yearned for, was a key determinant of their appeal, and in all probability he shared this attitude with many like-minded intellectuals.

Sartre's ex-cathedra pronouncements and certainties concerning the integral relationship between violence and rebirth[111] are the purest expressions of an overwhelming wish to believe that occasionally grips intellectuals in search of personal and political fulfillment. Sartre's views of rejuvenating violence are also among the best examples of an untroubled

you how we are going to defend ourselves from the Russians" (cited in *George Kennan and His Critics: Decline of the West?* Washington DC 1978, 32). While these remarks concerned Soviet–American relations, the underlying message was the same: we are not entitled to be critical of the Soviet (or any other) system given our own failings.

[109] Cited in Mosher, 134.

[110] Wolin 2010, 204, 205, 206, 207, 209, 127.

[111] Ibid., 208.

willingness to subordinate means to ends when the ends are of a utopian, secular-religious nature, even though there is no assurance whatsoever that the morally questionable means will accomplish the chosen ends.

Alain Badiou, comrade-in-arms of Slavoj Zizek (see Chapter 1), was another prominent French intellectual attracted to righteous political violence and "partial to violent philosophical imagery ... that goes hand in hand with his defense of bloodletting, or terror, in the name of 'progressive' political causes" such as the Russian Revolution, Stalin's Purges, and the Chinese Cultural Revolution. He also liked to cite Mao's warning that "the revolution is not a dinner party." Sartre doubtless agreed with his conviction (as Wolin paraphrased it) that "there is no need to renounce or to shy away from the sanguinary excesses of revolution, for violence is ... the necessary price of freeing humanity from the evils of democracy and capitalism."[112]

Badiou's profound, if muddled utopianism is further revealed in his convoluted justifications of the violence enacted during the Cultural Revolution:

> What about violence, often so extreme? The hundreds of thousands of dead? The persecutions, especially against intellectuals? One will say the same thing about them as about all those acts of violence that to this very day have marked the History of every somewhat expansive attempt to ... radically subvert the eternal order that subjects society to wealth and the wealthy, to power and ... to Capital and its servants and considers worthless ... the intelligence of workers ... and any thought that is not homogenous to the order in which the ignoble rule of profit is perpetuated. The theme of total emancipation ... is always situated *beyond Good and Evil ... The passion or the Real is devoid of morality ... Morality is a residue of the Old World.*[113]

The bottom line seems to be that violence used to bring about "total emancipation" (the goal of the Cultural Revolution, according to Badiou) deserves wholehearted support since it seeks to end age-old inequalities and injustices. The meaning of the last italicized sentence quoted above is far from clear, nor is that of "total emancipation" – a key to the utopian longings and fantasies of Badiou and others.

112 Ibid., 162, 163.

113 Badiou quoted in Wolin 2010, 164. More recently Mark Lilla wrote: "Badiou, now nearly eighty, still writes warmly about the Chinese Cultural Revolution ... It is not every day that one finds a defense of Mao's personality cult, and in quasi-theological terms." Badiou was also a "defender of the Khmer Rouge in the 1970s" (Mark Lilla: *The Shipwrecked Mind*, New York 2016, 92–93).

Louis Althusser (see also p. 31) was another once-famous French intellectual all too willing to subordinate means to the glorious ends enshrined in Marxism.[114] As he saw it, Marxist theory "contained absolute truth" and it did not matter if its attempted applications failed: "Stalin may have committed egregious crimes; the Soviet Union might be a degenerate workers' state; yet Marxism's pristine theoretical truths would persevere unscathed." Althusser was not concerned with the unity of theory and practice; the pristine theory was gratifying enough for him. In any event he approved of the "revolutionary vitality" of Mao's leadership and "one of the main reasons [he] ... admired Chinese communism was that its leaders remained unwavering Stalinists."[115]

China scholars and journalists often came to similarly dubious conclusions about conditions in communist China and the attributes of its leader. Joseph Kraft, the influential journalist, author and columnist for the *Los Angeles Times*, *Washington Post* and *New York Times*, syndicated for 200 newspapers, was among the journalists who accompanied President Nixon on his historic trip to China in 1972. Kraft intended to use the occasion to learn about Chinese society under Mao. While there is no evidence suggesting that (unlike many others visitors) he went to China with a highly favorable predisposition, it appears that ignorance, limited imagination, and the "techniques of hospitality" came to be the determinants of his assessments and generalizations the trip yielded. He wrote, among other things: "judging by what I saw and considering past hardships of this country and the standards of Communist leaders in other counties, I cannot believe that the rulers of China are the murderous butchers the American right wing is pleased to imagine."[116] Apparently, lack of information and imagination combined to give rise to his disbelief in the atrocities the Chinese authorities perpetrated before his visit. Nor can it be ruled out that his desire to disassociate himself from the American right created, or contributed to, a disposition to strive to be what he considered "fair," that is, to refrain from criticizing what he saw. It was an attitude he shared with other members of the press.[117]

[114] During the 1930s Althusser belonged to a militant Catholic organization. There was speculation, according to Wolin, that "following World War II ... [he] transposed his fervent quest for absolute truth from the Church to the Communist Party" (Wolin 2010, 121).

[115] Ibid., 120.

[116] Joseph Kraft: *The Chinese Difference*, New York 1972, 60.

[117] Mosher, vii.

The disposition to avoid being overly "judgmental" was not peculiar to Kraft. Ross Terrill, author of numerous books on China, cautioned that "a judgment about China's human rights record must be made, but only after choosing our yardstick with care. It is no good looking at your cherished values, labeling them universal values, then asking if the Chinese are human enough to adhere to such 'universal values'."[118] He shared this disposition with many sympathetic Westerners, and not only in regard to China but other repressive communist systems as well: they preferred not to criticize. It was a position apt to prevent outsiders from being critical of *any* human rights violation anywhere, as long as those violations were not in conflict with the indigenous values or customs of the perpetrators. By the same token one could take the position that Westerns should not frown on headhunters, cannibals, slavery, apartheid, clitoridectomy, the persecution of homosexuals, or any other human rights violation defined as culturally acceptable and customary in various parts of the world.

Terrill did not explain what moral or cultural standards would allow him (or anyone else) to make critical judgments of Chinese human rights violations as long as the latter were considered expressions of "cultural diversity." Simon Leys wrote:

> A logical extension of this principle would be to say that Nazi Germany should be perceived in a Hitlerian perspective, or that to understand the Soviet system we should adopt a Stalinist point of view ... Here we come to Terrill's fundamental philosophy ... Things happened in Maoist China that were ghastly by any standard of common decency ... Terrill maintains however that China being "different," such standards should not apply. Look at the cult of Mao, for instance – it was grotesque and demeaning and the hapless Chinese experienced it exactly as such. Not so, says Terrill ... being Chinese and thus different, they ought to have thoroughly enjoyed the whole exercise ... "The cult of Mao is not *incredible* as it seems outside China ... It is odd for us because we have no consciousness of Chinese social modes."[119]

Kraft was also under the impression that Maoist values "sunk roots" both "among the masses" and urban elites. Elsewhere he observed that "to a remarkable degree the Chinese accept and observe Maoist teaching." He was in no position to reach such a conclusion and offer

118 Ross Terrill ed.: "Introduction," in *The China Difference*, New York 1979, 7. Terrill, in order to illustrate cultural differences, compared American revulsion over the violence of the Cultural Revolution to Chinese condemnation of high rates of unemployment in the United States and the turning off of the electricity of some old people in New York City who could not pay their bills (ibid., 12).

119 Leys 1985, 204.

generalizations; he knew no Chinese and depended for any information about social-political conditions on his guides and the people they introduced him to. The latter included "a young woman scientist" in a May 7 School to which well-educated urban people were sent during the Cultural Revolution to be "reeducated." She assured him that "it is useful to spend time with workers and peasants. It is necessary to rotate jobs in our society ... I have benefitted from my stay here. It has remolded my whole world outlook." He also met in the May 7 School a woman who used to paint traditional scenes. She told him, "now I paint workers and peasants ... I have come to understand the real purpose of life." A middle-aged party functionary revealed to him how the Cultural Revolution taught him not to be selfish and "to serve the people body and soul." There was also "the living symbol of this Chinese miracle ... Chen Yung-kuei, an uneducated peasant ... held up by Chairman Mao as a model for all Chinese agriculture,"[120] whom Kraft also managed to meet in his remote mountain village, Tachai, that happened to be a model village where foreign visitors were regularly taken.

In the aftermath of his conducted tour Kraft concluded that "support from the countryside brought Mao to the top of the Chinese Communist party ... His historic achievement, as leader and thinker, has been to understand how peasant masses could be recruited for Communism. He is the supreme agrarian radical of world history." Kraft was also inclined to believe that the New Maoist Man was being born, or would be forthcoming, in the foreseeable future. In holding such beliefs he resembled the White House staff and the press entourage who accompanied Nixon to China in 1972 and "seemed to be accept[ing] ... the immense achievements of the Chinese revolution."[121]

Kraft's slim book (113 pages) suggests that either he was totally unaware of the so-called Great Leap Forward and the famine it led to, or if he was aware, he did not think that it was worth mentioning or had any noticeable impact on the life of the peasants and their admiration of Mao. He did learn a little of the Cultural Revolution, thanks to the carefully arranged meetings with informants (as noted above) who told him how they benefited from it and of the lessons it taught them, and who apparently made no reference to its irrationality and orgies of violence.

Mosher wrote of the same group of journalists that they "were of one mind about ... the beneficial impact of the Cultural Revolution on the

[120] Kraft, 63, 82, 83, 85, 112.

[121] Ibid., 12, 73.

institutions of society and on public mores; the eradication of human vices such as crime, drug addiction and prostitution ... [and] the creation of a new, selfless, Maoist man." In displaying such credulousness these journalists resembled American political activists such as Staughton Lynd and Tom Hayden (among others), who "on all things accepted the assurances of their hosts over the evidence of their senses."[122] Apparently, even Henry Kissinger was taken in (or perhaps pretended to be), referring to the Chinese leaders (Mao included) as "a group of monks ... who have ... kept their revolutionary purity."[123] Likewise Simone de Beauvoir was most impressed by what struck her as the authenticity of the Chinese leaders: "What is so winning about the Chinese leaders is that not one of them plays a part; they are dressed like anybody else ... and their faces are not deformed either by class mannerism or by ... the need to maintain front ... these are just faces, plainly and wholly human."[124] Doubtless she was unaware (as were the other sympathetic visitors) of the immense efforts the Chinese (and other communist) governments made to create favorable impressions on important foreign visitors[125] and the distance separating such visitors from the rest of the population.

In conclusion, it has to be pointed out that the admiration of Mao on the part of many Western intellectuals was different from, and rarely reached the level of, the domestic deification orchestrated by the Chinese authorities. Although the Western intellectuals' admiration did not amount to the kind of bizarre deification that was created in China, it is possible that some of them were influenced by it, impressed by the apparent adoration he received from his own people.

Mao also benefited from the widely held belief among his Western supporters that his brand of socialism avoided the mistakes and misdeeds of the Soviet version perpetrated by Stalin, and that communist China was imbued by an authentic revolutionary spirit.

Like the other dictators here discussed, Mao perfectly fit the image of the "redeemer" who not only improved the material living conditions of his people but also made their lives meaningful, and – like his Soviet predecessors – allegedly modernized society without the destructive by-products of capitalist modernization.

122 Mosher, 8, 121.

123 Quoted in Chang and Halliday, 587.

124 Simone de Beauvoir: *The Long March*, Cleveland and New York 1958, 429.

125 For a detailed discussion of these policies, see "Techniques of Hospitality," ch. 8 in Paul Hollander: *Political Pilgrims*, New York 1981.

As each and every dictator here considered, Mao too was seen as an incorruptible idealist using his power benignly in pursuit of self-evidently praiseworthy goals. Unlike the Western politicians held in great contempt by many Western intellectuals, he appeared to be the admirable embodiment of both the philosopher-king and the renaissance man. He wrote poetry, was a vigorous swimmer, had been both guerilla leader and military genius during the civil war, and never stopped advising and prodding his subjects about how to conduct their lives. However, he was not a genuinely charismatic leader and his oratorical skills were limited, especially in comparison with Mussolini, Hitler, Castro, and Chavez.

The basic determinants of the Western idealization and misjudgments of Mao were similar to those of the other dictators discussed before. The most important precondition for the rise of the wishful projections was dissatisfaction with Western societies, with capitalism and the problems of modernity, as well as specific crises during the 1960s such as the Vietnam War. The favorable predisposition was strengthened by lack of information and the misinformation that many intellectuals absorbed during the conducted tours of the countries concerned.

As noted earlier, the misapprehensions and misperceptions of the policies and the personality of Mao were among the most extreme, even as compared to similarly wrongheaded views of other dictators – the gap between his image and personality the widest. The language barrier and greater unfamiliarity with the social, historical, and geographical setting (compared to those of the other dictators) probably contributed to the illusions and misjudgments here sampled.

SHORT-LIVED ILLUSIONS ABOUT POL POT'S CAMBODIA

While Pol Pot, the dictator of Cambodia, was not the focus of interest among Western intellectuals, sympathetic misjudgments of his system, while short-lived and limited to a handful of Western intellectuals, did occur. These positive assessments are among the most spectacular political misjudgments of our times here sampled.

Cambodia under Pol Pot had some of the same attractions Mao's China possessed: it offered "a utopian vision of society … based on a … utopian, egalitarian ideology similar to but even more extreme than Maoism." Pol Pot visited China when the Cultural Revolution began and was "impressed by the purity of China's utopian revolutionary enthusiasm."[126] Likewise Jean-Louis Margolin pointed out that "the lineage from Mao Zedong to Pol Pot is obvious." He further suggested that "there is ... no doubt that traits discernible in his [Pol Pot's] personality correlate with the bloodiest excesses of his regime." There were further similarities between proclaimed ends and the unintended disastrous consequences, as the Cambodian regime too "claimed that its intention was to create an egalitarian society, in which justice, fraternity and altruism would be the key values, yet like other Communist regimes it produced a tidal wave of selfishness, inequality and irrationality."[127]

The Western misjudgments of Cambodia under Pol Pot are especially glaring because of their sheer implausibility and the extreme gap they exemplify between illusions and realities. We must remember that this political system was responsible for the death of a higher portion of the population (over 1.5 million) than any other system here discussed and these atrocities took place over a relatively short period of time. The country as a whole was converted into a large, highly regimented rural forced-labor camp.[128]

It was Noam Chomsky and Edward Herman who made the most determined attempts to deny or minimize the mass murders carried out by the Pol Pot regime, ridiculing and dismissing refugee accounts as untrustworthy "tales" designed "to defame the regime." Among other things, they wrote: "where evidence [of the mass murders – P.H.] is subject to some independent check it repeatedly and with remarkable consistency turns out to be fabricated."[129] Even Sydney Schanberg, the *New York Times* reporter who later did report the nightmarish conditions created by the Pol Pot regime, in his earlier reports had some illusions about the system. He wrote: "for the ordinary people of Indochina ... it is

[126] Daniel Chirot: *Modern Tyrants: The Power and Prevalence of Evil in Our Times*, New York 1994, 210, 220.

[127] Jean-Louis Margolin: "Cambodia: The Country of Disconcerting Crimes," in Stephane Courtois et al.: *The Black Book of Communism: Crimes, Terror and Repression*, Cambridge MA 1999, 577, 603, 629.

[128] See for example Francois Ponchaud: *Cambodia*, New York 1978; Ben Kiernan: *The Pol Pot Regime: Race, Power and Genocide in Cambodia under the Khmer Rouge 1975–1979*, New Haven CT 1996; for memoirs, see Pin Yathay: *Stay Alive My Son*, London 1987; Haing Ngor: *A Cambodian Odyssey*, New York 1987; Dith Pran (compiler): *Children of Cambodia's Killing Fields*, New Haven CT 1997. See also Margolin.

[129] Noam Chomsky and Edward Herman: *After the Cataclysm: Postwar Indochina and the Reconstruction of Imperial Ideology*, Boston 1978, 292, 293; see also by the same authors: "Distortions at Fourth Hand," *Nation*, June 25, 1977, esp. 789, 791, their critique of the refugee accounts.

difficult to imagine how their lives could be anything but better with the Americans gone." He was also highly skeptical about the possibility of "mass executions" to follow the communist take-over, and strained to see things through "Cambodian revolutionary eyes." He wrote: "is it possible that, seen through the eyes of the peasant soldiers and revolutionaries, the forced evacuation of the cities is a harsh necessity? Perhaps they are convinced that there is no way to build a new society ... without literally starting from the beginning."[130]

Richard Dudman (whom Chomsky quoted as an authority on Cambodia, to bolster his own views about the progress made under Pol Pot) shared Chomsky's skepticism about the reliability of refugee accounts. Dudman criticized William Shawcross for "accept[ing] uncritically the testimony of Cambodian refugees about life ... under the Pol Pot regime ... Two weeks of recent eyewitness observation [presumably his own – P.H.] inside Cambodia indicated that food, clothing and shelter were adequate ... and working conditions, while hard, seemed by no means intolerable."[131]

Less well-known have been the sympathetic views of George Hildebrand and Gareth Porter, who devoted an entire (slim) volume to the proposition that the forced evacuation of the capital Phnom Penh was a reasonable and humane response to conditions (mainly impending starvation) created by the United States.[132] Like Chomsky and Herman they too were indignant about what they considered Western slandering of the Pol Pot regime that they judged to be decent and praiseworthy. They ridiculed and dismissed *New York Times* reporter Schanberg and "his preconceived notion about a cruel and fanatical Cambodian leadership ready to carry out a genocidal purge of society." They were also fully persuaded that "human needs and long term economic conditions" justified the evacuation of Phnom Penh, as well as the necessity to "gain control over armed saboteurs and armed agents linked to the United States" lurking in the city. Following the style of Chomsky (who sprinkled outlandish assertions with words and expressions suggesting detachment and objectivity), they wrote:

A careful examination of the facts regarding the evacuation of Cambodia's cities show that the description and interpretation of the move conveyed to the

[130] Quoted in Mona Charen: *Useful Idiots*, Washington DC 2003, 66, 67, 68.

[131] Ibid., 71–72.

[132] George Hildebrand and Gareth Porter: *Cambodia: Starvation and Revolution*, New York 1976.

American public was an inexcusable distortion of reality. What was portrayed as a destructive ... policy motivated by doctrinaire hatred was actually a rationally conceived strategy for dealing with the urgent problems that faced postwar Cambodia.

According to these authors, the root cause of "the death and devastation" in Cambodia was "the US intervention" that was "neither an aberration nor an accident" but the outcome of deep-seated American hostility toward the progressive revolutionary movements in the region. They proposed that the USA preferred "human suffering," including "mass starvation," to "the failure of its anti-Communist policy in Cambodia."

These authors concluded that "only the revolutionary left ... had the will and capability to resolve" the food shortages, determined as it was "to meet the most elementary human needs" of the Cambodian people: "The revolutionary forms of organization which permitted the mobilization of the Cambodian people" was credited with averting famine.[133] Thy did not dwell on the nature of this "mobilization," probably because it had involved brutality and terror on a massive scale.

Slavoj Zizek (see pp. 27–31) praised the Cambodian regime "for attempting a total break with the past." He wrote: "The Khmer Rouge were in a way, *not radical enough*: while they took the abstract negation of the past to the limit, they did not invent any new form of collectivity." He nonetheless believed that "revolutionary violence should be celebrated as 'redemptive' and even 'divine.'"[134]

Since Pot Pot's exceptionally brutal and irrational dictatorship was short-lived (1975–1979) and was overthrown by another neighboring communist state, Vietnam, its sympathetic depictions sampled above were short-lived but nonetheless remarkable for the intensity with which they were held. I am unaware of expressions of regret on the part of the authors who so profoundly misperceived and misrepresented conditions in Cambodia and attempted to discredit the testimony of the refugees.

The case of Pol Pot and his domination of Cambodia is another reminder of the connections between political beliefs and practices, especially pronounced in dictatorships, and of the disastrous consequences of the exercise of power by erstwhile intellectuals, or quasi-intellectuals, such as Pol Pot and his associates.

[133] Ibid., 11– 12, 19, 41, 56, 93, 96.

[134] Quoted in John Gray: "The Violent Visions of Slavoj Zizek," *New York Review of Books*, July 12, 2012, 23.

6

Castro, Che Guevara, and Their Western Admirers

As Fidel spoke, I allowed myself to listen closely and feel that peculiar sensation I experience in his presence, as if meeting with a force of nature, a man so filled with the energy of the historical mission that he is almost a different species. Power radiates from him.

Saul Landau[1]

[Y]ou gave all of us who are alone in this country ... some sense that there were heroes in the world ... It was as if the ghost of Cortez had appeared in our century riding Zapata's white horse. You were the first and greatest hero to appear in the world since the Second War ... you gave a bit of life to the best and most passionate men and women all over the earth, you are the answer to the argument ... that revolutions cannot last, that they turn corrupt or total or they eat their own.

Norman Mailer[2]

[Che Guevara] presided over the Cuban Revolution's first firing squads ... [and] founded Cuba's labor camp system ... The present day cult of Che ... has succeeded in obscuring this dreadful reality ... Che was an enemy of freedom and yet he has been erected into a symbol of freedom. He helped establish an unjust social system in Cuba and has been erected into a symbol of social justice.

Paul Berman[3]

1 Saul Landau: "After Castro," *Mother Jones*, July/August 1989, 48.

2 Norman Mailer: "Letter to Castro," in *Presidential Papers*, New York 1963, 67, 68, 75. Mailer was apparently mistaken in his belief that Castro's approach to political violence was spontaneous and impassioned. Carlos Franqui, who knew Castro well and used to be among his close associates during the early years of the Revolution, had no such illusions as he contrasted Castro with Che Guevara: "Che never forgot that the enemy is a ... human being. Fidel was different: he had to kill, and he did it, in a cold way, without emotion" (*Family Portrait with Fidel, A Memoir*, New York 1981, 163). Jorge Dominguez suggested that the distinctions between Castro and Guevara have often been exaggerated: "Che was less saintly, [and] Fidel was not always evil. The gap was narrower" (personal communication, 2015).

3 Paul Berman: "The Cult of Che," *Slate*, September 24, 2004.

FIGURE 9. Instructing and exhorting his audience in an impassioned speech.

FIGURE 10. Clinking glasses with Shirley MacLaine, one of his numerous celebrity admirers who visited Cuba.

CASTRO'S CHARISMA AND CULT

The admiration of Fidel Castro by intellectuals and non-intellectuals alike stands out as one of the purest instances of political hero worship in our times. Castro was exceptionally well suited for this role: he was young (when his worship began and was most intense), handsome, dynamic, articulate, a powerful speaker,[4] a genuine revolutionary and guerilla fighter who overthrew an oppressive government. He was, in all probability, the most charismatic of all the dictators considered in this study. Georgie Anne Geyer noted his "unusual physical and psychological, propensities – the frenzied and ceaseless talking ... the manic energy that seemed almost superhuman as he often went days without sleeping."[5] He often met visitors from abroad late night or early morning (like Stalin), impressing them with his stamina.

Alma Guillermoprieto, a Mexican-American journalist and author, had this to say about the components of his charisma:

> Fidel has determined that he, and through him you, will be greater than any man, will defy history ... live for a dream ... of perfect equality and perfect justice such as Cuba will one day produce. Socialism will not be defeated! ... With Fidel at the helm, there is no cause for fear ... The ability to inspire feelings of intimacy and awe in equal measure are what kept Fidel Castro in power ...
>
> [I]n the end it is Fidel ... who, with his supernatural will, historic sense of moment and of mission, quick trigger finger and massive ego, has single-handedly led Cuba ... he was immune to self-doubt and possessed of the underdog's obsession with honor and dignity.[6]

Castro was the single major source of legitimacy of the political system that emerged from the Cuban Revolution. Enrique Krauze wrote:

> The history taught in Cuban schools exalts in the redeeming function of the Cuban Revolution but it also ... reduces that revolution to a biography of Fidel Castro. Castro also sought to use religious symbolism in support of his cult

[4] Castro's speaking habits and talents reminded an Italian journalist (a friend of Carlos Franqui) of Mussolini (see Franqui, 86). But Mussolini did not make speeches lasting for several hours. Castro's propensity to speak for hours to live audiences was among the reflections of his enormous ego, of his unshakeable conviction that all of his ideas deserved to be communicated at such great length, to huge and arguably captive audiences. (Participation in the giant rallies and mass meetings was highly organized, as were similar events in other totalitarian societies.)

[5] Georgie Anne Geyer: *Guerilla Prince: The Untold Story of Fidel Castro*, Boston 1991, 175. For another critical biography, see Juan Reinaldo Sanchez: *The Double Life of Fidel Castro: My 17 Years as Bodyguard to El Lider Maximo*, New York 2015.

[6] Alma Guillermoprieto: "Fidel in the Evening," *New York Review of Books*, October 22, 1988, 42, 44, 46.

making remarks such as "whoever condemns the revolution ... betrays Christ and declares himself capable of crucifying ... Christ once again." ... Castro had no belief in religious dogmas. Nevertheless he affirmed and imposed his beliefs as if they were ... new dogmas.[7]

Castro's appeals for Western intellectuals rested in large measure on his impassioned critiques of the United States, his fiery anti-capitalism, and his being the leader of a country that many considered a victim of American imperialism. For many of these intellectuals disappointed with the Soviet system, such as Regis Debray, French activist intellectual, Castro personified a new, youthful, and authentic revolutionary socialism. Debray wrote: "The worker and peasant masses everywhere crave socialism, but they don't yet know it because they are still in the power of Stalinist bureaucracies. Hence the latent spontaneity [*sic*!] of the workers must be awakened."[8] Debray was among the early devotees of Castro's Cuba and "a young protegee" of Castro, as well as of Louis Althusser, the French Marxist philosopher. Castro "spent months tutoring Debray in the concrete mechanics, philosophical orientation and above all ... the unique strategy of the Cuban Revolution." Debray was also involved in the futile and doomed attempts of Che Guevara to organize a guerilla movement in Bolivia. Years later "he showed up in Nicaragua in a Sandinista uniform on the last day of the 1979 revolution in Managua." Subsequently Debray became disillusioned with Castro's Cuba and Third World revolutionary movements. According to Tom Hayden, "The understandable error of Debray, shared with thousands of Westerners, was born of a sense of guilt that drove him to extremes of radical alienation."[9]

Castro was also acclaimed by Latin American intellectuals: "intellectuals in this part of the world have reflexively accorded him and other revolutionary, anti-American leaders – Daniel Ortega in Nicaragua, Hugo Chavez in Venezuela – immunity to the moral standards, applied to other leaders."[10]

As Dennis Wrong, the American sociologist, put it, Castro was "a natural hero for the New Left from the first ... a genuine hero in an

[7] Enrique Krauze: "Cuba: The New Opening," *New York Review of Books*, April 2, 2015, 51. His early education in a Jesuit school probably helped him to appreciate the value of dogmas (a point suggested by Dominguez, personal communication).

[8] Regis Debray: "Revolution in the Revolution?: Armed Struggle and Political Struggle in Latin America," *Monthly Review*, Special Issue, Vol. 19, No. 3, 1967, 36.

[9] Tom Hayden: *Listen Yankee! Why Cuba Matters*, New York 2015, 5, 85, 88, 96, 108–109.

[10] Larry Rohter: "In Latin America, the Cult of Revolution Wanes," *New York Times*, May 18, 2003.

age of characterless bureaucratic leaders."[11] Arthur Schlesinger, the historian, observed that on Castro's first visit to the United States in 1959 he "captured the kind of counterculture magic ... before a stadium full of Harvard students. 'They saw in him ... the hipster, who, in the era of the Organization Man, had joyfully defied the system.'"[12]

C. Wright Mills, the sociologist and prominent social critic, was a major representative and voice of the New Left for whom Castro was the kind of "natural hero" Dennis Wrong referred to. Mills was among the early supporters of the Cuban Revolution eager to see at first hand the invigorating changes taking place. He was also one of the Western intellectuals Castro considered important enough to meet and engage in an extended exchange of ideas. Mills spent "three and a half 18-hour days with Prime Minister Fidel Castro," talking and inspecting the political sights. The encounter made a deep impression on him and became a major source of his assessments of the new society. The visit led him to write a strange book that was supposed to present the views of an imaginary Cuban revolutionary (in his letters to the "Yankee"); in effect Mills sought to impersonate such an individual:

> My major aim in this book is to present the voice of the Cuban revolutionary, as clearly and emphatically as I can, and I have taken up this aim because of its absurd absence from the news of Cuba available in the United States today ... The facts and interpretations presented in these letters from Cuba accurately reflect, I believe, the views of the Cuban revolutionary ... The voice of Cuba today is the voice of revolutionary euphoria. It is also an angry voice.

It was an extraordinary conceit of Mills that he could transform himself into the representative voice, alter ego, and self-appointed spokesman of Cuban revolutionaries and express authentically their feelings, thoughts, and ideas. It was also an unusual instance of role-playing that probably reflected the longings of Mills to be part and spokesman of a revolutionary community. He was firmly convinced that he was capable of accomplishing this and could separate his own views from those of the Cubans. He wrote:

> it is ... necessary to know what the argument, the hopes, and the problems of the Cuban revolutionaries are. It is my task to state some of these. That is why,

[11] Dennis Wrong: "The American Left and Cuba," *Commentary*, February 1962, 99. Cuba's (and Castro's) appeals for the New Left diminished after 1971 as Cuba increasingly aligned itself with the Soviet Union (see Kepa Artaraz: *Cuba and Western Intellectuals Since 1959*, New York 2008, esp. 43–45).

[12] Quoted in Anthony DePalma: *The Man Who Invented Fidel: Cuba, Castro and Herbert L. Matthews of the New York Times*, New York 2006, 161–162.

in writing this book, I have thought the expression of my own views much less important than the statement of the Cuban revolutionaries' case. And that is why, insofar as I have been able, I have refrained from expressing a personal opinion ... Please know, then, as you read these letters, that it is the Cuban revolutionaries who are talking to you.

Mills made no attempt to explain what made him presume that he could become the authentic voice of Cuban revolutionaries, or what was the basis of his sense of entitlement for playing such a role.

The format of the book did not allow him to include recollections of the exciting days spent with Castro but it is most likely that he shared the conception of Castro expressed by one of his imaginary interlocutors:

From Fidel we have learned ... that you can go very far, if only you try hard enough ... "to fly high." Maybe that is utopian, but that *is* what Fidel has taught us and is teaching us all the time. To dream and to believe you can make the dream come true. The revolution is a way of defining reality. The revolution is a way of changing reality ... The revolution in Cuba is a great moment of truth.[13]

Castro's image and popularity abroad, and especially in the United States, greatly benefited from the famous and dramatically staged interview he gave in 1957 to the *New York Times* reporter, Herbert Matthews. He was invited to meet Castro in the Sierra Maestre mountains where he was waging guerilla war against Batista. Castro initiated the interview because he was looking for a foreign journalist who would generate favorable publicity abroad, and especially in the United States.[14] Both

[13] C. Wright Mills: *Listen Yankee: The Revolution in Cuba*, New York 1960, 8–9, 11, 12, 114. Tom Hayden considered himself a "lifetime student of Mills ... a rebel thinker" and was impressed by his lifestyle that included riding around on a motorcycle "and model[ing] himself on Ernest Hemingway. He was unquestionably macho, as was Fidel" (Hayden cited, 35). Hayden, a radical New Left activist, was also a lifelong supporter and admirer of Castro (whom he met several times in Cuba) and the system he created. He was a close, lifelong friend of Saul Landau, who devoted much of his life to proselytizing on behalf of Castro and his system. Hayden acknowledged and mildly disapproved of the authoritarian features of Cuban political system but held responsible for them US policies and hostility (see for example Hayden, 241–242). The book I cited from "was based in part on conversations with Ricardo Alarcon" [title page]. Alarcon was "a top leader of the Cuban Revolution, foreign minister, United Nations representative, and president of the National Assembly" (Hayden, xii). He was apparently a close friend of Hayden. More recently he shared with Hayden "the search for another New Left" (ibid., 39).

[14] John Wallach, an American journalist who reported from Cuba in later years, observed that "there are few modern political heroes on the world stage who have been more successful in manipulating media coverage of themselves than Castro" (quoted in William E. Ratliff ed.: *The Selling of Fidel Castro: The Media and the Cuban Revolution*, New Brunswick NJ 1987, 129).

Castro and Che Guevara "understood the value of Matthews' bias from the outset ... because both were masters of propaganda and manipulators of image." Anthony DePalma further wrote that "after studying what happened during that interview for a long time, I understood that Castro had carefully planned to mislead Matthews." Matthews, on his part, persisted "in his perception of Castro as an idealist long after he had transformed himself into a demagogue."[15] Castro's manipulations of Matthews were made easier by the fact that Matthews was and "remained a hopeless romantic who sought desperately to find and believe in causes."[16] Matthews found Castro's personality "overpowering. It was easy to see that his men adored him."[17]

Another critic of Matthews, John Chamberlain, observed that "his addiction to causes and his propensity to be dazzled by men of power have frequently put blinders on him."[18] Other critics of his 1969 book on Castro felt "that his infatuation with Cuba and Castro bled through every page."[19] Matthews' enduring support of Castro may also be explained by Castro's understandable warmth toward him and the privileged treatment he continued to receive during his numerous visits to Cuba over the years that followed the famous interview. On these trips "he was given a hero's welcome" and driven around in a chauffeured car. Matthews believed that "Fidel, his brother Raul and virtually all the revolutionary leaders do not look upon me as an outsider." He also declared "Cuba to be 'the friendliest spot on earth to me.'"[20] These feelings suggest that the appeals of Cuba included a sense of community he did not experience in his own society.

Broader historical trends stimulated the appeal of Castro among Western intellectuals. By the time he rose to power the Soviet system was largely discredited, a process greatly accelerated by Khrushchev's revelations of the crimes of Stalin in his famous speech at the Communist Party Congress in 1956. By the late 1950s the Soviet Union was increasingly seen by Western intellectuals as another modern, impersonal, inauthentic, oppressive industrial society, a superpower like the United States, hence the popularity of the convergence theory. In its optimistic version the Soviet Union was bound to become more pluralistic and democratic,

[15] DePalma, 83, 257, 266, 278.
[16] Geyer, 168.
[17] Matthews quoted in Ratliff, 150.
[18] Chamberlain cited in DePalma, 250.
[19] DePalma, 247.
[20] Matthews quoted in ibid., 208–209, 252.

while the pessimists (which included many leftist intellectuals) thought it was becoming just as exploitative and immoral as the United States. By the same token the appeals of Cuba began to wane as it became closely allied with the Soviet Union.

Under these circumstances many alienated Western intellectuals were ready to embrace a new, revolutionary incarnation of their hopes and longings. They found it in the Third World, in countries like Cuba, China, Vietnam, and later Nicaragua. The idea of the Third World itself had its own appeals that suggested that the countries in question were free of the defects of both the capitalist West and Soviet state socialism. From the earliest days of his rise to power, Castro made good use of these susceptibilities of Western intellectuals as he sought respectability and international support.[21]

The phenomenon of wishful projection was strikingly illustrated by Julian Bond's claim that "Castro's idealism reminded him" of the "connection between socialism and Christianity."[22] (Some Western visitors to the Soviet Union in the 1930s expressed similar sentiments.) Steven Spielberg, who met Castro in Havana in the fall of 2002, called the meeting "the most important eight hours of my life."[23]

Barbara Walters' observations of Castro further illustrate the way in which Castro's physical features and personality combined to create a winning impression:

> He is 6 feet 2 inches, a massive man, and this adds to his image. Add too, a keen sense of humor, an apparent warmth for the people he likes [surprising? – P.H.] and a gallantry with strangers ... He enjoys driving ... took the wheel of his Russian-made jeep, with his rifle across the dashboard ... He drives, talks and smokes all at the same time ... He is surprisingly soft spoken.

It is not clear on what grounds Walters also reached the conclusion that "many people in this country feel that Cuba is Fidel and Fidel is Cuba."[24]

Leo Huberman and Paul Sweezy (co-editors of the leftist *Monthly Review*) were impressed by Castro's apparent determination to uplift the masses: "First and foremost, Fidel is a passionate humanitarian ... in the meaningful sense that he feels compassion for human suffering, hates injustice ... He treats people ... kindly, sternly, implacably, according to

[21] See also Carlos Alberto Montaner: "The Cuban Revolution and Its Acolytes," in Irving L. Horowitz ed.: *Cuban Communism 1959–1995*, New Brunswick NJ 1995, 772.

[22] Bond quoted in Ratliff, 132.

[23] Spielberg quoted in Humberto Fontova: *Fidel: Hollywood's Favorite Tyrant*, Washington DC 2005, 154. The statement was disputed by Spielberg's office. See ibid., 207, note 14.

[24] Walters quoted in Ratliff, 141.

their potential role in the creation of the good society."[25] Such a view of Castro was compatible with a more critical assessment of his elitist disposition. Robert S. Leiken wrote: "Fidel considered himself indispensable to the revolution. He insisted that 'the people were not ready and that a revolutionary minority had to take it upon itself to impose socialism on the people.' ... the role of the people was to work and to obey unquestioningly."[26] Doubtless, Lenin would have approved.

Ignacio Ramonet, a French author and admirer of Castro, conducted 100 hours of (largely sycophantic) interviews for what became his huge "spoken autobiography,"[27] its introduction featuring the views of him that came to be embedded in his cult. Ramonet claimed to undertake the project "to allow one of the most implacably attacked figures in the world of the last fifty years, and at the same time the most censored, to have his say," as well as to show "his true humanity." He believed that Castro "has a place in the pantheon of world figures who have struggled most fiercely for social justice and ... came to the aid of the oppressed."[28] In the course of the lengthy interviews he discovered

> a private, almost shy Fidel, a polite, affable man who pays attention to each person he talks to ... is always attentive to others, aware of them as persons ... He is a leader who lives ... modestly ... His are the habits of a soldier-monk ... He sleeps about four hours a night ... His workday, all seven days a week, usually ends at five or six in the morning ... Seeing Fidel Castro in action is inspiring ... Fidel has a profound sense of himself in history ... he is a person who acts out of ambitions that are noble, out of ideals of justice and equity. This quality, which makes one think of those words of Che Guevara: "A great revolution can only be born out of a great feeling of love," made a great impression on American film-maker Oliver Stone. "Castro" he said "is one of the wisest man there are ... I admire his Revolution, his faith in himself and his honesty."[29]

If, and insofar as admirers of Castro and Cuba admitted it, the Cuban authorities restricted free expression and refused to tolerate dissent, it was "a reaction to the constant aggression against Cuba directed from abroad," Ramonet suggested. He also asserted that no fewer than 600

[25] Leo Huberman and Paul Sweezy: *Cuba, Anatomy of a Revolution*, New York 1961, 176.

[26] Robert S. Leiken: "Inside the Revolution," *New York Review of Books*, October 11, 1985, 3.

[27] Ignacio Ramonet: *Fidel Castro: My Life – A Spoken Autobiography*, New York 2007.

[28] Ibid., 18, 11.

[29] Ibid., 13, 14, 15, 16. The Cuban Revolution was not the only one Oliver Stone admired. In 1996 he visited "leftist guerillas," participants in an "Indian uprising two years ago" near San Cristobal De Las Casas in Mexico: "'I'm here because I believe in their struggle,' Stone said after meeting with 23 leaders of the Zapatista National Liberation Army" ("Oliver Stone Visits Mexican Rebels," *Daily Hampshire Gazette*, March 25, 1996).

assassination attempts were made against Castro.[30] Not surprisingly, for Castro and his supporters, self-defense became the time-honored justification of repression, as was the case for both Hitler and Stalin. It has continued to be the justification of repression in other communist states like China under (and after) Mao and North Korea. Castro's personality, possibly even more than Mussolini's and Hitler's (both of whom were also domineering and charismatic), was the preponderant influence on the nature and course of the Cuban revolution and the political system that emerged from it. In the opinion of one of his early supporters, Carlos Alberto Montaner, "Recent Cuban history is absolutely unexplainable if one forgets the psychological make-up of its principal and almost sole protagonist," that is, Castro. This "make-up" included "childish temper tantrums ... paranoia ... abnormal fits of anger ... insane jealousy directed toward any person who might stand out or might begin to win the people's love or admiration ... Fidel is a Messianic man with a sickly vocation for power and glory."[31] Maurice Halperin, a disillusioned former American supporter of both the Soviet Union and Castro's Cuba, made a similar assessment of Castro: "He has had an uncontrollable compulsion to lead and to dominate – the results of an innate compulsion of his superiority and of his destiny to make history ... His monumental ego does not admit errors."[32] Mario Llerena, a Cuban academic intellectual who supported Castro's struggle against Batista but subsequently went into early exile in the United States, wrote that

> many who have followed Castro's life trajectory ... see in him a clear case of psychopathic behavior ... Revolution ... came to be Castro's supreme vocation. Castro sees the revolution not as a last resort but as a channel for self-expression – an escape valve for his accumulated resentments and hates ... What primarily attracts him is the iconoclastic, destructive turbulence that inevitably accompanies the revolutionary process."[33]

According to Geyer, Castro as a young man had a great interest in modern dictators such as Mussolini, Hitler, Lenin, Stalin, and Peron and

[30] Ibid., 6. According to Dominguez, most of these attempts were made by Cubans, not the United States (personal communication).

[31] Carlos Alberto Montaner: *Secret Report on the Cuban Revolution*, New Brunswick NJ 1982, 46, 49.

[32] Maurice Halperin: *Return to Havana: The Decline of Cuban Society under Castro*, Nashville TN 1994, 162, 185.

[33] Mario Llerena: *The Unsuspected Revolution: The Birth and Rise of Castroism*, Ithaca NY 1978, 202–203.

studied their political style and behavior. He found especially appealing "the idea that the Fascist 'new men' were soldiers."[34]

Castro resembled other dictators here discussed in possessing abundant manipulative talents. Cabrera Infante, the Cuban writer, another former supporter who also chose exile in 1965, wrote: "Fidel Castro's real genius is in the arts of deception ... bluffing and holding his cards close to his olive green chest ... As a grand deceiver he is really extraordinary. But even more astonishing is the capacity of all concerned ... to let themselves be fooled willingly."[35] Halperin too noted Castro's talent for "projecting sincerity while concealing cunning calculations."[36]

CASTRO, NORMAN MAILER, AND LIBERATING VIOLENCE

Norman Mailer, who may be among those "fooled willingly," was eager to find and revere a powerful revolutionary hero; he was one of Castro's most ardent admirers. He instructively displayed the key impulses and attitudes predisposing to such a worship. He was convinced that his admiring "open letter to Castro" could have an "effect on history."[37] According to Mailer's biographer, "over the years, his belief in Castro's greatness never flagged and was strengthened when they met in Cuba decades later. Asked late in life to list the geniuses he met in person, Mailer named Ezra Pound, Charlie Chaplin, Muhammad Ali and Fidel Castro ... Che Guevara ... elicited similar admiration."[38]

Mailer's propensity to hero worship also found expression in admitting that "I'd like to be another Malraux."[39] This wish presumably originated in his admiration of Malraux for seemingly realizing the perennial desire of intellectuals, namely the linking of words and deeds. Malraux participated in the Spanish Civil War and the anti-German guerilla movement

[34] Geyer, 42.

[35] Guillermo Cabrera Infante: "Foreword," to Franqui, xvi.

[36] See Halperin, 185. Cabrera Infante called Castro "a man of infinite cunning and deceit" (see Guillermo Cabrera Infante: *Mea Cuba*, New York 1994, 59).

[37] He worked on this letter for three weeks and was preoccupied with getting it published at the time Adele, his wife, was hospitalized as a result of his stabbing her. A friend of his commented: "he stabbed his wife the night before and what was uppermost in his mind? Getting the letter published" (J. Michael Lennon: *Norman Mailer: A Double Life*, New York 2013, 285, 292).

[38] Mailer quoted in Lennon, 264.

[39] Mailer quoted in Renee Winegarten: *Writers and Revolution: The Fatal Lure of Action*, New York 1974, 294.

in France, and after World War II had access to real power as a minister in the government of Charles de Gaulle. Mailer's aspirations to political power were exhausted in his failed mayoral campaign in New York City.

Mailer's reverence for Castro, as well as his other political attitudes and actions, prompt reflections about the confluence of the personal and political attributes in the human psyche. Gore Vidal's observation of Mailer's personality may help us to understand why he fell for Castro: "His [Mailer's] drive seems to be toward power of a religio-political kind. He is a messiah without real hope of paradise on earth, or in heaven, and with no precise mission except that dictated by his ever-changing temperament."[40]

Mailer's attraction to and respect for what he considered authentic, liberating violence is likely to have played an important part in his admiration of Castro. The same impulses also found other, not as clearly political expression in his durable and fervent support of the convicted murderer, Jack Abbott (also an impassioned critic of American society). Abbott had corresponded with Mailer for several years before he was paroled with Mailer's help. Mailer believed that Abbott possessed great literary talents ("special abilities") that required a "special solution," i.e., parole.[41] His early release was soon followed by his committing another murder.[42]

In a remarkable feat of projection Mailer characterized Abbott as "an intellectual ... a potential leader with a vision of more elevated human relations in a better world that revolution could forge." In his introduction to Abbott's book (which he helped to get published) Mailer wrote: "There are moments when the voice [of Abbott, that is] ... is the clear descendant of Marx and Lenin ... the tone of Vladimir Ilyich Ulyanov [Lenin] rises out of these pages." Martin Amis aptly observed that Mailer had a "weakness for any killer who has puzzled his way through a few pages of Marx."[43]

40 Vidal quoted in Lennon, 262.

41 Lennon, 552.

42 Steven Pinker wrote: "Over the objections of prison psychiatrists who saw that Abbott had PSYCHOPATH written all over his face, Mailer and other New York literati helped him win early parole" (*The Blank Slate*, New York 2002, 262). For further discussions of the Mailer–Abbott relationship, see Naomi Munson and James Atlas: "On Norman Mailer and Jack Abbott: The Literary Life of Crime," *New Republic*, September 9, 1981; Lionel Abel: "Murder and the Intellectuals," *Commentary*, November 1981; and Michiko Kakutani: "The Strange Case of the Writer and the Criminal," *New York Review of Books*, September 20, 1981.

43 Lennon, 519; Martin Amis: *The War Against Cliche: Essays and Reviews, 1971–2000*, New York 2001, 276.

Mailer was not alone in grotesquely misreading the character and overestimating the literary talents of Abbott. Abbie Hoffman compared Abbott to Solzhenitsyn and Jacobo Timmerman.[44] These were the kinds of assertions that bring to mind Orwell's oft-quoted suggestion that only intellectuals are capable of believing certain kinds of nonsense.

Although saddened by Abbott's new murder, Mailer continued to support him and was "the least cooperative" with the police of all the people who knew Abbott well, according to the detective involved in the case. At a press conference following the court proceedings Mailer expressed opposition to a long sentence, pointing out that it would prevent Abbott from becoming a writer. He associated long prisons sentences with fascism, whereas "a democracy involves taking of risks." As his biographer pointed out, "Mailer never stopped believing that art can ennoble, and that it is possible to rise above one's errors and crimes."[45] As such and other remarks make clear, Mailer's romanticism greatly influenced his political attitudes and beliefs.

While Mailer was "Abbot's most devoted champion,"[46] he was not the only New York intellectual befriending him. Robert Silvers (still the editor of the *New York Review of Books*) and the novelists Jerzy Kosinski and William Styron were also Abbott's supporters and admirers.[47] Naomi Zack, a philosophy professor, actually married Abbott in 1990, following his imprisonment for the murder he committed while on parole. During his new imprisonment, Abbott was quoted saying that he tried "to behave like a 'real' intellectual." Zack divorced him after two years of marriage.

Mailer's fondness for violence (of the kind he considered well intentioned and liberating) also found expression in his notorious article, "The White Negro" (*Dissent* 1957), which glorified personalized criminal violence and, specifically, the murder of a fifty-year-old candy store owner

[44] Quoted in Lennon, 519, 567.

[45] Lennon, 560, 563, 565.

[46] Lennon, 552.

[47] A remarkably similar instance of admiration of a convicted career criminal, Roger Knobelspiess, by leftist intellectuals, celebrity actors, and politicians occurred in France in the 1980s. Like Abbott he too was seen by these admirers as "an outlaw hero" who became a writer of great talent while in prison. Michel Foucault, the philosopher and admirer of the Iranian theocracy (see Chapter 7, pp. 273–275), wrote a preface to his first book. He was pardoned by socialist president Mitterrand in 1981, but was arrested again in 1983 and 1987 in a bank holdup. Like Abbott he too denounced his society and the prison system. (John Vinocur, "Convict-Hero of French Left Now a Burden for Socialists," *International Herald Tribune*, June 15, 1983; Richard Bernstein: "Symbol of French 'Injustice' Held in Robbery," *New York Times*, April 8, 1987.) He spent a total of 26 years in prison and was released in 1990, according to Wikipedia.

by two young black men, who "dared the unknown" and displayed courage, as Mailer saw it. It was the kind of murder that, for Mailer, was morally sanitized since it involved the laudable rejection both of social conventions and of "the repression of instinctual urges that are noble and natural, a suppression that seemed likely to lead ... to ... regimes that would wield technology to eliminate opponents ... so efficient that Hitler and Stalin would resemble crude bully boys by comparison. Against the emergence of such regimes stands the hipster" – as Mailer's biographer interpreted his outlook.[48] There is little doubt that Mailer believed in the essential goodness of human nature (suppressed by modern society) and the noble savagery of violent criminals protesting meaningless or repressive social conventions.

What Mailer admired about the black underclass was its bold defiance of white middle-class norms (presumably including criminal law).[49] The white "hipster" imitated such black defiance and rebelliousness and embraced the existential rejection of the cowardly white middle-class conformity and its norms and values. Mailer also made a sharp moral distinction between the large-scale impersonal violence he deplored – such as bombs dropped by American planes from high altitudes – and the authentic and impassioned personal kind engaged in by human beings confronting one another, preferably in hand-to-hand combat and motivated by strongly felt emotions, whatever they were.

Such views of violence were widespread during the Vietnam War, when many critics of the United States made clear their preference for what they considered the authentic and just violence of the Vietcong guerillas using simple weapons, over the mass-produced, technologically advanced means of destruction used by the American military.[50] Mailer, like other Western intellectuals attracted to communist (and other) dictators and

[48] Lennon, 219, 221, 619.

[49] Even an admirer of Mailer acknowledged that "Mailer was evolving his own romantic theories about the outlaw style, the existential superiority of the street hoodlum who lived beyond the law. His extraordinary essay, 'The White Negro' is the best example of that romanticism" (Pete Hamil: "Norman Mailer," in Jack Newfield ed.: *American Rebels*, New York 2003, 4).

[50] Sartre embraced the same position: "I refuse to put on the same plane the actions of group of poor hunted peasants ... and the actions of an immense army supported by a super-industrialized country ... Besides it is not the Vietnamese who invaded America and caused a deluge of fire to descend on a foreign people" (quoted in Maurice Cranston: "Sartre and Violence," *Encounter*, July 1967, 19–20). He also took pride in refusing to equate the terrorism of Algerian rebels with the actions of the "richly equipped" French army.

their social-political systems, was animated by a strong romantic, anti-technological disposition. The latter was further reflected in Mailer's proposition that Eichmann would have deserved some moral credit if he "had killed 500.000 victims with his bare hands."

Mailer's attitude toward violence also manifested itself in his stabbing Adele, one of his six wives. As he recalled the incident, at a party announcing his run for mayor of New York, "Adele was going nuts ... And finally, in a rage, I took out my penknife and stuck it into her with the idea 'Here, you think you're tough, I am tougher' ... The idea was not to do her any damage, just give her a nick or two." However, he later averred, upon visiting her in the hospital, that he stabbed her because "I love you and I had to save you from cancer." He and Adele "wept together," but according to her "his tears were of self-pity."

Also relevant to Mailer's attitude toward violence was that he was able to find "morsels of redemptive gain in all risk-taking acts, even when they were criminal," and likewise he was able "to find things to admire in unsavory individuals, even one who assassinated a president," and even in Charles Manson. As his biographer wrote, "Mailer is unable to resist making Oswald [assassin of president Kennedy] more likeable, more tortured and more substantial than he was." A reviewer wrote of his book on Oswald that he felt "invited to place a sympathetic arm around the killer's shoulder."

In the final analysis Mailer's beliefs, sampled above, were rooted in a belligerent and resentful estrangement from his own country and in his inflated notions of self-realization: "For the rest of his life he would harp on his disappointment with the United States for failing to achieve its millennial promise, the Puritan idea of a 'city on the hill,' a beacon of hope for humankind." By the same token he felt that the United States ought to recognize the damage caused by its "huge, profit-making way of life" and it if does not " 'we are going to be the most hated nation on earth.' "[51]

CASTRO, SARTRE, AND THE PURSUIT OF AUTHENTICITY

Jean-Paul Sartre was another important and influential Western intellectual enthralled by Castro's charisma and apparent authenticity, and his putative ability to realize the fondest dream of intellectuals (like Sartre),

[51] Lennon, 221, 263, 285, 303, 304, 447, 684, 720.

that is, to bridge the gap between word and deed, theory and practice, the personal and the political. Sartre was particularly impressed by Castro telling him that he became a "professional revolutionary" because "I can't stand injustice." Sartre wrote: "What pleased me in this answer was that this man – who fought ... for a whole people and who has no other interests than theirs – first recalled for me his personal passions, his private life ... He learned *the inanity of words*."[52] The latter was an especially remarkable attribution, indeed, pure fantasy, given Castro's veritable addiction to his own words, expressed in his recurring harangues directed at his captive audiences and lasting for several hours.[53]

Sartre's irrepressible idealization of Castro led him to the conclusion that "Castro, for me was the man of everything, able to view the whole ... [but] he was also the man of the smallest detail ... he joined the detail and the whole inseparably." He was persuaded that Castro is totally "disinterested" in matters concerning himself but devoted to everything that concerns the welfare of his people and he "discovers personal joys, a moment of happiness in the most austere enterprise." He was persuaded that Castro became his friend.[54]

For Sartre, Castro (and Che Guevara) promised nothing less than the possibility of overcoming the limitations of the human condition, the triumph of the mind over the body. Sartre was revitalized by the energy and spirit of these supermen. A midnight visit to Che Guevara's office prompted these recollections:

> I heard the door close behind my back and I lost both the memory of my old fatigue and any notion of the hour. Among these fully awake men, at the height of their powers, sleeping doesn't seem like a natural need, just a routine of which they had more or less freed themselves ... they have all excluded the routine alternation of lunch and dinner from their daily program ... Of all these night watchmen, Castro is the most wide awake. Of all these fasting people, Castro can eat the most and fast the longest. [They] ... exercise a veritable dictatorship over their own needs ... they roll back the limits of the possible.

[52] Jean-Paul Sartre: *Sartre on Cuba*, New York 1961, 44 (emphasis added).

[53] Another view of Castro's speech-making is offered by Jacobo Timmerman: "Castro produces several of these statements daily and believes ... that he's creating a new kind of revolutionary conscience. When you go from city to city, from group to group, from person to person, it becomes clear that his rhetoric has produced a vacuum in the conscience of the Cuban people, substituting a stifling collective paranoia" (*Cuba: A Journey*, New York 1990, 116).

[54] Sartre, 123, 135, 140.

Sartre also believed that these feats of endurance, enthusiasm, and determination displayed by Castro and Che "encourage the workers of the island to liquidate fatalism."[55]

As dawn approached (on the day of the visit described above), these amiable supermen

> watch the day, the palm trees in the court, or the sea; they are happy. They return to their offices, leafing through another dossier ... Their first visitor finds them at 8 or 9 o'clock [in the morning, that is] fresh, smiling, shaved, with eyes already dimmed by the far off look of expectations. There is no affectation ... They are thoughtful, they question themselves ... The meeting ends. Everyone embraces.

Sartre's projections and wishful attributions were unstoppable: "it is the same high demand that is found in the rigorous conduct of their morals ... They hold themselves accountable to the nation ... they refuse to waste money."

Sartre discovered, while accompanying Castro on a tour of inspection, how warm and informal were "the human relations of the leader and the *campesinos*" (peasants). Castro mingled with them freely and with pleasure "because they were of the same family with the same interests and the same needs." All around him Sartre saw evidence of the emerging new society, one without alienation and saturated with sustaining communitarian bonds and sentiments. He observed (more likely, imagined) that "confidence is the primordial bond" in the new society and was elated by what he considered "a radical overthrow of human relations" produced by the regime.[56] He was certain that the new human relationships being forged were, or promised to be, far superior to the old ones.

Sartre's concerns and hopes transcended what is conventionally seen as the political realm: he craved a fundamental transformation of human beings and social relations. Political change was merely a step toward realizing his fantasies of utopia that were remarkably uninformed by the lessons of history. He concluded the book on the same note, having witnessed "the pageantry of a national holiday" and the outpourings of "revolutionary joy":

> This last nocturnal image will render better than any other ... the joyous and somber life of Cuba. The future is its hope. The island awaits its salvation ... [they] are fighting to safeguard ... the New Ark of the revolution, the confidence and friendship which unites them. I do not see how any people can propose today a

[55] Sartre, 99, 102, 103, 104.

[56] Ibid., 93, 92, 100–101, 104–105, 125–126.

more urgent goal nor one more worthy ... The Cubans must win, or we lose all, even hope.[57]

Arguably, when Sartre visited Cuba in 1960 there was more reason for such hopeful assessments and expectations than in later years, and it was easy to succumb to an atmosphere of joyful revolutionary spirit and the agreeable anticipations it engendered. Carlos Franqui wrote: "J.P. Sartre and Simone de Beauvoir arrived in 1960, during one of the best moments of the Cuban Revolution ... There was a party atmosphere throughout the island, a collective joy that manifested itself in singing and playing bongo drums."[58] De Beauvoir recalled: "Well-known performers danced or sang in the squares ... 'It's the honeymoon of the revolution' Sartre said to me. No machinery, no bureaucracy, but a direct contact between leaders and people ... It wouldn't last forever, but it was a comforting sight. For the first time in our lives, we were witnessing *happiness that had been attained by violence*."[59] It was this imagined unity of ends and means that thrilled Sartre and Beauvoir. According to Maurice Cranston, Sartre believed that "nothing valuable can be accomplished in politics unless one is ready to 'soil one's hands.' "[60]

Even if we make allowances for happier circumstances that prevailed during the early years of the Cuban Revolution, Sartre's (and Beauvoir's) complete suspension of their critical faculties and his blind utopianism remain astonishing. His projections illuminate with great clarity his own longings and fantasies, as well as his reverence for the supposed renaissance men of the revolution, who, he believed, had succeeded in overcoming their human frailties and limitations he himself would have liked to overcome. This was hero worship at its purest, only tangentially related to the social-political causes and transformations these supermen sought to bring about. It was Sartre's own craving for "total transformation to be accomplished by revolution" resembling "St. Paul's concept of spiritual resurrection"[61] that made him especially vulnerable to Castro and what he stood for.

Finally, it should be pointed out that Sartre (like Mailer) was also greatly attracted to "righteous," liberating violence and this

[57] Ibid., 146.
[58] Franqui, 68.
[59] Beauvoir quoted in Michael Casey: *Che's Afterlife: The Legacy of an Image*, *New York* 2009, 70 (emphasis added).
[60] Cranston, 21.
[61] Renee Winegarten: *Writers and Revolution: The Fatal Lure of Action*, New York 1974, 307.

presumably further contributed to his being impressed by Castro. He had displayed this propensity on the occasion of his enthusiastically endorsing Franz Fanon's call for Third World violence against the colonial powers, as well as in his sympathy toward the Baader-Meinhof group in Germany.[62] Like Mailer (and Zizek), Sartre believed that violence can be empowering, redemptive, invigorating, and therapeutic. Unlike Mailer, he endorsed and glorified political rather than criminal violence, provided of course that it was used to further causes he approved of. In his Preface to Fanon's *Wretched of the Earth*, he averred that anti-colonial violence enabled those carrying it out to "recreate" themselves and that

> the native cures himself of colonial neurosis by thrusting out the settler through force of arms ... the rebel's weapon is the proof of his humanity ... to shoot down a European is to kill two birds with one stone, to destroy an oppressor and the man he oppresses at the same time: there remain a dead man and a free man ... The child of violence, at every moment draws from it his humanity ... violence, like Achilles' lance, can heal the wounds that it has inflicted."[63]

Fanon himself exemplifies the politically committed intellectual who becomes an enthusiastic supporter of what he considers righteous, liberating political violence.

Sartre's eager endorsement of anti-Western Third World violence manifested itself against a background of his profound alienation from his own society and a toxic hatred of Western societies in general. In the same Preface he wrote: "With us, to be a man is to be an accomplice of colonialism, since all of us, without exception have profited from colonial exploitation"; North America is a "super-European monstrosity" full of "chatter" about "liberty, equality, fraternity, love, honor, patriotism ... Our precious sets of values begin to molt; on closer scrutiny you won't see one that isn't stained by blood." He proposed that "the only chance of our being saved from shipwreck is the very Christian sentiment of guilt."[64]

[62] Meir Seidler: "The Beauty and the Beast: J.P. Sartre and the Baader-Meinhof Gang," *Terrorism and Political Violence*, September–October 2013.

[63] Sartre in Preface to Franz Fanon: *Wretched of the Earth*, New York 1963, 21, 22, 24, 30. Sartre's and Fanon's views of liberating violence also impressed Stokely Carmichael, who found in them "doctrinal basis" for black movements in the United States (see Rafael Rojas: *Fighting over Fidel: The New York Intellectuals and the Cuban Revolution*, Princeton NJ 2016, 188–189).

[64] Sartre, in Fanon 25, 26, 27. Sartre also argued that "violence, like Achilles' lance, can heal the wounds that it has inflicted" (quoted in Paul Berman: *Power and the Idealists*, New York 2005, 50).

Sartre's characterizations of Castro and Guevara reveal far more about him than about the subjects of his enthusiasm. Unrestrained credulousness, readiness to discard critical faculties, the wish to believe, utopian hopes, capacity for projection, longing for community, reverence for power, and a blind hero worship determined and distorted Sartre's perceptions and judgments of Castro and the system he was in the process of creating.[65]

OTHER ADMIRERS OF CASTRO

Castro's charisma and perceived selflessness also made a deep impression on Elizabeth Sutherland, American journalist and arts editor of *The Nation* at the time. She wrote: "He [Castro] seems ... utterly devoted to the welfare of his people ... When he speaks, it is as if his own dedication and energy were directly transfused into his listeners with almost physical force. Possessed of an extraordinary instinct for rhythm and voice pitch, he builds his speeches ... like long poems."[66]

Journalists Frank Mankiewicz and Kirby Jones found Castro "one of the most charming and entertaining men either of us had ever met ... [he] is personally overpowering ... one of the truly electrifying personalities in the world in which his peers seem dull and pedestrian."[67] Mankiewicz was also impressed by Castro's "designer fatigues ... They're very light weight, well cut – I wouldn't be surprised if they were Oscar de la Renta." Last but not least Mankiewicz was struck by Castro's "height ... spontaneity and the 'softness' of his hands."[68]

Julius Lester, a black writer, believed (at any rate in 1968) in a mysterious convergence between the supreme leader and his people: "The West says a 'cult of personality' exists in the figures of Mao and Fidel. That

[65] Following the 1971 show trial of the Cuban writer Heberto Padilla, Sartre (and some other Western intellectuals) criticized the Cuban regime and its repression of free expression. According to Artaraz, "this infamous episode ... was met by an international campaign for Padilla's release and marked the separation between European progressive intellectuals and the Revolution" (Artaraz, 194).

[66] Elizabeth Sutherland: "Cubans' Faith in Castro," *Manchester Guardian Weekly*, December 7, 1961. I assume she is the same person referred to by Rojas as the "young Chicana socialist Elizabeth Sutherland Martinez" (Rojas, 234–235), an anthropologist and author of *The Youngest Revolution: A Personal Report on Cuba*, New York 1969.

[67] Kirby Jones and Frank Mankiewicz: *With Fidel: A Portrait of Castro and Cuba*, Chicago 1975, 9, 10.

[68] Mankiewicz, quoted in Ratliff, 131, 140.

is not true. Revolutionary consciousness and revolutionary commitment destroyed the ego in Mao and Fidel, and in that destruction they as men became free. Mao is China. Fidel is Cuba. China is Mao. Cuba is Fidel."[69] Identifying a particular leader with an entire people or nation was an integral part of their cult and quasi-religious legitimation. Such claims and sentiments were also expressed, with great confidence, by Hitler, Mussolini, and more recently Hugo Chavez,[70] as well as their followers and propagandists. The admirers of dictators failed to notice that their charisma and sense of mission was inseparable from megalomania.

Angela Davis was among those who had no doubts about the intimate bonds between Castro and the Cuban people. She reported that

> talking to almost any Cuban about Fidel, it soon becomes clear that they did not see him as being anything more than extraordinarily intelligent, exceptionally committed, and an extremely warm human being endowed with great leadership talents ... people loved him in large part because of his honesty with them. Fidel was their leader, but most important he was also their brother in the largest sense of the word.

She was pleased to see on the streets of Cuban cities that advertisements for American products, "trade marks of global exploitation," had been replaced by "warm and stirring symbols [political exhortations – P.H.] that had real meaning for the people." Her belief that Cubans were possessed of a boundless enthusiasm for manual labor was the purest example of wishful projection:

> It seemed as if every able-bodied resident of Havana was rushing to the fields as though to a joyous carnival. On these faces reigned the serenity of meaningful work – the passion of commitment. They were finished with the politics of race and class, done with the acid bile of outdoing one's neighbor for the sake of materially rising above them.[71]

Members of the Venceremos Brigade (American volunteers, mostly college students attracted to the new regime and intent on helping to harvest sugarcane) were also impressed by what they saw as the prevailing

[69] Julius Lester: *Revolutionary Notes*, New York 1968, 177.

[70] Venezuelan state television showed videos of Chavez supporters "hold[ing]up hand-lettered signs that say 'I am Chavez,' the president's voice is heard in one of them shouting, 'I demand absolute loyalty because I am not me, I am not an individual, I am a people' ... Many of Mr Chavez's followers speak of him in religious terms, as a god-like presence and the [television] campaign seems intended to feed those perceptions" (William Neuman: "With Chavez Ill and State in Flux, Videos Offer an Image of Stability," *New York Times*, January 8, 2013).

[71] Angela Davis: *An Autobiography*, New York 1974, 203, 204, 207.

spirit of egalitarianism: "There is so little condescension here. That is the most beautiful thing. Every man, no matter what he is doing, is contributing. Every man and woman, and Fidel brings this out constantly, is just as important as he, Fidel is."[72] The use of "Fidel" was officially encouraged and intended to create an aura of informal (and inauthentic) egalitarianism, a good example of false consciousness. This usage made a profound impression on sympathetic visitors such as Angela Davis, as well as Graham Greene, who claimed that "even his name is an object of veneration: Fidel 'whom no Cuban except an enemy calls by the name of Castro'."[73]

Castro, as the other dictators here discussed, had the reputation among the sympathetic intellectuals of being a brilliant fellow intellectual, not only an active, authentic revolutionary but a deep thinker. He made a point of having read (or claiming to have read) books written by some of his visitors from abroad and conducting lengthy discussions with the more important ones among them. He told C. Wright Mills, the American sociologist and social critic, "that his *Power Elite* had been a bedside book of most of the *guerrileros* in the Sierra Maestra. Castro invited him to come on a tour ... of the country."[74]

Elizabeth Sutherland suggested that Castro was "above all an educator of his people ... When he spoke in public, the scene often resembled a huge ... classroom ... A concern with morality, especially honesty dominated his teachings."[75]

Castro's allegedly encyclopedic knowledge and attention to detail were part of his image and personality, a trait that was also part of the image of other modern dictators, as well as the kings and emperors of the past. Kirby and Mankiewicz wrote:

> He does know ... the annual construction rate of schools, housing, factories and hospitals ... their scheduled dates for conclusion and the building plans projected for the next five to ten years. He knows the number of students at each level of the educational process ... He knows the water temperatures at the fishing ports and when they are most favorable for catching various fish. He knows how many feet can be spanned by concrete ... He knows, almost hourly, sugar's price on the world market.[76]

[72] Sandra Levinson and Carol Brightman eds.: *Venceremos Brigade: Young Americans Sharing the Life and Work of Revolutionary Cuba*, New York 1971, 160. Levinson was an SDS activist and admirer of Castro, whom Hayden interviewed (Hayden, 112).

[73] Quoted in Cabrera Infante, 297.

[74] K.S. Karol: *Guerillas in Power: The Course of the Cuban Revolution*, New York 1970, 58.

[75] Sutherland, 112.

[76] Jones and Mankiewicz, 217–218.

It is hard to think of a relationship between a dictator and a distinguished intellectual as intimate, durable, and mutually beneficial as that between Castro and Gabriel Garcia Marquez, the famous writer.[77] Marquez was not merely a foreign admirer visiting Cuba, he had easy and regular access to Castro and "was showered with privilege: his own institute of cinema in Havana ... a mansion, a Mercedes, a staff of servants."[78] He was "Panegyrist, court adviser, press agent, ambassador-at-large, plenipotentiary representative, head of foreign public relations ... all these things for Castro." In 1996 he told President Clinton "if you and Fidel could sit face to face, there wouldn't be any problem left"[79] – a proposition both wrong-headed and foolish. It is hard to know if Marquez actually believed it.

Marquez's loyalty survived each and every moral outrage or political setback Castro perpetrated or experienced, including occasions when some formerly admiring Western intellectuals could no longer tolerate and rationalize his repressive policies and especially the persecution of dissenters such as the writer Herberto Padilla. If and when Marquez had some qualms about Castro's policies it was not on account of their moral defect but because of the possibility that his enemies could use them to discredit him. Charles Lane wrote, "Castro has no more fervent defender than Garcia Marquez ... [who] never gave up the ambition of being useful to Castro ... 'Fidel is one of the people I love most in the world' he explained."[80] He regarded Castro's speech-making as an "inspiration, an irresistible blinding state of grace, which is only denied by those who have not had the glorious experience of living through it."[81]

Marquez also thought highly of Castro on account of his "needing only six hours of sleep after an intense day of work." Marquez's portrait of Castro, Jacobo Timmerman wrote, "is a Rambo ... who triumphs owing to his supernatural intelligence." According to Marquez, Castro's "rarest virtue is the ability to foresee the evolution of an event to its farthest reaching consequences ... no one can explain how he has time, or what method he employs to read so much and so fast." He even had time to read and make insightful observations about an orthopedic treatise, Marquez noted.[82]

[77] The same point was made by Enrique Krauze in "In the Shadow of the Patriarch," *New Republic*, November 4, 2009, see especially 38.

[78] Charles Lane: "The Writer and His Labyrinth," *New Republic*, August 25, 1987, 33.

[79] Marquez quoted in Krauze 2009, 46.

[80] Lane, 33, 38.

[81] Quoted in Ignacio Ramonet: "A Hundred Hours with Fidel," in Ramonet, 15.

[82] Marquez quoted in Timmerman, 34.

In 1959 Marquez was invited to cover the trials and executions of hundreds of former officers of Batista's army and "came away from this grim spectacle a believer, accepting an offer to help open a bureau of *Prensa Latina*, Castro's official wire service."[83] Krauze summed up his political disposition:

[Marquez] professed an absolute faith in the Revolution as it was incarnated in the heroic figure of the Commandante … in thirty four turbulent years [he] has never publicly detached himself from that epiphanic vision … What he saw … was what he wanted to see: five million Cubans who belonged to the Committees for the Defense of the Revolution, not as spies and enforcers of the Revolution but as its happy, spontaneous, multitudinous true force.

Marquez even claimed to believe that Castro established an "almost telepathic system of communication" with the people and that "His gaze revealed the hidden softness of his childlike heart [*sic*] … he has survived unscathed the harsh and insidious corrosion of daily power, his secret sorrows … He has set up a whole system of defense against the cult of personality …' Castro had managed to achieve the 'coveted and elusive' dream of all rulers: affection."[84]

In short, Marquez would have us believe that Castro miraculously escaped the corruptions of power. He also proposed – most implausibly – that Castro "is afflicted by 'shyness' and … is 'one of the greatest idealists of our time,' [and] a profound intellectual who 'breakfasts with no less than 200 pages of news from all over the world,' reads treatises on orthopedics in his spare time."[85]

If, as I suggested earlier, intellectuals are drawn to dictators because of their belief that they embody both idealism and power wisely used, for Marquez the attractions of power played an especially large part. Charles Lane wrote: "All his passions and his principles notwithstanding, Garcia Marquez has an unconquerable weakness for power … [his] power-worship was already evident on his early trips to Eastern Europe."[86] His biographer chronicled his

strange fascination with Stalin's embalmed corpse: "nothing impressed me so much as the delicacy of his hands … In no way did he resemble the heartless character Nikita Khrushchev denounced in a terrible rant." [Marqurez said] Martin [the biographer] also records … [Marquez's] "intoxication" at the physical

[83] Lane, 33.
[84] Krauze 2009, 44, 46.
[85] Marquez quoted in Lane, 34.
[86] Lane, 34.

proximity of Janos Kadar, the man who suppressed the Hungarian uprising whose deeds he strives to justify. Upon learning of the execution of ... Imre Nagy [head of the Hungarian revolutionary government] Marquez criticizes the act not in moral terms but as a "political mistake."[87]

As his long association with Castro and the numerous tasks he performed in his service indicate, the idealism of Marquez was colored by a thirst for power, influence, and recognition quite irrelevant to his literary accomplishments. His avid "collaboration with oppression and dictatorship" (as Krauze put it) is among the most notorious instances of what might be called "the treason of intellectuals."

Unlike the favorably disposed foreigners, numerous Cubans who knew Castro well, and had for substantial periods of time close working relations with him, had markedly different and far more negative views of him. These views paralleled their disillusionment with the political system he created and dominated. Insofar as they and most critics of the government considered Castro the predominant influence on the system, they held him responsible for its degeneration that included both political repression and economic mismanagement, resulting in crippling shortages and declining living standards.

CASTRO AND THE SYSTEM

The reverential views of Castro were an integral part of the positive, hopefully expectant disposition toward the new Cuban social-political system and the human beings it had supposedly shaped and improved. Even an author relatively restrained in his praise of Cuba under Castro believed that the ideology guiding the revolutionary transformations "placed mankind at its center" and that "the leadership's discourse was founded on building comradeship, solidarity, national pride and dignity – a new society based on a superior form of consciousness and a higher socialist morality ... that put man at the center."[88] Mr. Artaraz evidently did not reflect on the compatibility of comradeship, solidarity, and dignity with the encouragement and rewarding of institutionalized spying on one another by the residentially based Committees for the Defense of the Revolution.[89]

[87] Quoted in Krauze 2009, 42.

[88] Artaraz, 26–27.

[89] See Arch Puddington: "Revolutionary Defense Committees," in Irving Louis Horowitz ed.: *Cuban Communism 1959–1995*, New Brunswick NJ 1995.

Cuba also inspired high hopes among Western intellectuals who identified with the New Left and believed that the role of intellectuals in Cuba was going to be altogether different, that they would play an important role in building the new society. Artaraz wrote:

> One of the characteristics of the Cuban Revolution that did much to attract the progressive left-wing intellectual from the West was the special relationship developed between the state and the intellectual. The importance attached to intellectuals ... was evident from the Revolution's search for the support of the international intelligentsia ... This process began with the visit of Sartre and de Beauvoir ... in 1960.

Artaraz believed that the Cuban Revolution, and the political system it gave rise to, created a new type of intellectual, "a vanguard of intellectual workers ... part of the mass-scale drive to extend the population's internalization of some basic ideological precepts in conjunction with its [the Revolution's] political needs."[90] In less tortured prose he might have acknowledged that these new intellectuals were given the task of indoctrinating the population.[91] Paul Sweezy's favorable impressions acquired during his visit to Cuba were typical of the period: "To be with these people, to see with your own eyes how they are rehabilitating and transforming a whole nation, to share their dreams of great tasks and achievements that lie ahead – these are purifying and liberating experiences. You come away with your faith in humanity restored."[92]

Susan Sontag was similarly impressed by what she saw as the beneficial impact of political change on the demeanor and behavior of the people, her observations clearly shaped by what she disliked in her own society:

> The Cubans know a lot about spontaneity, gaiety, sensuality and freaking out. They are not linear, desiccated creatures of print culture ... The increase of energy comes because they have found new focus for it: the community ... the first thing a visitor to Cuba notices is the enormous energy level. It is still common, as it has

[90] Artaraz, 33–34, 37–38.

[91] The high hopes and expectations of New Left intellectuals regarding the rise of the new type of intellectual in Cuba – at once politically committed and independent – could not, and did not, endure. Beginning with Padilla's show trial and throughout the post-Soviet era, Cuba turned out to be, and has remained, one of the most intolerant political systems in existence, imprisoning, silencing, or expelling dissident, non-conformist intellectuals. These policies continued, in milder forms, after 2006, under Raul Castro, with short-term arrests replacing lengthy imprisonment.

[92] Quoted in Peter Clecak: *Radical Paradoxes: Dilemmas of the American Left 1945–1970*, New York 1973, 152.

been throughout ten years of the revolution, for people to go without sleep – talking and working several nights a week.[93]

Sontag did not disclose the basis of her sweeping and confident generalization about the sleeping habits of the Cuban population.

A British visitor, David Caute, detected in the wake of a (highly organized) demonstration a euphoric mood among the participants: "As we walk home ... the demonstrators are climbing into their trucks and buses, euphorically happy and proud as any festival's children could be. For us, Cuba has suddenly fulfilled her promise and we too are happy."[94] Michael Parenti, deeply estranged from American society and what he considered its debilitating preoccupations and values, found welcome differences in Cuba:

what struck me ... about the people of Havana was the absence of any kind of "struggle" one experiences in North American cities ... Cubans are not preoccupied with money anxieties of the kind that plague most Americans, and the absence of money problems and all related competitiveness, personal fears and aggressions has a palpable effect on social relations.[95]

Needless to say, these beliefs – rather, wishful fantasies and projections about the Cuban attitude toward money – had as much empirical basis as Sontag's ideas about how much Cubans slept.

Members of the Venceremos Brigade (mentioned earlier) were similarly detached from reality as they suggested that Cubans "were 'the most unalienated people [they'd] ever known.'"[96] Attributing the absence of alienation to people living in communist countries was among the most fanciful and widely held misconceptions of these societies and those who lived in them. It was also a reflection of the unmet desires for meaning, solidarity, and community of the admirers of these systems who were disposed to find what they were looking for.

Waldo Frank was among those who transferred his past enthusiasm for the Soviet Union to Cuba, succeeding, in both cases, in finding a connection between the new political systems and the heart-warming authenticity of ordinary people, to wit, "young men and women sparkling with animals spirits" in Cuba. He also believed that "a revolution such as

93 Susan Sontag: "Some Thoughts on the Right Way (for Us) to Love the Cuban Revolution," *Ramparts*, April 1969, 10, 14.

94 David Caute: *Cuba Yes?* New York 1974, 84, 85.

95 Parenti quoted in Ronald Radosh ed.: *The New Cuba: Paradoxes and Potentials*, New York 1976, 41.

96 Quoted in Levinson and Brightman eds., 238.

Castro's is nourished by the direct, almost physical embrace of leaders and people."[97] In Russia a few decades earlier, he came upon "happy workers, because they are whole men and women." In a Russian village he found "a homogenous world: man and animal and fruit, air and wood and earth were a single substance … I stood in the village mud and sensed the organic rhythm of this telluric world."[98]

Waldo Frank apparently succeeded in transmitting his political-ideological disposition to his grandson, Marc Frank, a self-described "tireless crusader for social justice" who moved to Cuba in 1984 and published two books defending "the economic, political and moral leadership of Fidel Castro" and blaming the United States for most of the economic (and other) difficulties of Cuba.[99] In his recent book he called Castro "the last of the romantic revolutionary figures" of the twentieth century and compared him to Nelson Mandela.[100] While not as starry-eyed as many other sympathetic Americans (including his grandfather), he was unable, or unwilling, to recognize or admit that systemic and determined repression was an essential source of the longevity and stability of the Cuban system. Thus he wrote that "the police and military do not systematically brutalize and bloody the population," overlooking the fact that in a well-established and efficient police state, such as Castro's Cuba, the population has internalized predictable punishment for any display of political nonconformity,

[97] Waldo Frank: *Cuba: Prophetic Island*, New York 1961, 149, 163. Frank was held in high regard by the Cuban authorities, Castro included, being seen as a major source of influence (like Sartre and Mills) on the thinking of American intellectuals. Castro gave him a gift of "a special wooden tobacco box." In a letter Frank "expressed gratitude to Castro for the 'generous and powerful new world' that the Cuban leader and his revolution were creating … The revolutionary regime took Frank's letter quite seriously … At Castro's order, Frank was hired [in 1959] by the Prime Minister of Education Armando Hart and Foreign Minister Raul Roa to write a 'portrait of Cuba' to be published by the Cuban government's Dept of Cultural Relations. Frank set his initial fee at $ 2500 but … he would request additional funds, in the end charging more than $ 5000." The book (I quoted from) was never published in Cuba since it apparently "diverg[ed] from Havana's expectations"; that is to say, Frank had some minor and mild reservations about "the radicalization of Cuba" and the book also contained "several factual errors" (Rafael Rojas: *Fighting over Fidel: The New York Intellectuals and the Cuban Revolution*, Princeton NJ 2016, 62–63, 64, 70).

[98] Waldo Frank: *Dawn in Russia*, New York 1932, 98, 99, 109, 127.

[99] See Enrique Krauze: "The New Cuba?" *New York Review of Books*, March 19, 2015, 24, 26 (review of Marc Frank: *Cuban Revelations: Behind the Scenes in Havana*, 2013).

[100] See Marc Frank: *Cuban Revelations*, 48.

hence there is no need for overt or regular displays of police brutality. Elsewhere he wrote that on the rare occasion of an unauthorized demonstration as in 1994, "there was no tear gas, and no riot police. Bused-in construction workers, some with metal rods in hand, quickly restored order." He did not make clear if he considered this more informal crowd control and intimidation, delegated to seemingly unorganized supporters of the regime, to be an improvement over tear gas administered by the uniformed riot police. He made the same point about the handling of a protest march of female relatives of imprisoned dissidents by "the mob" and policewomen, who removed the protestors by buses without recourse to "armed riot police, cops on horses or water canons." Again, it is not clear if he considered this a reflection of the moral superiority of the regime or just a more efficient way of dealing with public dissent.

The key to these questionable assessments is a confident core belief in the legitimacy of the system and in its wide popular support: "Most Cubans had adapted to an overregulated society through the decades. They believed that unity and discipline were prerequisites for development, social justice and defense of their country and revolution."[101] But it is problematic, to say the least, to reach such conclusions in regard to an "overregulated" (i.e., highly repressive) society where free expression and unorthodox political opinions have been systematically and powerfully discouraged over decades, and independent public opinion surveys or outlets for free expression don't exist. Most obviously, the legitimacy of the political system of any country is open to doubt when well over 10 percent of its entire population removed itself, legally and illegally, often taking huge risks in attempting to do so.

It should be emphasized that most of the highly enthusiastic assessments of Cuba (as those here referred to, or quoted above) were limited to the 1960s and 1970s. Cuba's increasingly close association with the Soviet Union (discredited by the New Left, as noted earlier) undermined its moral legitimacy and reduced its popularity among New Left and left-liberal intellectuals. This is not to suggest that the totalitarian or authoritarian features of the Cuban system resulted from its close ties with the Soviet Union. Arguably, Cuba under Fidel Castro was more intolerant of intellectual and personal freedoms than the Soviet Union in much of the post-Stalin period.

[101] Marc Frank, 15, 23, 200, 252.

THE SELF-CONCEPTIONS OF CASTRO

Given the plausible connection between the dictators' self-conception and their perceptions by others, it is of considerable interest what Castro thought of himself and his political roles.[102] As to the latter, Castro could not comprehend how anybody could conceive of him as a dictator: "I ... don't understand why I'm called a dictator. What is a dictator? It's someone who makes arbitrary, unilateral decisions, who acts over and above institutions, over and above the laws, who is under no restraint but his own decisions and whims." This was a good summary of many of the attributes of a dictator. Remarkably, Castro was persuaded (or pretended to be?) that these attributes did not apply to him:

> I don't make unilateral decisions. This isn't even a presidential government. We have a Council of State. My function as a leader exists within a collective ... the important decisions ... are always studied, discussed and made collectively. I can't appoint ministers or ambassadors. I don't appoint the lowest public official in this country ... I don't give orders or rule by decree.

These remarks are reminiscent of the Webbs' surrealistic assessment of the limited powers of Stalin noted earlier. One may wonder if Castro truly believed what he told his interviewer about his limited power, or whether those statements were part of a sustained effort at image building, or rather image preservation?

Of further interest is Castro's response – central to his self-conception – to accusations of his alleged cruelty: "I really think that a man who has devoted his entire life to fighting injustice, oppression of every kind, to serving others, to fighting for others, to preaching and practicing solidarity, I think that all of that is totally incompatible with cruelty." The reader may wonder why he bothered to address at all such a supposedly false accusation. There is no evidence to suggest that Castro enjoyed mistreating people he considered politically harmful. More likely such treatment was a reflection of subordinating means to ends. He certainly had no compassion for those who might have interfered with his plans and programs.

[102] I am unaware of any document comparable to Castro's *Spoken Autobiography* that would allow learning about the self-conceptions of the other dictators discussed in this book. Hitler's *Mein Kampf* has a few autobiographical details, but unlike Castro's reflections at the end of his political career, *Mein Kampf anticipated* Hitler's political programs and actions and is a collection of pieces about Hitler's political ideas and opinions on a wide range of subjects. Mussolini published an autobiography in 1928 dealing with his youth and struggle for, and early years in, power. To the best of my knowledge neither Stalin nor Mao produced autobiographies of any kind.

Castro's highly favorable view of himself and his historical role presumably helped him to engage in what can only be called blatant and brazen denial (see below) of the well-documented and widely experienced repression of the whole population over long periods of time. A key indicator of a popular response to this repression was the exodus of more than 10 percent of the entire population over the years, often under extremely hazardous conditions. To be sure, Cubans of different socio-economic background also sought to escape the dire economic conditions, not only the lack of political and personal freedom.

Castro had no hesitation in claiming that

> Here no one has ever been imprisoned for being a dissident or because they see things differently from the way the Revolution does. Our courts sentence people ... on the basis of laws and they judge counter-revolutionary *acts* ... we have followed a line of absolute respect for the physical integrity of the individual ... there is not a single case of physical maltreatment or torture in the entire history of the revolution ... There has never been a demonstration broken up by public law enforcement. No police officer has ever ... beaten a citizen during a demonstration.

As regards the 1998 show trial and execution of General Ochoa, a "Hero of the Republic of Cuba" and distinguished fighter for the revolution, as well as commander of Cuban forces in Ethiopia and Angola, who was charged with corruption and drug-trafficking – Castro resorted to the unoriginal, generic, and lame excuse for political repression favored by all dictators: "We had to mount a firing squad ... when we discovered grave acts of treason ... *there was no alternative*, the country was put in great danger, and we had to be harsh, and even more so with people from our own ranks who compromised the country and the Revolution." On another occasion he claimed that, unlike the Soviet Union, Cuba had nothing like Stalinism, no cult of personality, and no "abuse of power."

Contemplating in retrospect his entire political life, Castro was unwilling or unable to express any regrets and concluded his "spoken autobiography" on an implausibly and unrealistically optimistic note:

> I have not one iota of regret about what we've done in our country and the way we've organized our society ... I can say now, after forty-six years since the triumphs ... that what we've achieved is far greater than the dreams we could conceive back then and we were pretty good dreamers from the start! ... We aren't done by a long shot. We live in the best time in our history, with the greatest hope ever, and you see it everywhere ... You don't have to measure our elections by the number of votes. I measure them by the depths of sentiments, by the warmth that I've been seeing for so many years. I never saw faces so filled with hope, with

pride. And all that has been coming together ... There will be greater and greater participation and we will be a nation with a holistic, unified general culture.[103]

Castro routinely legitimated all his policies by his favorite abstraction "the Revolution," and it was he who determined what policies were to be pursued on its behalf, or in its spirit. A good example is his famous statement: "What are the rights of writers and artists, revolutionary or not revolutionary? Within the revolution, everything, against the revolution, no right."[104] It was a notoriously vague proposition, especially the key phrase "within the Revolution," which was subject to his interpretation.

Castro's unshakeable self-confidence and exalted self-conception converged with the needs and disposition of his supporters outside Cuba who were intent on locating and revering a self-proclaimed redeemer who would find new, uplifting ways to reorganize society, instruct people how to lead more meaningful lives, and, in effect, alter the human condition.

THE MYTH AND REALITY OF CHE GUEVARA

The inclusion of Che Guevara in this book requires explanation since he was not a dictator and his power did not approach that held by the dictators here discussed, including, especially, that of Castro. He was a close associate and helper of Castro, with whom he eventually developed ideological differences. Born in Argentina, where he trained as a physician, he was one of the small group of revolutionaries led by Castro who sailed from Mexico to Cuba in 1956 to start guerilla war against the Batista government, and he played an important part in it. Subsequently he was Supreme Prosecutor in La Cabana Fortress in Havana, President of the National Bank of Cuba (1960), author of a manual on guerilla warfare, and minister of industry (1961). None of these positions could have predicted the unique posthumous hero worship he became the subject of.

As one of his biographers wrote: "Rarely in history has a single figure been so passionately and universally accepted as the personification of revolutionary idealism and practice."[105] For Paul Sweezy and Leo

[103] Ramonet, 360, 367 (emphasis added), 571–573, 583, 622, 624.

[104] Quoted in Victoria Burnett: "Blurring the Boundaries between Art and Activism in Cuba," *New York Times*, *The Arts*, January 24, 2015, 6.

[105] Richard L. Harris: *Death of a Revolutionary: Che Guevara's Last Mission*, New York 1970, 2007, 20; Rojas, 104. For a collection of reverential writings about Guevara, see Marienne Alexander ed.: *Viva Che! Contributions in Tribute to Ernesto "Che" Guevara*, New York 1968.

Huberman, "Guevara personified the idea of the Cuban Revolution that was the closest to the New York Left's global view."[106]

In 1965 he led an expeditionary force in Congo to support a guerilla movement that failed, and in 1966 went to Bolivia to organize another one. The badly organized movement had little local support; he was captured and executed in 1967. In 1997 his remains were returned to Cuba and interred in a mausoleum.

According to the author of a book on the Cuban revolution and the New Left, Guevara was "considered not only an intellectual but the quintessential embodiment of the intellectual," as well as "the new poster hero of the New Left." Some of his statements were converted "into a near-religious experience for generations of would-be revolutionaries." Most importantly, he came to symbolize the erasure of the difference between "the intellectual as 'thinker' and intellectual as 'man of action.'"[107]

Although Guevara's efforts to stimulate guerilla movements in various parts of the world had failed, as did his domestic initiatives to create new, idealistic, and non-materialistic human beings, he became the subject of an unprecedented global hero worship, more enduring and widespread than all the others considered in this book. Moreover, this cult has been the most spontaneous, and the least dependent on official authorization and support.[108] He came to personify the authentic romantic revolutionary, "celebrated as a Byron, a Malraux, a Lawrence of the 1960s: Che in his beret, with his cigar, inspiration of a revolution that never arrived."[109] For Allen Ginsberg, unaware of, or temporarily overlooking, his homophobic disposition, "Guevara's early death naturalized him not as a leftist leader in the political realm, but as an icon in the poetics of the Beat Generation."[110]

Daniel Benveniste, an American leftist disillusioned with both communist Cuba and Venezuela under Chavez, could not understand

> how members of the counterculture who previously embraced the values of peace, love, nonviolence, free speech, tolerance of differences, human rights … could turn around and celebrate Che Guevara, who personally executed or oversaw the execution of about five hundred people … [and who] spoke of "hatred as an element of struggle; unbending hatred for the enemy, which pushes a human being

[106] Rojas, 104.

[107] Artaraz, 57, 73, 74, 171.

[108] Only after his death and the repatriation of his remains to Cuba did his cult become institutionalized in Cuba.

[109] William Pfaff: *The Bullet's Song: Romantic Violence and Utopia*, New York 2004, 284.

[110] Rojas, 163–164.

beyond his natural limitations, making him into an effective, violent, selective, cold-blooded killing machine."

Che also wrote: "I feel my nostrils dilate savoring the acrid smell of gunpowder and blood of the enemy."[111]

Especially startling and unexpected has been the posthumous commercialization of Guevara's image enlisted to sell "T-shirts, pants, caps, bandanas, lighters, key chains, coffee mugs, wallets and backpacks ... The image has been used to sell car air fresheners in Peru, snowboards in Switzerland, beer in Korea, and wine in Italy ... Smirnoff vodka and Converse sneakers ... mouse pads, doormats, beach towels, cigarette cases, condoms, lip balm, hair combs."[112] It is not easy to explain how and why this commercialization came about, who initiated it, and who determined that the image of this fierce critic of capitalism could and should advertise a wide range of consumer goods and services.[113] Jorge Castenada (one of his numerous biographers) suggested that he has become a symbol of the 1960s and a reflection of nostalgia for the idealism of that period, and that his "popularity today has little to do with his political views."[114] While it is certainly true that most of his posthumous admirers have not been familiar with the specifics, or even the substance, of his political beliefs and activities, his cult did have unmistakable political components, in addition to the diffuse utopian elements and longings for some fundamental transformation of existing social systems and human beings, even of human nature.

Arguably, Che Guevara has been especially appealing to intellectuals,[115] and possibly more so than any of the dictators considered in this volume. Christopher Hitchens explained this by pointing out that "he was one of those rare people for whom there is no real gap between

[111] Guevara quoted in Daniel Benveniste: *The Venezuelan Revolution: A Critique from the Left*, North Charleston SC 2015, 119.

[112] Casey, 29.

[113] This was especially ironic given Guevara's profound detestation of capitalism. Already in 1953, he wrote "how terrible these capitalist octopuses are. I have sworn before a picture of the old and mourned comrade Stalin that I won't rest until I see the capitalist octopuses annihilated" (quoted in Christopher Hitchens: *And Yet ... Essays*, New York 2015, 9).

[114] Castenada, quoted in Doreen Carvajal: "From Rebel to Pop Icon: 30 Years after His Death Che Guevara Has New Charisma," *New York Times*, April 30, 1997, B2.

[115] Apparently he was aware of this since during his ill-fated Bolivian campaign he expected their help, instructing Regis Debray, one of his most active Western intellectual supporters, "to contact J.P. Sartre and Bertrand Russell about organizing an international fund to help the Bolivian guerillas movement" (Harris, 124).

conviction and practice."[116] He was himself an intellectual, an authentic revolutionary, and a genuine idealist who proved his commitment by a willingness to die for the cause in a hopeless and poorly organized guerilla campaign. None of the other figures discussed in this study died on the battlefield in the attempted service of the ideals they championed; neither did any one of them become a symbol used to sell consumer goods and services in capitalist countries.

At the same time, and paradoxically enough, Guevara's cult offers a superb illustration of the religious, or secular-religious, wellspring of all these cults and the hero worship they entail. Mark Rudd, a 1960s radical activist who visited Cuba in 1968 inspired by Guevara, confessed in his autobiography: "Like a Christian seeking to emulate the life of Christ, I passionately wanted to be a revolutionary like Che, no matter what the price."[117] Michael Casey wrote: "In dying, Che rounds out his myth. We are left with a life similar to that of the prophets of the mainstream religions. A man, a teacher, lays down a code of personal conduct from which to build a just society, and then proceeds to live and die according to it." Photographed after being shot to death,

> Che exudes the wisdom of the dead. He looks at us with neither condemnation nor pity. This is "the gaze of the dead Guevara" wrote biographer Jorge Castenada, "looking at his tormentors and pardoning them because they know not what they are doing, and [looking] at the world, assuring it that one does not suffer when one dies for one's ideas."[118]

The suggested comparison with Christ could hardly have been more explicit.

As Casey reported, "the myth of divinity strengthened after his real death. Bolivian peasant women took locks from the hair of Che's corpse in the belief that these relics would protect them." When his grave was located and some of his material possessions found, "these items took on a status akin to religious relics" and were traded "as collector's items."[119]

[116] Christopher Hitchens: "Goodbye to All That," *New York Review of Books*, July 17, 1997, 22.

[117] Rudd, quoted in Hayden, 110. See also Paul Hollander: "Unrepentant," review of Mark Rudd: *Underground: My Life with SDS and the Weathermen* in *Claremont Review of Books*, September 2009.

[118] Castenada quoted in Casey, 60, 185. Religious projections were not limited to Guevara. Carleton Beals, another sympathizer with the Cuban Revolution, believed that "the young Sierra Maestra rebels entering Havana with their beards and crucifixes looked like biblical prophets approaching a new Mecca of justice and liberty" (Rojas, 231).

[119] Casey, 180.

Much earlier in his life, seven months after the revolutionary war ended, writing about the peasants' attitude toward the revolution: "Che employed religious symbolism, rendering their [the peasants'] travails as a kind of Pilgrim's Progress in which individuals found redemption through sacrifice, attaining final enlightenment by learning to live for the common good." Lee Anderson also noted that Guevara "idealized life in the sierra ... his evocation of a pastoral utopia wrought through armed struggle was a vision he sought to replicate on an international scale ... he identified war as the ideal circumstance in which to achieve a socialist consciousness ... socialism was the natural order of mankind, and guerilla war the chrysalis from which it would emerge."[120]

When Guevara died, Sartre proclaimed that "he was 'not only an intellectual but also the most complete human being of our age.' "[121] Anderson observed that "Che endured as a role model and as an almost mystical symbol of veneration. He inspired new generations of fighters and dreamers because of the revolutionary principles he represented – fearlessness, self-sacrifice, honesty and devotion to the cause."[122] Toward the end of his life, leading the small band of guerillas in Bolivia, Guevara said: "a struggle of this type gives us the opportunity to become revolutionaries, the highest step in the human ladder, and also allows us to test ourselves as men."[123] This was Guevara's version of self-transcendence by means of participation in lethal revolutionary struggle.

A key to Guevara's idealism *and* ruthlessness was his preoccupation with, and belief in, the possibility of creating a new socialist man. Harris wrote:

> Che was dedicated to living his life in accordance with his concept of the new kind of human being that would come into existence in the revolutionary struggle ... this new type would arise out of the revolutionary struggle to liberate humanity from the egoistic individualism, dehumanizing exploitation and social alienation of capitalism ... [he] felt that the struggle against capitalism and the construction of a new socialist order required a new type of human being ... committed to making personal sacrifices for the good of others.[124]

This belief was also emblematic of the totalitarian mentality: the ambitiousness of the project demanded and justified huge amounts of coercion and regimentation – the more lofty the ends, the less moral attention the

[120] Jon Lee Anderson: *Che Guevara: A Revolutionary Life* (rev. edn.), New York 2010, 285.
[121] Sartre, quoted in Anderson, 446.
[122] Ibid., xi.
[123] Guevara quoted in ibid., 691.
[124] Harris, 268–269.

means received and deserved. Guevara summed up the complete, serene politicization of his personality, writing that "there is no life outside the revolution."[125]

Shortly after Guevara's death Castro proposed that Guevara was the perfect role model for children who ought to become "'ardent revolutionaries. We want them to be like Che.' Ever since, Cuban school children have chanted each morning: 'Pioneers for communism! We will be like Che.'"[126] Castro also averred that "If we want to be the ... model of a human being who does not belong to our time but to the future ... such a model, without a single stain on his conduct ... is Che." These statements of Castro culminated in "Che's rehabilitation as a saintlike presence in Cuba."[127] As Geyer put it, "in this new resurrected life ... Ernesto Guevara became 'Che, of the heroic poster.' But it was a distorted image. 'That poster that was in the dormitory of every young man in the 1960s and 1970s' ... a friend of Che's mused many years later ... 'that is not Guevara, that is a myth.'"[128] His famous and endlessly reproduced photograph taken by Alberto Korda was credited with being "capable of stirring the forces of human imagination and tapping into deep-seated longings for a better world" and with encouraging people "to dream of defeating death."[129]

The cult and veneration of Che Guevara has been most memorably expressed by I.F. Stone, the journalist and social critic, who on this occasion readily abandoned his supposedly hardnosed, skeptical disposition:

> He was he first man I ever met whom I thought not just handsome but beautiful. With his curly, reddish beard, he looked like a cross between a faun and a Sunday School print of Jesus ... In Che, one felt a desire to heal and pity for suffering ... It was out of love, like the perfect knight of medieval romance, that he had set out to combat with the powers of the world ... In a sense he was, like some early saint, taking refuge in the desert. Only there could the purity of the faith be safeguarded.[130]

Eduardo Galeano, another admirer, discerned in the picture of the dead Guevara "the magnificent face of this Christ of the Rio Plata."[131]

[125] Guevara quoted in Harris, 269. As Guevara put it: "A true revolutionary sacrifices his wife, his children for the cause; that is why here is no life outside the revolution" (quotation supplied by Dominguez).

[126] Castro quoted in Casey, 101.

[127] Castro quoted in Anderson, 714, 726.

[128] Geyer, 318.

[129] Casey, 285, 342, 348.

[130] I.F. Stone: "The Legacy of Che Guevara," *Ramparts*, December 1967, 20–21.

[131] Eduardo Galeano: "Magic Death for a Magic Life," *Monthly Review*, January 1968, 13.

Doubtless Guevara was a genuine idealist but, as is often the case, this idealism had its dark side, stemming from the sense of entitlement to ruthlessness conferred by the strongly felt good intentions and selfless dedication to the cause. Harris wrote:

> Che was not a fanatic, and he did not have a pathological love of bloodshed or human cruelty. He was not, however, a normal and contented man. If he had been, he would never have become a revolutionary. He was a dreamer, an adventurer, and an unrelenting rebel against the established order of things ... deeply incensed by the social injustices that he saw in the world all around him ... He was the personification of the true revolutionary – a super-idealist who insisted on bringing heaven immediately to earth.

Even Harris admits that Guevara had a strong affinity with the violence of guerilla war: "Che wrote that ... combat is the most interesting event that befalls them [the guerillas, that is]. Combat, therefore, is both the climax and the greatest joy of the guerilla's life, and only through combat do they fulfill the purpose for which they exist."[132] This was precisely the type of mystified, romantic veneration of violence that would warm the hearts of Mailer and Sartre, a veneration that also animated the elite troops of Nazi Germany.

Cabrera Infante wrote: "Che, like Trotsky, advocated permanent revolution. But loving humanity, an abstract idea, he forgot all about people. He believed in the New Man but not in human beings, new or old."[133] As Casey pointed out, this kind of idealism could easily provide motivation for violent acts carried out with a clear conscience: "against an unjust imperial system, killing is not merely permissible; it is noble ... Thus he, the model New Man, is transformed into a religious hero, where the inherent contradictions of his own philosophy – love versus hatred – are wiped away." Che wrote that "we have no right to believe that freedom can be won without a fight."[134] A similar point was made by Anderson: "He [Guevara] had made a conscious leap of faith and entered a domain [that] could be taken for an ideal, and where the end *did* justify the means ... Che believed that the faith he had chosen was limitless. What he was doing had a historic imperative." Anderson further noted that "Che's habit of referring to the people ... as bits of machinery affords a glimpse of his emotional distance from individual reality. He had the coldly analytical mind of a medical researcher and a chess player." Che

[132] Harris, 50, 56. Guevara also believed that a revolutionary must become "a cold killing machine" (quotation supplied by Dominguez).

[133] Cabrera Infante, 315.

[134] Casey, 63, 225, 572.

referred to the dutiful and politically fulfilled citizen as "cog in the wheel, a cog that has its own characteristics and is necessary, though not indispensable, to the production process."[135]

These attributes of Guevara were either unknown or overlooked by his many admirers. Guevara's enduring idealization was reflected in Steven Soderbergh's nearly four-and-a-half-hour movie, *Che*, that made no reference to "his brutal role in turning a revolutionary movement into a dictatorship ... This ... allows Mr Soderbergh to preserve the romantic notion of Guevara as a martyr and iconic figure, an idealistic champion of the poor and oppressed ... this image seems at best naive and incomplete, at worst sentimental and dishonest," according to the *New York Times* film critic.[136] Another hagiographic movie made of him and based on his *Motorcycle Diaries* was given an enthusiastic ovation at the Sundance Film Festival by people who did not have the faintest idea what he was like and how he acted.[137]

Guevara's ruthlessness found unambiguous expression in his readiness to execute perceived political enemies, including those deemed to be traitors to the cause: "Che's narrative is as chilling as it is revealing of his personality. His matter-of-fact description of an execution [that he himself performed – P.H.], his scientific notations on the bullet's entry and exit wounds, suggest a remarkable detachment from violence." Not surprisingly, "he had acquired a reputation for cold-blooded willingness to take direct action against transgressors of the revolutionary code." Moreover, he "sought opportunities to mete out punishment as an example to others" and had no difficulty in justifying his punitiveness: "War is harsh, and at a time when the enemy was intensifying its aggressiveness, one could tolerate not even the suspicion of treason."[138] Such justification of terror recalls Stalin's assertions in the 1930s about the so-called cornered enemy that supposedly had become more aggressive and menacing, and therefore had to be dealt with a special, uncompromising severity.

Guevara's affinity with political violence found further expression in his untroubled vision of a nuclear war. Speaking at the First Latin American Youth Congress (1960) he said: "This people [Cubans] you see today tell you that even if they should disappear from the face of the earth because

[135] Che quoted in Anderson, 225, 572.

[136] A.O. Scott: "Soderbergh and Che, Provocateurs," *New York Times*, Art Section, May 23, 2008, 8.

[137] See Paul Berman: "The Cult of Che," *Slate*, September 24, 2004.

[138] Anderson, 223, 229, 230, 271.

an atomic war is unleashed in their names ... they would feel completely happy and fulfilled." It is a statement that reflects a remarkable egomaniacal trust of his own ability to divine and express the sentiments of the Cuban people (not consulted in the matter of nuclear war), in effect to speak for them – the key attribute of self-confident authoritarians.

On another occasion he advised, in the same spirit: "We should not fear violence, the midwife of new societies." Anderson commented, "once again, Che invoked the specter of death, now envisioned on a truly massive scale, to extol the beauty of collective sacrifice for liberation." Anderson also pointed out that "Che did not shrink from that outcome [i.e., nuclear war – P.H.], and he was telling others they should not, either. Many would die in the revolutionary process, but the survivors would ... create a new, just world order."[139]

While Guevara's cult has not only survived his death but was greatly boosted by it, it remains to be seen what impact the approaching death of Fidel Castro will have on his fading favorable image among many Western intellectuals. This will also depend on the nature of future political changes in Cuba that will probably follow his death and that of his similarly aged brother, Raul. If and when such changes take place, it is likely that widespread critical domestic reassessments of Castro will follow (as they did after the death of Stalin in the Soviet Union). Such probable domestic reassessments will make it more difficult for Castro's remaining Western admirers to retain their idealized image of him.

[139] Ibid., 455, 456, 550, 571.

7

Other Dictators and Their Admirers in More Recent Times

> Kim Jong Il is not the playboy, womanizer, drunk and mentally deranged fanatic "Dr Evil" of our press. He is a homebody who doesn't socialize much, doesn't drink much, and works at home in his pyjamas … He most enjoys tinkering with his many music boxes, sitting on the floor … He is prudish and shy, and like most Korean fathers, hopelessly devoted to his son.
>
> *Bruce Cumings*[1]

> Bashar [al Assad] is basically a principled man. He is very unassuming … His voice is not the commanding type, yet what he has to say holds our attention because of his appealing sincerity … he is essentially a morally sound individual, someone who has the best of intentions, even if clumsily pursued at times.
>
> *David W. Lesch*[2]

> [H]aving created a new model of popular revolution, based for the most part on non-violent tactics, Iran may yet provide us with a desperately needed model of human governance for a third world country.
>
> *Richard Falk*[3]

There have been no dictators in more recent times comparable to those discussed earlier, neither in regard to their impact and historical role, nor the amount of adulation they elicited from Western intellectuals and

[1] Bruce Cumings: *North Korea: Another Country*, New York 2004, 163.

[2] David W. Lesch: *The New Lion of Damascus: Bashar al Assad and Modern Syria*, New Haven CT 2005, 199.

[3] Richard Falk: "Trusting Khomeini," *New York Times*, February 16, 1979.

others. Nonetheless some dictators of lesser notoriety and impact did find a smaller number of devotees, and were targets of similarly misplaced reverence. This being the case, it is safe to say that the impulses and illusions that in the past gave rise to political hero worship persist, at any rate in an attenuated form.

Although the popularity of, and interest in, this miscellaneous group of dictators has been far more limited (with the exception of Hugo Chavez, who enjoyed great popularity), it is of some significance that their appeals and attractions closely resemble, and sometimes duplicate, those of the more widely admired figures of earlier times.

We will be looking here at a mixed group of dictators of different personalities, beliefs, and policies, but sharing strong nationalistic sentiments. Hugo Chavez of Venezuela and Omar Torrijos of Panama were self-styled radical socialists with strong anti-American attitudes who did not perpetrate large-scale political violence or create *highly* repressive political systems.[4] Torrijos was not nearly as well-known abroad and popular as Chavez, nor was he, like Chavez, an accomplished demagogue. Slobodan Milosevic of Serbia was an opportunistic, left-leaning Serbian nationalist; Saddam Hussein of Iraq and Bashar al Assad of Syria had no strongly held ideological positions (aside from their Arab nationalism) and it would be difficult to determine their place on the left–right continuum. Both have been responsible for huge amounts of political violence and repression without relying on legitimation by Muslim religious ideologies. There was an affinity between Assad and Chavez, reflected in Chavez "providing vital energy support [oil] to Assad and conducting business with Syrian firms blacklisted by Washington and Brussels."[5]

North Korea, rather than its specific leaders, also had some Western sympathizers, as did the Iranian theocracy and its founder Ayatollah

[4] However, Chavez strongly approved of political violence carried out in support of causes he supported. He "heaped praise" on his fellow countryman, Ilich Ramirez Sanchez, better known as Carlos the Jackal, whom he considered a "revolutionary fighter." Sanchez carried out numerous hijackings and terrorist attacks in Europe during the 1970s and 1980s and is serving a life sentence in France. Chavez called Sanchez (who converted to Islam in prison) "one of the great fighters for the Palestine Liberation Organization" (Simon Romero: "Chavez Offers Public Defense of 'the Jackal'," *New York Times*, November 22, 2009). The violent rhetoric of Chavez aimed at his opponents further encouraged mob violence. See Daniel S. Benveniste: *The Venezuelan Revolution: A Critique from the Left*, Charleston SC 2016, 123–124, 135–137, etc. Benveniste, an American clinical psychologist, lived and practiced in Venezuela between 1990 and 2010.

[5] Toby Young: "Hugo Chavez, a Venezuelan Spartacus? A Latin American Kim Jong-il, More Like," *Telegraph*, online, March 6, 2013.

Khomeini. Vladimir Putin of Russia, defined by his KGB background, nationalistic beliefs, and thirst for power, had defenders among a handful of American public intellectuals of different political persuasion.

NORTH KOREA AND ITS DYNASTIC LEADERS

In the twenty-first century, generalized affirmations of socialism, Marxism, and anti-capitalism remain widespread among Western intellectuals without anyone specifying *when and where* those ideals were, would, or could be realized. It is difficult at the present time to find academic intellectuals ready to identify and locate such a system. Bruce Cumings, a professor of history at the University of Chicago, is a rare exception. He personifies this implausible position, affectionately disposed as he has been toward the last remaining highly repressive totalitarian system, communist North Korea.[6]

While more concerned with portraying the admirable, or respectable, features of the North Korean system than the appealing qualities of its leaders, Cumings also managed to find some good things to say about them. In particular, he sought to humanize the founder of the dynasty, the late Kim Il Sung, who "was so deeply distressed by the drowning of his younger son in 1947 that he had a *mudang* (shaman) carry out rituals on the very spot a decade later; the 'captured documents' in the US archives contain long scrolls written by Buddhist monks, trying to assuage his loss and pain."[7]

Of all the states discussed in this volume, it is North Korea (and China under Mao) that developed and institutionalized the most extreme, quasi-religious cults of its leaders. According to one study:

> the North Koreans more than matched the long list of prefixes that characterized the Chinese adulation of Mao … the North Korean practice has surpassed any other campaign anywhere by Communists or non-Communists … the magnitude of adulation often borders on fanaticism. His [Kim Il Sung's] photograph is displayed ahead of the national flag and the national emblem; the song of Marshal Kim Il Sung is played ahead of the national anthem; the best institution of higher learning is named after him; [as is] the highest party school … and there are songs, poems, essays, stories and even a flower named after him.

On his sixtieth birthday, "a colossal monument" occupying 240,000 square meters was built to honor him, as well as an enormous museum

[6] Cumings: *North Korea*.

[7] Ibid., 138.

and, in addition, "sixty monuments in every province and every major city, factory, mine and agricultural cooperative." On the same occasion (his birthday), he "awarded himself a 'double hero gold medal' of the republic and the 'order of the national banner, first class,' the highest honors" available. To celebrate his seventieth birthday an "Arch of Triumph" was built, and to commemorate his political thought a 170-meter-high tower was erected, claimed by North Korea as the highest stone tower in the world.[8]

He was also referred to as "Peerless Patriot, the Ever-Victorious, Iron-Willed Commander, the Sun of the Nation, the Sun of Mankind, the Red Sun of the Oppressed People," among other things. His son and successor, Kim Jong Il, was often called "unique Leader, Wise Leader … Father of the People, Our Father … Leader of the Twenty First Century, Glorious Sun of the Twenty First Century, Sun of Mankind and Everlasting Sky," among others.[9] According to a more recent account, "everything positive – a decent harvest, nice weather, victory in a sporting event … is ascribed to the beneficence and wisdom of the leader … he is everywhere. Nothing passes his notice … He is a scientific genius, a great artist … [he] guarantees 'bumper harvests,' military glory and universal happiness of the Korean people."[10]

Andrei Lankov, a former Soviet exchange student to North Korea, was well positioned to observe the cult:

> Perhaps the most striking part of the North Korean "ideological landscape" from the late 1960s was a personality cult of Marshall (eventually Generalissimo) Great Leader Kim Il Sung, the Sun of the Nation, the Ever-Victorious General. Initially this cult was patterned on the cults of Mao and Stalin, but by the early 1970s it took on dimensions that were unprecedented in the modern world.

He further writes:

> Since 1972, all North Koreans above 16 … were required to sport a badge with Kim Il Sung's visage when they left their homes. [His] portraits needed to be placed at every office and every house; from around 1980 portraits of his son and successor Kim Jong Il were displayed alongside the father … There were (and still are) complex regulations that prescribe how the pristine conditions of the sacred images should be maintained. If the portrait were damaged the people responsible for their maintenance would be punished if found guilty of neglect. The North

[8] Dae-Sook Suh: *Kim Il Sung, the North Korean Leader*, New York 1988, 316, 319, 320.

[9] Michael Breen: *Kim Jong-Il: North Korea's Dear Leader*, Singapore 2004, 2, 121.

[10] Ian Buruma: "In North Korea: Wonder and Terror," *New York Review of Books*, June 4, 2015, 48. References to the cult are in one of the books reviewed, Suki Kim's *Without You There Is No Us…*

Korean media was (and still is) full of stories about the heroic deeds of North Korean citizens who willingly sacrificed their lives to save portraits of the Great Leader and his son.

Kin Il Sung's statues were erected across the country ... The statues were made centers of elaborate rituals ... on the Great Leader's birthday ... every North Korean was supposed to go to the nearest statues and after a deep bow lay flowers ...

... [T]he North Korean authorities built a "replica" ... of a log cabin where Kim Jong Il was allegedly born, and made it a site of obligatory pilgrimage.[11]

The distinctive features of North Korean totalitarianism also included the ban on radios that could be tuned to other than the official government stations and the destruction of privately owned foreign books. Even Soviet exchange students, such as Lankov, were strictly segregated from North Koreans: "We were not allowed to attend classes together with North Korean students. We could not visit private homes."

The number of inmates in the extensive system of prison camps was large and remained stable; in 2011 it was estimated to 154,000 or higher and "the ratio of political prisoners to the general population" was somewhat higher than corresponding figures in the Soviet Union in the last years of Stalin's rule. There was an estimated one informer for every fifty adults of the population, or 250,000 to 300,000 paid police informers. Obligatory military service for males is between seven and ten years. Last but not least, between 1945 and 1951 when this was possible, approximately 1.2–1.5 million people, or 10–15 percent of the entire North Korean population, fled to South Korea.

The unusually well-qualified author concluded that "it is fair to say that in the 1960s Kim Il Sung managed to create a society that was arguably the closest approximation to an Orwellian nightmare in world history."[12]

Even professor Cumings was constrained to admit that North Korea had some unpleasant features, being a "garrison state," although he convinced himself that such and other blemishes were to be blamed on the unfriendliness of the United States, the hostility of South Korea, various historical events, and on being generally beleaguered and victimized, even on inclement weather. The flaws of North Korea, he would have us believe, had nothing to do with its political system, its leaders, or their ideological convictions. Cumings' entire book here referred to

[11] Andrei Lankov: *The Real North Korea: Life and Politics in the Failed Stalinist Utopia*, New York 2013, 50, 51, 53.

[12] Ibid., 8, 43, 44, 45, 46, 49, 61, 71.

is an extended pleading for the proper understanding and urgent moral rehabilitation of this supposedly much maligned, misunderstood, and victimized North Korea, deserving of empathy. He wrote:

> There is another way of thinking of this country [i.e., less critical, ignoring its repressive character, etc. – P.H.]: as a small, Third World postcolonial nation that has been gravely wounded, first by forty years of Japanese colonialism and then by another sixty years of national division and war, and that is deeply insecure, threatened by the world around it.[13]

A similar therapeutic conception of the aggressive-repressive features of other communist totalitarian states, mainly the Soviet Union and its leaders, used to be common during the Cold War, always accompanied by a similar plea for their more sympathetic understanding.[14] There was little comparable readiness to extend such an understanding of the mentality of the Nazi leaders, although they too felt just as deeply threatened and victimized, both by imaginary evils and to a lesser extent by some realistic circumstances. Apparently rulers of the most repressive systems known in history felt, at some level and in some measure, threatened and insecure, unless it was a traditional society they ruled.

The determination to improve the image of North Korea found further expression in Cumings' attempts to obscure the fact that North Korea had invaded South Korea in 1950, thereby initiating the Korean War that he insists on calling "a civil war … fought for Korean goals."

The perception of North Korea as the victimized underdog country is probably the key to Cumings' idiosyncratic attitude and his unwillingness, or inability, to engage in any serious criticism of the morally reprehensible qualities of this regime, or even to recognize that they exist. He admits to being incapable of resisting feeling "empathy for the underdog," but he does not reflect on the peculiar choice he has made in defending an exceptionally repressive, rigid, intolerant, and militaristic regime. He deplores characterizations of North Korea as totalitarian or despotic and dismisses the information defectors provided as "fibs that even a moment in a good library would expose," claiming that "defectors are the main source of *tales* about the North."[15]

Cumings even attempts to humanize the North Korean gulag, writing that "conditions were primitive and beatings were frequent *but* the

[13] Cumings, 151.

[14] Paul Hollander: "Therapy for the Kremlin," review of S.F. Cohen: *Rethinking and Soviet Experience*, *Wall Street Journal*, December 24, 1985.

[15] Cumings, 6, xiii, viii, xii, 153 (emphasis added).

inmates were able to improvise much of their upkeep on their own ... The natural environs meant that small animals could ... be caught and cooked ... death from starvation was rare."[16] He delicately refrains from mentioning that these "small animals" were rats, as was disclosed by the author of the major English-language account of life in these camps.[17] The latter also made it abundantly clear that starvation *was* widespread and conditions were exceptionally brutal, including public executions inmates were obliged to attend. For minor infractions prisoners were squeezed into a "sweatbox" for days or weeks. Cumings doesn't dwell on such matters, preferring instead to make the wholly unsubstantiated claim that the same book, *The Aquariums of Pyongyang*, is *not* "the ghastly tale of totalitarian repression" (which it was) intended by its publishers. This totally groundless and bizarre assertion is immediately followed by a leap to moral equivalence, or rather the suggestion that American penal institutions are *worse*: "Meanwhile we have a longstanding, never-ending gulag full of black men in our prisons."[18] Anyone who read *The Aquariums of Pyongyang* (as I had) will rub his eyes in disbelief encountering Cumings' misleading and distorted characterization of the North Korean penal colony described in it.

He also sought, most unconvincingly, to relativize and obfuscate the exceptionally repressive character of the North Korean system by raising the rhetorical question: "Does this system promote human freedom? Not from any liberal's standpoint. But from a Korean standpoint, where freedom is also defined as an independent stance against foreign predators – freedom for the Korean nation – here the vitriolic judgements do not flow so easily."[19] How this alleged "stance against foreign predators" accounts for and legitimates the totalitarian character of North Korea he does not explain, satisfied as he is by calling "vitriolic" the critiques of the system and its self-evidently repressive character.

Cumings, like other sympathizers with dictatorships of the past, listed and praised the alleged accomplishments of the regime, such as "free education and health care to everyone." He quotes with approval an English author who reported that "the average North Korean lived 'an incredibly simple and hardworking life but also has a secure and happy existence, and the comradeship between these highly collectivized people is moving

[16] Ibid., 175 (emphasis added).

[17] Kang Chol-hwan and Pierre Rigoulet: *The Aquariums of Pyongyang: Ten Years in a North Korean Gulag*, New York 2005. See also chapter 9: "The Gulag," in Breen.

[18] Cumings, 176.

[19] Ibid., 151.

to behold ... Young people have plenty of (chaste) fun, dancing in public squares after big rallies.'" Cumings was also impressed by the capital Pyongyang, which "mixes the bucolic pace of Alma Ata [of Kazakhstan] with the clean efficiency of Singapore ... exceedingly orderly, smoothly functioning ... anything but drab." He was especially touched by "little old ladies [who] got out with brooms to clean the public streets,"[20] implying that this was a voluntary contribution to public hygiene, not something ordered by the authorities. His remarks about the activities of these ladies (as well as other passages of the book) suggest that Cumings was also drawn to North Korea because of the vestiges of a traditional society he observed and mistakenly conflated with the virtues of the new system.

Robert Scheer, a journalist, was another rare admirer of what he considered the progressive communism of North Korea. As Ronald Radosh recalled, at a much earlier date (in 1970), "For over two hours ... he [Scheer] talked [on Pacifica Radio] about the paradise he had seen during a recent visit to North Korea, about the greatness of Kim Il-Sung, about the correct nature of his so-called *juche* ideology ... Kim's redefinition of Marxism-Leninism in building communism against all obstacles."[21]

It may be recalled that in 1994 President Carter made an unofficial goodwill visit to North Korea and returned with excellent impressions of the country's leader and the prevailing conditions he observed. According to a report in the *New York Times*, "Mr Carter heaped praise on Kim Il Sung ... 'I found him to be vigorous, intelligent ... well-informed ... and in charge of decisions about his country.' Carter also managed, in the course of his short visit, to observe, 'the reverence with which they [the people of North Korea] look upon their leader.'"[22] Reportedly Carter also found "Pyongyang ... full of pep – its shops remind him of the 'Wal-Mart in Americus Georgia' and at night the neon lights remind him of Times Square."[23] If correctly quoted these observations are among the most memorable examples of projection and a vivid imagination.

Less surprising is that Nicolae Ceausescu, dictator of communist Romania, was inspired and influenced by North Korea, which he had visited. He modeled his own cult on that of Kim Il Sung as both leaders "presented themselves ... as gods incarnate – omniscient, omnipotent,

[20] Ibid., 135, 140, 143, 145.

[21] Radosh quoted in Mona Charen: *Useful Idiots*, Washington DC 2003, 117–172.

[22] Quoted in David E. Sanger: "Two Koreas Agree to Summit Meeting on Nuclear Issue," *New York Times*, June 19, 1994, 12.

[23] Quoted in George Will: "Carter Misreads North Korea's Kim," reprinted in *Daily Hampshire Gazette*, June 24, 1994.

models of perfection whose rule was the culmination of millennia of glorious national history."[24]

More recently a group of thirty women from fifteen different countries undertook a "peace mission" to North and South Korea that amounted to crossing from North to South by bus under conditions carefully controlled by the authorities of both countries. As their statements indicate, this "mission" was based on several highly dubious or totally mistaken premises: namely, that (1) a symbolic gesture by a self-elected group of idealistic women can influence the foreign and domestic policies of a totalitarian regime such as North Korea; (2) that on a visit to such a country they could actually meet and discuss politics with ordinary citizens who are not government functionaries or representatives and feel free to talk to foreigners; (3) that meeting such ordinary citizens and exchanging ideas with them could influence the government of their country; (4) that the political systems in North and South Korea are not substantially different from one another, as each allows ordinary citizens and public opinion to influence official policies; (5) that North Korea is interested in removing obstacles between the two countries and their people and in reducing current levels of hostility.

Greatly overrating the significance of this "peace mission," Gloria Steinem (a participant) said that the "women 'accomplished what no one said could be done – we were able to be citizen diplomats.' "[25] Abigail E. Disney, another member of the group (a film-maker and peace activist, Ph.D. in English from Yale University, and member of the Hollywood Disney family of fame and fortune), was indignant that a *Times* correspondent did not take the "peace mission" seriously enough. Ms. Disney could not discern any significant difference between the repressive policies of North and South Korea and focused on American "saber-rattling, sanctions and isolation" as the major explanation of the hostilities between the two countries. She suggested that it was President Bush's designation of North Korea as belonging to the "axis of evil" that made the regime more aggressive. Finally, she proposed that change in North Korea will come only when its people become "sufficiently dissatisfied with their own regime" – as if all it took was popular discontent to remove the government of an exceptionally ruthless totalitarian police state. Even more bizarre was her suggestion that the other requirement for regime change

[24] Daniel Chirot: *Modern Tyrants: The Power and Prevalence of Evil in Our Times*, New York 1994, 236.

[25] Quoted in Donald Kirk: "Women Crossing DMZ Praise Their Mission But Avoid Human Rights in North Korea," *Forbes Asia*, online, May 25, 2015.

is that the North Korean people cease to be "frightened that the rest of the world is looking to destroy them."[26]

In another statement the same group also asserted that "crippling sanctions against the government make it difficult for ordinary people to access basics needed for survival." Christine Ahn, a spokesperson of the group, in a newsletter blamed the sanctions for the shortages.[27] None of these statements made any critical reference to the policies of the North Korean government, its huge military expenditures, mismanagement of the economy, and distribution of resources (including foreign aid) that favors the elite groups.

Ms. Disney's letter and the other statements of the same group accurately reflect the survival of spectacular ignorance of conditions in North Korea, fortified by an apparently complete lack of imagination concerning the nature of repressive institutions and policies of totalitarian police states.

HUGE CHAVEZ OF VENEZUELA AND HIS AMERICAN ADMIRERS

The warmth and enthusiasm Hugo Chavez inspired among Western intellectuals illustrate the importance of certain personal qualities the numerous dictators here discussed had in common, as well as a persisting predisposition to misjudge both the character and the policies of these dictators. The prestige of Chavez also benefited from his close personal relationship with Castro, who supported and advised him, while Chavez provided substantial economic assistance to Cuba. Both benefited, in the eyes of their foreign admirers, from this friendship and the attendant mutual legitimation. Few of his Western admirers knew that approximately 1.3 million Venezuelans left the country since he came to power,[28] voting with their feet, as it were, to escape both his authoritarian rule and the results of his persistent economic mismanagement. Foreign admirers of Chavez were also unaware of the serious deterioration of public safety and soaring levels of crime since he came to power, with homicide rates four times those in the United States and the second highest in the world.[29]

[26] Abigail E. Disney: "Women on a Peace Mission to North Korea" [Letter], *New York Times*, June 2015.

[27] Quoted in "Women's Walk for Peace in Korea," online (accessed June 15, 2015).

[28] See Benveniste, 152.

[29] Ibid., 125–126, 151.

Chavez was less vicious and violence-prone than his better-known colleagues discussed earlier (including his mentor, Castro). At the same time, as Daniel Benveniste points out, he "threatened constantly and encouraged violent attacks on the opposition. Government sponsored violence brought well over two hundred deaths and four thousand injuries in the streets of Venezuela."[30] He was "an elected autocrat,"[31] "a democratically elected president rul[ing] in an antidemocratic way," and a skilled manipulator "of democratic processes to amass unchecked executive power."[32] However, fraud and intimidation also played an important part in his electoral successes. Benveniste wrote: "If Chavez won an election by getting more votes than the opposition he did so by threatening government workers with losing their jobs if they didn't vote for him," among dozens of other "fraud strategies" Benveniste specifies.[33]

The political disposition of Chavez was further revealed by his allies and friends abroad, which included not only Castro but also Quadaffi of Libya, Ahmedinajad of Iran, Mugabe of Zimbabwe, Kim Jong Il of North Korea, Assad of Syria, and Lukashenko of Belarus – every one of them unscrupulous authoritarian dictators. Chavez was also an enthusiastic supporter of the drug-trafficking FARC guerrillas of Columbia, the Basque terrorists in Spain, and Hezbollah in Lebanon.[34]

He appealed to Western leftists because, as Jon Lee Anderson wrote:

> Chavez revived the language and the spirit of leftist revolution in Latin America. He would remake Venezuela into what he called ... "a sea of happiness and of real social justice and peace." ... [He] often referred to himself as an artist and the revolution as an unfinished portrait ... there was something timeless in his all-encompassing persona of painter, singer, poet, horseman, warrior, father, teacher, thinker, leader.

Unembarrassed, he also thought of himself as a philosopher-king and "cast [Simon] Bolivar as a prototype socialist with sacred mission to transform Venezuela, a mission he himself would complete. Bolivar and Karl Marx, he said, were complementary architects for Venezuela. (Other times he added Jesus, making a triptych.)"[35]

30 Ibid., 123–124. On specific incidents of mob violence, see also ibid., 42–43, 49–50, 56, 59.

31 Rory Carroll: *Comandante: Huge Chavez's Venezuela*, New York 2013, 274.

32 William J. Dobson: *The Dictator's Learning Curve*, New York 2012, 90–91.

33 Benveniste, 154–159. Benveniste, who lived in Venezuela for eleven years, witnessed the fraudulent 2004 elections, noting that "A stunned country watched in horror as former president Carter gave his seal of approval to Chavez's fraudulent election" (ibid., 158).

34 See also ibid., 142, 163, 165.

35 Jon Lee Anderson: "Letter from Caracas," *New Yorker*, January 28, 2013, 42.

His fixation on being heir to Bolivar found expression in that "during his cabinet meetings, he always set an empty chair next to his own, symbolizing his claim that he governed in tandem with the spirit of Bolivar. Along the streets of Caracas it became common to see murals of Chavez together with Jesus Christ and Bolivar, the Holy Trinity of the Bolivarian Revolution."[36] It was written of him that "in death Chavez approximated Bolivar more than he did in life. Venerated as 'the Christ of America,' his colossal image flapping from Caracas skyscrapers ... El Commandante is finally as exalted as his hero."[37]

Unlike the other modern dictators, Chavez displayed a pronounced religious streak.[38] Described as a

> fervent Catholic [he] attributes his charmed existence to the scapular [small piece of cloth of religious significance] that he has worn since childhood. Thanking God for what he thought at the time was his recovery from cancer he visited Venezuela's most sacred Catholic shrine ... greeting worshipers, embracing priests, placing rosary beads around a statue of the Virgin ... stood by the altar with a microphone and announced he had come to give thanks for a miracle.[39]

Like his more murderous colleagues, Chavez too "was convinced that he was carrying out an earthly mission guided by superhuman force ... [he said] 'I get everything I need straight from the people, the people on the street.' " Enrique Krauze observed that

> [his] omnipotence is owed to his omnipresence ... Presiding over his silent, acquiescent ministers ... the Commandante tells stories from his life and ... about romantic adventures, gastric ailments, baseball games; he also sings, dances, recites, prays ... All of this has struck some American journalists – and movie people such Oliver Stone and Sean Penn – as folksy, authentic and even patriotic.[40]

His self-conception was captured and popularized by endless television appearances and presentations of his activities and opinions:

> They run around the clock on state television, highly polished videos of President Hugo Chavez hugging children, kissing grandmothers, playing baseball and reciting poetry. As supporters around the world hold up hand-lettered signs that say

[36] Enrique Krauze: "Bolivar: What Prize Glory?" *New York Review of Books*, June 6, 2013.

[37] Maries Arana: "Latin America's Go-To Hero," *New York Times* [op-ed], April 18, 2013.

[38] Putin has also shown some respect for religion, as embodied in the Russian Orthodox Church, but this has been, in all probability, a matter of political expediency and reflection of the traditional link between Russian nationalism and the Church rather than personal belief.

[39] Carroll, 3, 279.

[40] Enrique Krauze: "The Shah of Venezuela," *New Republic*, April 1, 2009, 31, 37.

"I Am Chavez," the president's voice is heard ... shouting, "I demand absolute loyalty because I am not me, I am not an individual, I am a people!"[41]

His thirst for publicity was insatiable: "Presidential events" such as "touring a tractor factory, greeting a Russian delegation, handing out medals would pop up in the middle of a televised movie, baseball game, or soap opera when the screen would abruptly change, showing [his] beaming face ... 'Good evening compadres ... I have something important to say.'" As Carroll wrote, "The images alone were the news. The commandante painting, the commandante reading ... taking breakfast ... hosting visitors: affairs of importance unfolding before our eyes."[42] In turn Benveniste recalled: "From downtown Caracas to distant jungles around the Upper Orinoco river, Chavez's face appeared on billboards, murals and even tree trunks." Like his mentor Castro, Chavez too "typically talked for five hours or more,"[43] reflecting an extraordinary belief in the importance of everything he had to say, or that came into his mind.

Chavez was also popular with American protestors of the Iraqi war such as Cindy Sheehan, who, while attending a rally in Caracas, literally and figuratively embraced him. As the *New York Times* noted, "Mr Chavez has become a voice for many opponents of the Bush administration policies who are drawn to his self-styled socialist revolution and his close alliance with ... Fidel Castro."[44] More generally speaking, Chavez appealed to all those on the left who considered American society hopelessly unjust and inhumane and saw his regime as greatly superior. Not surprisingly, Tom Hayden, former 1960s radical, was among these admirers. He declared: "As time passes, I predict, the name of Hugo Chavez will be revered by millions."[45] Cornell West, the prominent academic social critic, stated: "I love that Hugo Chavez has made poverty a major priority. I wish America would make poverty a priority." West visited Venezuela in January 2006 with the delegation that included Harry Belafonte and Danny Glover (actor, film director) and met Chavez.[46]

[41] William Neuman: "With Chavez Ill and State in Flux Videos Offer an Image of Stability," *New York Times*, January 8, 2013.

[42] Carroll, 184, 271. See also Dobson, 109–112.

[43] Benveniste, 34, 71.

[44] "Antiwar Campaigner Speaks on Chavez Broadcast," *New York Times*, January 29, 2006. See also Juan Forero: "Visitors Seek a Taste of Revolution in Venezuela," *New York Times*, March 21, 2006.

[45] Hayden quoted in Beneviste, 148.

[46] West quoted in Benveniste, 153. On their visit, see ibid., 143–144. Benveniste devotes chapter 5 to "The Venezuelan Revolution and the Popular North American Left," 116–162.

Glover also received $18 million from the government of Venezuela to make a movie of the slave uprising in Haiti.[47] Following the death of Chavez, Glover said "We all embraced Hugo Chavez as a social champion of democracy, material development and spiritual well being."[48]

Admirers of Chavez included Noam Chomsky and Tariq Ali, the British author/activist of long-standing leftist credentials,[49] as well as Hollywood celebrities such as Oliver Stone, who made a documentary after his death in 2014 entitled *My Friend Hugo*, and the actor Sean Penn, who also visited him several times. At his 2006 United Nations appearance Chavez praised Chomsky and brandished one of his books, advising his audience to read it and learn from it about the iniquities of the United States. Chavez and Chomsky had a warm relationship of mutual admiration, doubtless based in large measure on their shared fervent anti-Americanism.[50] Chomsky visited Venezuela and appeared with Chavez at rallies, while Chavez was fond of quoting Chomsky in his speeches. The relationship soured when Chomsky expressed criticism of the arrest and jailing (without trial) of Maria Lourdes Afiuni, a judge accused of releasing a critic of the government.[51]

Istvan Meszaros, a Marxist philosopher of Hungarian origin, also enjoyed a relationship of mutual admiration and "personal friendship" with Chavez. Chavez designated Meszaros the "pathfinder of socialism" and wrote the foreword to one of his books; he also gave him the "Bolivar Award for Critical Thought" in 2009 on one of his numerous visits to Venezuela. In turn Meszaros harbored boundless admiration for Chavez.[52] Apparently his experiences in Soviet-dominated Hungary failed to immunize him against the promises of another Marxist utopia.

Barbara Walters, who was also impressed by Castro (see p. 211), following her interview with Chavez reached the conclusion that "He cares very much about poverty, he is a socialist. What he's trying to do for all of Latin America, they have been trying to do for years, eliminate poverty. But he is not the crazy man we've heard ... This is a very intelligent man."[53]

47 See Glover in Wikipedia (accessed February 15, 2016).

48 Glover quoted in Benveniste, 144.

49 See Tariq Ali: "Diary," *London Review of Books*, June 21, 2007 and "Celebrity Fans," *Newsweek*, September 3, 2007. See also Forero.

50 Carroll, 248–249.

51 See also John McDermott: "Lunch with Chomsky," *Financial Times*, March 15, 2013.

52 John Bellamy Foster: "Istvan Meszaros: Pathfinder of Socialism," *Monthly Review*, April 30, 2013.

53 Walters quoted in Benveniste, 140. This "very intelligent man" claimed that the United States used its "high technology" to cause the earthquake in Haiti "to create an excuse for its 'military invasion' of Haiti" (Benveniste, 78).

Eva Golinger was a major and influential American admirer of Chavez who moved to Venezuela and became his personal advisor and propagandist:

> [She] first came to Venezuela in the 1990s to research her family history, has created a unique niche for herself here: an American with the president's ear ... She has since emerged as one of the most prominent fixtures of ... state propaganda ... Her zeal evokes earlier waves of political pilgrims in Latin America ... like the volunteers who cut Cuban sugar cane in the 1960s, or the Sandalistas ... who flocked to Nicaragua in the 1980s ... to support the Sandinistas ... She accompanied Mr Chavez on a seven-country tour that included visits with ... Ahmadinejad, president of Iran. "Chavez presented me as his defender to Ahmadinejad" said Ms Golinger describing the Iranian leader as "gentle".[54]

Reportedly, Golinger "imbibed progressive causes from a young age." After attending Sarah Lawrence College "she obtained a law degree specializing in human rights." She lived in Venezuela in the 1990s before becoming a political activist teaching English, singing in a jazz band, and learning Spanish. ("'It was an adventure and I fell in love with the country.'") In 2004, using the Freedom of Information Act, she "found evidence that the United States was funding anti-Chavez groups. She packed the documents into a bulging suitcase and flew to Venezuela to inform the Commandante." She succeeded in meeting him: "There was an instant connection. The first time you meet him is pretty overwhelming. There is magnetism, a powerful presence ... also gentleness and vulnerability."

It may be noted here that she also projected gentleness upon Ahmadinejad, the Iranian head of government at the time. Apparently gentleness and vulnerability were attributes she learned to value growing up in the increasingly therapeutic culture in the United States – attributes she readily projected on the political figures she admired.

Golinger settled in Venezuela and wrote several books about alleged American attempts to undermine Chavez. She was proud to be his advocate and became a regular presence on Venezuelan television, "where she accused opposition figures of being US collaborators." She considered her job to be "defending the revolution and the president." Subsequently she became the editor of the international edition of a state newspaper. "Her crowning moment was addressing ministers, governors, generals and ambassadors at a special event ... 'Here is the light that has opened the path for a better world' she told them ... 'Here is the nucleus of the

[54] Simon Romero: "In Venezuela, an American Has the President's Ear," *New York Times*, February 4, 2011.

battle for global social justice ... The future of humanity is here; that is what I profoundly believe.'" In the same speech she also alleged that "the opposition media ... were in cahoots with the US empire." She urged the assembly to outlaw foreign funding of NGOs and political parties. "'Fatherland, socialism, or death!' she cried." She also averred that "The changes under way are incredible ... Venezuela is truly a beacon of the world."[55]

Golinger's case was unusual since she moved to the country whose political system and leader she admired, and committed herself to its support. She became a highly placed political functionary as well as the proverbial true believer who came to identify without any reservation with the chosen dictator and his political system.

OMAR TORRIJOS AND GRAHAM GREENE

The appeals of General Omar Torrijos of Panama had some similarity to those of Chavez based as much on his personality as his politics, but far fewer Western intellectuals knew of him or were interested in him. It is the unusual relationship he had with Graham Greene that deserves attention and stands out as another case study of the idealistic intellectuals' attraction to supposedly (or genuinely) idealistic men of power. While Greene also thought well of Castro[56] and regarded the Sandinistas as friends,[57] he was exceptionally close to Torrijos. It was a relationship Torrijos initiated, inviting him to Panama and sending him first-class airline tickets. Greene came to consider him a close friend; he devoted an entire book to him "as a tribute to a man whom ... I had grown to love" and saw him as "a teacher as well as friend." Greene also believed that the General knew him better than he knew himself. When Greene learned of the death of Torrijos in 1981, "it was as though a whole section of my life had been cut out."

Greene was also impressed by Torrijos's "respect for literature," which did not extend to similar sentiments toward intellectuals, as reflected in his remark that "'intellectuals are like fine glass, crystal glass, which can

[55] Golinger quoted in Carroll, 197, 198, 199.

[56] In 1958 Greene "carried warm clothes to Santiago for Castro's men in the Sierra Maestra." See Graham Greene: *Getting to Know the General: The Story of an Involvement*, New York 1984, 221.

[57] Earlier he sympathized with the Soviet system. In a letter to the London *Times* (September 4, 1967) he averred that if he "had to choose between life in the Soviet Union and life in the United States I would certainly choose the Soviet Union."

be cracked by a sound. Panama is made of rock and earth.' "[58] Greene was not bothered by this opinion and probably shared the general's ambivalence about intellectuals, as he too preferred "doers" (such as the general) to talkers. According to Alan Riding, Greene was drawn to Torrijos because he was "a man of instinct rather than ideology" and "united by a form of raw idealism"[59] – a man of certain romantic traits that Greene appreciated. Gabriel Garcia Marquez was another writer Torrijos trusted and was close to.

Torrijos was well-suited to be the recipient of the admiration and affection, indeed, of the hero worship Greene felt for powerful and well-intentioned political figures, especially if they were revolutionaries, or professional military men such as Torrijos. Greene believed that "the United States was lucky to be dealing with Omar Torrijos, a patriot and an idealist who had no formal ideology, except a general preference for Left over Right and a scorn for bureaucrats."

Torrijos was handsome, personable, arguably charismatic, and a bit of a womanizer who liked to drink (as did Greene). According to Greene, his eyes "came to express an almost manic humor, an affection, an inscrutable inward thought, and more than all other moods, a sense of doom."[60] That is to say, he was a tragic hero (as Greene saw him), who died at an early age in a plane crash that might have been engineered by the United States, Greene and other critics of the United States thought.

Torrijos was the least dictatorial and intolerant of the figures here discussed. His authoritarianism was restrained and he was described as a "de facto dictator," or "dictator like," possessing "near absolute power." More ominously, "never officially elected," he was titled (in the 1972 Constitution) "the Maximum Leader of the Panamanian Revolution."[61] He revealed his darker side in a peculiar, mafioso-style offer he made to Greene to "'send a man to France to teach a lesson to this fellow who is troubling you ... I am sure he [someone obligated to Torrijos] could arrange to have the man dealt with. He owes me a debt of gratitude.'" Greene at the time had some problems with what he vaguely described as an "undesirable character in Nice" who threatened a friend's daughter. Greene did not take up the offer. The quixotic ideas of Torrijos – "another of the General's romantic notions" Greene called it – included a plan "to rescue Senora Peron from her house arrest in Argentina." Greene did not

[58] Greene, 34, 43, 95, 128, 211.

[59] Alan Riding: "His Man in Panama," *New York Times*, November 4, 1984.

[60] Greene, 33, 139, 211.

[61] Wikipedia on Omar Torrijos (accessed July 20, 2015).

explain why the general sympathized with Eva Peron, and presumably with her husband as well.[62]

Greene's relationship with Torrijos was one of mutual admiration and trust, and it made Greene's life more interesting and colorful for a period of time. He felt a "sense of adventure" as he embarked on his first visit to Panama in 1976. Torrijos took him on tours of inspection in the countryside, "meeting with farmers and rural representatives." Greene believed that Torrijos practiced "a direct form of democracy," proven by his visits to remote villages and talking to ordinary people without condescension.[63]

Time and again planes or helicopters were sent to fetch Greene to various destinations, including the general's country homes, or idyllic tropical islands Greene was interested to visit. Greene had become fond of Panama, "captivated by it ... this bizarre and beautiful little country ... which had become, thanks to the General, of great practical importance in the struggle for liberation taking place in Nicaragua and El Salvador." He was exceptionally well-treated and could go anywhere he wanted by plane (including the private jet of the general), helicopter, or car, and not only in Panama but also to Belize, Nicaragua, and Costa Rica. He was more than a recipient of the "techniques of hospitality" since the general was also interested in specific political services he could render. To wit, Torrijos included Greene in the Panamanian delegation sent to Washington DC to sign the Canal treaty, providing him with a Panamanian diplomatic passport. All this was obviously heady stuff for a sedentary writer not used to consorting with powerful political figures. In 1983 Greene was awarded the "Grand Cross of the Order of Vasco Nunez de Balboa" by the President of Panama.[64]

The general also "arranged an invitation from Tomas Borge," the notorious minister of internal affairs of Nicaragua in charge of the police, security forces, and prisons. Greene reported that he became a "good friend" of his, notwithstanding Borge's prominent role in domestic repression. Greene was ready to give him the benefit of the doubt and seemed satisfied with Borge's explanation of the mistreatment of the Miskito Indians:

> Borge ... himself admitted to me that the Sandinistas behaved clumsily [*sic*]. They had not explained to the Indians ... the reasons for removing them into

[62] Greene, 180, 206–207.

[63] Greene, 27, 74, 106.

[64] Greene, 13–14, 82, 119–120, 220.

camps ... However, the American nun had visited the camps and she denied ... their ill-treatment. She found them well housed and well fed and better cared for medically than they had ever been before.[65]

Greene obviously preferred to believe these reports to those that detailed the serious human rights violations. Mark Falcoff observed that Greene accepted "wholly and without the slightest reservation everything the Sandinista *commandantes* told him," and, more generally speaking, he could not "distinguish between fact and fiction and ... [did] not even try."[66]

Borge introduced Greene to Lenin Cerna, head of state security, who showed him allegedly American-made explosives disguised as a Mickey Mouse picnic box, supposedly used by the anti-Sandinista guerillas. Greene's Sandinista "friends" included Ernesto Cardenal, minister of culture, who welcomed him at the airport on his arrival to Managua. He also met the leader of the Salvadorian guerillas, Marcial (or Cayetano Carpio), in connection with his involvement as mediator in negotiations about the kidnapped South African ambassador held by the Salvadorian guerillas.

Greene's political bias was further revealed in his explanation of the defection of Eden Pastora, one of the heroes of the Sandinista revolution, as due to his wounded vanity. He could not conceive of any other (good) reason for becoming disillusioned with the increasingly repressive regime. Likewise, Greene could not understand why Archbishop Obando, another former supporter of the Sandinistas, became their critic, and once more fell back on the "wounded vanity explanation."[67]

Greene was both a devout, if tormented and unorthodox, Catholic and a leftist – not an unusual combination in times past in Europe. He was briefly a member of the British Communist Party while a student at Oxford, and "he kept up a residual form of Catholic fellow-traveling to the end of his life." Christopher Hitchens wrote of him that he was "always at odds with authority." But such anti-authoritarianism was selective and obviously did not interfere with his relationship with the general or his sympathy for the rulers of Nicaragua.[68] Greene was also a lifelong friend of Kim Philby, the British master spy (in the service of the Soviet Union), and wrote a warm introduction to his memoirs. Given

[65] Greene, 158, 184, 226–227.

[66] Mark Falcoff: Review of "Getting to Know the General," *American Spectator*, April 1981.

[67] Greene, 88, 158, 181–184, 222–223, 230.

[68] Christopher Hitchens: "I'll be Damned," *Atlantic*, March 1, 2005.

these attitudes it is not surprising that he was attracted to left-wing dictators and their political systems, but his choice of Omar Torrijos was unusual.

The anti-Americanism of Torrijos and his conflict with the United States over the control of the Canal added to his appeals for Greene, himself "unwaveringly hostile toward the United States," as Hitchen put it.[69] For Greene, the Panama–US confrontation was a case of the virtuous underdog, bravely confronting a vacuous, bloated topdog. Greene was also drawn to Torrijos because he "was a lone wolf" – getting no support from the other, authoritarian generals in Latin America. More unusually,

> he [Torrijos] was a friend and admirer of Tito (of Yugoslavia) and on good terms with Fidel Castro, who kept him supplied with excellent Havana cigars ... and gave him advice to be prudent, unwelcome advice which he followed with reluctance. His country had become a haven ... for refugees from Argentina, Nicaragua and El Salvador and his dream ... was of a social democratic Central America.

If true, the latter certainly set him apart from radicals such as Castro and the Sandinistas who despised social-democrats. But when he decided to found a party it was called the Democratic Revolutionary Party.[70]

It is not difficult to detect a confluence of Greene's religious and political impulses and leanings. Michael Korda's observations are salient and help us to understand his relationship with Torrijos:

> In spite of his Catholicism [or perhaps because of it? – P.H.] he was always trying to discover sainthood in secular figures ... his later works are a kind of pilgrimage in search of a different kind of faith ... He was a sentimental leftist when it came to Africa, Cuba, Panama and Vietnam but a man of old-fashioned Tory attitudes when it came to England.[71]

BASHAR AL ASSAD OF SYRIA AND DAVID LESCH

Another, more recent example of the willingness of some intellectuals to give the benefit of the doubt to dictators is provided by the respectful treatment of Bashar al Assad of Syria by Jurgen Todenhofer, a German writer, former judge, and former member of parliament. He called "the

[69] Ibid. According to David Pryce-Jones, Torrijos initiated the relationship with Greene because of his anti-American credentials and the help he was expected to provide in the campaign to bring the Canal under Panamanian control ("Cracked by a Sound: Graham Green in Panama," *Encounter*, February 1985).

[70] Greene, 37–38, 151.

[71] Michael Korda: "The Third Man," *New Yorker*, March 25, 1996, 50.

Western press ... unfairly hostile to Mr Assad" and favoring the opposition. He interviewed Assad repeatedly, considering it "an opportunity for Mr Assad to explain himself ... 'I thought it was important that we listen to this guy whether we hate him or not.' " He obviously did not hate him and thought that he was the victim of a Western "disinformation campaign."[72]

Well before the Syrian civil war, David Lesch, an American professor of Middle Eastern studies, devoted an entire book to Assad, seeking to improve his image and that of his political system. It was his avowed intention to combat what he considered the unfair and biased treatment he received from Western opinion-makers. In 2004 he spent three weeks in Syria conducting interviews with Assad and his highly placed associates; in 2005 he met him again. He also maintained email correspondence with him. Lesch had easy access to Assad and had many conversations with him – undoubtedly the Syrian authorities were aware of his favorable disposition. He averred that he undertook to write about Assad because he "was interested in finding out who Bashar really was."[73]

The apparent point of departure of this undertaking was the author's conviction that Syria was misunderstood by the Western powers and public opinion and unfairly blamed for events it was not responsible for, such as the 1983 attack on the US marine barracks in Beirut and conditions in Lebanon. Lesch believed that "Syria is not a rogue state" and has been anxious to cooperate with the international community. If not a democracy, that is because "Syria is in a dangerous neighborhood ... surrounded by real threats." Bashar inherited "a corrupt, inefficient, broken-down system" and it is unrealistic to expect rapid improvements. Even so, "the margins of freedom [in Syria] are much wider than popularly perceived." He claimed that Syria is "the third safest country in the world in terms of the incidence of crime."[74] This is a claim many police states can make, having monopolized means of violence and having successfully intimidated the population.

Lesch also tried to mitigate Assad's anti-Israeli statements, admitting that "his language regarding Israel ... did indeed consist of fairly harsh rhetoric ... [but] It was probably to be expected that a young, relatively untested leader such as Bashar would stake out a tough line." It was

[72] Rick Gladstone: "Writer Defends His Handling of Interview," *New York Times*, August 6, 2012.

[73] David W. Lesch: *The New Lion of Damascus: Bashar al Assad and Modern Syria*, New Haven CT 2005, viii.

[74] Ibid., 110, 119, 120.

more difficult to rationalize Bashar's comparing Israel to Nazi Germany, but then "unfortunately this type of verbiage has become commonplace in Arab discourse." Moreover, "because of the asymmetry of power arraigned against them, the only weapon that many Arab leaders have at their disposal ... are angry words."[75]

Lesch was most favorably impressed by what he saw as the good intentions of Assad, "the type of person who has wanted to help people his entire life" and had "a vision for the future of his country." His personal qualities were similarly impressive:

> Bashar is basically a principled man. He is very unassuming, his laugh that of an innocent young man. His voice is not the commanding type, yet what he has to say holds your attention because of his appealing sincerity ... he is essentially a morally sound individual, someone who has the best of intentions even if clumsily pursued at times. People who meet him usually come away struck by three things: his politeness, his humility and his simplicity ... I truly believe that Bashar is attempting to set an entirely new tone for the country ... He sees himself as the compassionate healer ... Bashar wants his moral character, his integrity to be the guiding lights that generate loyalty, effort and hope among the Syrian population.[76]

A similarly benign portrait (what might be called a "puff piece") focused on the first lady, Mrs. Assad ("glamorous, young and very chic"), and the Assad family, appeared in *Vogue* magazine more recently. The article noted as a matter of fact, and without skepticism, that Assad was elected with 97 percent of the votes in 2000. He was characterized as "a precise man, who takes photographs and talks lovingly of his first computer, [he] says that he was attracted to eye surgery [while living in England, before becoming president of Syria – P.H.] 'because there is very little blood.'" His household was run "on wildly democratic principles" and the first lady's "central mission" was to promote "active citizenship" among the young. The article concluded with a heart-warming description of the Assads visiting a Catholic orphanage where Assad hands our little bells to the children, remarking "this is the diversity you want to see in the Middle East ... This is how you can have peace."[77]

Lesch believed that he

> really got to know the man as well as the head of the country, and this is in no small measure due to Bashar's own unpretentious and extremely personable demeanor. He was very welcoming. I think being close in age also helped, as we

[75] Ibid., 157, 160.

[76] Ibid., 199, 200, 230–231.

[77] Joan J. Buck: "A Rose in the Desert," *Vogue*, online, March 2011.

could discuss socio-cultural affairs from a similar generational perspective and background. He was also very cooperative in setting up meetings with other leading Syrian figures as well as some of his lifelong friends, childhood teachers, and family members.

Did Lesch truly believe that these "leading Syrian figures," friends and family members, were a reliable source of information who would reveal anything about Assad that was not favorable? As to his conversations with Assad: "No questions were off-limits, and I believe he tried to answer every question in as straightforward a way as he could ... I was immensely pleased with his forthrightness and the extemporaneous way in which he responded to my queries." Lesch was convinced that "I maintained my objectivity; in fact what has drawn me to Bashar on a personal level is all part of a package that I believe bodes well for Syria in the long run ... If I am reading him correctly, his own personal success would be good for Syria."[78] As of this writing (late 2014), Lesch might admit that he did not read him correctly.

Lesch's interaction with the Syrian dictator and his associates resembled numerous other occasions when Western intellectuals suspended the use of their critical faculties in the course of encountering various dictators. We do not know what were the sources of his favorable predisposition toward Assad and his regime. As other admirers of dictators, Lesch was impressed by him because he believed that he was committed to modernization, and such intentions seemed to him incompatible with being a dictator. He obviously overlooked the precedents of other authoritarian modernizers like Stalin and Mao, whose modernizing policies were pursued by inhumane authoritarian methods. Lesch wrote: "The combination computer nerd, ophthalmologist, devoted family man, westernized pop-culturist, outgoing and caring friend, humble and reluctant leader, avid photographer, health and fitness advocate and lurking reformer had all of a sudden become a Middle Eastern dictator"[79] he did not want to be, Lesch was firmly convinced.

Lesch inclined to believe that Assad would not remain a dictator for long, or if he did, he would be a benevolent one, well suited to lead and modernize a backward country. Lesch also reported, without any surprise or skepticism, that in 2000 Bashar got 97 percent of the votes (of the valid 99 percent cast).

[78] Lesch, x.
[79] Ibid., x.

Finally, Lesch rather absurdly claimed to believe that "if President George W. Bush and President Bashar al-Assad were ever to meet in person, they would find that they have a lot in common." According to Lesch, Assad would also inspire the feeling among Americans that "this is someone with whom you could really have a gregarious discussion over dinner and who would be a very loyal and devoted friend." It was a view nurtured by the optimistic, popular, and wrongheaded American cultural belief that face-to-face communications can solve virtually all problems between hostile parties, be they ordinary citizens or heads of state, hence the desirability of summit meetings of world leaders. On such occasions (many Americans believed) the participants, basically good people, regardless of their nationality, ethnicity or class position, would learn that they have much in common. Lesch strongly believed (at any rate when he wrote his book) that Assad

> needs to have a conversation with America because in lieu of this the floor is being monopolized by groups that want nothing but the negative side of Syria to be publicized ... Allowing someone such as myself access to him in order to write this book was also the right thing to do, but he needs to do much more.[80]

While Lesch was not nearly as worshipful of Assad as some other intellectuals used to be of other dictators at earlier times, his feelings had the familiar components of credulousness, naiveté, projection, and the wish to believe. Lesch came to think well of the policies of a dictator who had made a good personal impression on him. There is no evidence I know of that would suggest that Lesch's friendly attitude toward Assad and Syria arose out of an estrangement from American society (Lesch advised US government officials about the Middle East), or that he regarded Syrian social-political arrangements as inspiring and worthy of emulation. More likely his judgments might have been influenced by the disposition to take a favorable position on the political system and its leader he wished to study – an attitude that obviously makes it easier to gain access to such systems and their leaders.[81]

[80] Ibid., 234, 237.

[81] A critic of Lesch wrote: "So enchanted was he with the promise of the British-trained ophthalmologist ... that Lesch resolved to pen Bashar's biography. Not surprisingly, Bashar agreed to cooperate ... Lesch is not alone among scholars who premise their work on repressive states on access to elites. Academics and analysts studying ruthless authoritarian regimes routinely rely on inside sources ... the regimes keep track of the author's publications and if the coverage is not suitably flattering future access is curtailed" (David Schenker: "The New Arabists," *Commentary*, November 2012, 51–52). Schenker also pointed out that Lesch spent much of his time in Syria with "Bashar's inner circle and the pro-regime elites" (ibid., 52) – not exactly unbiased sources of information.

In subsequent years, under the impact of the intensifying civil war in Syria Professor Lesch revised his views of Assad. He wrote:

the authoritarian Syrian system proved too difficult to overcome. Assad morphed into a real-life tyrant … in the beginning I was generally impressed with Bashar and the promise of his leadership … However, I clearly detected changes in Assad as he became more ensconced in power … Instead of creatively and courageously embracing the future, Assad chose a bloody path that is well beaten by an impressive list of brutal dictators from Middle East history.

In the same volume he also wrote that

Bashar was different from the typical Middle Eastern dictator, and this led many people (including me) to hope for the best – and maybe even indulge in a little wishful thinking … somewhere along the road … Assad lost his way … I do believe that, at first Bashar was genuinely interested in serious reform … Soon enough, Bashar found that all he could do was to make some cosmetic changes … He retrenched and retreated into a typically Syrian authoritarian mode of survival.[82]

SADDAM HUSSEIN, RAMSEY CLARK, AND OTHER SYMPATHIZERS

Saddam Hussein was probably the most implausible candidate in recent times for the reverence of Western intellectuals, and admittedly few of them harbored such sentiments toward him. Nonetheless the fact that *any* notable intellectual or public figure could have had any positive feelings about him and his political system is noteworthy, as well as perplexing and compels reflection. Saddam Hussein was one of the most unscrupulous and ruthless dictators in recent times: exceptionally brutal in repressing potential or imaginary dissent; megalomaniacal and insatiable in accumulating power; and unprovoked aggressor, attacking his neighbors Iran and Kuwait. He demanded and basked in a suffocating cult of himself. He created, Kanan Makiya wrote, "a polity that has put enormous resources into the systematic invasion of privacy, denial of individuality and generation of fear … The range of cruel institutional practices … confession rituals, public hangings, corpse displays, executions and finally torture – are designed to breed and sustain widespread fear." In 1979 in the course of a purge he orchestrated and personally directed, the filmed confession of an accused Revolutionary Command Council member was shown to an audience of party leaders:

[82] David W. Lesch: *Syria: The Fall of the House of Assad*, New Haven CT 2012, vii–viii, 211–212, 239–240.

A grief-stricken Saddam addressed the meeting with tears running down his cheeks. He filled in the gaps in Rashid's testimony [the confession] and dramatically fingered his former colleagues. Guards dragged people out of the proceedings and then Saddam called upon the country's top ministers and party leaders to themselves form the actual firing squads. Neither Stalin nor Hitler would have thought up a detail like that.

As to some specifics of his cult, Makiya wrote:

A large painted cutout figure of Saddam Husain towers over the entrance of every Iraqi village; often at night it emits a lurid fluorescent glow. A thirty-foot high version can be seen near Bagdad city center. Photographs adorn every shop, school, police station, army barracks and public building, and can be seen in people's offices and living rooms and overhanging streets from the parapets of houses. No official will appear before a camera without a picture of the president in the background, and his name is evoked in every public address.[83]

This was the man Ramsey Clark, former attorney general of the United States, considered a great leader, decent human being, and innocent victim of American power, "demonized" by the United States.[84] He deserved his legal assistance when brought to trial in Iraq after the war.

Clark has undergone one of the most improbable political transformations of recent times. As Christopher Hitchens described it:

From bullying prosecutor he mutated into vagrant and floating defense counsel, offering himself to the *genocideurs* of Rwanda and to Slobodan Milosevic [of Yugoslavia], and using up the spare time in apologetics for North Korea. He acts as front-man for the Workers World Party, an especially venomous little Communist sect, which originated in a defense of the Soviet invasion of Hungary in 1956.[85]

In the words of John Judis, writing in 1991:

today Clark, 64, inhabits the furthest reaches of the fevered swamps of American politics. He has become not simply a critic of American administrations, but the best hope of their foreign adversaries, from Libyans to the Iraqis. As a lawyer ... [he] turned into a legal 911 for a tawdry collection of accused terrorists and neo or ex-Nazis ... He threw himself at every exotic cause and became a mark for every domestic and foreign liberator and liberation movement ... went to North Vietnam to condemn the US bombing over the "Voice of Vietnam." ... [He served] as a flack for a number of despots who sought his services. In Khomeini's

83 Samir al-Khalil (Kanan Makiya): *Republic of Fear: The Inside Story of Saddam's Iraq*, New York 1989, 67, 72, 110.

84 Ramsey Clark: "Why I'm Willing to Defend Hussein," *Los Angeles Times*, January 24, 2005.

85 Christopher Hitchens: "Sticking up for Saddam," *Slate Magazine*, December 1, 2005. See also Hitchens: "Saddam's Chief Apologist," *Los Angeles Times*, December 8, 2005.

Tehran in June 1980, while American hostages were in their eighth month of captivity, he joined in a forum on "Crimes of America" ... [He] also went to Grenada to advise Bernard and Phyllis Coard, leaders of the clique that was accused of murdering Maurice Bishop.[86]

As these quotations indicate, Saddam Hussein was only one of several exceedingly unappealing political figures Clark decided to champion. His impassioned political activities culminated in volunteering his legal services to both Saddam Hussein and Slobodan Milosevic, both of whom he regarded as admirable human beings and innocent victims of the United States. Clark attended the funeral of Milosevic and received in 1999 an honorary doctorate from Belgrade University.

In a letter to Kofi Annan, Secretary General of the United Nations, Clark wrote about the Milosevic trial:

the spectacle of this huge onslaught by an enormous prosecution team with vast resources pitted against a single man [Slobodan Milosevic], defending himself, cut off from all effective assistance, his supporters under attack everywhere and his health slipping away from the constant strain, portrays the essence of unfairness, of persecution ... there was no more conciliatory leader than President Milosevic who avoided all out war as Slovenia, Croatia, Bosnia and Macedonia seceded of Yugoslavia ... The former president of Yugoslavia is on trial for defending Yugoslavia ... In contrast the President of the United States, who has openly and notoriously committed war of aggression ... against a defenseless Iraq killing tens of thousands of people, spreading violence there and elsewhere, faces no charges.[87]

Those whom Clark defended (both legally and morally) included the PLO "against a suit brought by the family of Leon Klinghoffer" – the disabled passenger in a wheelchair pushed into the sea by the Palestinian terrorists who hijacked the ship in the Mediterranean.[88]

Not only did Clark consider Iraq and Saddam Hussein to be victimized by the United States, he also brought charges of genocide to the International Court on Crimes Against Humanity.[89] He wrote that the United States "demonize[d] Saddam Hussein" and he implied that charges of Iraqi use of chemical weapons against the Kurds were groundless. He further wrote:

86 John B. Judis: "The Strange Case of Ramsey Clark," *New Republic*, April 22, 1991, 23, 28.

87 Quoted in *The Defense Speaks for History and the Future*, International Action Center, New York 2006, 9, 11, 13. See also Clark, "Why I'm Willing to Defend Hussein."

88 Judis, 29.

89 "Criminal Complaint against the United States and Others..." in Adam Jones ed.: *Genocide, War Crimes and the West: History and Complicity*, London and New York 2004, 270–275.

the United States, a technologically advanced superpower has created weapons systems and executed plans to devastate a small and defenseless country ... first with a direct assault by fire, then with the more deadly ice of enforced isolation, malnutrition and impoverishment ... US technology smashed the cradle of civilization and George Bush called it liberation ... There was no war. No combat. There was only a deliberate, systematic genocide of a defenseless population.[90]

As these statements indicate, Clark came to entertain a starkly polarized global scenario of good and evil, of the underdog and topdog, of overwhelming malignant power and virtuous powerlessness. As Judis wrote, "he became incapable of distinguishing between self-appointed representatives of victims and the victims themselves."[91] Such a disposition was not limited to Clark; some other leftists also misidentified Milosevic and Saddam as victims.[92]

The pronouncements and beliefs of George Galloway, former Labour member of the British parliament, rivaled Clark's quixotic political misjudgments. He too exuded warmth toward an assortment of radical leftist dictators of the twentieth century including Stalin, Mao, Castro, and Saddam Hussein. He wrote to Saddam Hussein: "I salute your courage, your strength, your indefatigability. I can honestly tell you that there was not a single person to whom I told that I was coming to Iraq and hoping to meet with yourself, who did not wish me to convey their heartfelt fraternal greetings and support."[93] Evidently Galloway inhabited a subculture of Saddam supporters. He fully agreed with Clark about the malevolence and power of the forces of evil (the United States and its president) and the identity of its innocent victims, Saddam Hussein and Milosevic, noble and powerless. In a television interview, "he refused to describe Saddam as an evil force. He merely said 'I don't judge people as good or evil'," proceeding immediately to blame the United States for the invasion of Panama and Kuwait and the resulting loss of life. It was patently untrue that he did not judge people, or political systems, as good or evil, as many of his statements here quoted also make clear. According to a friend of his, he displayed "sympathy for the underdog and contempt for the overdog," each unambiguously designated as good vs. evil.[94] As has often been the case when people are consumed by political

[90] Ibid., 7, 9, 10, 21.
[91] Judis, 27.
[92] Christopher Hitchens: "So Long Fellow Travelers," *Washington Post*, October 20, 2002.
[93] Quoted online in Discoverthenetworks.org/A Guide to the Political Left (accessed January 4, 2015).
[94] Quoted in Judis, 26; Judis, 27.

or religious passions, his designations of victim and aggressor become highly idiosyncratic and groundless. Invariably and automatically Clark designated each and every adversary of the United States, regardless of its policies, actions and power, as virtuous and innocent victims.

A combination of selective perception and a disposition to overlook or reject dissonant information allowed Clark to take these quixotic positions. One may wonder, was he aware of the Serbian treatment of Albanians under Milosevic? Of the Srebrenica massacre committed by the Yugoslav forces while Milosevic was in power? Of the hundreds of thousands of people Saddam Hussein had killed, tortured, or imprisoned? Of his use of chemical weapons against Kurdish civilians? If he was aware of any of these atrocities it is likely that he regarded them as matters of justifiable self-defense and as morally insignificant compared to those committed by the United States.

It is likely that well before Clark took his bizarre positions in support of highly repressive, violent, and intolerant political systems and their leaders, he came to the conclusion that the United States was the most dangerous and reprehensible source of evil in the world. This overarching belief led to the reflexive sympathy and support for all the enemies and alleged victims of the United States. They included dictators of different ideological persuasion noted above, whose inhumane qualities and policies Clark was unable to discern or acknowledge, let alone condemn. It was sufficient for Clark's moral accounting that if these dictators were opposed to (and allegedly victimized) by the United States, they deserved and earned his sympathy.

There was even an International Committee to Defend Slobodan Milosevich (ICDSM) that was supported by numerous Western intellectuals including Ramsey Clark, Peter Handke, Edward Herman, Harold Pinter, Michael Parenti, Valenti Rasputin and Alexander Zinovev among others.[95] See ICDSM websites online.

While there were few major Western intellectuals or public figures who shared Clark's and Galloway's strong sympathy for Saddam Hussein, Clark's positive feelings about Milosevic were shared by Peter Handke, an Austrian writer well known in Europe. He was described as "one of the most prominent defenders" of Milosevic; he attended and spoke at his funeral in Belgrade and earlier had attended his trial in the Hague and

95 "Artists' Appeal for Milosevich," drafted by Canadian poet Robert Dickinson, online (accessed June 12, 2015).

denied its legitimacy. Handke excused the atrocities of Milosevich on the ground that he "had been forced to 'defend his country's territory' and that 'anyone in his position' would have acted as Milosevic had done."[96]

FRIENDS OF THEOCRATIC IRAN

Further back in time, the Iranian Revolution of 1977–1978 provides another case study of misplaced admiration and profound political misjudgment on the part of some Western intellectuals. Maxine Rodinson summed up the initial interest of many leftist intellectuals in that revolution:

> The hope for a world revolution that would abolish exploitation and the oppression of man by man, for a long time dead or moribund, resurfaced ... Could it have been that this hope now found itself incarnated in the most unexpected way in the Muslim Orient, up to now not a very promising location for it; and ... in this old man [Ayatollah Khomeini] lost in a universe of medieval thought?
>
> High flying intellectuals hurled themselves toward Iran ... They wanted to see with their own eyes, to witness ... this astonishing revolutionary process, to study it ... The establishment of the new government ... only increased the interest of Western intellectuals. Their trips to Iran multiplied.[97]

Of all these hopefully expectant visitors Michel Foucault was the most deeply committed to and most laudatory of the new regime. He visited Iran twice in 1978, and subsequently "wrote and spoke enthusiastically and uncritically of the revolution."[98]

As the new Iranian authorities began in 1979 to repress "feminists, ethnic and religious minorities, liberals and leftists – all in the name of Islam," Western enthusiasm diminished. Foucault persisted in his ardor and sympathy, his attitudes exemplifying one of the most singular of all the political infatuations discussed in this volume. He further personifies an especially striking convergence of political and religious impulses and needs that led to his unconstrained admiration of the Iranian political system and its leader. As Afary and Anderson write, "his writings on Iran represent the most significant and passionate political commitment of his life."[99]

[96] Michael McDonald: "The Apologist," *American Scholar*, 2007.

[97] Rodinson in Janet Afary and Kevin B. Anderson eds.: *Foucault and the Iranian Revolution: Gender and the Seduction of Islamism*, Chicago 2005, 267–268.

[98] Ibid., 2.

[99] Ibid., 8, 163.

Among all the Western intellectuals dealt with in this volume who visited the countries whose political systems and leaders they admired, Foucault stands out as the most literal pilgrim – political as well as religious. More than most others, he self-consciously sought a society that would satisfy his intense spiritual-religious needs. Again as Afary and Anderson write, "his earlier work had shown a consistent … affinity for the Orient and the more traditional social norms of the East as well as a preoccupation with messianic Eastern thought." He went to Iran " 'to be there at the birth of ideas' " in the belief that "the new 'Muslim' style of politics could signal … a new form of political spirituality." This idea of "political spirituality" was the product of a muddled, wishful, utopian yearning, a fantasy that combined the best of all possible worlds – legitimate, traditional religious authority somehow adapted to the modern world and embraced by popular consent, religiously authenticated community and the vanishing of the boundaries between the private and public, or the personal and the social-political realm.

Foucault endorsed the new regime in Iran because it "aimed at a fundamental cultural, social and political break with the modern Western order." It is an understatement to suggest that he was not "immune to the type of illusions that so many Western leftists had held with regard to the Soviet Union and later, China." His errors, as those made by the admirers of communist systems noted above, were born of wishful thinking that overpowered common sense and the critical faculties. The major determinant of his thinking was "a search for alternate forms of non-Western modernity that could rejoin spirituality and politics." He steadfastly confused and conflated the religious authoritarianism of the Iranian theocracy with "political spirituality" and the embodiment of "political will." He distrusted legalistic ways of governing and instead put his "faith in the creativity of Islam."

His wishful projections were boundless and vague. He proposed that "the Iranian Revolution was beyond politics, an expression of a totally unified society … 'constitut[ing] a perfectly unified collective will…'."[100] It was characteristic of Foucault (and many intellectuals similarly enthralled by idealized political systems and their leaders) that he required and

[100] Ibid., 2, 3, 4, 5, 10, 90, 98. Lilla helps to understand Foucault's mindset as he observes that "his life and writings show … what happens when an essentially private thinker, struggling with his inner demons … projects them out onto the political sphere" (Mark Lilla: *The Reckless Mind: Intellectuals in Politics*, New York 2001, 158).

possessed little solid evidence to back up his sweeping assessments. As another of his critics wrote,

Foucault … placed excessive hopes in the Iranian Revolution. The great gaps in his knowledge of Islamic history enabled him to transfigure events in Iran, to accept for the most part the semitheoretical suggestions of his Iranian friends, and to extrapolate from this by imagining an end of history that would make up for disappointments in Europe and elsewhere.[101]

Foucault's admiration and respect of Ayatollah Khomeini was an integral part of his misapprehension of the Iranian revolution and its aftermath. Afary and Anderson noted that

as a keen admirer of Nietzsche Foucault might have been more cautious about supporting a revolution led by a religious ascetic … perhaps Foucault was also impressed with Khomeini because he went beyond the role of ascetic priest. Khomeini knew how to exploit the religious sentiment of guilt … [he] was the personification of Nietzsche's "will to power," a ruthless historical figure.[102]

Foucault was apparently susceptible to Khomeini's charisma that overshadowed what Rodinson called "his [Khomeini's] serene indifference to the sufferings caused by his senile stubbornness and vindictive fury."[103] Foucault's benign views of Khomeini may also be contrasted with the assessments of the Iranian psychologist, Fathali M. Moghaddam, who wrote that "Khomeini … clutched and clung to absolute power until his dying breath … He sought to bolster his power by religious-spiritual claims: "This leader interprets the word of God for the people … show[ing] the people the right path according the holy scripture."[104]

It is of some interest that another French author believed that there was "something similar in the charisma of Mao Zedong and of Khomeini; there is something similar in the way the young Islamic militants speak of Khomeini and the way the Red Guards spoke of Mao."[105]

In further contrast to the assessments of Foucault, Bruce Mazlish characterized Ayatollah Khomeini as one of those political, or political-religious, figures who "appear detached from normal human emotions" and whose capacity for love "shifted away from persons onto an abstraction – the People, the Revolution, Humanity – which is all perfect and can never disappoint.

[101] Rodinson in ibid., 270.
[102] Ibid., 36.
[103] Rodinson in ibid., 269.
[104] Fathali M. Moghaddam: *The Psychology of Dictatorship*, Washington DC 2013, 12, 113.
[105] Pierre Blanchet in Afary and Anderson, 253.

This permits what I call the 'revolutionary ascetic' to break all normal emotional ties in the name of the cause; he can now send his best friends to the guillotine."[106] Khomeini said in an interview that "the Iranian revolution was the most humane in history; not a single person was killed by the revolutionaries. When the surprised journalist asked about the death penalties publicized in the media, Khomeini calmly replied: 'Those that we killed were not men, but criminal dogs!' "[107] Such a disposition was shared by most of the other dictators here discussed, as was the following characterization of Khomeini: "beneath Khomeini's control of feeling lay hidden ambition and rage of monumental proportions ... he was also an excessively suspicious person ... convinced that plots, conspiracies and treacheries abounded ... So too, the theme of poisoning was omnipresent in Khomeini."[108]

Richard Falk, professor emeritus of international relations at Princeton University, with a long record of sympathy for political movements and systems hostile to the United States and Israel,[109] was among the small number of Western intellectuals who harbored positive sentiments for the Iranian theocracy and its founder Ayatollah Khomeini. He suggested that there was no trace of religious fanaticism in Khomeini, that he was "defamed by the news media" and falsely associated with "virulent antisemitism." Falk was also confident that the "non-religious left will be free to express its views in an Islamic Republic and to participate in political life." He averred that "to suppose that Ayatollah Khomeini is dissembling seems almost beyond belief." His depiction "as fanatical ... and the bearer of crude prejudices seems certainly and happily false," he also wrote.[110]

This was not the only occasion Falk chose to express confidence in the tolerant and enlightened disposition of the Iranian theocracy. He also assured readers of *Foreign Policy* about "a new and more representative governmental system for Iran," one that will not "necessarily be

[106] Bruce Mazlish: *The Leader, the Led and the Psyche: Essays in Psychohistory*, Hanover NH 1990, 144–145. Hannah Arendt's characterization of revolutionaries is applicable here: "Since the days of the French Revolution, it has been the boundlessness of their sentiments that made revolutionaries so curiously insensitive to reality in general and to the reality of persons in particular, whom they felt no compunctions in sacrificing to their 'principles,' or the course of history, or the cause of the revolution." Such revolutionaries "lost the capacity to establish and hold fast to rapports with persons in their singularity" (*On Revolution*, New York 1965, 85).

[107] Quoted in Slavoj Zizek: *Violence*, New York 2008, 54–55.

[108] Mazlish, 146, 147.

[109] Falk's aversion to the United States and Israel approaches and approximates the corresponding dispositions of Chomsky both in duration and intensity. They also share a style of writing that seeks to create a semblance of judiciousness and impartiality.

[110] Richard Falk: "Trusting Khomeini," *New York Times*, February 16, 1979.

inherently anti-American, let alone a fanatical theocracy." He had high hopes for "the prospects for a moderate and human governing process" supported by "respected secular nationalist figures" in the government. He also believed that "the entourage around Khomeini ... has had considerable involvement in human rights activities and is committed to a struggle against all forms of repression ... Khomeini's Islamic republic can be expected to have a doctrine of social justice at its core; from all indications it will be flexible in interpreting the Koran."[111]

It is hard to know what led Falk to these ideas aside from wishful thinking and probably the false assurances by Iranian officials he met in Iran. As many other intellectuals of a similar disposition, it is likely that he could not resist the attractions of a government he considered both a victim and righteous opponent of the United States. What is most striking about his assessments and expectations is not only that every one of them proved to be wrong, but the complete suspension of critical faculties that led to them. He never expressed regrets in public about his profoundly mistaken analysis of the Iranian authorities and Khomeini in particular.[112]

More recently two former State Department officials came to display what a critic called "deep affection for the Islamic Republic of Iran" and became "across-the-board apologists for an inefficient and often ruthless regime," making an "eerie effort to whitewash the Islamic Republic" and trying to create in their book a "mythology of a benign Iranian order loved by its citizens." These authors believe that Iran's government "may well produce 'a wider range of choice for Iranian voters than the United States' two-party system offers American voters.' "[113] The same authors also sympathize with the Syrian regime. Roger Cohen wrote: "The Leveretts, whose empathy with human suffering is on the shallow side, continue to fawn before Bashar al-Assad. They dismiss his brutality much as they did that of the post-election crackdown in Iran."[114]

Going to Tehran is a lengthy, polemical apology for the Iranian regime and its founder Ayatollah Khomeini, whose "revolutionary commitment to restore Iran's sovereignty and defend its independence was grounded

[111] Richard Falk: "Khomeini's Promise," *Foreign Policy*, Spring 1979, 28, 31, 32.

[112] See "UN's Richard Falk Justifies His 1979 'Trusting Khomeini" NYT op-ed," *Human Rights Council* (UNHRC), October 12, 2012, online (accessed July 10, 2015).

[113] Leveretts quoted in Roger Cohen: "Ruthless Iran: Can a Deal Be Made?" *New York Review of Books*, June 6, 2013, 64, 66; the book in question: Flynt Leverett and Hillary Mann Leverett: *Going to Tehran: Why the United States Must Come to Terms with the Islamic Republic of Iran*, New York 2013.

[114] Roger Cohen: "Reply," *New York Review of Books*, July 11, 2013.

in the underlying principles of justice, equality among peoples and nations, and unity among the *umma* (the community of Muslim believers)." He is neither "a dogmatic authoritarian" nor "the quintessential fundamentalist."[115]

These authors were not the only ones entertaining favorable views of Ayatollah Khomeini: "Andrew Young saw Khomeini as a saint and Richard Falk regarded him as a worthy visionary."[116]

The Leveretts argue with great vehemence that Americans and Westerners are incapable of properly understanding Iran (presumably making an exception for themselves), and more generally the Muslim world, their views being conditioned and distorted by "orientalism," as Edward Said argued and whose idea they invoke. These alleged false attributions and misperceptions of the Muslim world were not innocent mistakes but were devised to help to "legitimize ... regional interventions" of the colonial powers.

The authors' point of departure is that the United States, its elites, and policy-makers have been both unwilling and incapable of understanding the true nature of the Islamic Republic of Iran and consequently created a myth designed to legitimate their hostile policies toward it, based on ignorance and ill will. This ignorance is "a source of grave danger, for the United States ... courting strategic disaster by persisting in a fundamentally hostile posture toward the Islamic Republic." This theme is embedded in a broader view of the world in which the United States is depicted as engaged in a ceaseless, ruthless, conspiratorial pursuit of hegemony, its policies in recent times inspired and determined by a small, malevolent group of neoconservatives. American policy-makers and journalists are predisposed "to see foreigners resisting American hegemony not as rational actors with real interests but as irrational and illegitimate." The entire Cold War is reduced to the American pursuit of global power. They write: "In the post-World War II period, the United States conducted its Cold War struggle against the Soviet Union as part of a massive exercise in empire building."[117] There is only one genuine aggressor and menace to peace and harmony in the world, and that is the United States, assisted by its ally and regional aggressor, Israel.

115 Leverett and Leverett, 31, 33.
116 Mazlish, 139.
117 Leverett and Leverett, 1, 9, 234, 288.

By contrast Iran's foreign (as well as domestic) policies have been determined by being encircled, besieged, and threatened by the United States and its allies, including especially Israel. Iran has borders with fifteen states, none of them "a natural ally." The authors write: "Opposition to domination and the defense of legitimate rights" define Iranian foreign policy. Iranians believe that "other powers would like to eliminate" their state. Their military policies (with special reference to reliance on ballistic missiles) is governed by "a fundamentally defensive logic."[118]

If and insofar as the authors acknowledge anything unseemly in Iranian political positions and policies, it is always the outcome of a fully justified defensiveness. It is a view that recalls and resembles past attempts to defend the aggressive and repressive policies of the Soviet Union by Soviet sympathizers and apologists. It is also a position regularly and predictably taken by virtually every repressive government and its supporters, as they convert aggression into self-defense.

The relationship between Iran and Israel is a major case in point: "Tehran's objective is to contain what Iranian leaders ... have seen as Israel's ambition to weaken and subordinate its Muslim neighbors" and its pursuit of "regional dominance." Hence Iran's choice to support Hamas and Hizballah "are far from irrational." Moreover, unlike Israel, Iran "does not seek ... regional dominance" and has no "hegemonic ambitions."

Also reminiscent of the apologists' approach to virtually all totalitarian systems of the past, the Leveretts plead for a proper "understanding" of the Iranian theocracy and endlessly warn against the folly and danger of evaluating it by Western liberal standards. For example: "To understand the Islamic Republic's unique approach to balancing external threats, it is necessary to look more deeply into Iran's geographic, historical and cultural setting." Not once do they acknowledge that similar circumstances may also require consideration and understanding of the concerns of Israel and its defensive needs. Against overwhelming evidence, they assert that Hizballah "and other Iranian proxies" are *not* "irrationally committed to terrorizing Israelis."[119] Were they rationally committed to terror? The Leveretts don't say.

As to Ahmedinajad threatening to wipe Israel off the map – it was "a pernicious legend" based on a poor translation of what he said. In fact, he only quoted a statement of Ayatollah Khomeini who said that

[118] Ibid., 35, 40, 45, 79.

[119] Ibid., 19, 21, 30, 55, 64, 71.

"this regime occupying Jerusalem must disappear from the page of time." But later they suggest that "Ahmedinejad's rhetoric about Israel and the Holocaust needs to be understood" in the context of "a virtual state of war" between Israel and Iran that includes covert attacks and threats by Israel. In using this rhetoric, "he is tapping into a deep anger throughout the Middle East." Thus they seem to imply that, after all, these circumstances justify threatening to wipe Israel off the map – whatever the precise expression was to convey this intention.

A particularly unappealing instance of the endless efforts to cleanse the Iranian regime of any wrongdoing was the assertion that one of the demonstrators (Neda Soltan) gunned down during the protests against the 2009 electoral fraud was shot "at least a kilometer away from the nearest demonstration" and not by "the security forces." They insinuate, referring to unnamed official Iranian sources, that she might have been shot by members of a movement opposed to the regime (MEK), "with Israeli and/or Western support," who infiltrated the protests "to galvanize popular support for overthrowing the Islamic Republic."

These authors have nothing but contempt for the domestic opponents and critics of the regime (Greens) and insist that the government has broad and deep popular support testified to by "methodologically sound polls taken during the 2009 election and after ... both sufficiently large and random to minimize sampling error."[120] They fail to note that neither of these features of the polls cited could be expected to eliminate the justified apprehension of respondents in a police state. As a critic wrote:

> They [the Leveretts] cite opinion polls conducted on insecure phone lines from outside the country. That's because no independent polling agency has operated in Iran since 2002, when pollsters were sentenced to nine and a half years in prison for publishing results the regime didn't like, and for cooperating with Gallup and Zogby, which the judiciary regarded as collaboration with an enemy state. Now imagine you are an ordinary Iranian taking a phone call from a stranger who identifies himself with a Western polling outfit and wants to know about your political views ... Until they [the polls cited by the Leveretts] are replicated under conditions free from fear, no one knows what they really mean.[121]

To support their belief in the legitimacy of the Iranian system they quote (of all people) Michel Foucault: "Visiting Iran in October 1978 Foucault reported that in response to the question 'What do you want?' four out of five respondents – including 'religious leaders, students,

[120] Ibid., 19, 92, 238, 263.

[121] "Laura Secor Replies" (to the Leveretts' letter protesting her March 3 review of their book), *New York Times Book Review*, March 31, 2013.

intellectuals' – and 'former guerilla fighters' – answered, 'An Islamic government.' " They do not disclose the total number of those who responded to the question and while they admit that it was not "a scientific sample," they nonetheless regard these responses as confirmation of widespread "popular backing" for Khomeini's "Islamist vision." Nor do they have any doubt that the regime delivered "a better life," relying on Iranian official statistics. They have no criticism of the large number of death sentences that Iran carries out and is the second largest number in the world after those in China. They only observe that "the judicial system vigorously applies the death penalty to drug dealers and traffickers."

As to the brutal suppression of demonstrations protesting the 2009 elections and the show trials of those arrested that followed, they admit that occasionally "security actions exceeded public tolerance" and "some detainees were physically abused and others murdered," but they are satisfied that the government dealt appropriately with the perpetrators of such abuses. They hasten to add: "The political significance of the security forces' behavior after the June 2009 presidential election should be considered in the context of Iran's history." What they mean is that bad things also happened in the past, that more demonstrators were killed in 1979 under the Shah, and "in comparison the government's response in 2009–2010 was relatively restrained."[122] Even if this was the case (and it is hard to consider the authors a reliable source), it is a feeble and morally dubious justification.

We do not know what circumstances disposed these authors to produce this biased book and to take a totally uncritical and sympathetic position toward the theocratic dictatorship of Iran. Their conviction that the United States is the sole genuinely malevolent imperialist power in the world is certainly a part of the explanation, a firmly held belief they share with other apologists of repressive political systems and their leaders. Such a lopsided and oversimplified view of the world and international relations itself requires an explanation that is not available to this author.

VLADIMIR PUTIN AND STEPHEN F. COHEN

While Vladimir Putin's popularity in his own country is not difficult to explain, it is far less obvious why he has stimulated positive

[122] Leverett and Leverett, 162, 187–194, 194, 270, 271.

sentiments from a handful of American intellectuals of different ideological persuasion.

Somewhat unexpectedly Pat Buchanan, the prominent old-style conservative author and public intellectual, appreciated him as a critic of Western decadence and fighter for traditional moral values, especially those embedded in Christianity. He wrote: "Nor is [Putin] without an argument when we reflect on America's embrace of abortion on demand, homosexual marriage, pornography, promiscuity and the whole panoply of Hollywood values."[123] Sympathy for Putin as a fighter against secular decadence combined with and was fortified by the conservative isolationism in international affairs.

But it has been a man of the left, Stephen F. Cohen (professor emeritus of history, Princeton and New York University), who has emerged as "the most prominent apologist for Putin," according to Jonathan Chait, a liberal journalist.[124] Another writer, Cathy Young, called Cohen the "Kremlin's No.1. American apologist" and expressed dismay at "seeing Cohen – once a serious scholar ... – sink to the level of repeating Russian misinformation."[125] Isaac Chotiner also considered him "Putin's American apologist" determined "to defend him [Putin] from the evil American media," and a strong supporter of Putin's policies regarding Ukraine.

Cohen even found merit in Putin's complaint that the United States sent "only a low level delegation [to the Sochi Olympics] including retired gay athletes."[126] On several occasions Cohen was indignant about Putin being "personally villainized" in the American media and he repeatedly called for ending his "demonization," much of which, he claimed, "originat[ing] with his personal enemies."[127]

Under these circumstances it is not surprising that Cohen has been a frequent guest on *Russia Today*, "the primary hub of Russian propaganda in the West ... an English-language, Kremlin-funded propaganda outlet." Cohen was not alone in being attracted to *Russia Today*. Chait wrote:

[123] Buchanan quoted in Ron Radosh: "The New Apologists for Vladimir Putin – on the Right and the Left," March 15, 2014 (pjmedia.com/ronradosh).

[124] Jonathan Chait: "The Pathetic Lives of Putin's American Dupes," *New York Magazine*, March 14, 2015.

[125] Cathy Young: "Putin's Pal," *Slate*, June 24, 2014.

[126] Isaac Chotiner: "Meet Vladimir Putin's American Apologist," *New Republic*, March 2, 2014.

[127] Radosh cited; Stephen L. Cohen: "Stop the Pointless Demonization of Putin," *Reuters*, online, May 7, 2012; also in *Nation* September 16, 2013.

the central appeal of RT is to leftists, libertarians, conspiracy theorists and other marginalized groups. The main thematic work of RT is to paint the West in the worst possible light, as decadent, corrupt and failing ... [it] offers a platform to critics who are denied respectful treatment in the US media ... The demise of communism has left a void in the place where socialist fervor once animated Soviet dupes. In the absence of any positive motivating force, Putin's Russia, which has positioned itself as America's main rival, has sponged up whatever motley collection of outsiders it can find. Russia is not the vessel for their ideological fantasies, but merely a placeholder for their accumulated discontent.[128]

Cohen has not been one of these marginalized outsiders, given his elite academic positions, numerous publications, and frequent appearances on mainstream television. The likely explanation of Cohen's sympathy for Putin's Russia and Putin himself is more complex than Buchanan's and different from those of the marginalized groups referred to by Chait. While it appears that Cohen's affinity with Putin has been increasing in proportion with his rising indignation about the United States and its foreign policies, it may also have deeper and more distant roots. His positive sentiments may originate in the old leftist view of Russia as the perennial victim of the West and the corresponding sympathy for a strong leader, such as Putin, determined to overcome the alleged victimization. In this long-standing perspective *both* Soviet-Russian domestic repression *and* aggression abroad are explained as forms of legitimate collective self-defense. In other words, what strikes other observers as self-evident aggression – such as the use of Russian military force against Georgia and in the Ukraine – in Cohen's view is appropriate defense against Western encroachments on Russia's sphere of interest. As a *Nation* editorial argued, "Russia is merely reacting to Western expansionism."[129] More specifically, Cohen also claimed that Obama "has unilaterally declared a new Cold War against Russia," that "twenty years of NATO's eastward expansion has caused Russia to feel cornered," and that "future historians will note that in April 2014, the White House declared a new Cold War on Russia."[130]

The cognitive dissonance between Cohen's position as a man of the left and his defense of what Ioffe calls "a revanchist, nationalist, imperialist, conservative Putin who established an oligarchy in Russia" can best be explained by the felt urgency and importance of supporting the enemy

[128] Chait.

[129] Quoted in Alec Torres: "*The Nation:* America's Russia Apologist," *National Review online*, March 4, 2014.

[130] Quoted in Julia Ioffe: "Putin's American Toady at the *Nation* Gets Even Toadier," *New Republic*, May 1, 2014.

of his enemies. Cohen's disposition may be traced to several sources, the most immediate and pressing being his rising anger at American policies, or as Ioffe put it, "the moral imperative of sticking it to Washington and American hegemony."[131]

Cohen's unembarrassed support of Putin and Russia probably has a more indirect connection with frustrated past hopes about the survival and transformation of the Soviet Union into a benign and authentic socialist system under Gorbachev. The roots of such hopes may be found in Cohen's lifelong admiration of Nicolai Bukharin, who, in Cohen's view, might have created such a system had he not been murdered by Stalin.[132] That is to say, it is likely that Cohen harbored lifelong hopes about the possibility of the creation of a decent socialist system in the Soviet Union. He was repeatedly disappointed and this contributed to his growing anger at the United States, seen as the major obstacle to the realization of such hopes.

Chait offered another interpretation of these attitudes, suggesting that Cohen "carried on the mental habits of decades of anti-anti-communism ... into a new career of anti-anti-Putinism."[133] The proposition may also be associated with Vietnam-era Soviet revisionism that had some impact on Cohen[134] and with the widely shared, enduring belief of the period that an aggressive, militarized United States has been responsible for most global problems and conflicts.

Being married to the editor-in-chief of *The Nation* (Katherina vanden Heuvel), and having ready access to its pages, may also have some relevance to Cohen's increasingly radicalized political beliefs and attitudes. This is not to suggest that Ms. Heuvel has been a major influence on his outlook, but rather that the marital bond confirms and reflects his own deep-seated convictions that he shares with his wife.

SEAN PENN AND EL CHAPO

The political sympathies of the American celebrity actor, Sean Penn (noted above), provide unexpected insight into the connections and overlap between political and non-political hero worship, and hero worship in general. While Penn's admiration of Fidel Castro and Hugo Chavez

[131] Ibid.

[132] Stephen L. Cohen: *Bukharin and the Bolshevik Revolution: A Political Biography*, New York 1980.

[133] Chait.

[134] See Hollander 1985.

has been well-known and long-standing, and shared with many other Hollywood celebrities,[135] his recent embrace of the Mexican drug lord Joaquin Guzman (better known as El Chapo) was far more unusual and revealing.

Penn was a frequent visitor of Cuba under both Fidel and Raul Castro and Venezuela under Chavez, meeting each of them several times. He also visited Iraq under Saddam Hussein and considered the country a victim of American imperialism. He harbored great admiration for Fidel Castro and Chavez, convinced that both were devoted to the best interests of their people and the creation of a social-political system far superior to the American. In his view these great leaders were misunderstood by the American public and slandered by American policy-makers and the media.

Penn's recent interest in and sympathy for El Chapo, while at first glance rather implausible, on closer inspection reveals a pattern and affinity with his admiration of Castro and Chavez. These three disparate figures had in common attributes of great importance to Penn: an apparent authenticity, charisma, huge personal power, and, perhaps the most important, a profound, animating hostility to the United States and capitalism that he shared with them. It was also possible to project upon each the image of the underdog who had brilliantly and heroically overcome great difficulties and deprivations. Castro and Chavez were revolutionaries, overthrowing an unjust social-political system, while Guzman defied the arbitrary and oppressive social norms of his society by establishing a huge and powerful criminal enterprise and becoming, in Penn's eyes, the "other president" of Mexico. Like the political leaders Penn was drawn to, Guzman impressed him with his authenticity – an especially alluring attribute for a privileged Hollywood celebrity caught between an abiding sense of entitlement and pervasive guilt over his unearned privileges bestowed upon him by the unjust social-economic system he detested.

Penn's visit and interview with Guzman (for *Rolling Stone*) was an exciting adventure, an arduous clandestine journey arranged with the help of the Mexican actress, Kate del Castillo, Guzman was attracted to and sought to enlist in a movie about himself. Penn's favorable predisposition toward Guzman was unmistakable from the outset of his adventurous visit, as was his pride in being able to do "the first

[135] See for example Sean Penn: "Conversation with Chavez and Castro," *Nation*, November 25, 2008.

interview El Chapo had granted outside an interrogation room." Penn saw him as "This simple man ... from a simple place, surrounded by the simple affections of his sons to their father, and his toward them, [he] does not initially strike me as the big bad wolf of lore." Quite to the contrary, he was "a Robin Hood figure who provided much needed services in the Sinaloa Mountains." He became the biggest drug dealer in the world because there were no other alternatives; it was the only way to support his family.

At the time of Penn's and del Castillo's joint visit, Guzman was hiding in a remote area, surrounded by his faithful and heavily armed bodyguards and troops, and it required complex cloak-and-dagger arrangements for Penn to reach him. One of Guzman's sons piloted a plane for the local flight. He was received by Guzman with great warmth, wined and dined; he felt comfortable and secure in his company, profoundly impressed by what he called "the otherworldly experience of sitting with a man so seemingly serene." He wrote that upon arrival

> He pulls me into a "comprador" hug, looks me in the eyes and speaks lengthy greeting in Spanish ... Throughout my interactions Chapo smiles a warm smile ... The trust that El Chapo had extended to us was not to be fucked with ... My only genuine cards to play were to expose myself as one fascinated and willing to suspend judgement ... I give in to the sense of security offered by the calm of Chapo and his men ... He greets Kate [the actress] like a daughter returning from college. It was important to him to express warm affection in person that until now he had only occasion to communicate from afar ... He is entirely unapologetic ... whatever villainy is attributable to this man ... he is also a humble, rural Mexican.

As these lines and others make clear, Penn had no difficulty to suspend moral judgment, he proudly and successfully resisted what he considered his "moral conditioning" by his "puritanical and prosecutorial culture" and refused to attribute "soullessness" (or any moral failing) to his amiable host. Penn believed that American society is "complicit in what we demonize" and raised the rhetorical question he readily answered: "Are we saying that what's systemic in our culture ... shares no moral equivalency to these abominations that may rival narco assassinations in Juarez?" That is to say, we are no better than him, as a matter of fact, a lot worse.

It is apparent that Penn's great capacity for moral indignation, readily displayed in regard to the inequities of his own society, vanished when it came to the "narco assassinations in Juarez." The moral inequities of El Chapo's vast criminal enterprise are quickly neutralized by his conviction that the evils of the United States dwarf anything El Chapo (or anyone else) might have done, and by his belief that "El Chapo is a businessman first and only resorts to violence when he deems it advantageous to himself and his business interests." How did he know? El Chapo told him.

He readily embraced (a skewed) moral relativism concerning the misdeeds of El Chapo: "As much as anything it's a question of relative morality ... what of the tens of thousands of Americans ... locked down in facilities where unspeakable acts of dehumanization and violence are inescapable."[136] These images instantly relieved Penn of the slightest inclination to be judgmental of El Chapo and his doings.[137]

In a subsequent electronic interview,[138] Penn asked El Chapo if he thought that drugs were destructive (he did); if "he considered himself a violent person" (he did not; "all I do is defend myself, nothing more"); about his relationship to his mother ("perfect ... [one of] respect, affection and love"); of his "dreams and hopes" ("to live with my family the days God gives me"). It is not easy to grasp what Penn hoped to accomplish by these questions, seemingly calculated to elicit bland or agreeable responses.

It is not difficult to come to the conclusion that Penn's sympathetic portrayal of El Chapo was rooted in the same impulses that led to his admiration of Castro and Chavez and the profound rejection of American society. While his political infatuations were encouraged by the left-leaning Hollywood celebrity subculture of which he was an integral part, it is not wildly speculative to suggest that his father's political

[136] Sean Penn: "El Chapo Speaks: A Secret Visit with the Most Wanted Man in the World," *Rolling Stone*, January 28, 2016, 144–155. See also Dave Itzkoff: "Sean Penn's Excursions into Writing Often Mix Activism with Journalism," *New York Times*, January 11, 2016, A6.

[137] Penn expressed misgivings about the *Rolling Stone* article in a 60 Minutes interview with Charlie Rose (January 17, 2016). He thought that the article was "a failure" and misunderstood. In response to Rose's prodding as to why he undertook it, the only explanation he would offer was that somehow it was supposed to help to better understand and solve the drug epidemic in the United States by "observing another human being," i.e., Guzman. He was unable to explain how the interview might have helped to accomplish this. Also notable was that he reaffirmed, in a convoluted way, his reluctance to be judgmental of El Chapo. On the whole he was defensive, evasive, and somewhat incoherent. The interviewer didn't ask him about his favorable impressions of El Chapo.

[138] See online, "Watch El Chapo's Exclusive Interview," January 12, 2016, www.RollingStone.com.

sympathies and blacklisted status in the McCarthy period might have been another powerful influence on the evolution of his political attitudes and beliefs.

While the attitudes sampled in this chapter have not been widespread (compared to those inspired by the dictators dealt with earlier), they illustrate the variety of political figures and systems intellectuals (and others) may select as the repository of their hopes and expectations. They also testify to the durability of the political misjudgments the hero worship inspires and entails.

8

Conclusions: The Personal and the Political

> Men, it appears, would rather believe than know.
>
> *Edward O. Wilson*[1]

> [T]he dream of a better world holds out such a compelling attraction that some will become determined to kill everyone who stands in the way of its realization.
>
> *Alan Wolfe*[2]

> [W]hen belief in a divinity gives way, a reserve army of idols stands ready to take its place – ideas, dogmas, leaders, movements.
>
> *Mark Lilla*[3]

This book was devoted, for the most part, to attempts to better understand why many Western intellectuals thought well of various contemporary dictators and the political systems they created and dominated. Since in my earlier work (*Political Pilgrims*) I examined such misjudgments that pertained only to communist states, this time I was interested in finding out if dictatorships of different ideological foundations and histories were also similarly misperceived and idealized. Italian fascism, Nazi Germany, and dictatorships in the Arab world, among others, allowed broader comparisons. It became apparent that there was no shortage of similar misjudgments and illusions inspired by these regimes and their leaders. These findings suggest that the beliefs and dispositions

[1] Edward O. Wilson: *On Human Nature*, Cambridge MA 1978, 171.

[2] Alan Wolfe: *Political Evil*, New York 2011, 5.

[3] Mark Lilla: "Daniel Bell (1919–2011)," *New York Review of Books*, April 7, 2011, 26.

in question have deep roots that transcend the attractions of specific (mostly leftist) ideologies and the political systems that sought to realize them. These sentiments, and the associated misjudgments, originate in a combination of ignorance, idealism, high expectations, wishful thinking, and possibly some other shared personal traits (yet to be identified) of the individuals we call intellectuals.

As to ignorance, Anthony Daniels (whose opinions I respect) disagrees:

> one of the myths of the twentieth century is that many Western intellectuals sympathized with the Soviet Union because they were unaware of the true nature of the regime ... lack of information allowed ... them to fix their mind on the regime's declared ideals ... Nothing could be further from the truth ... books published in Britain, France and the United States in the 1920s and 1930s ... prove that ... every class of atrocity, if not every atrocity itself, was made known in the West as soon, or after it occurred.[4]

Doubtless such information was available but not widely disseminated, and those favorably disposed toward the regimes concerned were not anxious to seek it out, and if encountered preferred to question it.

As always, it is difficult, if not totally impossible, to identify and separate the personal from the social, or sociological, motives and circumstances that gave rise to the disposition that was central to the subject of this book. Whatever part the personality of the protagonists played, the misjudgments were highly patterned, quite standardized, and had discernible social-historical roots and determinants. The widely shared political illusions reflected longings and discontents that intensified at times of crises, mainly economic in the 1930s, political and cultural in the 1960s and 1970s. But during the same periods such political sentiments among intellectuals (and other strata of the population) were not uniform, or evenly distributed, suggesting the limits of the social determination of political attitudes.

In addition to the preoccupation with the political attitudes of a portion of Western intellectuals, this book also reflects my long-standing interest in human beings – such as dictators – whose life is devoted to the pursuit, accumulation, and maximization of political power. These

4 Daniels quoted in Thomas Sowell: *Intellectuals and Society*, New York 2011, 216. George Watson held the same view and strongly believed (at any rate about the Soviet Union under Stalin) that Western intellectuals were *not* ignorant of its true character and supported it because they believed in its objectives and were not bothered by the means used to accomplish them. According Jeffrey Hart, for many of these intellectuals, the Soviet system had "the mark of the authentic, the sincere" (Introduction to George Watson: "Were the Intellectuals Duped?" *National Review*, November 7, 1975).

are individuals possessed of extraordinary self-regard, convinced of their momentous historical role and mission. At the same time, this was not an undertaking designed to shed new light on the mentality, personality, or rise to power of dictators, on the outlook of the relatively small number of people whose life is devoted to the pursuit and exercise of power. Nor did I attempt to explore the social and political conditions that might explain the uneven distribution of the thirst for power. Nonetheless, I had hoped that a comparison of the perceptions and misperceptions of the dictators and the cults they themselves initiated and encouraged might shed some light on their actual personalities, as distinct from their images.

It is difficult to know whether or not, and if so to what degree, the highly organized and institutionalized cults of the dictators influenced the intellectuals' perceptions of the dictators. Correspondingly, it is difficult to tell whether or not the sympathetic intellectuals were aware of the difference between genuine popularity, or the spontaneous outpourings of affection on the part of the citizens, and the elaborate cults of the dictators, orchestrated by the propaganda apparatus at their disposal.

MODERNITY, RELIGION, AND THE DICTATORS

The central idea of this book that I kept returning to was that the individuals who were inclined to make the political misjudgments and admire the dictators, harbored, and sought to gratify, unacknowledged religious needs and impulses.[5] The latter found expression in (among other things) the importance attributed to good intentions and ideals that seemed to guarantee the moral legitimacy and integrity of the dictators and their political system.[6]

Slavoj Zizek provides the most striking present-day example of such unconditional devotion to ideals, that is, utopian fantasies of "emancipation" at the expense of human and social realities. Roger Scruton wrote:

> Zizek praises the "humanist terror" of Robespierre ... not because it was in any way kind to its victims but because it expressed the enthusiasm, the "utopian

[5] As Arthur Koestler put it: "In our age those who felt most deeply that paradise was lost, were the first to be attracted by the ersatz-kingdoms of heaven: the World Revolution, Soviet Russia or the Thousand-Year-Reich" (*The Trail of the Dinosaur*, New York 1970, 230).

[6] Sartre and Merleau-Ponty declared that "we should judge communism by its intentions and not by its actions" (quoted in Francois Fejto: "Sartre, the Illustrious Innocent," *Encounter*, April 1985). Most intellectuals who shared the same belief didn't go this far, making it explicit.

explosions of human imagination" of its perpetrators. No matter that the terror led to the imprisonment of half a million innocent people, and the death of many more. The statistics are irrelevant ... What is relevant is the way in which ... Robespierre "redeemed the virtual content of terror from its actualization." In this way, *for Zizek, thought cancels reality ... It matters less what you do than what you think you are doing, provided what you think you are doing has the ultimate goal of emancipation.*[7]

Zizek personifies the most extreme, willful blindness about the consequences of the pursuit of certain ideals, and a perverse disregard of the abyss between ends and means.[8] He is one of many intellectuals who showed far less (if any) interest in the actual accomplishments of particular governments and their policies, oblivious of the tension, or gap, between ends and means and the unintended consequences that come to haunt and contaminate even the best-intentioned social and political undertakings.

Intellectuals attracted to certain ideals (and to the political systems or movements seeking to implement them) rarely if ever asked why their realization was so difficult. Nor did they seem to consider the possibility that the notorious discrepancy between ends and means could have been a reflection of the nature or substance of the ideals, the ends themselves. This is a point forcefully made by a former Marxist-Leninist, pro-Soviet historian, Eugene Genovese:

The horrors [perpetrated by communist systems – P.H.] did not arise from the perversions of radical ideology but from the ideology itself. We were led into complicity with mass murder and the desecration of our professed ideals not by Stalinist or other corruptions of high ideals ... but by a deep flaw of our understanding of human nature ... social movements that have espoused radical egalitarianism and participatory democracy have begun with mass murder and ended in despotism ... The allegedly high ideals we placed at the center of our ideology and politics are precisely what need to be reexamined.[9]

For many Western intellectuals the appeals of socialist theories and programs converged with a more diffuse, flattering self-conception of

[7] Roger Scruton: *Fools, Frauds and Firebrands*, London 2015, 268–269, 274 (emphasis added). Scruton further noted that Zizek "found his undaunted confidence in revolution on principles so abstract and arcane that no empirical disproof could possibly dislodge them" (Ibid., 291).

[8] Scruton also wrote: "They [radical leftist intellectuals] desire to leap from the tainted world that surrounds them into the pure but unknowable realm of total emancipation. This leap into the Kingdom of Ends is a leap of thought, which can never be mirrored in reality" (Ibid., 274).

[9] Eugene D. Genovese: "The Question," *Dissent*, Summer 1994, 375.

being decent and generous human beings, upholding idealistic political beliefs, different from all those infected by the greed and selfishness of capitalism. Perhaps it was the vagueness and generality of socialist ideals that made them so attractive for intellectuals. As Solzhenitsyn put it: "no precise, distinct socialism exists; instead there is only a vague, rosy notion of something noble and good, of equality, communal ownership and justice: the advent of these things will bring instant euphoria and a social order beyond reproach."[10] A similar point was made by Scruton: "The Communist Party appealed not because of its concrete policies or any believable program of action ... It appealed because it addressed the *inner* disorder of the intellectual class, in a world where there was nothing real to believe in."[11]

While the ideals and theories of Nazism and fascism were far less attractive, Hitler and Mussolini too were given credit (for much shorter periods of time) for their good intentions.

The centrality of good intentions and their close connection to the idea of authenticity may also be traced to the durable influence of Romantic ideas described by Isaiah Berlin:

> What people admired was wholeheartedness, sincerity, purity of soul, the ability and readiness to dedicate yourself to your ideal ... motive counts more than consequence ... the greatest virtue of all – is what existentialists call authenticity, and what the romantics called sincerity.[12]
>
> [T]he romantic movement ... preached ... the importance of motive, the importance of character, or at any rate of purpose, over consequences ... what matters is ... the sincerity of one's beliefs, readiness to live and die for a principle, which counts for more than the validity of the conviction or the principle themselves.[13]

As we know all too well, the preoccupation with authenticity has also become a hallmark of present-day American culture. A *New York Times* "trend spotter" wrote: "Authenticity seems to be the value of the moment, rolling off the tongues of politicians, celebrities, Web gurus, college admission advisers, reality television stars ... The word has been

[10] Alexander Solzhenitsyn: "Foreword," to Igor Shafarevich: *The Socialist Phenomenon*, New York 1980, viii. These attitudes are also captured in the following observation: "the main pay-off for middle class radicals is that of a psychological or emotional kind – in satisfactions derived from expressing personal values in [political] action" (Frank Parkin: *Middle Class Radicalism*, Manchester, UK 1968, 2).

[11] Scruton, 19.

[12] Isaiah Berlin: *The Roots of Romanticism*, London 1990, 9, 139, 141.

[13] Isaiah Berlin: *The Crooked Timber of Humanity*, New York 1991, 230.

bandied about for ages, be it by politicians or Oprah Winfrey, who popularized the notion of discovering your 'authentic self.' "[14]

James Billington discerned a connection between romanticism and the radical political beliefs of intellectuals, suggesting that "the revolutionary faith was shaped not so much by the critical rationalism of the French Enlightenment (as is generally believed) as by the occultism and proto-romanticism of Germany."[15]

The free-floating religious, or quasi-religious, needs and impulses of intellectuals (and others) found further expression in the projection of attributes upon the dictators that they did not possess. The Western intellectuals in question were looking for "a morally superior breed of leaders,"[16] superior to the politicians of their own society, who would create just and purposeful social systems. They were also looking for ways to make their own lives more meaningful and stimulating, and for social-emotional support from an authentic community they could belong to. As Irving Howe suggested, " 'the hunger for community has been one of the deepest and most authentic of our century...' [Howe] never doubted that our deepest desire is a collective one, a wish for a 'bonding fraternity' that was 'both the most yearned for and most treacherous of twentieth-century experiences.' "[17]

The underlying source of the intellectuals' dissatisfaction was a painful awareness of the inability of Western pluralistic, capitalist societies to deliver sustaining values and beliefs that would enable them to confront and weather the endemic crises and frustrations of life, and especially modern life. While the emergence of these modern, pluralistic societies was closely linked to the rise of secular intellectuals, they found the growing meaninglessness and moral relativism disturbing and difficult to tolerate. Daniel Bell tersely summed it up: "the real problem of modernity is the problem of belief." Irving Kristol's observation further elucidates the phenomenon:

> The real trouble is not sociological or economic ... It is that ... bourgeois society falls short of responding adequately to the full range of man's spiritual nature ... it

[14] Stephanie Rosenbloom: "You Call Yourself Authentic? Really?" *Cultural Studies*, *New York Times*, September 1, 2011.

[15] James R. Billington: *Fire in the Minds of Men: Origins of the Revolutionary Faith*, New York 1980, 3.

[16] Stephen Pinker: *The Blank Slate: The Modern Denial of Human Nature*, New York 2002, 295.

[17] Howe quoted in Edward Mendelson: "My Grasping Greedy American Soul," *New York Review of Books*, March 5, 2015, 44.

is this weakness that generates continual dissatisfaction, especially among those for whom material problems are no longer so urgent ... it is a religious vacuum – a lack of meaning in their own lives, and the absence of larger purpose in their society – that terrifies them and provokes them to "alienation" and unappeasable indignation.[18]

There was an unmistakable congruence between the idealized images of the dictators and the conventional, religiously inspired conceptions of God. The similarity could be found both in the kinds of attributes projected (or imagined), and in the circumstance that in neither case was there a verifiable basis for these projections. To be sure, the projected characteristics of God have been entirely imaginary, whereas the idealistic misconceptions of the dictators occasionally had some empirical foundations. The dictators were, after all, real human beings, whose existence was not a matter of conjecture or fantasy, even if they were little known by their admirers. In both cases imagination, or projection, played a considerable part, endowing both God and the dictators with attributes of a divine or quasi-divine entity that promised decisive and much longed for solutions to age-old, as well as more recent, human problems and dilemmas. The congruence between the image of God and those of the dictators was apparent in the specifics of their cult, in the institutionalized claims of infallibility, omniscience, omnipresence, sense of justice, and kindness.

While at the beginning of this study I suggested that the dictators' rise to power (and perception as charismatic) was connected to the rejection of, or ambivalence toward, modernity, this proposition needs reconsideration and modification. The original proposition certainly applies to Mussolini and Hitler, who gave voice to those who associated modernity with decadence, meaninglessness, alienation, the weakening of the moral fiber of society, and the decline of a sense of community. At the same time these dictators energetically promoted the material, technological,

[18] Bell quoted in George Urban: "A Conversation with Daniel Bell," *Encounter*, February 1983, 13; Kristol quoted in Elie Kedourie: "Is 'Neo-Conservativism' Viable?" *Encounter*, November 1982, 28. In the same spirit, Andrew Delbanco suggested that "the most striking feature of contemporary culture is the unslaked craving for transcendence" (*The Real American Dream*, Cambridge MA 1999, 114). This deeply rooted craving for meaning, transcendence, spirituality, and their religious, quasi- or secular-religious expressions have also been addressed in Norman Cohn: *The Pursuit of Millennium: Revolutionary Millenarians and Mystical Anarchists in the Middle Ages*, New York 1957, 1970; Joshua Muravchik: *Heaven on Earth: The Rise and Fall of Socialism*, San Francisco 2002; Richard Landes: *Heaven on Earth: The Varieties of the Millennial Experience*, Oxford 2011.

and organizational modernization of their countries that was essential for strengthening their political and military power which they intended to use for nationalistic, collective self-assertion.

What Mussolini and Hitler claimed, and tried to accomplish, was a resuscitation and melding of wholesome traditional sensibilities and ways of life with technological-industrial modernity. Their countries, and especially Germany, required far less modernization – in the material-technological realm – than Russia or China.

Insofar as modernization is conventionally linked to progress and the growth of rationality, it is difficult to associate it with totalitarian systems driven by irrational ideologies, such as Nazi Germany. Hence the useful concept of "reactionary modernism," introduced by Jeffrey Herf.[19]

The communist regimes' approach to modernity was less ambiguous. Stalin and Mao in particular have been generally seen as bold and decisive modernizers, and thought of themselves as such, rather than as critics of modernity. They came to power in largely traditional, pre-modern societies that they intended to transform fundamentally. They were not sentimental about traditional values, beliefs, and institutions. At the same time they too deplored soulless capitalist modernity, sharing with Hitler and Mussolini the contempt for modern capitalism, considered decadent, rotten, immoral, and unjust.

Castro too was a communist modernizer, but his anti-American nationalism was a major preoccupation and distinctive determinant of his beliefs and policies. Castro could also be classified as a national socialist, the label invented by Hitler, which is also applicable to the aspirations and policies of numerous post-World War II Third World dictators.

As these observations suggest, the dictators' attitude toward modernity varied depending on their conceptions of modernity and the material-economic conditions prevailing in their countries. Each of them was eager to adopt modern technology and believed that the material-technological modernization of their society could be accomplished without the detrimental social-cultural side-effects of the process observed in capitalist systems.

The intellectuals' attitude toward modernity was also ambivalent. While they were impressed by the programs and pace of material-technological modernization in the communist states and were repelled by the by-products of modernity under capitalism, they also harbored nostalgic

[19] Jeffrey Herf: *Reactionary Modernism: Technology, Culture and Politics in Weimar and the Third Reich*, Cambridge MA 1986.

sentiments about traditional societies and their apparent authenticity, especially as manifested in personal relationships and values. Among the many exemplars of such a disposition, Marxist Rosa Luxemburg's effusions capture a characteristic blend of apolitical romanticism, rejection of modernity, and wishful projection. She found on one occasion

> simple perfection … on primitive Corsica … [and] an ideal alternative "to the Europe of today", a place to satisfy that deep desire of revolutionaries … to simplify things … [She] recalled recovering "the silence of the beginning of the world" amidst rural purity and finding the archetypical unspoiled "people" in a poor peasant family that passed silently by "precisely in harmony with the landscape." She felt inspired "to fall on my knees as I always feel compelled to do before some spectacle of finished beauty."

Luxemburg's idealized image of rural Corsica brings to mind later generations of "revolutionaries [who] have also pursued a geographical quest for some ideal place where the 'holy other' could be wholly present."[20]

It is an intriguing paradox that most of the dictators admired by portions of Western intellectuals were both modernizers *and* critics of modernity (or aspects thereof) – a disposition that probably increased their appeal. Daniel Chirot too noted "the contradictory feelings of admiration and hatred of European modernity" among, but not limited to, the Nazis. He wrote:

> The Nazis could present themselves as technological and scientific virtuosi … at the same time Wagnerian nostalgia for a fantasized past and contempt for bourgeois democracy appealed to all those alienated by the vagaries of modern market forces and the seeming collapse of traditional communal solidarities. Communism, which may seem to be so different, is pretty much the same in this respect. In its most extreme form, such as Pol Pot's Khmer Rouge, communism abandoned modernity entirely in favor of a return to communal, rural solidarity … the Khmer Rouge believe[d] that they could work miracles by returning their population to its pristine rural condition and breaking all contacts with the outside world … The cities were the home of corruption and foreign influence.[21]

It is not an accident that these extreme and irrational policies in Cambodia were devised and implemented by "a group of Francophone middle-class intellectuals, known as the Angka Leu ('the Higher Organization'). Of its eight leaders five were teachers, one a university

[20] Luxemburg quoted in Billington, 7, 501–502. The same "geographical quest" was the subject of *Political Pilgrims*.

[21] Daniel Chirot: *Modern Tyrants: The Power and Prevalence of Evil in Our Times*, New York 1994, 2, 218.

professor, one a civil servant and one an economist."[22] A similarly murderous, radical-utopian political movement inspired and led by intellectuals was the "Shining Path" in Peru, its founder Abimael Guzman a former philosophy professor at a provincial university.

The problems of modernity and the estrangement they inspire – what a writer called "an inchoate rage against modernity" – also motivate and mobilize at the present time the fanatical and militant supporters of radical Islam. Ken Malik argued that "many strands of contemporary thought, including those embraced by 'deep greens' and the far left, express aspects of such discontent. But it is radical Islam that has become the lightning rod of this fury."[23]

While the attractions of radical Islam for secular Western intellectuals remain, for obvious reasons, limited, some of them sympathize with its anti-modernist thrust and find its fierce rejection of Western capitalist societies congenial and refreshing. These sentiments have prompted some Western intellectuals to reconceptualize supporters of radical Islam as the new virtuous victims of the West, and even to feel some sympathy for Islamic notions of blasphemy. Thus John le Carre reproached Salman Rushdie "over the publication of 'The Satanic Verses.' Nobody has a God-given right to insult a great religion and be published with impunity," he opined. Similar attitudes came to light in the Western critiques of the cartoons published in the French magazine, *Charlie Hebdo*, that inspired the notorious outburst of Islamist murderousness in Paris. Garry Trudeau, the American cartoonist, among others, disapproved of "mocking things sacred" to the Muslim true believers, and suggested that the cartoonists were "punching downward ... attacking a powerless, disenfranchised minority ... ridiculing the non-privileged."[24] It was a peculiar notion of what constitutes powerlessness, given the self-evident, lethal power of the

[22] Paul Johnson: *Intellectuals*, New York 1988, 246.

[23] Kenan Malik: "Radical Islam, Nihilist Rage," *New York Times* [op-ed], January 4, 2015.

[24] Le Carre quoted in "The Spy Who Came in from the Cold" [review of *John Le Carre: The Biography*, by Adam Sisman], *The Economist*, October 31–November 6, 2015, 77; Trudeau quoted in Ross Douthat: "Checking Charlie Hebdo's Privilege," *New York Times*, April 18, 2015. In a similar spirit some American writers condemned the alleged "cultural intolerance" of the same magazine and disapproved of the PEN Club's decision to award its annual Freedom of Expression Courage Award to the same publication ("6 PEN Writers to Skip Gala After Charlie Hebdo Award," *New York Times*, April 27, 2015). Such solicitousness toward Islamic true believers has also been reflected in the strenuous efforts of numerous academic intellectuals and some politicians to deny that there is *any* connection between acts of violence and Muslim religious beliefs. See also Thomas L. Friedman: "Say It Like It Is," *New York Times* [op-ed], January 21, 2015; Paul Hollander: "Marx and the Koran," *Weekly Standard*, February 23, 2015.

well-armed terrorists resolved to determine which characterizations or depictions of Islam are permissible, and punish the offenders accordingly. The notion of Garry Trudeau (which he shares with many liberal Western intellectuals) that Muslim radicals are recruited from a disenfranchised, powerless minority is incorrect. There is a great deal of, and growing, evidence that "young people from relatively prosperous, educated backgrounds have long been over-represented in jihadist causes" and among suicide bombers.[25]

THE PERCEPTIONS AND IMAGES OF THE DICTATORS: A SUMMARY

The dictators, their perceived personality and intentions, played a major part in legitimating the political systems they dominated. It is hard to imagine that any of these systems would have been admired without their deified, heroic leaders. Even a less charismatic, or pseudo-charismatic, leader was essential for symbolizing the alleged blessings of these systems.

It has been a notable finding of this study that the perceptions and appeals of the various dictators, and especially their *personal qualities*, turned out to be far more similar than I expected, despite the differences between their ideologies and policies. Their institutionalized cults were also highly similar.[26] It is more difficult to generalize about the appeals and perceptions of the lesser figures discussed in Chapter 7, but those too had much in common.

These dictators also shared qualities that were not matters of projection and veneration, qualities their admirers did not discern and would not have appreciated if discerned: an immense hunger for power, belief in their own historical role and importance, a sense of mission, megalomania, and ruthlessness. Their sense of mission rested on what could only be described as a pathological self-confidence and readiness to attribute false-consciousness to the masses who had different ideas about their true interests than the dictators.

Isaiah Berlin eloquently grasped the essential, psychological mechanism that allowed the most ambitious dictators to coerce and repress their

[25] Maajid Nawaz: "The Education of 'Jihadi John'," *New York Times*, op-ed, March 3, 2015. See also Simon Cottee: "Pilgrims to the Islamic State," *Atlantic*, July 2015.

[26] Chirot wrote: "there is little difference between the deliberate, mendacious cult of Hitler, Kim Il Sung, Ceausescu, Saddam Hussein, or of Stalin" (Chirot, 159).

people with a clear conscience. It was the "mythology of the real self, in the name of which I am permitted to coerce people." He also wrote:

> The Jacobins, Robespierre, Hitler, Mussolini, the Communists all use this very same method of argument, of saying that men do not know what they truly want ... [therefore] when I bend human beings to my will ... I am not merely doing something which is good for them ... I am doing that which they truly want, though they may deny it ... Therefore I speak for them, on their behalf ... They do not know what their true self is, whereas I, who am wise, who am rational, who am the great benevolent legislator – I know this.[27]

The unappealing traits of the dictators are relevant to the larger issue of the relationship between the personal and the political realm that this study also attempted to shed some light on. As Chirot asked: "Was it perhaps just an unfortunate accident that these ideological movements were taken over by such vicious leaders?"[28] That is to say, was there an *affinity* between the personality of the dictators and the political systems they created and dominated? Did individuals with an exceptional hunger for power and diminished capacity for empathy gravitate toward particular political movements and systems, and positions of leadership in them? Did their personal qualities complement the institutions and policies they created and dominated? Apparently they did, but it doesn't follow that the personality of these dictators by itself explains the intolerant, repressive character of these systems.

In any event, each of the major dictators here discussed fulfilled – at least for certain periods of time – the hopeful expectation of numerous intellectuals both in their own countries and abroad. They were believed to be "revolutionary idealists," possessed of "an absolute sense of moral superiority based on an ideology that claims to explain everything ... This sense of certitude can justify the worst horrors in the name of sanctity, purity and the general improvement of life for the multitudes."[29] The dictators were also seen by their admirers as exceptionally impressive and attractive human beings devoted to the well-being of their people, or even mankind as a whole, committed to ending (or drastically reducing) injustice, inequality, alienation, scarcities of various kinds. Most importantly, they seemed to make the lives of their people meaningful. It was more difficult to give credit to Hitler or Mussolini for such aspirations and achievements since their ideas and ideologies were not universalistic, their benevolence was confined to their own nation or certain selected racial and ethnic populations.

[27] Isaiah Berlin: *Freedom and Its Betrayal: Six Enemies of Human Liberty*, Princeton NJ 2002, 47, 48.

[28] Chirot, 123.

[29] Ibid., 16–17.

As emphasized earlier, at the core of the idealized conceptions of the dictators was the image of the redeemer, endowed with a glowing sense of mission. This image was most readily and plausibly projected upon the charismatic dictators – Hitler, Mussolini, Castro, and Chavez – rather than on the questionably charismatic or pseudo-charismatic ones: Stalin, Mao, and the other lesser figures. As to Mao, Simon Leys pointed out that "for a leader of such stature, Mao had very little personal charisma. He was a poor speaker, with a high-pitched, unpleasant and monotonous voice."[30] Stalin too was an unimpressive speaker and rarely addressed large audiences, unlike Hitler, Mussolini, Castro, and Chavez. But even in the absence of overwhelming or indisputable charisma, Stalin and Mao too managed to impress the sympathetic intellectuals (and many of their own citizens) of their quasi-divine qualities, or at least of being wise father figures, benign care-givers, morally and intellectually superior to the political leaders in other societies, especially those in Western countries.[31]

John Gray reminds us that

> the needs that are met by tyrants are as real as those to which freedom answers ... tyrants promise security – and release from the tedium of everyday existence ... the perennial romance of tyranny comes from its promising its subjects a life more interesting than they can contrive for themselves ... [the] Dictators ... unspoken promise is that they will relieve the boredom of their subjects.[32]

The dictators also had in common (to different degrees) the renaissance man image, supposedly excelling in a wide range of scholarly, artistic, managerial, military, and physical capabilities and activities. In this incarnation they appealed to the Western intellectuals' craving for "wholeness." They were perceived as towering above the emotionally stunted, fragmented, and over-specialized human beings supposedly damaged by the pressures and demands of capitalist modernity – a process intellectuals deplored and somewhat exaggerated.

Sartre's assessment of Che Guevara was typical of such fantasies of wholeness, as he averred that "he was 'not only an intellectual but also the most complete human being of our age.' "[33] It is difficult to know what

[30] Simon Leys: *Broken Images*, New York 1970, 63.

[31] For example, G.D.H. Cole, a British economist, wrote in 1942: "Much better to be ruled by Stalin than by a pack of half-witted and half-hearted social-democrats" (quoted in George Watson: "Were the Intellectuals Duped?" *National Review*, November 7, 1975, 1235).

[32] John Gray: *Straw Dogs: Thoughts on Humans and Other Animals*, London 2002, 124.

[33] Sartre quoted in Jon Lee Anderson: *Che Guevara: A Revolutionary Life*, New York 2010, 446.

exactly Sartre had in mind, presumably that Guevara was an incarnation of revolutionary warrior, statesman, political philosopher, and secular saint. The absence of "wholeness" (or the claim of its absence, whatever its exact meaning) has been a major critique of modernity, or its capitalist version. Sartre probably would have agreed with Isaiah Berlin's sketch of the romantic hero (applicable to Guevara): "a man who has dedicated himself to an ideal, who has thrown away the world, who represents the most heroic, the most self-sacrificing, the most splendid qualities which a human being can have."[34]

More recently Vladimir Putin has sought to project a protean image of wholeness, and especially its physical dimensions, "shown [in the Russian mass media] dressed as a fighter pilot, swimming in a river, shooting a Siberian tiger with a sedation dart, and ... tagging a polar bear."[35] Reportedly he also excels in martial arts and is an accomplished scuba diver.

Less was known and said about the physical sides and accomplishments of Hitler and Stalin, but they too disdained regular hours of sleep, allegedly needing far less than ordinary mortals; that was also the case with Mao.[36] The reader may recall how impressed Sartre was by the modest amount of sleep Castro and Guevara supposedly required.

In their quasi-sacralized or deified images, these dictators were also endowed with a unique and boundless capacity of love for other human beings and all of mankind. I.F. Stone (reputed to be a hard-nosed journalist and fact-finder) deserves credit for what might have been the most grotesque and far-fetched of such attributions, as he proposed that

> in Che [Guevara], one felt a desire to heal and pity for suffering ... It was out of love, like the perfect knight of medieval romance, that he had set out to combat with the powers of the world ... he was like an early saint, taking refuge in the desert. Only there could the purity of the faith be safeguarded.[37]

These images and beliefs were bolstered (for those favorably predisposed) by the avowals of the dictators themselves that they had embarked on "a moral mission." Of the latter, Fathali M. Moghaddam, an Iranian psychologist, wrote: "The moral mission can take many different forms,

[34] Berlin 1999, 13.
[35] David Satter: *Russia's Road to Dictatorship*, New Haven CT (forthcoming) 2015, ch. 3, 1 [manuscript].
[36] See Chirot, 207.
[37] I.F. Stone: "The Legacy of Che Guevara," *Ramparts*, December 1967, 20–21.

from the Nazi ideology of the revival of the master race, to the holy moral crusade of Stalin in the name of the people, to Mao's perpetual revolution to maintain the purity of the people's revolution, to the religious crusades of Khomeini and other Islamic dictators and would-be dictators."

Time and again these dictators sought to legitimate themselves by claims of sacredness, or virtual sacredness: "Mussolini, Stalin, Mao, Khomeini and, many other dictators ... were not only obeyed, they also became infallible. To question their word was equivalent to questioning the word of God."[38]

In their incarnation as philosopher-kings the dictators promised to find solutions for all the seemingly intractable problems of their society, or even those of mankind as a whole. As Berlin put it, "if one believes that such a solution is possible, then surely no cost would be too high to obtain it: to make mankind just and happy and creative and harmonious for ever – what could be too high a price to pay for that?"[39]

It may be further argued (as was done in Chapter 1) that the appeal of the dictators reflected the discontents of modernity and the attendant proliferation of the sense of victimhood, or victimization, that the dictators were expected to alleviate or altogether banish. While in the second half of the twentieth and the early twenty-first century there have been fewer suitable candidates to play the role of such a powerful redeemer, the sense of victimhood and victimization has been spreading and was embraced even in the more tolerant and democratic Western societies. Ian Buruma wrote:

> What is alarming ... is the extent to which so many minorities have come to define themselves as historical victims ... Sometimes it seems as if everyone wants to compete with the Jewish tragedy ... Chinese-Americans are not the only ones to be prey to such emotions. The idea of victimhood also haunts Hindu nationalists, Armenians, African-Americans and homosexuals ... Why has it come to this? Why do many people wish to identify themselves as vicarious victims?[40]

38 Fatali M. Moghaddam: *The Psychology of Dictatorship*, Washington DC 2013, 81–82, 96.

39 Berlin 1991, 15.

40 Ian Buruma: "The Joys and Perils of Victimhood," *New York Review of Books*, April 8, 1999, 4; see also Joel Best: "Victimization and the Victim Industry," *Society*, May–June 1997; David Rieff: "Victims All? Recovery, Co-dependency, and the Art of Blaming Somebody Else," *Harper's*, October 1991; Paul Hollander: "We Are All Victims Now," *Wall Street Journal*, January 18, 1995; Paul Hollander: "The Pursuit of Identity, Community and Social Justice: The Cult of Victimhood Revisited," in *Discontents: Postmodern and Postcommumist*, New Brunswick NJ 2002.

There have been numerous reasons for the attractions of victimhood, some of them more tangible than the malaise or alienation associated with modernity. Uncontested, widely acknowledged victimhood is a gratifying source of identity in modern societies where many people find it difficult to satisfactorily determine their identity. The victim status also helps the certified victims to occupy the moral high ground. Certified victimhood may also contribute to political influence and legitimate demands for compensatory measures.[41]

Political hero worship and the discontents of modernity may also be linked by the apparent relief the dictator provides from the fragmentation and disharmony of modern mass societies by the promise of "the spiritualization of politics." These dictators assume the mantle of "a salvationary Great Leader able to communicate directly with all people."[42]

Probably the most compelling attraction of the dictators (at any rate for intellectuals) was their alleged ability to unite theory and practice, being "practical idealists" (as Edgar Snow called Mao), not merely talkers but doers, who put ideas to good use. This celebrated and longed-for synthesis has been the ultimate aspiration of many intellectuals who consider it their duty to generate ideas. But unless the lofty ideas are put to good use their time is wasted, their social function, sense of identity, and importance are called into question.

The highly valued qualities projected upon the dictators, in addition to idealism, kindness, sincerity, wisdom, and sense of justice, included the capacity for the just and creative use of power and an exceptional understanding of history and human nature, essential for bringing about the long-awaited moral regeneration of their society and human beings.

Attention to detail was another praiseworthy trait, rather than an expression of obsessive involvement with the exercise of power and control and mistrust of subordinates. The dictators' legendary managerial

[41] Taking a highly unusual position, Joseph Brodsky (Noble Prize-winning poet of Russian origin) in a commencement address advised against embracing the victim role: "No matter how abominable your condition may be, try not to blame anything or anybody: history, the state, superiors, race, parents ... childhood, toilet training etc. ... The moment you place blame somewhere, you undermine your resolve to change anything." But he understood that the "victim status is not without its sweetness. It commands compassion, confers distinction, and whole nations and continents bask in the murk of mental discounts advertised as the victim's conscience. There is an entire victim culture, ranging from private counselors to international loans" (*On Grief and Reason, Essays*, New York 1995, 144–145).

[42] Irving Louis Horowitz: "Preface," to *Radicalism and the Revolt against Reason: The Social Theories of Georges Sorel*, Carbondale IL 1968, x.

talents found expression in their alleged capacity to master every detail relevant to the huge social engineering projects undertaken, including their superb grasp of data and statistics, familiarity with details of the economy, and excellence in devising military strategy when needed. (As it became subsequently clear, the dictators were also capable of making huge blunders and demonstrated spectacular incompetence in various undertakings, military or civilian.)

It appears that the imputed authenticity, heroic qualities, and other *personal attributes* made a deeper impression on the intellectuals than the dictators' specific beliefs, ideologies, and policies.

Last but not least, the sympathetic intellectuals often claimed, most implausibly, that these dictators were exceedingly modest, even humble human beings, notwithstanding their cult and the compulsory reverence it entailed.[43]

The physical appearance and attributes of dictators here considered did not appear to be a major factor in their appeal and charisma. By contrast, dictators such as Nasser and Peron were "stirring speakers with a flair for the dramatic ... Projecting vigor, good looks, meticulous grooming and charm, Juan Peron cut a dashing figure in his uniform ... The tall athletic Peron, flashing his famous smile, stood out in any crowd. Nasser was cut from a similar mold."[44] Hitler, while physically unimpressive, was nonetheless undeniably charismatic, as was evident in his capacity to make a great emotional impact on his audiences; Mussolini was more impressive physically and similarly capable of impressing his audiences. Mao's interest in swimming was given vast publicity as proof of his physical prowess, but by itself was a limited source of charisma. The best example of the combination of physical attractiveness and oratorical skill in the projection of charisma was provided by Castro.

HUMAN NATURE AND THE NATURE OF INTELLECTUALS

A major underlying determinant of the political disposition of intellectuals here discussed has been their conception of human nature, or rather the implicit denial that there was such a thing. The clearly articulated political-ideological preference for the "blank slate" conception of

43 Stalin's inflated self-conception and interest in his own cult (documented in Jan Plamper's *The Stalin Cult*, New Haven CT 2012, see esp. 120–135) is applicable to the other dictators.

44 Barry Rubin: *Modern Dictators*, New York 1987, 71.

human nature has been rooted in the belief that the evolutionary, biologically determined conceptions of human nature could be misused to support a wide range of inequalities and undermine notions of progress and ideals of human perfectibility. As Steven Pinker wrote: "To acknowledge human nature, many think, is to endorse racism, sexism, war, greed, genocide, nihilism, reactionary politics and neglect of children and the disadvantaged."[45]

Notwithstanding its well-meaning, idealistic aspects, the blank slate approach proved to be highly congenial with repressive political systems committed to the fundamental and coercive transformation of societies and human beings. As reflected in their enormous investment in propaganda, these systems made good use of the premise that human beings are malleable, their character easily shaped by a variety of external, environmental, or situational stimuli and influence. Again, Pinker wrote:

> the Blank Slate had, and has a dark side. The vacuum that it posited in human nature was eagerly filled by totalitarian regimes ... Its corollary, the Noble Savage ... blinds us to our cognitive and moral shortcomings ... The romantic notion that all evil is a product of society has justified the release of dangerous psychopaths ... And the conviction that humanity could be reshaped by massive social engineering projects led to some of the greatest atrocities in history ... the ambition to remake human nature turned ... leaders into totalitarian despots and mass murderers ... Inborn human desires are a nuisance for those with utopian and totalitarian visions, which often amount to the same thing. What stands in the way of most utopias is ... human behavior.[46]

In a somewhat contradictory manner, the blank slate conception of human nature is often combined with a belief in, and nostalgia for, the Noble Savage of pre-industrial, pre-literate societies, especially popular with anthropologists. The Noble Savage is uncorrupted by civilization, that is, by Western values and ways of life – he is authentic, unselfish, generous, and communal. Rousseau was a major proponent of this pleasant fantasy that gained renewed popularity in the 1960s. It was embraced by angry social critics such as Noam Chomsky, presumably motivated in part by the strongly felt contrast between the possibility that such noble human beings could (and did) exist, and the reality of greedy, selfish individuals proliferating and dominating modern capitalist societies. Pinker observed that "Chomsky implies that people are born with fraternal

[45] Pinker, viii.

[46] Ibid., x–xi, 169–170 296, 421. Joseph Brodsky was also among the critics of the Noble Savage fantasy and a believer in the timeless human capacity for evil. See for example Brodsky, 217–218.

feelings toward their social groups and that the feelings are driven out of their heads by training."[47]

Ramsey Clark (discussed in the previous chapter) also subscribed to a benign conception of human nature that may help to explain his sympathy for virtually every movement and political system opposed to the United States, which was, in his opinion, responsible for corrupting and dehumanizing human beings worldwide. These conceptions of human nature found expression in his view of criminals and their treatment, and in the conviction that punishment should be altogether replaced by rehabilitation:

> The theory of rehabilitation is based on the belief that healthy, rational people will not injure others, that they will understand that the individual and his society are best served by conduct that does not inflict injury, and that a just society has the ability to provide health and purpose and opportunity for all its citizens. Rehabilitated, an individual will not have the capacity – cannot bring himself – to injure others or take or destroy property.[48]

Unfortunately, as Pinker points out, "history shows that plenty of healthy, rational people can bring themselves to injure others and destroy property because, tragically, an individual's interests sometimes *are* served by hurting others ... Conflicts of interest are inherent to the human condition."[49] By contrast, integral to all utopias is the hope and conviction that all such conflicts can be resolved and abolished, as well as the boundary between the private and public domain, and their discrepant interests, following the restoration of the mythical wholeness of human beings.

The dictators and their ideologues too subscribed to an idealistic conception of human nature, but only in the long run – a belief made most explicit in the Marxist theory of the withering away of the state, reaffirmed by Lenin (in *State and Revolution*, 1917) and more recently by a Soviet textbook (V. Afanasyev: *Marxist Philosophy*, 1968). Thus, if and when communist society is established – following the abolition of private property, exploitation, and inequalities of all kinds – it will be accompanied by a vast improvement in the disposition and behavior of human beings. If so, the state and its coercive bureaucratic apparatus will no longer be required for the maintenance of social order.

The short run was a totally different matter, reflecting a different belief of these rulers and ideologues, namely, that human beings had to

47 Ibid., 247.

48 Clark quoted in Pinker, 313.

49 Ibid.

be disciplined, regimented, and coerced, to deter them from (or punish them for) bad behavior and to root out false-consciousness responsible for undesirable behavior.

As the reader approaches the end of this study, it needs to be reaffirmed that its major findings and propositions were limited to a certain (unquantifiable) portion of Western intellectuals analyzed and quoted in the preceding pages. However, it should be kept in mind that other contingents of distinguished Western intellectuals can also be readily identified who had *never* been attracted to authoritarian or extremist movements, or totalitarian political systems, and their ideologies. A second, probably larger group of intellectuals not discussed in this study consists of those who, after periods of sympathy with or commitment to such movements or systems, became profoundly disillusioned with them (and their ideologies).[50] A third group, natives of the dictatorial societies, became the most rapidly and decisively disillusioned (if indeed they had any illusions to begin with). It was their experience of daily realities that undermined and destroyed their earlier hopes and expectations, as the gap between theory and practice, or ideals and realities, became impossible to ignore or rationalize.[51] Many of these intellectuals, and especially those in the last group, significantly contributed to the delegitimation of communist systems.

Probably the best-known and most vocal of these anti-totalitarian and anti-communist intellectuals had been the *former* leftists, fellow travelers, sympathizers of different degrees of involvement and commitment. They include Daniel Bell, Saul Bellow, Albert Camus, Whittaker Chambers, Howard Fast, Lewis Feuer, Andre Gide, Maurice Halperin, Christopher Hitchens, Sidney Hook, David Horowitz, Irving L. Horowitz, Irving Howe, Arthur Koestler, Irving Kristol, Doris Lessing, Andre Malraux, George Orwell, Jean Francois Revel, Ignazio Silone, Susan Sontag, Stephen Spender, Richard Wright, and Bertram D. Wolfe, among many others.

Other prominent anti-communist intellectuals in the West had familial roots in communist countries, or grew up in them and defected, or were

[50] Here I am only referring mainly to communist movements and systems and their former supporters among intellectuals, since Nazi and fascist movements and states attracted far fewer intellectuals and for much shorter periods of time (as discussed earlier) and generated no comparable (if any) literature of disillusionment.

[51] For a comparative study of disillusionment with communist movements and systems, see Paul Hollander: *The End of Commitment: Intellectuals, Revolutionaries and Political Morality*, Chicago 2006.

exiled. They include Thomas Aczel, Reinaldo Arenas, Joseph Brodsky, Jorge Dominguez, Leszek Kolakowski, Victor Kravchenko, Wolfgang Leonhard, Eugen Loebl, Georgi Markov, Tibor Meray, Czeslaw Milosz, Carlos Montaner, Heberto Padilla, Richard Pipes, Victor Serge, Sidney Rittenberg, and Adam Ulam.

Finally, there have also been prominent anti-totalitarian, anti-communist Western intellectuals (both liberal and conservative) who had no prior involvement or association with leftists movements or causes (as far as I know), and had no roots in or personal experience of conditions of life in the countries concerned. They include Anne Applebaum, Raymond Aron, Peter L. Berger, Isaiah Berlin, Paul Berman, William F. Buckley, Alan Bloom, Pascal Bruckner, Robert Conquest, Richard Crossman, Friedrich Hayek, Eric Hoffer, Alex Inkeles, Melvin Lasky, Bernard-Henri Levy, Simon Leys, S.M. Lipset, Steven Mosher, Edward Shils, and Leonard Schapiro, among others.

These lists suggest that the most powerful incentive for resisting or repudiating illusions about communist movements or systems has been a close personal familiarity with them, with their realities or practices, as experienced by the individual. It is far more difficult to propose any generalization about the motivation and political attitude formation of the anti-totalitarian intellectuals who had no personal experience of or connection with the systems or movements concerned and developed critical sentiments about them *without* such experiences.

This brief detour to anti-communist intellectuals of different generations, nationalities, occupations, public renown, and political attitudes ought to make clear that those discussed in this book did not have a monopoly over the political-cultural discourse of their society, although they often exercised disproportionate influence, especially in educational and cultural institutions and the mass media.[52]

[52] By the twenty-first century there remained few American (or Western European) intellectuals publicly supporting communist systems or movements. Instead, the prevailing attitude – traceable to the late 1960s – has been anti-anti-communism. It amounted to the conviction that while communist systems had some undesirable aspects, anti-communism was worse, a largely irrational disposition, more harmful than communism. Michael Parenti was a leading exponent of this view (see his *The Anti-Communist Impulse*, New York 1969). Almost half-a-century later Gloria Steinem still considered anti-Communism "a mental disease," as she wrote: "We got on the wrong side in Afghanistan ... because we had anti-Communism as a mental disease" (Gloria Steinem: "By the Book" column, *New York Times Book Review Section*, November 1, 2015).

In all probability it is the belief in the benign and virtually unlimited human potentials that has been the major component and driving force of the idealism and high expectations of many intellectuals here discussed, motivating them to search for alternatives to the dispiriting conditions they have been familiar with. Wishful thinking and projection supported these aspirations and gave rise to the political illusions, misperceptions, and self-deception.

In addition to their high expectations, intellectuals also differ from the rest of humanity by taking themselves more seriously, being more individualistic, and often harboring grandiose aspirations of self-realization. But the desire for self-realization may also take more prosaic and unexpected forms, as David Brooks suggested:

> There is no longer a small, rarified intelligentsia living ... in bohemian neighborhoods ... Now there is a massive class of educated analysts and "opinion leaders" who have made the old bohemian neighborhoods unaffordable for anybody without stock options or large royalty checks ... Now writers and cultural studies professors embrace mass culture and devote conferences to Madonna or Marilyn or Manson ... Intellectuals have come to see their careers in capitalist terms ... They compete for attention ... So the social role of the intellectual really has been transformed. Once the aloof member of a secular priesthood, she is now ... comfortable member of a large class of people who are interested in ideas. Once the radical who sought to challenge the rule of mammon, she is now the worldly player, building a reputation and climbing the ladder of success.[53]

Nonetheless, even in their more recent, prosperous, and well-integrated incarnation Western intellectuals are likely to think of themselves as idealistic social critics and the conscience of society. They often succeed in finding their social conscience and criticism compatible with a respectable social status and high income.

The individualism of intellectuals coexists with their longing to be part of some idealized community. As Paul Johnson (among others) argued, the idealism of intellectuals is also compatible with condescension to specific human beings and indifference to their mundane but genuine problems, as distinct from a devotion to abstractions such as mankind, the nation, social class, and, of late, (dubious) conceptions of identity groups. Admittedly, such contradictory characteristics are not peculiar to intellectuals; most human beings are governed, and often torn, by conflicting impulses and desires, but intellectuals, and especially public intellectuals,

[53] David Brooks: *Bobos in Paradise*, New York 2000, 148–149, 185–186.

display these contradictory attitudes and impulses more conspicuously and frequently.

Critics of intellectuals (such as those quoted in the first chapter) also charge them with an unseemly hunger for power that plays a part in their rejection of their own society, supposedly depriving them of their just share of power and influence they feel entitled to. Some of these intellectuals believed that in the societies they admired intellectuals were far more powerful and influential than in their own.

While they admired powerful philosopher-king dictators and believed that their counterparts in various dictatorships were taken far more seriously, it does not follow that these Western intellectuals actually aspired to hold and exercise political power. It is difficult to think of specific intellectuals who attained positions of significant and durable political power in the societies Western intellectuals admired. The rare intellectual who ascended to high positions of power or influence in the countries concerned (for example, Goebbels, or Gentile, or the Hungarian Joseph Revai) rapidly divested himself of the defining characteristics of the intellectual. At the same time, the powerlessness of intellectuals in these dictatorships was not necessarily the result of their own reluctance to occupy positions of power but more likely the consequence of the dictators' aversion to and mistrust of intellectuals noted earlier (see pp. 102, note 68).

While it is impossible to prove or disprove sweeping generalizations about the disposition of intellectuals about the possession of political power, most intellectuals wish to be recognized and exert some cultural or public influence without a compelling hunger for exercising political power. This may be the case in part because of their often noted lack of practical talents and aversion to bureaucracy. It is not power-hunger as such,[54] but the desire to find meaning, purpose, and justice in the world that is the key characteristic of intellectuals, originating in meaning-seeking, quasi-religious impulses. Capitalist modernity, including secularization, undermined traditional forms of religious belief and activities, but at the same time stimulated and reinforced formless religious or quasi-religious longings

[54] There has been another theory that may account for the motivation of some of these intellectuals, or quasi-intellectuals, at any rate as regards the attractions of the Soviet Union. John Gray suggested that the group of Englishmen who attended Cambridge University in the 1930s and 1940s and became Soviet spies "were convinced that it [the Soviet Union] was about to become the world's dominant power ... The Great Depression discredited capitalism and it seemed obvious that the future lay with planned economy ... Burgess felt the 20th century would belong to Russia ... Philby's decision to spy for the Soviet Union ... [was] a switch from a declining to a rising power" (John Gray: "High Tea and Treason," *New Statesman*, September 25–October 1, 2015, 67).

among intellectuals. Indisputably, capitalism brought "disenchantment" to the world (as Weber put it) and has demystified it, causing considerable discomfort to many who witnessed and were exposed to the process. The political systems personified by the deified dictators raised hopes about restoring an equilibrium between a benign rationality that progressive intellectuals initially associated with modernity, and the retention or recreation of a social system that would entail elements of the sacred that traditional societies possessed.

THE PERSONAL AND THE POLITICAL

It has been one of the central, underlying themes of this study (not fully articulated) that the roots of the political attitudes and illusions here dealt with may be found at the intersection of conflicting personal and political impulses and concerns. Correspondingly it has been suggested that the political commitments of intellectuals are colored by their emotional disposition. Tibor Szamuelly wrote: "The other striking – and paradoxical – aspect of 'progressive' intellectuals' involvement in politics is the fundamentally *non-intellectual* nature of their commitment ... it is almost invariably an emotional attitude, owing very little, if anything, to the process of reasoning and study that one usually associates with word 'intellectual'."[55]

As I had written earlier, "political attitudes and beliefs often stem from non-political sources ... [from a] self-conscious orientation toward self-transcendence, self-expression, personal problem-solving through political action and immersion."[56] That is to say, the intellectuals dealt with might have sought answers and solutions for personal problems and discontents not likely to be found in the public or social-political arena, or in public policies. But this proposition too needs instant qualification, given the much-lamented difficulty of drawing the line between personal and social-political realms and problems, their origins, and interaction.[57]

[55] Tibor Szamuelly: "Intellectuals and Just Causes," *Encounter*, September 1967, 13–14.

[56] Paul Hollander: "New Light on the Roots of Radicalism," *Encounter*, April 1984, 68–69.

[57] A recent article reporting the complaints and grievances (such as a sense of isolation, invisibility, marginalization, lack of social bonds, meaninglessness, etc.) of highly privileged students at Amherst College, in Massachusetts, reflects the difficulties of separating the personal from the social-political concerns and circumstances (see Anemona Hartocollis: "With Diversity Comes Intensity in Amherst Free-Speech Debate," *New York Times*, November 29, 2015).

The long-forgotten musings of a 1960s radical suggest one way of looking at this relationship between the personal and the social-political realm and its interaction:

> We have an irreconcilable tension in our existence ... Blowing up a bad thing will relieve much of that tension. So that the preceding sentence doesn't become evidence for any of the rampant psychological theories about radicals, it should be pointed out that the psychological problems most of us have are very directly capitalism's fault ... The very virtue of terrorism, in fact is that it allows a spontaneous release of the frustrations caused by capitalism.[58]

This young man had no doubt at the time that it was the unjust social-economic system, capitalism, that disfigures our personalities, and is to be blamed for all our personal, psychological problems. The contrary belief, he sought to refute, was that radicals are neurotic malcontents who blame society for their personal problems that have little to do with the nature and defects of the social system or the social-political environment they live in. Hyland obviously subscribed to a version of what Pinker called "environmental determinism."[59]

Another noteworthy instance of the attractions and justifications of violence that are difficult to explain by purely impersonal, political motives or circumstances was provided by Antonio Negri, the Italian academic intellectual and vocal advocate of political terror. He wrote:

> Nothing better reveals the enormous historic positivity of the workers' self-valorisation than this role of the sniper, the saboteur, the deviant, the criminal that I find myself living [he wrote in *Dominion and Sabotage*.] Whenever I pull on my *passapontagna* [a knitted face-mask worn by terrorists and mountain climbers] I feel the heat of the proletariat. Nor does the eventual risk offend me: it fills me with feverish emotion as if I were waiting for a lover.[60]

[58] Richard E. Hyland quoted in Sidney Hook: "The Ideology of Violence," *Encounter*, April 1970.

[59] Pinker cited a *New York Times* report that illustrated this mindset: "Tiffany F. Goldberg ... was struck on the head with a chunk of concrete by a stranger ... Afterward she expressed concern for her attacker speculating that he must have had a troubled childhood. Graduate students in social work at Columbia [University] called Ms Golderg's attitude consistent with their outlook on violence. 'Society is blaming individuals' ... said one of the students" (Pinker, 178).

[60] Negri quoted in Alexander Stille: "Apocalypse Soon," *New York Review of Books*, November 7, 2002, 49. See also Claire Sterling: "Italian Terrorists," *Encounter*, July 1981, 24. Negri was convicted by an Italian court for his role in various assassinations and served a prison sentence. He was a minor academic celebrity in the United States following the publication in 2000 (by Harvard University Press) of the book *Empire*, which he co-authored with Michael Hard.

Paul Johnson, the prolific British author, also believed that there is a highly patterned relationship between the personal and political realm, but the causal connection he postulated was diametrically opposed to that embraced by Hyland. Johnson argued that "the private lives and the public postures of leading intellectuals cannot be separated: one helps to explain the other. Private vices and weaknesses are almost invariably reflected in conduct on the world stage." As opposed to Hyland, he believed that social critics tend to blame society for their personal failings and shortcomings that have little to do with the flaws and injustices of the social-political system, or the mode of production. He argued that Marx is "an outstanding example" that the "massive works of the intellect do not spring from the abstract workings of the brain and the imagination; they are deeply rooted in the personality ... his pent-up rage passed into his books, which always have a tone of intransigence and extremism." In the same spirit Johnson suggested that Ibsen's plays "in which anger usually simmers and sometimes boils over were a vast therapeutic exercise" and reflect "a huge burden of unappeasable resentment." Johnson further argued that Tolstoy is

> another example of what happens when an individual pursues abstract ideas at the expense of people ... Tolstoy destroyed his family, and killed himself by trying to bring about the total moral transformation he felt imperative ... he also yearned for ... a millenarian transformation of Russia ... not by gradual and painstaking reforms of the kind he despised, but in one volcanic convulsion.[61]

A more nuanced view of the relationship between the personal and social-political realm was taken by James Billington, who suggested that the Russian intelligentsia conceived of itself "as a classless moral force seeking to be closer to the suffering of common people." Even more relevant for the present discussion, he also believed that "the [Russian] intellectual retained ... the ability to identify his unhappiness with that of all society."[62]

While the specifics of Johnson's psycho-biographical approach may well be disputed, he does offer an unambiguous conception not only of what he sees as the preeminent personal qualities of intellectuals (none of them flattering), but also the part these traits play in creating the predisposition for the social-critical, adversarial mindset and role. His book here quoted begins with Rousseau, "the first of the modern intellectuals, their archetype and in many ways the most influential of them all." In

[61] Johnson, 69, 71, 91, 137, 274.

[62] Billington, 400–401.

Johnson's view, Rousseau established the secular tradition of "tell[ing] mankind how to conduct its affairs ... [and] proclaimed, from the start, a special devotion to the interests of humanity ... the first intellectual to proclaim himself repeatedly, the friend of all mankind."[63] For Johnson, concern with the welfare of mankind is an important marker of intellectuals, exemplified by several of them (dealt with in his book) who professed a love of mankind but had serious difficulties relating to actual human beings.

None of the dozen individuals Johnson chose to discuss appeared to be attractive human beings. They were self-centered, self-righteous, masters of self-promotion, detached from physical human realities, often deficient in warmth and kindness. They personified a vast gulf between their ideas and ideals on the one hand, and behavior on the other, notwithstanding their preoccupation with and yearning for authenticity.

The obvious problem with Johnson's thesis is that it is based on a minuscule sample that includes only those with an unappealing or unimpressive personality (except for Edmund Wilson), who were selected precisely because they illustrated the point Johnson wished to make.[64] He did not reveal how he selected this group, members of which had in common only two obvious traits: first, the claim that they were able to "diagnose the ills of society and cure them ... [and] could devise formulae whereby not merely the structure of society but the fundamental habit of human beings could be transformed for the better."[65] Second, they shared (according to Johnson) an unattractive personality and failure to live up to their professed ideals. The group included four philosophers (Marx, Rousseau, Bertrand Russell, and Sartre); six writers (Bertolt Brecht, Lilian Hellman, Hemingway, Ibsen, Shelley, and Tolstoy); one literary critic (Edmund Wilson); and an influential British publisher (Victor Gollancz).

On further reflection it appears that the positions taken by Hyland and Johnson may be reconciled: the broader social setting, the type of society one lives in indirectly contributes to what seem to be purely personal problems and dispositions – social isolation, a confused or uncertain sense of identity, lack of purpose, and sense of meaninglessness. The latter tend to be associated with or intensified by the processes of modernization, or more generally with rapid social change. But it is also true that

[63] Johnson, 1, 2, 10.

[64] Michiko Kakutani made the same criticism in "An Argument for Paying No Mind to Intellectuals," *New York Times*, February 21, 1989. See also my review of Johnson's book in *Society*, September–October 1989.

[65] Johnson, 1–2.

individuals, including intellectuals, may choose to blame society (or some of its institutions) for specific personal flaws and difficulties that have no apparent or plausible connection with the broader social-political environment – such as the mode of production, types of social stratification, the characteristics of political institutions, or the rates and nature of social change. Personal problems and difficulties have a multiplicity of sources – in upbringing, unique personal experiences and relationships, and especially traumatic experiences of various kinds, as well as in one's genetic endowment including the physical features of the individual. Prominent among the sources of personal problems is the gap between aspirations and achievements, created and stimulated *both* by modernity – and the growth of individualism it entails – and by unique personal proclivities of complex, unclear origin. The difficulties of calibrating the relative weight of personal as distinct from social-political variables preclude sweeping generalizations about the determinants of personal beliefs and behavior. We are constrained to fall back on the cautious suggestion that, as is generally the case, a wide range of factors shape and determine human beliefs and behavior, some more readily observable than others.

The instances of political hero worship and the associated misjudgments of political systems and ideologies sampled in this study demonstrate and confirm that the ranks of true believers have not substantially diminished in our times and continue to include intellectuals. These attitudes make clear that rationality – a precarious and much-challenged human quality – remains in short supply.[66] Its scarcity or absence is reflected in the dubious political beliefs here surveyed, probably at least in part inspired by deeper discontents, which the political positions taken sought to alleviate.

Another conclusion to be drawn is that it is extremely difficult, if not altogether impossible, to separate sources of discontent found in objective, empirically verifiable conditions (i.e., material deprivation, political repression, poor health, scarcities of various kinds) from those that originate in the deepest recesses of the human psyche, in subjective dispositions

[66] Orwell wrote: "We shall get nowhere unless we start by recognizing that political behavior is largely non-rational" ("In Front of Your Nose," *Collected Essays*, Vol. IV 1945–1950, New York 1968, 249). Religious beliefs can bolster such irrationality and enable terrorists to commit acts of violence with a clear conscience. Even rape can be seen as divinely sanctioned. A rape victim in Iraq reported that "'Every time he came to rape me, he would pray' said F., a 15-year-old girl ... 'He kept telling me this is ibadah' she said using a term from Islamic scripture meaning worship. 'He said that raping me is his prayer to God'" (Rukmini Callimachi: "Enslaving Young Girls, the Islamic State Builds a Vast System of Rape," *New York Times*, August 14, 2015, 1–12).

and expectations that often have no discernible or ascertainable connection with such objective, external conditions and difficulties.

The concept of "relative deprivation"[67] introduced by the American sociologist Robert Merton helps to connect the external and internal (or the personal and social) sources of discontent, and also helps us to understand the discontent of intellectuals that is often shaped and stimulated by high expectations. Merton conceived of relative deprivation as the result of comparing one's circumstances with those of others, either in the same status group or with any group that functions as a "reference group" deemed to be the most relevant for evaluating comparatively one's position in society. In traditional societies it is the group one is born into, its relevance for evaluating one's station in life taken for granted. In modern societies there is far more latitude for such choices. Accordingly, people may often feel deprived not so much because of certain discernible, objective deprivations (such as mentioned above) but as a result of comparing their condition with those of others (in their chosen reference group). The comparison may originate in, or confirm, a sense of entitlement, leading to frustration and grievance. Such comparisons were unknown or rare in traditional societies where social position was unambiguously defined and fixed, social mobility was non-existent or minimal, and people of different classes or status groups had little contact with one another and little knowledge of their respective ways of life. It is the idea of open-ended possibilities, as opposed to such seemingly immutable conditions, that differentiates – among other things – modern from traditional societies and ways of life.

The gist of the theory of relative deprivation is that what matters most in accepting or rejecting one's place or position in society is *how the individual feels* about it. Such feelings originate in comparing one's position with that of others who are not considered more deserving. While Merton did not use these ideas to account for the sensibilities and discontents of intellectuals, the idea of relative deprivation has an obvious relevance and applicability to their discontents. In the first place, intellectuals criticize and reject their society not because they themselves are deprived or underprivileged (most of them are not), but on behalf of other groups subject to the obvious deprivations. Second, the intellectuals' or the social critics' concern with, and indignation over, these deprivations and injustices originates in, or is stimulated by, their conceptions of alternatives.

[67] Robert K. Merton: "Contributions to Reference Group Behavior," in *Social Theory and Social Structure*, Glencoe IL 1957.

The deprivations observed or felt are *relative to their ideas, expectations, and conceptions of superior attainable alternatives*. These expectations are, in turn, embedded in a belief in the changeability of conditions that in the past seemed to resist change or modification.

The idea of relative deprivation explains, among other things, why American social critics are especially outraged by poverty and inequality in America, an outrage intensified by contrasting it with (or relative to) the overall wealth of the society, and the wealth of a small group of very rich people, and by the perceived possibility of social arrangements that could alleviate or eliminate poverty. Relative to such wealth, and to conceptions of a more egalitarian income distribution, poverty is all the more intolerable morally. The same concept accounts for the impassioned critiques of inequality, contrasted with (or compared to) the aspirations and hopes of the Founding Fathers.

More generally speaking social injustices and deprivations are more difficult to behold and tolerate when alternative conceptions – moderate or utopian – of social justice and social organization are available. The key sentiment underlying and magnifying moral indignation is the conviction, and the requisite imagination, that conditions could be different. Intellectuals are the most capable of entertaining and elaborating such conceptions of alternative social organizations and arrangements.

These reflections lead back to the tantalizing question of what are the deepest roots of the beliefs and political judgments discussed in this book, and to the subsidiary question of what the individuals who held them had in common, aside from these beliefs and judgments? What shared attributes precede and give rise to the political beliefs and attitudes here considered? Is it higher expectations that primarily define and differentiate intellectuals from other human beings?

While it was not among the goals of this study to find definitive answers to such questions, it may be reaffirmed that idealism, high expectations, a propensity for discontent, and an enlarged capacity for moral indignation are among the distinctive attributes of intellectuals that account for many of their attitudes and beliefs examined in this book.

This study also confirms that many intellectuals, like human beings in general (and perhaps more so), need the kinds of illusions that promise a more meaningful and satisfying life. Their imagination, idealism, and urge for self-transcendence make them especially vulnerable to the allure of the good intentions that heroic leaders in their alleged pursuit of social justice personify.

Index

Orwell, George, 150, 216, 308, 316

Lightning Source UK Ltd.
Milton Keynes UK
UKOW01f0409230817
307798UK00016B/182/P

9 781107 415072